M000248070

# Blood & Kinship

# Blood & Kinship

*Matter for Metaphor
from Ancient Rome to the Present*

*Edited by*

Christopher H. Johnson,
Bernhard Jussen,
David Warren Sabean,
Simon Teuscher

*Berghahn Books*
New York • Oxford

Published in 2013 by

*Berghahn Books*

www.berghahnbooks.com

**Library of Congress Cataloging-in-Publication Data**

Blood and kinship : matter for metaphor from ancient Rome to the present /
edited by Christopher H. Johnson...[et. al.]. — 1st ed.
   p. cm.
Includes bibliographical references and index.
ISBN 978-0-85745-749-3 (hardback : alk. paper)
  1. Kinship—Europe—History. 2. Family—Europe—History. 3. Blood—
Symbolic aspects—Europe. 4. Europe—Civilization. I. Johnson, Christopher H.
  GN575.B56 2012
  306.83094—dc23

2012013692

**British Library Cataloguing in Publication Data**

A catalogue record for this book is available from the British Library

Printed in the United States on acid-free paper.

ISBN 978-0-85745-749-3 (hardback)
ISBN 978-0-85745-750-9 (ebook)

# Contents

*Chapter Thirteen*

# Figures

# Preface

The nexus of kinship and blood has a taste of age-old ideologies. Today, the connection between kinship and blood is little more than a metaphoric one. But current notions of kinship still owe a great deal to ideas about the physiological connections between kin and what these imply: ideas about shared and exchanged matter and bodily substances, about combining and genes, DNA-sequences, or about passing on characteristics, abilities, and diseases from one generation to the next. What are the continuities and ruptures in conceptions of physiology of kinship—and of metaphors of blood? This book wants to contribute to a history of the substances of relatedness. Its particular focus is on blood, and on how blood went in and out of the ways in which kinship was imagined, conceptualized, attributed relevance and meaning—and related to broader communities such as religious communities, estates, nations, and ethnic groups. It takes up a number of critical moments in these developments between ancient Rome and the present, focusing its gaze for the most part on Europe.

*Blood and Kinship* has grown out of an extended discussion among an international group of historians who want to take kinship seriously as an approach to the history of Europe. These discussions have, besides individual publications, led to several collective volumes representing stages in the group's work. The initial volume, *Kinship in Europe: Approaches to Long-Term Development (1300–1900)* took issue with ideas about the long-term development of kinship implied in most modernization narratives, namely that kinship in Europe over centuries lost ever more of its importance. Instead we sketched alternative models of long-term development and pointed to how kinship played a productive role in processes usually associated with modernization such as state building, migration, or industrialization. The subsequent volume, *Sibling Relations and the Transformations of European Kinship, 1300–1900*, took a closer look at developments of one particular dyad to show how kinship organization went through major transformations between the Middle Ages and the nineteenth century. The recently published volume *Transregional and Transnational families in Europe and Beyond: Experiences since the Middle Ages*, relates kinship organization to patterns of migration and thus demonstrates the role of kinship in highly dynamic social processes. The decision to do a fourth volume on blood came as response to the observation that genetics and technologies of fertility today provide some of the principal occasions to debate kinship—and to do so, once more, in terms of bodily substances.

We would like to thank Bernhard Jussen for the funding generously financed by his Gottfried Wilhelm Leibniz Prize Project, "Pre-modern Kinship." Among the many people who contributed greatly to our discussions and planning for this volume, we would like to thank, in particular, Rachel Fuchs, Karin Gottschalk, Max Sebastian Hering Torres, Michaela Hohkamp, Adam Kuper, Margreth Lanzinger, Jon Mathieu, Eric Porquerres i Gené, Jan Rüdiger, Francesca Trivellato, Karl Ubl, Rhiannon Noel Welch, and John Waller. We owe thanks to many others who helped to make this book possible: The staff at Berghahn Books, particularly Ann Przyzycki DeVita, Nathalie Büsser, Julia Heinemann, Thomas Meier, and, more than anybody else, Ellen Wilson.

# Introduction

## David Warren Sabean and Simon Teuscher

Cultural assumptions about how kinship is related to physiology and sexual reproduction have come in for reexamination in light of a series of new issues. The rapid acceleration in decoding DNA together with progress in reproductive technologies has brought renewed interest in the biological dimensions of parenthood, heredity, and filiation. Around such questions as medical genealogies, paternity testing, new reproductive technologies, and race-specific medicine, a new direction in social anthropological research has developed, calling itself the "New Kinship Studies."[1] This renaissance in research also comes in the aftermath of the 1984 critique by David Schneider, which had already destabilized kinship studies, once at the core of social anthropology.[2] Schneider claimed that traditional anthropological research was inevitably compromised by its tendency without reflection to project assumptions about "American" or "Western" kinship onto foreign cultures—in particular, assumptions about common physiological substance, blood, or genetic material. The new kinship studies pick up the challenge by reconceptualizing processes of "relatedness" and reexamining how different cultures construct an understanding of the substances that are thought to determine who kin are and how people are related to one another.[3]

While anthropologists have taken on a new research agenda for non-Western cultures and occasionally turn their attention today to Western subjects, they have not yet begun historical critical work on Western categories themselves. Schneider failed to notice that kinship in Europe has been anything but a stable entity, that it has gone through numerous reconfigurations over the centuries, that is has been the topic of controversies, and that it has always been the subject of comment in one way or another by theologians, lawyers, physicians, philosophers, and scientists. And today's anthropological studies of Western constructs such as "blood," "substance," and "relatedness" display the same ahistorical point of view. Yet these ideas also have complex historical stories necessary to a balanced understanding and waiting to be told. This book takes on the task of following the career of that substance, "blood," that appears to offer the most difficulty for cultural analysis. It is meant to open up discussion about mapping the use of blood in representations of family and kinship relations from the ancient world to the present, with a primary, reflective focus on Europe.

We can now see that anthropologists, writing in the 1980s, were symptomatic of a shift in research that affected more than one discipline. At the same time, historians began to reconceptualize the study of the family in the West by boldly—or perhaps naively—taking up the concept of "kinship," just as anthropologists were losing heart.[4] Historians found the idea to be a genial construct with which to think through a critique of the modernization paradigm and the self-sufficiency and exceptionality of the West. There had been a configuration of fields in the nineteenth century, consolidated during the first three quarters of the twentieth, which had understood the history of the family in the West essentially to be tied up with a progressive narrowing down of people related to each other and a steady shrinking of households to essentially "mom, dad, and the kids." The "rise of the nuclear family" was closely tied up with schemes of modernization and histories of the development of individualism and capitalism. The discipline that had taken over the responsibility for tracking the changes was sociology. In the meantime, the non-Western world was described as having kinship, and its investigation had been relegated to anthropology. The result was a sharp contrast in studies between the sociology of the family inside the West and the anthropology of kinship for the rest. One of the things that historians have been busy doing is challenging the old assumptions that anthropologists held about their own societies.

The three representatives of New Kinship Studies who write chapters in this book—Janet Carsten, Kath Weston, and Sarah Franklin—are led, each in her own way, to ask questions about history. Franklin, for example, argues that the current debate over the cultural consequences of genetics and the new reproductive technologies has become "blooded." By this she means that even in the discourses about revolutionary scientific discoveries, traditional ideas about physiologically founded ties are mobilized by notions of "blood communities," "pure blood," or "mixing of blood." Blood awakens associations with ancient ideas. But the problem is that we know very little about the history of thinking about blood and kinship in Western cultures. We do know, however, that there have been radically different notions in medical, theological, and juridical thought that have shaped how blood has been conceptualized and what roles it has played. Long before any excitement about genetic technologies, there were central themes, around 1500, for example, which for lack of a better word might be summarized as "proto-racism." Here, blood became the core of intensive debates about hereditary nobility or about essential differences among groups with different descent. While these ideas can be seen at work in the discrimination against Christians of Jewish descent in Iberia that developed around the notion of *limpieza de sangre*, they were also marshaled to rethink notions of connectedness, group recruitment and cohesion, and the distribution of rights and duties in many different ways throughout all the European cultural areas. In some ways, the "work" that blood came to do—which Franklin recognizes in the new genetics discourse—began its historical development in this period.

Anthropologists were quick to talk about popular or "folk" ideas of reproduction in the West without knowing much about them—much less about their history. And the anthropological literature has taken from a cursory, thoroughly ahistorical consideration of canon law the idea that the West "always" or "essentially" has been dominated by "cognatic" structures, bilineality, and "ego-focused" reckoning, notions that preclude the formation of groups through descent. These various terms imply that Western notions of kinship have always rested on an equal mixing of maternal and paternal blood, and that, therefore, lineage constructs, such as those based on agnatic or uterine descent, are impossible. This is simply false, as has been demonstrated by a growing number of historical studies of conceptions and practices of kinship in Europe from the Middle Ages to the present time. In three earlier books, the editors of this volume called on scholars to explore aspects of kinship in their regional and temporal complexity, always with an emphasis on social interaction.[5] Perhaps it is safe to say that their conceptual apparatus was largely developed through reflection on the long, "pre-crisis" anthropological scholarship and a concern with social practices. Yet, clearly, the time has come to engage more directly with the New Kinship Studies and to explore ideas of "relatedness" and offer an historical, critical account of the ways "substance"—in this case "blood"—has been employed in the European past to make connectedness.

This collection of current scholarship is a first attempt to reflect on many of the ways that kinship and substance have been thought about and put into play in Europe from ancient societies to the present. There is no attempt to cover all of the issues. On the contrary, the further we opened up the theme, the clearer it became that it raises many new questions for further reflection. We could not really clarify but only point, for example, to the important arc from the early discussions of evolutionary biology after Darwin and the rise of a scientific discourse about heredity in the early twentieth century to advances in cell theory, hematology, and the physiology of reproduction, current research in reproductive technologies, and the many implications of DNA research for biological identity. We know very little about the interplay between medical and biological research and popular ideas of blood and sexuality, the dissemination of ideas, and the epistemological filiations of metaphors. One of the desiderata of future research might well be to understand just how anthropologists from the late nineteenth century until the present have been situated within these variable discourses. But there is a further problem that needs to be taken into consideration as well. It is now becoming clear that European history is marked by structural breaks and regional and class distinctions within its kinship practices and cultural constructions. Parallel to the scientific reworking of the physiology of human substance has been a reordering of the dynamics of kinship. Recent work in nineteenth-century kinship dynamics needs to be brought into direct confrontation with current analyses of regional kinship by anthropologists who have turned their gaze to their own societies in order to begin to take up the quite recent historical construction of European kinship practices. New models of relationship, filiation, and blood, new social relationships among kin: there is a need to situate the anthropologist and the historian in their own particular contexts by thoroughgoing critical historical research that relates developments in the natural and the social sciences.

The project of this book is "reflexive" in that it takes as its point of departure the questions that anthropologists are now asking about how thinking about substances in different societies produce either "kinship"—where that is still considered to be a relevant category—or "relatedness," if one wants a more neutral term. Certainly any answer must be approached from a radically historical perspective. "Blood" has come and gone in European culture, just as kinship has constantly been reconfigured. Both have been moving, sometimes in parallel and sometimes in divergent directions. And both have taken on quite different meanings over time. Indeed the current understandings of blood in European culture emerged only gradually within the past 150 years.

The long tradition in the anthropological and historical literature was to assume that Europe had always had a particular form of kinship. European kinship was thought to be based on the idea that an individual is composed of a substance—more or less explicitly thought of as blood—that comes in equal parts from two parents. Most of the evidence for this position comes, as noted above, from a cursory reading of canon law proscriptions about marrying within prohibited degrees, since counting degrees proceeds equally through paternal and maternal lines. But there are at least three different problems with the tradition of reading canon law as indicative of "the" kinship system.

First of all, modern observers did not take canon law on its own terms, for there, what we call "affinal" relationships presented the same problem of forbidden marriage as those we bring under the heading of "consanguinity." If you were forbidden to marry a first cousin, you were not only forbidden to partner with the children of your aunts and uncles but also to marry a first cousin of a previous spouse. In other words, in canon law kinship has always been understood as constructed in the sense that marriage and affinal relations in principle present the same problematic as relations through descent. Second, canon law, despite its frequent use of the term "consanguinity" (from the Latin *sanguis*, blood) during its many centuries of formulation, rarely insisted that the substance that connected people was "blood." With regard to both of these issues, it is well worth quoting the regulations issued in 1215 at the Fourth Lateran Council, where the rules were clarified and simplified: here, the prohibition of marriage included the fourth degree (third cousins) of "consanguinity and affinity" without any distinction between the two kinds of relationship. It is clear from the quote below that it follows a logic that is rather different from contemporary Western notions of blood-relatedness. There *were* bodily substances mentioned, but nothing particular about blood—just the humors and the number "four": "The number four agrees well with the prohibition concerning bodily union about which the Apostle [1 Cor. 7:4] says, that the husband does not rule over his body, but the wife does; and the wife does not rule over her body, but the husband does; for there are four humors in the body, which is composed of the four elements."[6] And that is all the explanation that is given. Furthermore, this definitive statement of canon law from the High Middle Ages comes from a period in which blood was seldom used to model kinship. And, as Anita Guerreau-Jalabert shows in chapter 3 in this volume, *consanguinity*, a term borrowed from antiquity, was mostly deployed to gloss relations that were described as based on "flesh." Her chapter, as well as those by Simon Teuscher and Gérard Delille, chronicles the semantic shifts during the later Middle Ages and explains the importance of paying close attention to the language of the "natives."

There is a third problem with taking canon law as the starting point
for depicting a "European model" of kinship. By putting that law in the
first place in thinking about the construction of kinship relationships,
anthropologists have failed to take into consideration the complexity
of substances that connect people down the generations or to see all
the ways that those substances flow differentially or disproportionately.
Certainly, in studying non-Western societies, anthropologists would
take notions and practices of property devolution, naming practices,
familial claims to office and estates, ideas of reproduction, and the like
into consideration when commenting upon the dynamics of kinship for
any particular society. If the same questions also are asked about Europe, its kinship systems appear as composite and convoluted. It can be
shown, for example, that kinship came to be organized around agnatic
lineages throughout large parts of Europe during the early modern period. Moreover, a sharp break with such structures issued in the modern
period, along with a horizontalization of relationships, fostered by new
emphases on cousinship, repeated marriages within well-integrated kin-
dreds, and a new valence given to in-law relationships. And it also can
be shown that the systemic endogamy characteristic of the nineteenth
century began to break up in the decades around World War I. How a
person might find him or herself inscribed within a web of kinship varied substantially over time, with descent, marriage, residence, guardianship, tutorship, god parentage, gender, class, neighborhood, and milieu
playing varied roles.

While this book is mostly not about "substance" in general but con-
fines itself to issues of blood, it might be interesting to explore briefly
some of the other kinds of "things" that have been understood to be
crucial for mapping the circle of relatives. Anthropologists for the most
part have worked with a narrow construction of "substance," proceeding
from Schneider's critique and, as becomes evident when one surveys the
history of the profession, thinking of substance as a matter of physical
incorporation. In some societies, the woman who gives a child her milk
creates a special bond; any children who receive milk from that woman
become "siblings" by that very fact. In much recent work, emphasis has
been placed on nurturing and feeding as creating the ties of relatedness.
All of this, it seems to us, stems from a desire to continue the idea of
kinship arising from reproducing bodies. But it is important to think of
substance in much more complex ways, since after all, it might be property that offers bonds of inclusion or matrices of exclusion, to offer an
oxymoron. Anthropologists nowadays place great emphasis on all of the
practices that *construct* kinship or relatedness. Whereas feeding might be
thought of as progressively communicating the kind of substance that

incorporates, nurturing describes a more diffuse set of actions that attach people to each other, offering one basis for inclusion and exclusion and for the many shifts that alter status over the lifetime of individuals. Once it is possible to broaden the scope of kinship studies in this way, then the path is open to examine all the material actions that bind people together. In a curious way, an historian of nineteenth-century bourgeois society might want to develop a metaphor of ink: witness the flood of correspondence during the central decades of the nineteenth century that circulated between individuals, especially women, who managed to continuously construct and reconstruct kinship through patterns of reciprocal communication. Anyone who emphasizes the way food builds kinship in flexible ways in Southeast Asian or Pacific societies might well find parallels in the way the exchange of letters shaped familial ties in nineteenth-century Europe, since each letter was often thought of as a gift and many of them continuously conveyed moral, practical, and emotional claims.

Of course, the flow of letters might be seen as stretching a point. However, it does seem important to consider a wealth of both material and abstract things that mediate relations, and even more important to get away from the somatic assumptions built into anthropological treatments of the subject. After all, blood and other physical substances are usually only one of several interdependent ways of making kinship bonds plausible and "visible." Discourses about blood and the like always operate in conjunction with other "things": "matter" and "concepts" that shape kinship structures and provide the means for incorporation and exclusion. An impressive example is provided by the founding of Registered Family Associations (*eingetragene Familienvereine*) and their notion of "names," in Germany, toward the end of the nineteenth century.[7] These associations were founded expressly for the purpose of locating and bringing together family members, doing genealogical research and publishing family histories, promoting family solidarity and networks, helping young relatives with education and career opportunities, caring for the elderly, and periodically assembling everyone. What makes these associations interesting for our purposes is that, stereotypically, the "substance" that bound the relatives together was the name. Many of the association constitutions make it clear that the central purpose was to support the honor and reputation of the family surname. What entitled a person to membership in the association was in the first instance descent from a common ancestor—sometimes expressly named, typically someone alive at the turn from the seventeenth to the eighteenth century. By the fact that it was the name that bound people together, the main criterion was descent in the male line. And yet there were interesting inclusions and exclusions. Daughters could be fully fledged members until they married and took the name of another lineage (*Geschlecht*): of course, their children would be excluded from the association. Furthermore, illegitimate children with the name were excluded, since they would have acquired the name by virtue of their mother and thus not through agnatic descent. On the other hand, those women who married in and took their husband's name were expected to join, leaving the association once again, not immediately upon widowhood but upon subsequent remarriage.

There are several points to notice here. Clearly, such a phenomenon provides a very good example of "making kin." In so many of these cases, the people who came together had not had significant social dealings with each other, and in others, had not even had prior knowledge about the existence of one another. Furthermore, this provided a discourse about family that only in the rarest of instances employed the terminology of *blood*. Names mediated relationships and set up new fields of exchange—i.e., they worked much like blood or other substances in the previous examples. Finally, by the very fact that each generation in principle branched, diversified, and proliferated, we can imagine the clan or lineage as a pyramid with apex pointed back to a single ancestor and with all the descendants providing an increasingly widening base. When "blood" began to make its way back into familial discourse in the early twentieth century, it reversed the pyramid, with the apex focused on the individual, concerned as it was with the flow of substance to the individual and with the nature of personal identity—whether in racial identity, medical genealogies, or transfusion.

Agnatic descent could, of course, work quite differently from the nineteenth-century German instance of family societies. In early modern Europe, for example, where property, in the form of an estate or an office, mediated descent, one finds a variety of practices, but never the relatively undifferentiated sense of a family cohesion passed down generations like with the German nineteenth-century emphasis on the name, which, of course, is easier to share than an estate. The substance of property differentiated sharply among siblings and organized kinship around privilege. Still it was all a matter of descent. In England, for example, in a general process from the late Middle Ages, brought to completion by the late seventeenth century, first daughters and then younger sons were excluded from landed estates. Much of the dynamic of the novels of Jane Austen or Anthony Trollope works around agnatic inheritance issues and the relationships between senior and cadet branches of a family. But the key point is that a dynamic interaction within a group, perhaps over several generations, was constituted around the devolution of property, distributing claims, rights, duties, names, resources, expectations, standing, and the like, more-or-less around a line of descent that sloughed off kin in every generation. In his study of Italian noble families during the early modern period, Delille distinguishes sharply between different kinds of goods, real and movable property, offices, statuses, seniority, and so forth.[8] In lineages more and more characterized by primogeniture, the senior branch, rigorously selected through agnatic succession, became sharply differentiated from junior branches. Delille describes a situation in which the sets of cities and towns were differentially ranked as well, such that the senior noble branch would occupy the chief central city, while junior branches were distributed in each generation to centers of ever less prestige and importance. Should a senior branch die out, the next most senior branch took over the noble status, name, offices, rank, and residence. Those scholars who read canon law as reflecting the constitution of a self through blood equally mediated through both parents cannot understand how different kinds of substances such as names, real property, statuses, and offices each provide complex ways of connecting and differentiating kin.

Blood, of course, does show up frequently in Western culture as a substance that connects a person to parents and siblings. But several caveats are in order. There are different discourses, in some cases, which may be operating at the same time, but which cannot be seen to cohere in a single viewpoint. It is quite possible for a strictly agnatic lineage property system to develop and coexist with marriage prohibitions that interdict alliances with both paternal and maternal kin; or for medical science to model heredity in one way, while jurists model it in quite another. For example, in the seventeenth century, there were schools of medicine that followed Aristotle's understanding of generation, whereby the male contributed form and the female matter. Sperm from the male was brought under the category of thought, while the material contribution from the female was conceptualized as "blood." And yet, in the same culture, and sometimes by the very figures who followed Aristotelian notions of generation, blood could be thought of as a matter of agnatic descent. All of the categories seem to have been unstable. Rival schools of Galenic medicine thought of sperm (both male and female) as a form of blood, and many described milk as substantially blood under different accidents. One example of the complexity of meaning possible here is an interesting seventeenth-century treatise from a Bavarian official, Aegidius Albertinus, who "translated" an original Spanish text by Juan de la Cerda.[9] The point of the argument was to encourage women to breastfeed their own children. Indeed, so went the text, any child sent out to a wet nurse could be considered a bastard, an illegitimate child as far as paternal descent was concerned. The milk given to a child is nothing more than the mother's blood, but that blood is constituted by her husband through the act of generation. The wet nurse, therefore, cannot impart the power of the father of the child through her milk. And she becomes the real mother, while the woman who bore the child can only be a "stepmother." The child then is not only *not* hers but also cannot be the child of the father. By engaging a wet nurse, the mother essentially smuggles into her family, as the paternal heir, a child whose blood contains the power not of her husband, but of another man. But there were many other ways of thinking about blood and descent in the seventeenth century. Harvey, for one, in his empirical study of generation came to the conclusion that there was no blood relationship, indeed no relationship of substance of any kind between either parent and their progeny. A very different set of assumptions on how blood was passed on through descent, marriage, and sexual intercourse lay behind the politics of *limpieza de sangre*. Laws demanding "purity of blood" were first issued to keep converts from Judaism and Islam out of official positions. But these notions were also part of the baggage Portuguese and Spanish administrators brought overseas and used in developing visions and divisions of the new societies, drawing lines between indigenous populations, descendants of slaves imported from Africa, and various kinds of "mixed-bloods." These categorizations anticipated important elements of the kind of racism that later developed in the Americas. There is a growing literature on *limpieza de sangre* and related lines in the genealogy of modern racism. But how ideas about kinship and blood are operative in these concepts is one of the many important questions remaining to be addressed.

As David Warren Sabean shows in chapter 7, blood became a central category for descent and alliance in seventeenth-century discourse. Where medieval discourse, for example, had talked about the fleshly relationship between the Virgin Mary and Christ, baroque treatises made the relationship a matter of blood. Guerreau-Jalabert argues, in part, that "blood" became coded as something that could have spiritual content and could be configured as "pure," with the possibility of transmitting inherent qualities. Theologians found this to be a genial construction for thinking through the notion of the Immaculate Conception and understanding the intimate connection between Mother and Son. Indeed, a theologian such as Jacques-Bénigne Bossuet went so far as to argue that the salvific blood that Christ shed on the cross was uniquely and univocally Mary's blood. And blood could be fitted for alliance, as well, with the idea that the blood shared in the Eucharist is also Mary's blood. Secular texts would talk about two lineages "mixing" their blood through the marriage and carnal intimacy of a particular pair, and Bossuet drew an analogy between sexual intercourse and partaking of the Eucharist—both forms of incorporation. Sabean argues that the new theological representations were closely allied with seventeenth-century notions of lineage, which in turn were modeled on a semantics of blood descent; that Mary was seen as a conduit for the blood of Old Testament kings to reach her son. And yet there were ambivalences about just whose blood was understood to flow in the veins of a son. Bossuet himself in an unpublished text emphasized the bloodline as agnatically structured. Blood in the seventeenth century, therefore, could do complex duty, emphasizing descent, identity, purity, stability, paternity, or maternity. What it never seems to do is offer a model for cognaticism or bilineality.

A crucial term that shows up throughout the history of Western culture is *consanguinity* or *consanguinitas*. It is often simply taken for granted that the word means "blood relation" and, further, that it stands for connections that flow equally from both parents—a person is just as much the blood relative of a mother as of a father. This is one of the issues that concerns the first two chapters in this volume, by Ann-Cathrin Harders and Philippe Moreau, which deal with Roman law and culture. Moreau shows that the term emerged in law in a very precise context that had to do with intestate inheritance, designating the sons and daughters of one father. Indeed anyone adopted by a *pater familias* was part of his *consanguinitas*, and in the rare institution of *manus*, where a wife assumed the character of a daughter, she too became part of the *consanguinitas*. Thus in Roman culture, consanguinity was constructed as a subcategory of agnatic kin within the dynamics of absolute domestic power (*patria potestas*). The extensive exogamy rules in Roman society had nothing to do with blood. Rather, they were founded on social values that encouraged extensive intertwining of different families. As both Moreau and Harders argue, blood (*sanguis*) is not the point in "consanguinity." Still, as a large number of literary texts make clear, blood *was* a substance that descended bilineally. By the Middle Ages, the term *consanguinitas* has taken on quite different meanings, among them, as Guerreau-Jalabert points out, the rather diffuse one of "kin in general." The concept of "blood" very rarely was used as a metaphor or thought of as a substance for kinship relationships. Filiation was a matter of "flesh" (*caro*), and consanguines were those who partook of the same flesh. The related term *consanguineus* covered all those who were near kin, including affinal relatives, in an undifferentiated manner. (A French translation of Gratian's Decretals uses the single word *lignage* to translate *consanguineus, consanguinitas, cognatio, propinquitas*, and *parentela*.) Simon Teuscher follows the term *consanguinitas* from flesh to blood during the late Middle Ages and argues that *consanguinity* from the fifteenth century onward became confined to notions of descent. In Teuscher's conceptualization of the problem, blood is delimiting, and is precisely *not* that which connects people bilineally, but rather that which marks out a group through filiation. Where the discourse of flesh had been mostly concerned with marriage and sex, blood was largely a matter of descent. He argues that the differentiation in terminology reflected crucial changes in the vision of kinship, with the emergence of a greater emphasis on descent, linearity, historical depth, and agnatically structured lineages. He shows that only in the fifteenth century were the lines between affinity and consanguinity clearly drawn. Then blood took on new meaning as people began to speak of lineages mixing their blood upon the conclusion of a marriage alliance.

In order to understand the fate of blood during the Middle Ages, the historian has to pay close attention to a series of semantic shifts. Guerreau-Jalabert undertakes a careful philological study of the key terms used in the Middle Ages to deal with kinship. She shows that the early binary opposites, *caro* and *spiritus*, became mapped on to social categories. In complex ways flesh and spirit were called into play to differentiate the laity from the clergy, and with time flesh and blood reflected this same opposition—in the Eucharist, for example, blood was reserved for the priest, and the emergence of the notion of *sanc royal* (royal blood) in the fourteenth century was a semantic move to claim spirituality for the royal family. Teofilo Ruiz and Guillaume Aubert, as well as Teuscher and Delille, follow the fortunes of blood as a spiritualizing or socially valorizing idea to further aristocratic claims for purity of blood. And these contributors point to an important aspect of the development of blood discourse in the early modern period—it was associated with power and with assertions of rightful rulership, with hierarchies of value, and with ascriptive rights based on descent and purity of blood.

During the nineteenth century, as new forms of legitimate authority emerged, blood became increasingly associated with the nation and race, rather than with kin and succession. Aubert follows notions of blood in early modern France as aristocratic notions of purity, agnaticism, and pollution were reconfigured in the French colonies, where initial projects of creating a single blood from French males and native females collapsed. By the time of the French Revolution, fears of contaminating "French blood" in France itself through black and native immigrants shifted the focus of blood away from the family to the nation. Christopher Johnson continues the story, chronicling the disappearance of blood metaphors for family relations with the "horizontalization" of kinship structures and the fall of lineage ideologies. Johnson documents the centrality of blood in everyday familial discourse, particularly in the exchange of letters, in seventeenth-century France, but he shows that its use fades during the eighteenth century. Utilizing an extensive sample of familial correspondence, he is able to show how blood disappears from kinship discourse. Family constructs became useful for the new ideology of the nation, and blood shifted its focus to the ethnic group, race, and nation.

The philosopher Georg Wilhelm Friedrich Hegel pointed toward a number of transitions in social structures and political ideas at the turn of the nineteenth century. He had grown up in Württemberg where, like most European states during the eighteenth century, systems of kin-coordinated politics had developed at every level, from village councils to courts, parliaments, state, and county governments. Just as many other liberal commentators at the turn of the century, he was busy worrying about the conflation of private and public interest and with the "corruption" that confused family and kinship concerns with government. In 1798, commenting on the political organization of the Württemberg state, he ridiculed the entire structure of family-coordinated government as a "feeding trough." He became a powerful spokesman for a rationally constructed state constitution that reconfigured the private possessions of the prince as public property and denied officials, in turn, any familial, patrimonial stake in political institutions. Throughout Europe during the early modern period, the holding of office had more or less officially or legally become tied up with agnatic succession, with the property rights of family syndicates or the patrimony of lineages or clans. The decades around 1800—a central political slogan of the French Revolution was "careers open to talents"—witnessed at different speeds the dismantling of "old corruption" and the construction of "rational" systems of bureaucratic recruitment throughout Europe. However, a close look at state administrations during the nineteenth century shows that the class of officials continued to reproduce itself and provide access to positions within a completely reconfigured structure of kinship. This reordering of familial ties has been characterized as a move from vertical to horizontal relationships, from a system distributing rights through patrilineal succession down the generations to a much more fluid set of networks constructed through marrying endogamously, mobilizing affinal kin, and building obligation within "sibling archipelagos."[10]

This is neither the place to consider the broad shift in the nature of kinship from the eighteenth to the nineteenth century, nor to consider the reasons for the change or explore its ramifications. What is of interest here is the disappearance of "blood" during those same decades, as a metaphor for family and kinship relationships. And Hegel, once again, is a central witness to the reframing of the language of kinship. In fact, as

the chapters in this volume show, blood as a metaphor for kin or referenced as a substance shared by descendants had a rather short and very
discontinuous life in European history. Seldom used in the Middle Ages,
it developed during the early modern period in parallel with the rise of
agnatically structured lines and lineages, then lost its relevance for marking relatives as kinship began to be horizontalized in the late eighteenth
century. But that did not at all mean that blood lost its usefulness for
designating connections altogether. Rather it was refitted for a new kind
of "public," ethnic groups and nations, at about the same time that it lost
its place in the private sphere. Judith Butler has persuasively noted the
Hegelian texts that marked the shift in the valence of blood: "For Hegel,
kinship is precisely a relation of 'blood' rather than one of norms. That
is, kinship is not yet entered into the social, where the social is inaugu-
rated through violent supersession of kinship."[11] Hegel discussed some
of these issues in dealing with the case of Antigone and her conflict with
her uncle over the rights of kin and the power of the state. Antigone represents the claims of "blood," of the "household gods," while Creon, the
head of the state, represents the temporal order of law and justice—and
kinship must give way to the state. The question for us is not whether
Hegel got the terms of trade between the family and the political order
right. What he stands for is at once a critique of the old order of kinship
and a devaluation of the symbolic importance of "blood." He caught the
temper of an era that no longer needed a metaphor of blood to track
moral and physical dimensions of kinship.

By the end of the century blood had returned once again for family,
now in the context of newly emerging notions of heredity, and at the
beginning conflating family and nation. Scientists were busy trying to
figure out just how procreation worked and often borrowed categories
from inheritance law to apply them to the study of physiological heredity. But the development of scientific thinking about heredity, blood, and
race between the mid-nineteenth and the mid-twentieth century is one
important subject that this book can only point to and that remains to
be further explored. One outcome of the development was a consensus
around evolutionary biology, from Charles Darwin to Gregor Mendel to
August Weismann, which came to dominate both scientific and popular literature. Yet as shown in chapter 10 by Cornelia Essner, well into
the first decades of the twentieth century there were many contend-
ing understandings of procreation and connection. Certainly racial ideas
and ideas of the nation played a central role in imagining kinship. Her
chapter is of great interest in showing how widely disseminated notions
such as *Versehen* (the imagination of the mother having physical consequences for the fetus) and telegony (inheriting characteristics of a pre-

vious mate of the mother) still played a crucial role in figuring out not only how the individual was connected to his or her heredity but also how the individual was connected to encompassing constructs of nation and race. Essner explores the debate in National Socialist Germany over how much blood constituted the "German" or the "Jew." Weston, in turn, also calls attention to the issue of "blood quantum" in determining who is a Native American and to the early concerns about intermingling the blood of different races in transfusions. Late-twentieth-century anthropology has developed a model of Euro-American kinship, as Franklin points out, which bases that relation on "natural facts," genealogy, blood relations, and interconnectedness determined by sexual relations. In turning to field work within Western societies, anthropologists are examining values and models that have clearly been strongly influenced by medical and life sciences as they have developed since the late nineteenth century.

The consequence is a deepening of this contemporary version of naturalized kinship. In examining the configuration of nation and family during the first half of the twentieth century, Essner has underscored the understanding of blood as conferring an unchanging identity and of inherited blood as substance that defines the self. It is just that complex of ideas that Carsten, centering her focus on the British Isles, finds still dominant at the end of the twentieth and beginning of the twenty-first century in Europe. She offers an ethnographic contrast with Malaysian ideas in which blood is something that is constructed over time through maternal care and the sharing of food. It is not, as in the UK, an idiom of continuity, an inherited substance. Weston examines the idea in late Western culture that blood is the source of consanguinity, where kinship is understood as something derived from nature, the location of unalienated attachment. In her study, the quest for synthetic blood is closely tied up with the attempt to flee kinship demands and to negotiate either new possibilities of belonging or complexities of ambivalent obligations. Franklin follows the interconnection between blood and genes, and like Carsten and Weston, emphasizes blood as the paradigmatic European substance of kin connection. Biogenetics, like evolutionary biological constructs from the late nineteenth century, are posited upon an essential, blood-based bilateralism. In effect, scientific and medical notions of genes have been "blooded" through the dominance of blood as the main idiom of shared identity.

And so the question of what blood does arises again. We may need to look not only into ruptures but also into a few continuities. Despite profound changes, it seems possible to trace the genealogies of the association of blood with legitimate order, power, and stable identities fairly far back in time. As our contributors together have shown, blood came into play during the late Middle Ages precisely when lineage groups began to form, and it proved adept at stabilizing kin-based identities, in part by elevating kinship above the temporal world with its associations to flesh and decay. The language of blood provided kinship with a touch of spiritual dignity and virtue, turning the construct and institution into an instrument of describing and prescribing legitimate forms of social organization and hierarchies among groups.

In the growing formulation of the split between public and private around the turn of the nineteenth century and as the nation came to be the receptacle of identity and the center of political imagination, blood, along with obligation, seems to have been relocated from the lineage to the nation, thus tied in a new way to political power. Then, during the late nineteenth century, blood made its way back into kinship. Within a new discourse about heredity, under the pressure of evolutionary biology but in dialogue with and through the prism of race and nation, the assumption continued that blood confers an unchanging identity, based in nature and essential to the definition of self.

The model of blood-based bilateralism and inheritance has determined the discourse of biogenetics. Yet in Europe, blood was for centuries understood more often than not as something that attaches fathers to children. What happened to the pre-modern shape of Western ideas about blood, as blood came back in twentieth-century discourses about identity? The interaction between reconfigurations of kinship in twentieth-century Europe and America and the constructions of scientific ideas of blood and genes, together with their popularization, provides the agenda for the next stage of research into the historical development of Western kinship practices.

# Notes

1. See, for example, *Relative Values: Reconfiguring Kinship Study*, ed. Sarah Franklin and Susan McKinnon (Durham, NC, 2001) and Ladislav Holy, *Anthropological Perspectives on Kinship* (London, 1996). More citations and discussion of the recent literature in kinship studies are to be found in Sarah Franklin's chapter in this volume.
2. David M. Schneider, *A Critique of the Study of Kinship* (Ann Arbor, 1984).
3. See *Cultures of Relatedness: New Approaches to the Study of Kinship*, ed. Janet Carsten (Cambridge, 2000).
4. A summary of the trend for historians is found in *Kinship in Europe: Approaches to Long-Term Development (1300–1900)*, ed. David Warren Sabean, Simon Teuscher, and Jon Mathieu (New York and Oxford, 2007).
5. The three studies are *Sibling Relations and the Transformations of European Kinship 1300–1900*, ed. Christopher H. Johnson and David Warren Sabean (New York and

Oxford, 2011); *Transregional and Transnational Families in Europe and Beyond: Experiences since the Middle Ages,* ed. Christopher H. Johnson et al. (New York and Oxford, 2011); and the aforementioned Sabean, Teuscher, and Mathieu, *Kinship in Europe.*

6. http://history.hanover.edu/texts/trent.html.

7. David Warren Sabean, "Constructing Lineages in Imperial Germany: Eingetragene Familienvereine," in *Alltag als Politik—Politik im Alltag. Dimensionen des Politischen in Vergangenheit und Gegenwart,* ed. Michaela Fenske (Berlin and Münster, 2010), 143–57.

8. Gérard Delille, *Le maire et le prieur: Pouvoir central et pouvoir local en Méditerranée occidentale (XVᵉ–XVIIIᵉ siècle)* (Paris, 2003).

9. Juan de la Cerda, *Weiblicher Lustgarten,* Teil 1, trans. Aegidius Albertinus (Munich, 1605).

10. The phrase is Christopher H. Johnson's, in Johnson and Sabean, *Sibling Relations.*

11. Judith Butler, *Antigone's Claim* (New York, 2002).

# Chapter 1

# *Agnatio, Cognatio, Consanguinitas*

**Kinship and Blood in Ancient Rome**

## Ann-Cathrin Harders

## Family Matters

In her autobiography, *A Backward Glance,* first published in 1934, Edith Wharton takes the reader to the New York of her birth in the 1870s:

> My mother, who had a hearty contempt for the tardy discovery of aristocratic genealogies, always said that old New York was composed of Dutch and British middle-class families, and that only four or five could show a pedigree leading back to the aristocracy of their ancestral country. These if I remember rightly, were the Duers, the Livingstons, the Rutherfurds, the de Grasses and the Van Rensselaers (descendants, these latter, of the original Dutch "Patroon"). … My own ancestry, as far as I know, was purely middle class; though my family belonged to the same group as this little aristocratic nucleus I do not think there was any blood-relationship with it. The Schermerhorns, Joneses, Pendletons, on my father's side, the Stevenses, Ledyards, Rhinelanders on my mother's, the Gallatins on both, seem all to have belonged to the same prosperous class of merchants, bankers and lawyers.[1]

After placing her family in the group of families that came from British colonies other than New York and arrived in Manhattan later than the original Dutch and British settlers, Wharton turns to her great-grandfathers, paternal and maternal. To describe the heart of New York's society, she looks to family and family matters.[2] As the protagonists of her novels bitterly must learn, the ramifications of kinship networks placed individuals in a web of social expectations and obligations that they could not escape without facing grave consequences; their own doings and wishes were outweighed by the claims of genealogy and affinity.

Social arbiter Samuel Ward McAllister famously coined the expression "the Four Hundred" to describe the set of fashionable people and families that ruled New York society. Within this illustrious group, rank and distinction were determined by kinship ties. *Ab origine* families, such as the Duers, Livingstons, and Rutherfurds, set themselves apart as a special group within this elite by rejecting the attempts of newer families, the Whartons among them, to integrate by intermarrying with them and establishing blood relations. The oldest Manhattan aristocracy thus constituted an exclusive nucleus that founded its identity on consanguinity and antiquity.

Very much like the aristocracy of New York's Gilded Age, the nobility of republican Rome can be described as a "Four Hundred"—not only in numbers, but also in terms of self-regard. Also, like its modern counterpart, the republican Roman nobility used kinship to structure hierarchies within its ranks and marriage to integrate newcomers into the group, or the refusal of marriage to draw firm boundaries. Therefore, when Edith Wharton started her autobiography by referring to her paternal and maternal ancestors, thus distinguishing her agnate from her cognate descent, she was using strategies and speaking in terms that the great biographers of Roman antiquity, Suetonius and Plutarch, would have recognized. The same observation holds true of her references to families whose links through affinity would lead in the next generation to cognate relations. Wharton, in short, unfolded a social map that any Roman could easily have read.[3]

In republican Rome, kinship not only created family groups, but also helped to constitute the aristocracy and to distinguish that group as one of privilege and rank in the social structure. Affiliation to a specific kinship group allowed a Roman aristocrat to position himself within Roman aristocracy. He could refer to the honor of his ancestors, the prestige of his name, and, of course, he could count on his kinsmen, his clients, and his *amici* for help during his run for office—the Latin term *honor*, quite aptly, meant both "honor" and "political office."[4] On a macro-level, through belonging to the larger aristocratic "family," he could assure himself that he was different from the ordinary people, possessed of high-ranking social status, enjoying a spot at, or very near the top, of his society.[5]

Given the social importance of family and kinship, it is surprising that Roman society never settled on definitive concepts of kinship and family, but rather developed several concepts of each. The resulting variety makes it difficult for modern historians to define *the* Roman family or the larger Roman kinship group. Scholarly debates about the social importance of agnate and cognate relations, or about the outlines of the Roman household, the *domus*, ramify from these failures of definition. The aim of this chapter is first to discuss the various configurations of kinship in republican and imperial Rome and their social functions, and second, to analyze the significations and functions assigned in these concepts to the idiom of blood.

## *Agnatio* and *Cognatio*

The Latin language lacks a specific term to distinguish the nuclear family from larger kinship or household groups: usually terms like *necessarii* and *propinqui*, literally "those near in relationship," are used to describe relatives, but there is no differentiation of degrees, of maternal from paternal kin, or of relatives acquired by marriage (*adfines*) from those related by birth. Equally important, neither the modern concept of the nuclear family nor the modern terms *family, famille, famiglia*, and *Familie* directly translate the Latin term *familia*. Moreover, the precise meaning of the Latin has actually been debated since antiquity. At the beginning of the third century CE, for example, the Roman jurist Ulpian gave no fewer than five definitions of the term, while highlighting the important structures of Roman kinship groups: *agnatio* and *cognatio*.

According to Ulpian, *familia* refers to persons and property both. Freed men (*liberti*) belonged to the *familia* of their patron and former master, as did slaves, who were considered property.[6] *Familia*, therefore, exceeded the modern understanding of a group of related persons, although Ulpian is very careful also to define *familia* as a specific kinship group, a body in its own right, defined by an agnatic principle.[7] The *agnatio* (group of agnates) was a kin structure defined exclusively by patrilineal descent, which was seen as the core of the larger kinship group, *cognatio*. In legal terms, the *agnatio* was described as *cognatio legitima* or *civilis*, a subdivision of the *cognatio*. The *cognatio* (group of cognates), in contrast, was defined bilaterally and ascribed to natural law.[8] Though basically defined by patrilineage, agnatic kinship was not, in fact, transmitted via the biological act of procreation. Rather, the status resulted from the application of the legal concepts *paterfamilias* and *patria potestas*. Agnates were those who would have been subject to the power of the *paterfamilias* while he was alive.

There were actually many different ways of entering or leaving a *pater*'s power, the boundaries of which were determined by the distinction in Roman law between a *genitor* and a *paterfamilias* or legal father. The *genitor* was simply a biological father whose claim to *patria potestas* was restricted to his children born within the bounds of legal marriage; he had no claim to children born to a concubine or in any other way outside of wedlock. The *paterfamilias*, in contrast, was a legal status not directly tied to biological fatherhood. It could be granted to a *genitor* but also to underage boys, or to eunuchs or other men unable to sire children.[9] The *patria potestas* of the *paterfamilias* derived from his position as head of the household or *familia;* a *pater* thus exercised power over a broader group of people than a genitor did. Both emancipation and adoption were legal means of transferring *potestas* from one male to another: in the first case, an emancipated son left the *patria potestas* of his father and became a *pater* in his own right and head of his own *familia;* in the second case, an adoptee entered the *familia* of the adoptive father and became *agnatus* to him and to the other persons under his power as *paterfamilias*.[10] The legal character of kinship by adoption was emphasized by the fact that an adoptee was not considered a *cognatus naturalis* and therefore could not claim any relation to the wife of the adoptive *pater*.[11] Furthermore, with his "birth" *familia* an adoptee retained nothing but cognate relations. The situation for wives was different altogether. Motherhood brought a woman only a cognate relationship to her children, unless she had celebrated a special kind of marriage, the so-called *conventio in manum*. This form of marriage—exceedingly rare in the late republican and imperial eras—brought a wife under the legal control of her husband, the so-called *manus*, who replaced her biological father as her *paterfamilias*. Upon legally and ritually leaving the agnatic family unit of her birth, with which she afterward had but a cognate relationship, she became an *agnata* to her husband and children.[12]

Clearly the constitution of a *familia* was not based on procreative relations, and the biologically based idea of bilateral filiation was rejected in favor of a complex logic rooted in a legal concept. Why did the Romans make matters so complicated? In part, as I shall indicate below, it is because differentiation between agnatic and cognatic kinship served to constitute the *familia* as a distinct group and to construct its identity in many ways.

First, the family name was handed down from *pater* to son. The Roman name system was unique among the societies of antiquity in that

it identified the kinship group by a *nomen gentile* rather than by a patro-
nymicon derived (usually) from the agnatic lineage. The Roman *nomen
gentile* marked its bearer as a member of a certain *gens* (clan); an adoptee
accordingly was obliged to assume the clan name of his adoptive father.[13]
The origins and social significance of the *gens* remain obscure, and by the
time of the late republic, common usage no longer strictly distinguished
between *gens* and *familia;* both were structured by patrilineage and descended from a common ancestor. The *gens* was regarded as the larger
and older group, containing branches or subdivisions, the *stirpes*, which
were marked by a third name, the *cognomen*. According to ancient authors, the main distinction between *gentiles* and *agnati* lay in the fact
that agnates could still prove their relation to one another whereas clan
members could only assume it on account of their common name.[14]

Second, the family cult was passed down from one generation to the
next by patrilineal descent: thus agnates also formed a specific group
ritually. In performances of family rites, the *sacra familiae*, the *paterfamilias* was the focal point. The *Parentalia*, the most important festival,
which entailed sacrificial offerings to the ancestral dead, took place at
the end of February. Unlike the *Lemuria*, a festival to appease the spirits
of the dead, the *Parentalia* did not contain any apotropaic aspects; the
agnatic *divi parentum*, the spirits of the *parentes*, were considered benevolent: Only if a son were to act against his father, would that son for-
feit the grace of his ancestors' spirits. Another aspect of family cult that
strengthened the position of the *paterfamilias* was the worshipping of
the *pater*'s *genius*. Considered his procreational force, the *genius* was celebrated on the *pater*'s birthday by the *familia*, the slaves, the freedman,
and the clients. Furthermore, if those under the power of the *pater* had
to take an oath, they swore on his *genius*—the *pater* thus represented
"the trustworthiness of their actions."[15]

Third, and of greatest importance, agnatic descent determined the
transmission of property: the Roman law of inheritance clearly favored
agnates, who took priority over *gentiles* and *cognati*. According to the
Twelve Tables, Rome's earliest law code, dating from the 450s BCE, when
a *paterfamilias* died intestate, family members who became *sui iuris* (legally independent) as a consequence of that death were privileged as *sui
heredes* (his heirs). Sons and daughters of the deceased were given equal
shares in the estate and were denoted *consanguinei*—another specific
relationship in Roman law that will be discussed in the next section and
is treated in depth by Philippe Moreau in this volume.[16] A wife who
had entered the power (*manus*) of her husband was treated legally as
his daughter (*filiae loco*) and was therefore counted among his heirs.[17]
After the *sui heredes*, the next to inherit were the *proximi agnati* (clos-

est agnates).[18] Until the second century BCE, male and female agnates of this category were entitled to the same share, but after the issuing of the *lex Voconia* on female legacies in 169 BCE, female agnates other than the narrowly defined *consanguinei* were excluded. At the end of the republic, the praetor granted cognates a right of inheritance (the *bonorum posses-sio*), albeit only after agnates, emancipated sons, and clan members.[19] Agnates were also the first to be considered as tutors for underage children (*tutela impuberum*) or women (*tutela mulieris*). As legal guardians, they had to take care of their wards unless the *paterfamilias* declared otherwise in his will.[20]

The agnatic principle thus established unambiguous rules for the transmission of family property, name, and cult within the kinship group. Through unilateral filiation, every Roman was assigned to a single family unit and could claim no rights of any kind from another agnatic *familia*. This unambiguous classification of distinct family units was highly useful in a society as complicated and economically sophisticated as Rome.

Yet the distinguishing factor of the Roman agnatic system was not its mechanisms for the transmission of property, cult, and name by patri-lineage, all of which can be found in most classical and early modern societies, but the extensiveness of the *paterfamilias*'s powers, which ex-ceeded by far those of his Greek counterparts. The *patria potestas* is described by Roman jurists as uniquely Roman. It must be understood as an absolute power; indeed it is described as an *ius vitae necisque:* quite concretely, a *paterfamilias* held the power of life and death over those in his *potestas*. Unlike the Greek head of the family, the *kyrios*, the Ro-man *paterfamilias* did not transfer his position and power during his lifetime. Only after his death could sons still under his power become le-gally autonomous *patres* themselves.[21] Despite a few, very few, examples to the contrary, modern scholarship has long eschewed the idea of the cruel and controlling *paterfamilias* who tyrannized his household with the threat of death and occasionally killed his own children. Indeed, the concept of *patria potestas* must be seen as a means of disciplining both Roman sons and male heads of households.[22] This power was not to be wielded by whim but rather according to political needs; a *paterfamilias* who killed his sons for minor offenses was censured.[23] The *pater* actu-ally acted as a magistrate in his own house on behalf of the *res publica Romana*, which in turn granted him absolute power in his domain.[24] But the *pater* clearly had to place common interests before those of his lineage: if, for example, a son acted contrary to the interests of the *res publica*, the *pater* was obliged to punish him, even when the death of that son meant the end of his line.[25] Through their *potestas*, especially their powers to discipline, the Roman *patres*, as heads of agnatic *familiae*,

were thus part of the Roman political system. It was they who took care
that the magistrates' commands were obeyed.[26]

Given the extent of the power of the *pater* and his political-disciplin-
ary role, it was essential to define unambiguously the group of persons
who had to submit to it, in order to prevent confusion. The concept of
an absolute domestic power that transcended the limits of "public" and
"private" would not have worked in a kinship system based on bilateral
descent; a clearly defined *familia* that did not bend to disputable, biologically based logic was a prerequisite to the success of the system.

Because of the preference for the agnatic principle in Roman law,
modern scholars have generally argued for the prevalence of agnatic kin
also in social life and have relegated the larger cognate kin group to
a secondary role, even though the legally underprivileged *cognatio* and
*adfines* (kin acquired by marriage) can be seen to have played important
roles in daily life, especially in the raising of children and the establishment and maintenance of cooperative political, social, and economic
activities. These links were displayed in family festivals such as the *Matralia* and the *Cara Cognatio*, where cognate kinsmen met or performed
important ritual functions.[27] Bilaterally configured kindred were, in fact,
significant in Roman society, as Philippe Moreau has emphasized recently, even though the Latin language does not provide a precise term
for this group of relatives.[28]

The "horizontally" orientated *cognatio* and *adfinitas* served critical social functions outside the purview of the agnatically structured, essentially political *patria potestas*. The early republican system of structuring
marriage, which essentially prevented agnatic *familiae* from remaining
exclusive family units, provides the clearest example. Neither agnates
nor cognates were allowed to enter marriage within the sixth degree,
i.e., the fourth degree by modern reckoning. Such alliances were considered *incestus* and *nefas*, defiled and contrary to divine law, and were forbidden.[29] Marriages to stepchildren, children-in-law, and parents-in-law
were also prohibited, even after the spouse who had brought *adfinitas*
had died.[30] In contrast, in classical Athens, members of the *anchisteia*,
the legally defined kinship group including first cousins once removed,
were the preferred marriage partners. In order to protect the continuity of the household (*oikos*), even marriage between half-siblings was
allowed. The Greek practice of endogamy has been interpreted as an
attempt to strengthen the *oikos* and to guarantee that its property was
transmitted intact. This family strategy is most notorious in the case of
the daughter as heiress, the *epikleros*. Usually women were not able to
inherit or hold property, but when an Athenian died without male issue, his property was attached to his daughter, who then had to marry

the closest agnate, often an uncle or first cousin. In this way the *oikos* remained linked to the agnatic lineage.[31]

Roman society, in a strategy unique in antiquity, proscribed familial endogamy, opting instead for exogamy and the building of large kinship groups, even if this meant that property was diffused and the agnatic lineage thus weakened. Prescriptive marriage regulations were never developed, but Romans still knew perfectly well the boundaries distinguishing acceptable marriage alliances from misalliances. Familial exogamy was combined with social endogamy. Though it was forbidden legally to choose marriage partners from among agnatic or cognatic kin, it was nevertheless expected that spouses would be selected from a specific social group: matrimonial matches were judged on these grounds as *dignus* (worthy), *splendissimus* (most splendid), *par* (of equals) or *impar* (of unequals), or even *sordidus* (sordid).[32] Unlike aristocrats in early Greece, who married beyond the limits of their *patris*, Roman aristocrats concentrated on Rome. Given the limited number of appropriate families and the strict marriage regulations, the options of a Roman aristocrat seeking a marriage alliance were rather few. This "marry-go-round" within the peer group led to the building up of a complex network of intertwined familial relations and ultimately to the creation of one overwhelmingly aristocratic family. On the macro-level, the creation of *adfinitas* should therefore be seen as an important factor in the integration of Roman aristocrats and the constitution of the Roman aristocracy as a group. Marriage alliance, or in Lévi-Strauss's terms, the exchange of women within a certain group, was one element in a wider set of relationships built on exchange—of children for adoption, of property by dowry or legacy, and of sons, whose education was entrusted to peers.[33] This whirl of exchanges produced obligations, bonds, and relationships that were constantly woven into a social web. Roman aristocrats who operated in this network were at once confirmed as a group of peers and secluded socially from the lower ranks of society. Representing an exchange of persons, obligations, and property, these ties helped to secure cohesion in a group that was constantly challenged from inside by the stresses arising from aristocratic competition for fame, honor, and rank.[34]

Strains on aristocratic cohesion, however, as well as the beginning of the disintegration of the Roman elite during the third and second centuries BCE, coincided with changes in Roman marriage regulations. There is not enough source material to reconstruct precisely the relationship between changes in the building of kinship groups and in socio-political structures during the Roman Republic, but it is known that during the third century BCE, marriage restrictions were relaxed up to the fourth degree, thereby allowing first cousins to marry. Kinship groups could thus become more exclusive and refuse intermarriage with other families—very much like the families of Edith Wharton's New York. The most famous examples of this practice can be found within Rome's most illustrious family, the Cornelii Scipiones, where the daughter of Scipio Africanus, the conqueror of Hannibal, married her first cousin once removed; and Scipio's adoptive grandson, Aemilianus, married his first cousin, Sempronia, herself a granddaughter of the famous general. Despite such examples, however, marriage between cousins never became frequent within the Roman aristocracy.[35]

Let me summarize the main points so far: Roman society opted for a bilateral kinship system, in which different social functions were governed by contrasting principles. On the one hand, a strict agnatic principle was put forward by Roman jurists to regulate unambiguously the transmission of property, power, cult, and name, and to define the group of persons who were subject to the absolute power of the *paterfamilias*. This principle created small family units. On the other hand, an exogamous principle regulated marriage and enforced the building of large kinship groups. This cognate network was cultivated by family rituals, familial cooperation, and certain social expectations that shaped behavior among kinsmen.[36] In neither case were what we would call "blood" relationships supreme. Nevertheless, the Romans had a term for such relationships, *consanguinitas*, and understanding how they used that term offers another path for investigating their conceptions of kinship.

## Consanguinitas

Unlike ancient Greek, the Latin language possesses an abstract term, *consanguinitas*, to describe the sharing of blood. Its meaning, however, was never clearly defined in antiquity.[37] The actual character of blood as a substance was long debated in ancient medicine, but no standard theory ever prevailed.[38] Aristotle considered semen "foam of blood," and his views on blood and on the different roles of male and female in procreation influenced both late imperial-Roman as well as medieval authors.[39] In 623 CE, for example, Isidor of Seville, in his *Etymologies*, defined *consanguinei* as "those of one blood, i.e. those who are of one father's semen. For the semen of man is the foam of blood [*spuma sanguinis*]."[40] *Consanguinitas* is thereby confined to sons and daughters of one father. In her analysis of Roman blood ties, Gianna Pomata refers to this medical view and contemplates how medical ideas shaped the legal notion of *consanguinitas*. Roman law defined *consanguinei* as a special group of agnate heirs; according to Pomata, this legal logic can only be understood within the "context of the concomitant idea on the origin of the semen" as foam of blood. Accordingly, blood ties have to be seen as semen ties, a view that serves to establish the primacy of paternal, agnatic blood in both medical and legal contexts. Yet Pomata leaves aside alternative medical debates on the character of blood as well as the specific implications of legal definitions of Roman kinship, especially those that contradict biological-medical definitions of *consanguinitas*. Although she briefly admits the existence of contradictory literary evidence, she does not contemplate the actuality that in Latin literature neither the physical character of blood nor its actual transmission by the act of procreation is discussed. Given the ambiguities in linguistic and literary evidence, Walter Burkert thinks that to understand Roman kinship, it is best to leave aside the biological aspect of blood and to focus instead on its "quasi-magical impact."[41]

Gianni Guastella has shown the ways and contexts in which blood was thought of as a vehicle for constituting groups in general and kinship groups in particular: "the most elemental kinship relations were just considered 'relations of blood.'"[42] Blood in this sense was thought to be a substance transmitted bilaterally, that is through both mother and father. *Sanguis*, he goes on to demonstrate, was also seen by the Romans as a substance that metaphorically transmitted certain qualities, both physical and ethical, down through a lineage, and that defined group identity. It transcended the relationship between parents and children, being shared as it was by a much larger group of kinsmen of undefined grades.[43]

As *sanguis* is a very broad criterion for constituting groups, the precise meaning of the terms *consanguinei* and *consanguinitas* is difficult to grasp. In the hands of Roman jurists writing of intestate inheritance, the term *consanguinei* usually refers to siblings. The same holds true in Roman poetry.[44] It may, however, also refer to any member of a group constituted by common *sanguis*, thus to members of family groups, social groups like *ordines*, or even ethnic groups; and it is also used to make an anthropological distinction between human beings and animals. Given the vagueness of the parameters of the group defined as *consanguinei*, Guastella concludes that *consanguinitas* has a "rather widespread functional scope and may refer to entities of diverse dimensions."[45]

Although an important factor in constituting kinship groups—Guastella gives ample evidence from various authors and literary genres—it is striking that blood is not a prominent concept in the works of Latin authors, especially not in the works of that most gifted linguist, Cicero. It is therefore more instructive to analyze his uses of the idiom of blood than it would be to collect the usages of *sanguis* by ancient authors of lesser linguistic acuity.[46]

*Sanguis* as a substance enjoys a prominent role in Cicero's work. Usually it is spilled by monstrous adversaries, like the brutal governor Verres who kills brave Roman citizens.[47] In a few passages it is a substance that runs within a lineage, thereby transmitting personal qualities. In such instances blood is an explicitly bilateral concept.[48] Yet it can be noticed that the abstract *consanguinitas*, to describe a kinship group, appears less frequently than other descriptors of kinship such as *cognatio*, or *agnatio*, or the relatively "neutral" *propinquitas*. In his oeuvre of philosophical, rhetorical, and political treatises, his speeches, and in his correspondence as well, Cicero refers to *cognates* and *cognatio* about eighty times, to *propinqui* or *propinquitas* about sixty times. *Consanguinitas*, however, is mentioned only six times.[49] Due to its rarity, it is instructive to analyze the passages in which it does occur.

In August 59 BCE, Cicero wrote to his friend Atticus on the matter of the precarious protection from his political enemy Clodius being provided by Pompey Magnus.[50] The style of the letter is archly elevated: Cicero refers to Clodius's sister Clodia and to Pompey himself by using pseudonyms, Boōpis and Sampsiceramus respectively. Boōpis (literally, "cow-eyed") recalls the Homeric epithet associated with the goddess Hera; Sampsiceramus alludes to Pompey's achievements in the East, the real Sampsiceramus having been an Aramaic chieftain who infamously killed the last Seleucid king, Antiochos XIII, at Pompey's request. In this context, Cicero also refers to Clodia's brother not as her *frater*, as he usually does, but as her *consanguineus*. The term, clearly meaning "sibling" here, could evidently be regarded as comically pompous.[51]

In a more serious vein, in his rhetorical work, *De inventione*, Cicero, ranking the most horrible crimes that men can commit, puts those against kinsmen in first place: "These were those done with cruelty towards one's parents [*parentes*], children [*liberi*], spouses [*coniuges*], relations [*consanguinei*], or suppliants [*supplices*]."[52] It is not perfectly clear which group of kinsmen is referred to by the term *consanguinei*; we can say that consanguines/relations are distinguished from parents, children, and spouses, but that is as far as we can go. Cicero may be referring to siblings but also to cognates in general.[53] His other uses of the term—also to be found in *De inventione*—are more precise. He emphasizes the need to distinguish persons by their people (*natio*), homeland, *cognatio*, and age. To make his point he further distinguishes these categories: "homeland, whether Greek or barbarian; fatherland, whether Athenian or Lacedaemonian; kindred [*cognatio*], who are his ancestors [*quibus maioribus*] and who are his relations [*quibus consanguineis*]; age, whether a boy, a youth, an adult, or an old man."[54]

*Cognatio* is an overarching concept that is differentiated into *consanguinei* and *maiores;* Cicero twice combines these categories in *De inventione* to describe the widest range of *cognatio*.[55] Given the context, *maiores* seems to refer to "vertical" kinship organized in time, a diachronic lineage including the dead, whereas *consanguinei* indicates kinsmen still living and describes the bilateral, "horizontal" kinship group. Although Cicero's use of *consanguinitas* is not uniform and rather rare, a semantic tendency to denote the living cognate kinship group of an individual can be detected.

A few decades after Cicero's death, we have another Latin author with an enormous oeuvre: Titus Livius (Livy), whose *Ab urbe condita libri* covers the period from the foundation of Rome to the year 9 CE. Like Cicero, Livy uses terms like *cognati/cognatio* or *propinqui* far more frequently than *consanguinitas,* but he employs the concept of common blood in a different way.[56] In his narrative of the conflicts between Rome and the Etruscan cities, Livy describes relations in the latter as founded on *consanguinitas. Sanguis* serves to connect the otherwise autonomous cities and to constitute the Etruscans as an ethnic group distinct from Rome.[57] During the Latin War, Livy reports, the Latin L. Annius employed *consanguinitas* in a political argument which relied on the alleged blood relationship of Latins and Romans to validate Latin demands for one of the two consulships in the *res publica Romana.* The Roman consul Titus Manlius Torquatus famously rejected the Latin demand in 340 BCE, and both consulates remained in Roman hands.[58] Livy reports the same argument being used in 216 BCE, during the Second Punic War, by Decius Magius from Capua, who argued against a Punic occupation and reminded his fellow Capuans—without success—that the Romans were their "oldest allies and blood-brothers [*consanguinei*]."[59] The reconstruction of kinship ties between two political units such as cities or *ethnē* was not uncommon in antiquity: usually common descent from a famous ancestor or *heros* was claimed, which allowed for "kinship diplomacy."[60] But in Livy's account, Decius does not name a specific common ancestor. Instead he just refers to the more diffuse concept of *consanguinitas.*

Whereas in relating the story of the Etruscans and Latins, Livy shows *consanguinitas* being harnessed to the task of constituting political relations as one *natio,* in other narratives, he uses "plain" *sanguis* to constitute specific descent groups. In the cases of Hannibal, the Carthaginian, and Perseus, the Macedonian king, for example, a bloodline is envisioned that connects three generations of men. This common line means that the fathers and grandfathers of these noted individuals share certain qualities—bravery and enmity toward Rome—which they, in turn, pass down to their sons.[61] In another case, the Roman Titus Manlius proudly presents war spoils to his father, the commanding officer, as evidence that he is "descended from your blood [*tuo sanguine ortum*]." However, because Titus has disobeyed both his father and the consul, the elder Manlius orders his death, referring to the common blood running in their veins as an explanation for this harsh treatment.[62] Livy also uses the metaphor "royal blood" twice—but far more often he refers to "royal descent [*regii generis*]" or "stock [*regum stirps*]."[63] It is telling, however, that in modern translations the blood metaphor is preferred to Livy's original use of *genus* or *stirps*.

Yet the sharing of *sanguis* plays an important role in Livy's account of the Canuleian rogation to allow intermarriage between patricians and plebeians in 445 BCE. He reports that the patrician refusal to grant *conubium*, the right to intermarry, was strongly associated with the fear of mingling and thus contaminating patrician with plebeian blood: "Gaius Canuleius, a tribune of the plebs, proposed a bill regarding the intermarriage of patricians and plebeians, which the patricians believed would corrupt their blood (*sanguis*) and would confuse the rights of the clans." Canuleius attacked this position and argued that the patrician caste was not founded on blood, but rather on cooptation.[64]

As Guastella noted, *sanguis* was used to constitute the patricians as a distinct social and religious group.[65] Livy did not choose the word *cognatio* to describe the patrician group, despite the likelihood that the ramifications of kinship allowed patricians to recognize each other as cognates to some degree. Rather, he chose the concept of *sanguis* and in this way associated the patrician order with an organism that could be harmed. By referring to blood, Livy was evoking an image similar to the one that Edith Wharton would adopt millennia later in *A Backward Glance*. Like her New York aristocrats, Livy's Roman patricians tried to ensure their exclusiveness by refraining from intermarriage with "commoners," thus protecting the pureness of their blood and, at the same time, defining their circle by its "untainted" bloodlines. Blood not only establishes the patricians as a group but also guarantees the social hierarchy that differentiates patricians from plebeians. As Brigitta Hauser-Schäublin has shown for Hindu societies, blood can serve as a political instrument to naturalize hierarchies and stabilize class societies. She also points out that sexual relations of women are controlled in such a system because a woman who has relations outside the group would taint the blood and threaten the group's identity. The exclusiveness of the group is paralleled by the purity of blood, which legitimizes and enforces social endogamy.[66]

According to Livy, patrician identity depended on the purity of their blood; therefore opposition to the Canuleian bill was strong, though ultimately futile, because the bill was passed. The emphasis on blood in Livy's account must be seen as a peculiarity. In other narratives of the same incident, the blood issue is not mentioned, nor does purity of blood enter into Livy's descriptions of patrician-plebeian conflicts in other contexts.[67]

As we have seen, Livy uses *sanguis* and *consanguinitas* to constitute descent groups as well as large social or national groups, but his usages do not conform to Cicero's or to those of the Roman poets or jurists; in fact, overall, the concept *consanguinitas* proves to be rather flexible, open to interpretation.[68] Furthermore, in Livy's works, and in Cicero's in this instance, *consanguinitas* does not compete with *cognatio* and *agnatio* as a rival concept. Why is that so? It seems that *consanguinitas* was well suited to identify broad groups as kinship groups but was inferior to *cognatio* and *agnatio* in other, more important, social, legal, and political contexts.

In some respects the concept of consanguinity was too narrow, as when it collided with legal definitions of the elements of the kin group. This problem is revealed quite clearly in the cases of adoption and *manus* marriage. Adoption was a strategy for guaranteeing one's lineage, but also a means of cultivating relations built on exchange between aristocratic *familiae*.[69] Accordingly, a Roman *pater*, unlike an Athenian *kyrios*, could adopt even when he already had his own sons, and in this way he could bring someone unrelated by blood into his agnatic *familia* and *gens* and under the purview of his *patria potestas*. Similarly, by the institution of *manus* marriage, he could extend his power over a woman from another kin group; she was no longer part of her biological father's agnatic *familia*, although she still had a cognate relationship to her parents and siblings. Instead, in marriage, she had the same legal status in her husband's family as one of his daughters.

Had the everyday Roman bilateral conception of *consanguinitas* been applied to inheritance, adoptees and wives *in manu* would not have been recognized as kin and thus also would not have received inheritances upon the intestate death of the *paterfamilias*. But such practices would have weakened the *familia*, thereby undercutting its important functions within the Roman polity. Consequently in the context of intestate legacies, Roman jurists tried to accommodate *consanguinitas* and *agnatio*, devising definitions that still puzzle modern scholars. Cassius, for example, defined *consanguinei* rather tautologically as *"eos qui sanguine inter se conexi sunt"* (those who are related by blood), while the majority of Roman jurists subordinated *consanguinitas* to the agnatic principle.[70] The common meaning of *consanguinitas* was not flexible enough to account for the shifting of the *patria potestas* in cases of adoption, emancipation, or *manus* marriage, leading Roman jurists to define *consanguinitas* in the context of intestate legacies as unilaterally derived from *patria potes-tas* and thus detached from its biological implications: on the legacy of *spurii* (children born outside legal marriage and hence without *paterfa-milias*), Ulpian clearly states that biological siblings may not claim a *ius consanguinitatis* since it derives from *patria potestas*.[71]

Although it was possible to define the *consanguinei* as a subspecies of cognates, as Cicero did in *De inventione*, it was also possible to under-stand shared blood as constituting much larger and more diffuse groups: Livy demonstrates that social groups like the patricians and *nationes* like the Etruscans, Romans, or Latins could be defined by their consanguin-ity. Yet as a potential legal criterion of kinship in a system that charged the basic kin group with critical social and political duties and functions, *consanguinitas* was much too broad a concept to be useful. The func-tions of kinship, therefore, were connected—in law, but also in other so-cial and political contexts—with the more precise concepts of *cognatio*, *agnatio*, *adfinitas*, *gens*, or *domus*. Especially in regard to the disciplinary functions of *patria potestas*, bilateral concepts of *consanguinitas* could not be applied. The boundaries of the *pater*'s absolute power over life and death had to be strictly and clearly defined and limited, in order to avoid competition between *patres* (the father and the mother's father) with rivaling claims to the *filius familias*. In a legal context, such as intes-tate succession, Roman jurists had to restrict the group of *consanguinei* to the sons and daughters of the deceased. Thus, according to the Twelve Tables, emancipated sons did not inherit and were excluded from the *sui heredes*, although no one would have doubted a consanguineous relation to their siblings in a common sense. Around the time of the *lex Voco-nia*, legal provisions were also made that likewise denied aunts, cousins, and nieces of the deceased the right to claim any legally defined "blood relation." *Consanguinitas* was confined within the limits of the agnatic principle, restricted in such a way as to become a subcategory within the class of agnatic kin.[72]

In the end, it would seem that consanguinity really did not play much of a role in Roman legal kinship. It has been said above that the Ro-man Republic developed marriage regulations with the most complex incest taboos in classical antiquity and that these regulations enforced exogamy. Ancient authors discussed exogamy for its social benefits, not for any biological reasons.[73] As Philippe Moreau has shown, medical ar-guments against incest touching on the health of the progeny of an in-cestuous relationship cannot be found in ancient literature; the only bar to marriages between a father and his daughter, or between a son and his mother, is the difference in ages, considered a problem since one spouse might be too old to sire or to bear healthy children.[74] Incest was not thought of in terms of the blood contamination evoked in a term like the German *Blutschande*. The social implications of the marriage prohibitions are most obvious in the matter of regulating marriages between persons not related by blood. Unions between *adfines* were forbidden; also between siblings by adoption. The prohibition against the latter derives, at least for Ulpian, from the agnatic relation.[75]

The relaxation of the marriage prohibitions that allowed the marriage of Emperor Claudius to his niece Agrippina neither stemmed from discussions of consanguinity nor inspired any such discussions. When the recently widowed Claudius chose to marry the daughter of his brother Germanicus in 49 CE, he most likely had in mind dynastic aims, which collided with Roman incest rules: Agrippina brought Claudius, not only the illustrious prestige of her great grandfather Emperor Augustus, but also that of her father, a renowned and well-loved general. To accommodate the emperor's wishes, the precedent of a Roman knight marrying his brother's daughter was created and sanctioned by the senate, and it was this general relaxation of marriage prohibitions that allowed Claudius to marry Agrippina. Tacitus explicitly states that marriage between uncle and niece in general—i.e., marriage within the third degree—was not allowed, except between a niece and her father's brother (*patruus*).[76] Marriage between a mother's brother (*avunculus*) and his niece, or between aunts and nephews, was still forbidden.

## Possibilities and Limits of Blood in Roman Configurations of Kinship

*Sanguis* and *consanguinitas* have to be recognized as important to the constitution of kinship groups in Roman society. Blood, as a bilateral concept, informed the normative, everyday view of kinship among Romans, despite the preeminence of the agnatic principle in Roman civil law. Yet *consanguinitas* was at once too broad and too narrow to aptly describe the social and political functions connected with the Roman family and its *paterfamilias*—such as the disciplinary function that the *pater* would not delegate to a "public" institution like the magistrates. Nonetheless, *consanguinitas* complemented Roman views on the constitution of kinship groups, since *sanguis* was viewed as a substance that could be shared by large groups. Apart from medical texts, however, the character of the substance "blood" was hardly debated or pondered by Roman authors. In his philosophical treatise *De officiis*, Cicero discusses the role and meaning of kinship and affinity for the formation of society in general:

But a still closer social union exists between kindred; ... the first union is that of matrimony itself; the next that to children; then one home, with everything in common. And this is the foundation of the city, the nursery, as it were, of the state. Then follow the bonds between siblings, and next those of first and then second cousins; and when they can no longer be contained in one home, they go out into other homes as into colonies. The rights to intermarry [*conubia*] and affinities [*affinitates*] follow and from that even more kinship relations; and this propagation and offspring is the origin of states. These bonds of common blood [*sanguinis coniunctio*] hold men fast through good-will and affection. For it is important to enjoy the same ancestral monuments [*maiores*], to practice the same rites [*sacra*] and to have common burial places.[77]

Cicero's emphasis on *conubia* and *affinitates* is a Roman peculiarity; these concepts are not mentioned by Aristotle in the passage on the origins of society on which Cicero obviously draws.[78] The creation of affinity is presented as a strategy for integrating the basic units, *familia* and *domus*, into a greater, super-domestic context: Cicero concludes further that by interlinking isolated households through marriage, thus creating *cognatio*, a *res publica* emerges. He mentions *sanguis* last: it proves to be a concept flexible and broad enough to embrace *cognatio*, *adfinitas*, and *domus*. Yet Cicero does not contemplate the actual physical character of blood and its substantial quality; and it is the sharing of rites, of ancestors, and of burial places that concludes his thoughts.[79] Kinship is presented, not as a given natural fact, but as a social process. *Consanguinitas* thus contributed to and complemented the range of possible kinship relations but did not replace legal and social concepts of kinship in Roman society.

# Notes

1. Edith Wharton, *A Backward Glance* (Teddington, 2008), 10–11.
2. On the composition of New York's elite see Frederic Cople Jaher, "Nineteenth-Century Elites in Boston and New York," *Journal of Social History* 6 (1972): 32–77, esp. 45–46, 61, and 67–68 on Edith Wharton and other commentators on social life.
3. See, for example, Pliny's recommendation of young Minicius Acilianus (*Epistulae* 1.14).
4. Cf. Aloys Winterling, *Politics and Society in Imperial Rome* (London, 2009), 9–34, on the interdependency between political career and social rank.
5. Cf. Ann-Cathrin Harders, *Suavissima Soror. Untersuchungen zu den Bruder-Schwester-Beziehungen in der römischen Republik* (Munich, 2008), 318–21.
6. Ulpian *Digest* 50.16.195.1 and 50.16.195.3.
7. Ulpian *Digest* 50.16.195.2.
8. Gaius *Institutiones* 1.56; Ulpian *Digest* 1.4.24.1. A woman could become not only a cognate but also an agnate of her husband if she married him under the special

provisions of *conventio in manum*. On *agnatio*, see Gilbert Hanard, "Observation sur l'*adgnatio*," *Revue international des droits de l'Antiquité* 27 (1980): 169–204, here 177–83.

9. Ulpian *Digest* 50.16.195.2; Gaius *Institutiones* 1.103.

10. On emancipation, see Gaius *Institutiones* 1.132. On adoption see Paul *Digest* 1.7.23. See also Max Kaser, *Das römische Privatrecht. Erster Abschnitt: Das altrömische, das vorklassische und klassische Recht*, 2nd ed. (Munich, 1971), 65–71; Jane Gardner, *Family and Familia in Roman Law and Life* (Oxford, 1998), 10–19, 114–208.

11. Gaius *Institutiones* 1.156; 3.10; Paul *Digest* 1.7.23. Yet, if the wife of the *paterfamilias* had legally become a part of her husband's *familia*, the adoptee could claim agnate relations to her as well.

12. If the husband's *paterfamilias* were still alive, he became the wife's new *pater* and she legally occupied the position of a granddaughter. On *manus*, see Kaser, *Privatrecht*, 76–81; Susan Treggiari, *Roman Marriage: Iusti Coniuges from the Time of Cicero to the Time of Ulpian* (Oxford, 1991), 16–32.

13. A person's name was assumed to indicate his legitimate clan identity, and the assumption of a false name was considered a crime (Papinian *Digest* 48.10.13); see also Papinian *Digest* 22.3.1; cf. Hanard, "Observation sur l'*adgnatio*," 203. The former *nomen gentile* was usually added as a suffix in a filiated form (-*anus*); but during the first century BCE, onomastic changes occurred, and many adoptees kept their former clan names or combined them in a unique way; see David R. Shackleton Bailey, *Two Studies in Roman Nomenclature*, 2nd ed. (New York, 1991), 54–57. Clan members were entitled to inherit after agnates (Gaius *Institutiones* 3.17); they were also considered as tutors for women or underage children.

14. Varro *De lingua Latina* 8.4; Cicero *Topica* 6.29; Festus, ed. Lindsey, 94. Ulpian refers to common usage in his definition of the wider sense of *familia* as those persons who can claim a "blood relation" to a common *genitor* (Ulpian *Digest* 50.16.195.4); this meaning of *familia* echoes the definition of the *gens*; the blood relation is treated as a unilineal concept.

15. Jochen Martin, "Das Vaterland der Väter. Familia, Politik und cognatische Verwandtschaft in Rom," in Jochen Martin, *Bedingungen menschlichen Handelns in der Antike. Gesammelte Beiträge zur Historischen Anthropologie*, ed. W. Schmitz (Stuttgart, 2009), 311–27, esp. 315. See also Celia E. Schultz, *Women's Religious Activity in the Roman Republic* (Chapel Hill, NC, 2006), 123–31. On the *Parentalia*, see Ovid *Fasti* 2.533–70; Festus, ed. Lindsey, 260; cf. Howard H. Scullard, *Festivals and Ceremonies of the Roman Republic* (London, 1981), 74–75; Dorothea Baudy, "Parentalia," *Der Neue Pauly* 9 (2000): 330–31; see also Hanard, "Observation sur l'*adgnatio*," 186. Upon leaving the natal *familia*, an adoptive son lost claims to the *sacra familiae* of that family and belonged to the ritual group of his adoptive father. On the religious consequences of adoption, see Jörg Rüpke, *Die Religion der Römer*, 2nd ed. (Munich, 2006), 36–37; English trans., Jörg Rüpke, *Religion of the Romans* (London, 2009), 29–30.

16. See also Hanard, "Observation sur l'*adgnatio*," 189–97, and esp. 191.

17. Gaius *Institutiones* 3.1–7. On Roman laws of inheritance, see Kaser, *Privatrecht*, 95–104.

18. XII Tables 5.4.

19. Gaius *Institutiones* 3.25. On the *bonorum possessio*, see Kaser, *Privatrecht*, 698–701.

20. See XII Tables 8.20b. On the *tutela*, see Kaser, *Privatrecht*, 85–90; Hanard, "Observation sur l'*adgnatio*," 201–2; on the *tutela mulieris*, see Jane Gardner, *Women in Roman Law and Society* (London and Sydney, 1995), 14–22.

21. On *patria potestas*, see XII Tables 4.1b; Dionysius of Halicarnassus *Antiquitates* 2.26–27; Gaius *Institutiones* 1.48–55; 1.127. A woman was not able to wield *potestas* over others: *Digest* 50.16.195.5; Gaius *Institutiones* 1.104. Cf. Yan Thomas, "The Division of Sexes in Roman Law," in *A History of Women*, vol. 1, *From Ancient Goddesses to Christian Saints*, ed. P. Schmitt Pantel (Cambridge, MA, 1994), 83–138.

22. For examples from the archaic past, see Dionysius of Halicarnassus *Antiquitates* 2.26; Valerius Maximus 5.8.1–3.

23. XII Tables 4.1b; see Marcian *Digest* 48.9.5 on Hadrian: the emperor had a *pater* exiled who had killed his son for committing adultery with his stepmother.

24. See Yan Thomas, "*Vitae necisque potestas*. Le père, la cité, la mort," in *Du châtiment dans la Cité. Supplices corporels et peine de mort dans le monde antique. Table ronde organisée par l'École française de Rome avec le concours du Centre National de la Recherche Scientifique (Rome 9.–11. novembre 1982)* (Rome, 1984), 499–548; Jochen Martin, "Formen sozialer Kontrolle im republikanischen Rom," in *Demokratie, Recht und soziale Kontrolle im Klassischen Athen*, ed. D. Cohen (Munich, 2002), 155–72, here 158–60, 166–67.

25. The *pater* did not decide on his own; it was expected that kinsmen, friends, and, later, possibly also the emperor would counsel him; cf. Kaser, *Privatrecht*, 61–62.

26. Cf. Martin, "Vaterland," 311–27.

27. On the *Matralia*, see Livy *Ab urbe condita libri* 5.19.6; Ovid *Fasti* 6.481–82; 6.551–58; Plutarch *Quaestiones Romanae* 16; *Camillus* 5.2; cf. Scullard, *Festivals*, 150–51; Dorothea Baudy, "Matralia," *Der Neue Pauly* 7 (1999): 1027–28. On the *Cara Cognatio*, see Ovid *Fasti* 2.617–38; see also Scullard, *Festivals*, 74–76; cf. Martin, "Soziale Kontrolle," 160–61.

28. Philippe Moreau, "Domus Augusta: L'autre maison d'Auguste," in *L'expression du pouvoir au début de l'Empire. Autour de la Maison Carrée à Nîmes*, ed. M. Christol and D. Darde (Paris, 2009), 28–38, here 29–33.

29. Cf. Gaius *Institutiones* 1.59–64; Paul *Digest* 23.2.39.1. See also Tacitus *Annales* 12.6. During the second half of the third century, marriage between cousins became possible; see Livy, fragment 12, in Livy, *History of Rome*, vol. 14, *Summaries. Fragments. Julius Obsequens. General Index*, trans. A. C. Schlesinger (London and Cambridge, MA, 1959). On Livy, see Maurizio Bettini, *Familie und Verwandtschaft im antiken Rom* (Frankfurt am Main and New York, 1992), 164–65; Philippe Moreau, *Incestus et prohibitae nuptiae. L'inceste à Rome* (Paris, 2002), 181–86; Carla Fayer, *La familia Romana*, vol. 2, *Aspetti giuridici ed antiquari, sponsalia, matrimonio, dote* (Rome, 2005), 393n216; Harders, *Soror*, 23–25.

30. Gaius, *Institutiones* 1.63; Gaius *Digest* 38.4.3–7. During the fourth century CE, marriage prohibitions were extended to collateral affinal kin of the first degree, i.e., the brother's wife or the wife's sister; family exogamy was thus enforced (*Codex Theodosianus* 3.12.2).

31. Though endogamy was practiced, there is no evidence of prescriptive marriage regulations concerning cousin marriage in Athens. On the *epikleros*, see Cheryl A. Cox, *Household Interests: Property, Marriage Strategies, and Family Dynamics in Ancient Athens* (Princeton, NJ, 1998), 95–99; on marriage between cousins, see Wesley E. Thompson, "The Marriage of First Cousins in Athenian Society," *Phoenix* 21 (1967): 273–82.

32. See Treggiari, *Roman Marriage*, 89–94; Harders, *Soror*, 44–50.

33. See Jochen Martin, "Zur Anthropologie von Heiratsregeln und Besitzübertragung. 10 Jahre nach den Goody-Thesen," *Historische Anthropologie* 1 (1993): 149–62, here 161. See Oswyn Murray, *Early Greece* (London, 1993), 41; Elke Hartmann, *Heirat,*

*Hetärentum und Konkubinat im klassischen Athen* (Frankfurt and New York, 2002), 71–75, on marriage strategies of Greek elites in contrast to peasants. Civic endogamy in Athens was not enforced until Periclean legislation in 451 BCE.

34. See Harders, *Soror,* 318.
35. During the second century BCE, *manus* marriage lost importance and divorces were easier to obtain; see Harders, *Soror,* 41–44.
36. Cf. Harders, *Soror,* 6–8; see also Jochen Martin, "Zwei Alte Geschichten. Vergleichende historisch-anthropologische Betrachtungen zu Griechenland und Rom," *Saeculum* 48 (1997): 1–20, here 6–13.
37. In Greek literature, the term *homaimosyne* is found in just one poem, which can be found in the Planudean anthology: see *Anthologia Planudea*, entry no. 128, in *Anthologia Palatina*, bk. 16; for a Greek text with English translation, see *The Greek Anthology*, trans. W. R. Paton, vol. 5 (London and Cambridge, MA, 1918). See also Walter Burkert, "'Blutsverwandtschaft': Mythos, Natur und Jurisprudenz," in *Mythen des Blutes*, ed. C. von Braun and C. Wulf (Frankfurt am Main and New York, 2007), 245–56, here 250, 252.
38. See Danielle Gourevitch, "Le sang dans la médecine antique," *La Recherche* 254 (1993): 510–17.
39. Cf. Gourevitch, "Sang," 517; see also Jane Fair Bestor, "Ideas about Procreation and their Influence on Ancient and Medieval Views of Kinship," in *The Family in Italy from Antiquity to the Present*, ed. D. I. Kertzer and R. P. Saller (New Haven and London, 1991), 150–67, here 152, 156–67.
40. Isidor of Seville *Etymologies* 9.6.4. See Bestor, " Ideas about Procreation," 155; Burkert, "Blutsverwandtschaft," 246.
41. Gianna Pomata, "Blood Ties and Semen Ties: Consanguinity and Agnation in Roman Law," in *Gender, Kinship and Power: A Comparative and Interdisciplinary History*, ed. M. J. Maynes et al. (New York and London, 1996), 43–64, here 57; cf. Gianna Pomata, "Legami di sangue, legami di seme: consanguineità e agnazione nel diritto romano," *Quaderni Storici* 86 (1994): 299–334. On Pomata, see the chapter by Philippe Moreau in this volume; cf. Burkert, "Blutsverwandtschaft," 248.
42. Gianni Guastella, "La rete del sangue. Simbologia delle relazioni e modelli dell'identità nella cultura romana," *Materiali e discussioni per l'analisi dei testi classici* 15 (1985): 49–123, here 76. On the semantics of the Latin terms for blood, *cruor* and *sanguis*, see Francesca Mencacci, "*Sanguis/Cruor.* Designazioni linguistiche e classificazione antropologica del sangue nella cultura romana," *Materiali e discussioni per l'analisi dei testi classici* 17 (1986): 25–91; and Philippe Moreau, "Sangs romains. Taxinomie du sang dans la Rome ancienne," in *Penser et représenter le corps dans l'Antiquité. Actes du colloque international de Rennes, 1–4 septembre 2004*, ed. F. Prost and J. Wilgaux (Rennes, 2006), 319–32.
43. See Guastella, "La rete del sangue," 76–84, with its ample evidence from ancient sources.
44. See Hanard, "Observation sur l'*adgnatio*," 196; Pomata, "Blood Ties and Semen Ties," 49–50; and the chapter by Philippe Moreau in this volume. *Consanguinei* in Roman poetry, for example, Catullus 64.118; see Guastella, "La rete del sangue," 87 and passim for further evidence.
45. Guastella, "La rete del sangue," 95; cf. Mencacci, "Sanguis," 56.
46. Bestor, "Ideas about Procreation," 155, for example, cites one passage from Cicero *De inventione* 2.22.66, in order to attest the importance of the concept in Roman society.
47. Cicero *In Verrem* 2.1.9; 2.3.56; 2.4.26; 2.5.130; 2.5.139.

48. Cicero *Pro Roscio Amerino* 66; *De lege agraria* 2.1; *Post reditum in senatu* 15, 25.
49. In *De divinatione* 1.44, Cicero quotes from Accius's *Brutus* on two rams of the same blood (*duos consanguineos arietes*).
50. Cicero *Ad Atticum* 2.23.3.
51. *Frater* appears in Cicero *Pro Caelio* 32, 36, 78; *Pro Sestio* 16. He also uses *soror,* not *consanguinea* in *Pro Milone* 73, *De domo sua* 25, 92, and in *Ad Atticum* 2.1.5. It is implausible that Cicero referred to the allegedly incestuous relationship between Clodius and Clodia by picking on their blood relation, since incest was not considered a *crimen sanguinis* then; see, for example, Papinian *Digest* 48.5.39 [38], cf. Marie-Luise Deissmann, "Inzest," in *Antike Medizin. Ein Lexikon,* ed. K.-H. Leven (Munich, 2005), 462–63, here 463.
52. Cicero *De inventione* 1.103; see also *De inventione* 2.66. and 2.161 on "piety to those being related by blood" (*pietas per quam sanguine coniunctis*) referring to cognates in general.
53. Cf. Guastella, "La rete del sangue," 87.
54. Cicero *De inventione* 1.35.
55. Cicero *De inventione* 2.29; 2.107. See also Cicero *De officiis* 1.54.
56. Livy refers thirty-three times to *cognati/cognatio,* in comparison to seven references to *consanguinei.*
57. Livy *Ab urbe condita libri* 1.15.1; 5.17.9; 5.35.4; 7.19.6. See also 2.6.3; 2.9.1 (here only *sanguis*).
58. Livy *Ab urbe condita libri* 8.4.3; 8.5.4.
59. Livy *Ab urbe condita libri* 23.7.6.
60. On the Greek *syngeneia,* the sharing of a descent group, as an instrument of diplomacy, see Christopher P. Jones, *Kinship Diplomacy in the Ancient World* (Cambridge, MA, and London, 1999), 6–16; and Olivier Curty, *Les parentés légendaires entres cités grecques* (Geneva, 1995) with a catalog of epigraphic evidence.
61. Livy *Ab urbe condita libri* 21.10.3; 45.7.3.
62. Livy *Ab urbe condita libri* 8.7.13; 8.7.19.
63. Livy *Ab urbe condita libri* 1.46.6, versus 2.2.6; 24.25.11; 24.26.9; 27.19.8; 35.36.7; 35.47.7; 40.5.10; 42.51.8.
64. Livy, *Ab urbe condita libri* 4.1.1–2; 4.4.7. See also 6.40.6 on a Claudius reference to his patrician blood.
65. Cf. Guastella, "La rete del sangue," 49–56; on the socio-political implications, see Harders, *Soror,* 35–36.
66. Brigitta Hauser-Schäublin, "Politik des Blutes. Zur Verkörperung sozialer Ungleichheit als naturgegebene Verschiedenheit am Schnittpunkt zwischen Geschlecht, Klasse und Rasse," *Zeitschrift für Ethnologie* 120 (1995): 31–49, here 35–37, 40–42. She points out that membership in a group constituted through blood also involves control over women, since a woman's sexual relations with someone outside the accepted circle can taint the bloodline.
67. Cicero *De re publica* 2.63; Florus 1.17.1; Ampelius 25.3; cf. also the Greek Dionysius of Halicarnassus *Antiquitates* 10.60.5. See, for example, Livy *Ab urbe condita libri* 6.34 on the patrician Fabia's sorrow at being married to a plebeian.
68. See Guastella, "La rete del sangue," and the chapter by Philippe Moreau in this volume.
69. See Martin, "Heiratsregeln," 156–61.
70. For Cassius' definition, see *Digest* 38.16.1.10; see also Paul *Digest* 1.7.23. See Gaius *Institutiones* 3.24; 3.33a, on *manus* marriage; Ulpian *Digest* 38.8.1.4; Gaius *Institu-*

*tiones* 3.82 and 3.84 on adoption; cf. Guastella, "La rete del sangue," 86; Burkert, "Blutsverwandtschaft," 254.

71. See Ulpian *Digest* 38.8.4.
72. Paul *Sententiae* 4.8.20[22]. Hanard, "Observation sur *l'adgnatio*," 196, therefore argues that *consanguinei* as a distinct group of agnates was created rather late, in the context of the *lex Voconia*.
73. Cf. Harders, *Soror,* 31–44.
74. Moreau, *Incestus,* 64. Moreau dates the beginnings of a discourse on possible sterility of incestuous marriages at the beginning of the seventh century; cf. Deissmann, "Inzest."
75. Gaius *Institutiones* 1.63; Justinian *Institutiones* 1.10.5–7; Ulpian *Digest* 1.7.23.
76. Tacitus *Annales* 12.6–7; cf. Suetonius *Claudius* 26.3.
77. Cicero *De officiis* 1.53–55.
78. Cf. Aristotle *Politica* 1252a–b.
79. Cf. Burkert, "Blutsverwandtschaft," 253.

# Chapter 2

# The Bilineal Transmission
# of Blood in Ancient Rome

## Philippe Moreau

## The Debate

During the past several decades, historians of Rome have been considering a series of questions raised by anthropologists about the symbolic
meanings of bodily humors, especially blood. It is becoming evident
that in ancient Rome, blood—the fluid substance linked with filiation
and the transmission of identity—was the object of a set of perceptions
much more complex than used to be thought.[1] Useful studies comparing the biblical and patristic conceptions have been conducted by the
Centro Sanguis Christi in Rome, but the principal contribution is the
remarkable work of Gianni Guastella, to which can be added the study
by Jane Fair Bestor covering both antiquity and the Middle Ages.[2] Both
scholars have concluded that in republican and imperial Rome, blood
was understood to be transmitted bilineally; that is, a child of either
sex received *sanguis* from father as well as mother. Both also relied on
literary texts—especially texts of public utterances (speeches, dramatic
works), which can reasonably be assumed to have conveyed widely appealing ideas and values, to access the abstract representations, notions,
and beliefs characteristic of Roman culture.[3] This method is essential for
any case of retrospective anthropology focusing on a historical society,
but it is important always to keep in mind that it relies on an apparently

paradoxical assumption; namely, that the beliefs common to a whole society can be reconstructed accurately from the literary artifacts left behind by that culture's elites.

The conclusion of both Guastella and Bestor, that the Romans believed in bilineal blood transmission, coincides with what we know of the Roman system of kinship, that it was cognatic (non-unilinear): it was believed that each parent transmitted to their child his or her own identity, metaphorically represented by a substance.[4] In confirmation of this thesis, which has been perfectly established in my opinion, I will only quote four texts. These present the advantage of clearly associating the transmission of *sanguis* with that of values and qualities, and they have either not been mentioned in previous studies or have been interpreted, in my opinion, in questionable ways.

The first of these texts is by Cicero. In an attack on his enemy Lucius Calpurnius Piso Caesoninus, consul in 58 BCE, whose father belonged to the prestigious *gens Calpurnia* (of which Cicero's son-in-law, Gaius Calpurnius Piso Frugi, was also a member, as the orator recalls in this passage), but whose mother was of a much lower rank, being the daughter of a Gaul, Caluentius, Cicero writes: "I knew through my relationship with the Pisos how transalpine maternal blood had alienated him from this family."[5] Thus, Cicero expressed in the Senate, in front of members of the Roman aristocracy, the idea that maternal *sanguis* could alienate a noble Roman from the hereditary values of his paternal lineage.

The second of my texts shows maternal *sanguis* delivering an entirely different effect. Here Cicero recalls the way Senator Publius Seruilius Vatia Isauricus used an appeal to the solidarity created by common blood to persuade his relative Quintus Caecilius Metellus Nepos, consul in 57 BCE, to stop objecting to calling Cicero back from exile. He writes: "Then, this outstanding man—a true Metellus—burst into tears and even entirely submitted himself to P. Seruilius while he was still talking. Being of the same blood, he could no longer resist this divine nobility, full of ancient traditions."[6] Now the "same blood" in question was that of the Caecilii, transmitted to Nepos in the patrilineal line from his grandfather, Quintus Caecilius Metellus Balearicus, consul in 123 BCE, and to Vatia by his mother who was Balearicus's sister. Thus, in this public speech (the point is important for the diffusion and reception of these symbolic representations), Cicero again stresses the effect of solidarity created by the transmission of blood along two lines of filiation.

These texts obviously draw on a conception of filiation and of symbolic transmission of identity associated with the aristocracy, but my third text, offering a general biological and philosophical view, describes a form of filiation universal in its relevance. Lucretius, the Epicurean poet, attempting to explain the physical resemblance of children to one, or the other, or both parents, points to an effect presumed to come from the double transmission of *sanguis*, from the father and mother: "But those who resemble the one and the other, mixing the features of their parents, develop from the blood of their father and mother."[7] This text obviously reflects the point of view of the philosophical school of Epicurus, which professed the pangenesis of the sperm and equal contribution of the paternal and maternal seed to the formation of children, but it is nevertheless significant that Lucretius claims to be addressing all Romans, and indeed all humankind.

My fourth text, by Seneca, avoids rigorous philosophical frameworks, instead referring to a specific genealogy well known to everyone, that of the *domus Augusta*, the imperial house, and drawing only on popular conceptions of filiation. Satirizing the deification of Claudius, Seneca recalls that this emperor was linked by kinship to two deified mortals, two *diui*, Augustus and his spouse Liuia Augusta: "since the divine Claudius is linked by blood to both divine Augustus and divine Augusta, his grandmother."[8] Now, the blood line that links Claudius to Augustus runs through two women; on the one hand, Octavia, Augustus's sister, transmitting to her daughter, Antonia, Claudius's mother; on the other hand, Liuia transmitting to her son Drusus, Claudius's father; therefore the blood, which, in this parodic text carries with it a calling to deification, clearly follows matrilineal lines.

The received, bilineal-transmission thesis, which the examples above only confirm, was partly questioned by Gianna Pomata in an article published in Italian, in 1994, then in an abridged version in English, in 1996. Pomata tries to prove that, for Roman jurists (*iuris prudentes*), the *sanguis* that transmitted identity and provided a symbolic basis of filiation was that of the father, passed down to his children, while that of the mother transmitted nothing.[9] Yet she does not question the idea that in common Roman thought blood transmission was bilineal, and she actually quotes a certain number of texts mentioning the *sanguis maternus* of such and such a character, or referring to a *sanguis* common to two individuals related by a woman in a context of symbolic transmission.[10] She also tries to establish a correlation between the conception that she holds as characteristic of Roman jurists and the one of ancient medical theorists, according to which the sperm came from blood.[11] The principal questions in this debate, therefore, are the following: Did Roman society have two opposite conceptions of the transmission of *sanguis*, as Pomata suggests; one, widely spread in Roman society and ascribing blood transmission equally to male and female ascendants; and the other, specific to a small group of learned men, namely the jurists, influenced by a group of learned doctors, and restricting the transmission of *sanguis* to the patrilineal line? Or, on the contrary, as I will try to demonstrate in the following pages, did Roman jurists actually subscribe to the common opinion? Such a debate might seem limited, but it seems important to me for several reasons: In Rome, abstract thinking about the physical and social world was as much the field of jurists as of philosophers, and probably even more so. Furthermore, given the major intellectual influence of Roman law on the societies of medieval and early modern Europe, it is useful, in a broad historical perspective, to define exactly the position of the *iuris prudentes* in imperial Rome. Lastly, the position adopted by Pomata raises a theoretical question about the extent to which two opposite symbolic visions of filiation can coexist in one and the same society. It is to resolve this question that it has seemed useful to take up Pomata's demonstration, to examine its method, principles, and results. Since the author has placed herself on the ground of Roman law, the demonstration will necessarily involve the exegesis of legal texts, rather austere one must admit: I hope the reader will take this into account.

## *Consanguinitas* for Roman Jurists

To prove that Roman jurists restricted the transmission of blood to the patrilineal line, Pomata analyzes their use of the terms *consanguineus* and *consanguinitas*, which etymologically express community of blood.[12] The word *consanguinitas* first appears in the second page of her article. And it is only after that, significantly, that she asks herself what *sanguis* in *consanguinitas* means.[13] Clearly, she assumes that the analysis of the latter notion will explain the Roman jurists' conception of the transmission of *sanguis*. Since she has chosen a lexical approach to the question—in itself legitimate—one can wonder why she did not conduct her survey directly on the occurrences of *sanguis* but rather chose to focus on two terms derived from this word. A few elements of her survey will be presented below, but first, we shall deal with the question of the meaning given by jurists to *consanguinitas*, in order to measure its actual relevance to the question asked. I think that to understand the meaning and relevance of this word, the mere description of the principles and functioning of the system is not enough; it is essential also to study the historical conditions of both the appearance and abolition of the concept.

The notion of *consanguinitas* was devised by jurists in an extremely precise and limited context, and they seldom used the word, at least in the Classical Age (second and third centuries CE) outside the context of *ab intestato* succession.[14] In the system of ancient civil law based on the Twelve Tables (449 BCE, according to the tradition), succession could be transmitted to three categories of heirs, by order of priority: firstly to the *sui*, male and female descendants of the deceased under his paternal power (*patria potestas*) at the time of death; in their absence, to the nearest of the *agnati*, male and female collaterals in the patrilineal line, who, in addition, had to meet a demand other than the simply genealogical one—the tie created by *patria potestas* and submission to it had never to have been broken between any of the individuals making up the links of the genealogical chain between the deceased and the *agnatus* liable to succeed to him; lastly, to the *gentiles*, members of the *gens*, who would inherit collectively from the deceased if neither of the first two categories was represented.[15] At an unknown date, the system that treated the male and female heirs-to-be among *sui* and *agnati* in an egalitarian way was modified to the detriment of the women in the category of *agnati*. Emperor Justinian's *Institutiones*, in a brief historical excursus intended to justify the recent abolition of this discriminatory system, hold "the jurisprudence of the intermediate period" responsible for the introduction of discriminatory succession laws, arguing that they were promulgated after the Twelve Tables but before the first imperial constitutions (first century CE). A statement of Paul, the jurist, seems to delimit this period further. According to him, the *iuris prudentes* devised the reform by following the logic of the *lex Voconia*, a plebiscite of 169 BCE that restricted women's inheritance capabilities in the case of testamentary succession: thus the jurists are thought to have extended to *ab intestato* succession a restriction that before 169 BCE had applied only to testamentary succession.[16] The conclusion is that restrictions on inheritance by women had only applied between the time of the plebiscite and the issuance of the first imperial constitutions. At the very least, it can be said that the notion *consanguineus* was known to the jurist C. Cassius Longinus, consul in 30 BCE.[17]

Whatever the date of the original restriction of testamentary succession, it was then decided that women would also no longer succeed to a deceased *ab intestato*, unless they were his very close relatives—defined according to Roman conceptions as his sisters by the same father (including those with a different mother), either by birth or adoption; or as a mother or stepmother (*nouerca*) under the *manus* (marital authority) of the deceased and given the same status as a daughter in succession matters.[18] So among the *agnati*, the patrilateral aunts and nieces of the deceased, as well as all the more distant patrilineal collaterals, were excluded. Conversely, men retained successoral rights *ab intestato* to the patrimony of their female *agnati*, whether close to them or distant.[19]

*Consanguinitas* then was a dissymmetric and biased relation, having a restrictive effect on women but none on men.[20]

The result of the jurists' reform was that for purposes of intestate inheritance, the old category of *agnati* was split into two: the newly created category of *consanguinei* and a new one that kept the name *agnati*, but which, unlike its predecessor, excluded the brothers and sisters of the deceased. In their presentation of *consanguinei*, ancient jurists thus hesitated between two attitudes: either considering them as a specific category of persons, which was legitimate from the point of view of the logic and functioning of the system, or as a sub-category of *agnati*, which was justified from a historical point of view, the new class resulting from the splitting of the old one.[21] The system remained in force for several centuries and was only abolished in 531 CE by a constitution of Emperor Justinian, which, with his *Institutiones*, is an important source, as we have seen: in the name of respecting the law of the Twelve Tables the emperor was restoring the right of women to inherit *ab intestato*, whatever their degree of proximity to the deceased, and thus was abolishing the category of *consanguinei*.[22]

Some uses, a small minority, diverge from the framework just discussed and have actually been signaled by Pomata.[23] One can agree with her analysis of three occurrences: in *Cod. Theod.* 5.1.1 (Constantine, between 317 CE and 319 CE), *consanguinitas* is clearly used in the sense of *agnatio;* in *Cod. Theod.* 5.1.2 (Valentinian I, 369 CE) the *filius consanguineus* is opposed to *per adoptionem quaesitus*, with the obvious meaning of "begotten, natural"; in *Cod. Iust.* 10.35.1 (Theodosius II, 442 CE) *consanguinitas* is applied to patrilineal filiation and not to collaterality: an obvious semantic extension. Other occurrences, though, call for some discussion. In the phrase "in feminis tutelam legitimam consanguineus patruus non recuset," from *Cod. Theod.* 3.17.2 (Constantine, 326 CE), there is no need to follow Pomata in understanding *consanguineus patruus* as a reference to patrilineal consanguinity. Nor is there a need to see in this term an extension of the use of the adjective *consanguineus*, since *patruus* by itself refers to the "paternal uncle," by contrast with *auunculus* (maternal uncle), and since what is in question is legitimate guardianship, i.e., that which fell to *agnati:* the use of the adjective would be unnecessarily redundant were we to adopt such an interpretation.[24] One should rather understand *consanguineus* as an adjective noun and *patruus* as indicating an asyndeton, for there is a constitution of Leo (472 CE), expressly referring to the one of Constantine, which indicates that the *consanguineus*, namely the brother with the same father, and the *patruus* are both designated for legitimate guardianship.[25] In this case, the term *consanguineus* would therefore be used in its common meaning (brother with the same father). The interpretation of *Cod. Theod.* 14.4.5 (Valentinian II, 389 CE), which deals with the hereditary transmission of membership in the professional union of the pork merchants in the city of Rome, is very tricky: the end of the constitution invites the prefect of the city to remind those close to the pork butchers, the *suarii*, of the obligation they have, owing to their family tie, to replace a *suarius* in the association and trade: "in full equity and justice you should also order *consanguinei* or (*uel*) those who are bound to do so by birth [*originales*] to attach themselves to the title and function of those named above."[26] If *uel* is to be given an explicative value, which is the most probable reason for its appearance in this quote, then *consanguinei* are one and the same with *originales*, and, in that case, the former term refers to "sons" as related to either their father or mother (since the obligation of membership was transmitted from father or mother to the sons), which constitutes an extension, from collaterality to filiation. But if *uel* has a disjunctive value and differentiates two categories, then the meaning of *consanguinei* is not clear.[27]

These are only semantic extensions that stretch the terms *consanguineus* and *consanguinitas* to filiation, or patrilinearity, in general. But to go back to the specific meaning, several conclusions can be drawn from its history and description as given above.

(1) The new category of *consanguinitas* was devised in an extremely limited context, that of *ab intestato* succession, which was just one of the many fields in which kinship produced legal effects, and it only concerned patrilineal relatives. Given that in the *ab intestato* inheritance system of the civil law, both old and modified, only patrilineal relatives (qualified in addition by the ties of *patria potestas*) were concerned, *consanguinitas* could in no way aim at setting patrilineal relatives against matrilineal ones, the latter not being involved anyway.[28] The point was not to distinguish two lines of filiation, patrilineal and matrilineal, but two sexes, and, secondarily, among women, to differentiate between close patrilineal relatives and distant ones.

(2) It is clear that the category of *consanguinitas* only applies to collaterality, between brothers and sisters or assimilated children, never to filiation: a son or a daughter succeeds to his or her father in the quality of *sui*, not of *consanguinei*. It is not therefore the symbolic transmission of *sanguis* from one generation to the other that is directly at stake in the category under discussion.[29]

(3) *Consanguinitas*, for jurists, is a category largely disconnected from biological filiation: adoption, which is a form of exercising *patria potestas*, creates it, just as *manus* (marital authority) does.[30] Organic

and naturalist metaphor seems then to have a rather limited part in the elaboration of the concept.

(4) The category of *consanguinitas* thus concerns the closest *agnati:* to understand the term, it is necessary to give at least as much importance to the prefix, *con,* which expresses association, as to the radical, *sanguis.* The term opposes close *agnati* (mainly female) to distant *agnati.*

(5) Lastly, if, believing that the category of *consanguinitas* reveals the Roman jurists' conception of the transmission of *sanguis,* one wanted to extrapolate from *consanguinitas* to the notion of *sanguis,* it would indeed be legitimate to conclude from this case that, for Roman jurists, brothers and sisters with the same father had their father's *sanguis* in common, but in no way, following strict logic, could it be argued that they did not have their mother's *sanguis* as well. One would also have to accept that, for example, a paternal aunt (excluded from the *consanguinei*) did not share blood with her own brother's children, a surprising conclusion. Moreover, one would have to maintain that a stepmother (*nouerca*), a mere relative by marriage (*adfinis*) of a deceased, shared his blood, since she was entitled to succeed to him according to *consanguinitas,* provided she had been under the *manus* of the father of the deceased. Finally, one would have to conclude that a mother equally *in manu* of the father of the deceased, and therefore entitled to inherit his property in the same category, had *sanguis* in common with the deceased, which would prove that, for the jurists, matrilineal transmission of *sanguis* was possible.

These different aporias invite us to refuse to look for the Roman jurists' conception of the transmission of *sanguis* in the mere analysis of the notion of *consanguinitas,* as Pomata did. It is undeniable that *consanguineus,* in a successoral context (and mainly in imperial constitutions), was used restrictively with patrilineal collaterals, and that it referred expressly to patrilineal collaterals, not matrilineal ones; still it is more through a direct study of the occurrences of *sanguis* itself in legal texts that answers to the question posed are likely to be found.[31]

## *Sanguis* and its Bilineal Transmission for Roman Jurists

We shall therefore study a certain number of occurrences of *sanguis* in the texts of classical legal advisors and of imperial constitutions, which are known to have been written by the jurists in imperial offices and transmitted by compilations, specifically the Theodosian Code and the Justinian Code.[32] The texts, which cover the period from Gaius to the Justinian Code, fall into two categories (jurists' commentaries and imperial normative texts) and have been chosen for chronological and typological reasons. Given that the belief in patrilineal transmission of *sanguis* is not questioned, we will focus on occurrences supporting the idea of matrilineal transmission. This method, more economical than the examination of all the occurrences, will not permit us to measure the relative representation of each conception, but the male bias, typical of the Roman society and its jurists, makes the answer obvious: male transmission of blood is represented more often, which is confirmed empirically by a cursory reading of texts.[33]

The first example is a passage by Gaius, compiled in the *Digest* under the title *Vnde cognati*, which commented on the clause of the praetorian edict of that name, by which the praetor corrected the civil successoral *ab intestato* system, which was, as we have seen, entirely patrilineal. The praetor guaranteed possession of hereditaments to bilateral relatives designated as *cognati*.[34] Gaius does not comment directly on the praetor's edict, valid in Rome, but on an edict along the same principles, enforced by the provincial governors:

> In this part [of his edict], the proconsul, driven by a natural sense of equity, promises the possession of property to all *cognati* who are entitled to succession in consideration of blood, although they do not qualify according to civil law. Thus, even illegitimate children can claim the possession of their mother's property, and a mother the possession of the property of such children; in the same way, brothers, illegitimate children themselves, can claim possession of each other's property under this part [of the edict], because they are reciprocally *cognati*.[35]

The mention of illegitimate children is quite significant: having no legal father, no patrilineal transmission is possible for them.[36] The important point is that for Gaius, along with the sense of fairness that drives the proconsul to grant the same rights both to patrilineal and matrilineal relatives (evidence that, at that time, the bilateral conception of kin was widely spread), it is the *ratio sanguinis* (taking blood into account) which makes bilateral relatives liable to inherit: this *sanguis* has, therefore, been transmitted by at least one woman, if not several.

Ulpian deals with another case of *ab intestato* succession, that of the emancipated son. We know that the act of *emancipatio*, following the pattern of *manumissio* by which a master freed his slave, could resort in a purely formal way to a third party called *extraneus manumissor*, who carried out the final action emancipating the son from paternal power.

Under the civil law of the Twelve Tables, this *manumissor* would acquire the position of patron toward the emancipated son, with a right to succession *ab intestato*, except if the emancipated man had legitimate descendants. In order to correct this system and grant a few close relatives the right to inherit from an emancipated man who had died intestate, the praetor's edict granted the "possession of property" to ten *cognati*, whom Ulpian enumerated, explaining the praetor's motivation:

> And if the deceased has been a free man and not freed following remancipation, the law of the Twelve Tables granted civil succession to the man who has been in charge of the emancipation, but the praetor, driven by a sense of equity, gave priority to the following ten categories of *cognati*: the father, the mother, the son, the daughter, the grandfather, the grandmother, the grandson, the granddaughter, the brother, the sister, to prevent anybody from prevailing over the blood ties by taking advantage of purely legal circumstances.[37]

The praetor thus thought that *sanguis* passed from mother to children, creating bonds that legal procedures were not to break. The same applied to the mother's parents and her children, since the text does not specify that the grandparents and grandchildren must belong to the patrilineal line, and the ten persons concerned are expressly designated as *cognati*. A passage in Justinian's *Institutiones* makes the point clear:

> In third line, the praetor [granted possession of the property] to ten categories of people, to whom he gave priority over the outsider who had effected the emancipation. And the ten categories of people are the following: the father, the mother, the grandfather, the grandmother, paternal as well as maternal, plus the son, the daughter, the grandson, the granddaughter from the son as well as the daughter, the brother, the sister, either consanguineous or uterine.[38]

There appears in this text an undeniable occurrence of *consanguineus* in the sense of "from the same father," since it is opposed to *uterinus*. But we also see, since, according to Ulpian, the praetor's decision is based on his wish to take *sanguis* into account, that the uses of this adjective are not sufficient to inform us about the jurists' conceptions regarding blood transmission.

Another of Ulpian's texts transmitted by the *Digest* deals with the *obligation alimentaire*, that is, the obligation between ascendants and descendants in the male line to provide food and other sustenance (alimony). Its extension to the mother and her ascendants was under discussion in Ulpian's time, and Ulpian indicates that, in his own opinion, it is clear that a judge ought to accept a request for food, at least for the benefit of the mother:

It is necessary to examine the question whether we are obliged to provide food only to our father, our paternal grandfather, our great-grandfather, the father of our paternal grandfather and to all our other male ascendants or if we are also obliged to do so for our mother and all the other ascendants with whom we are linked by a female bond. On the one hand, it is preferable that the judge should intervene in both cases, to meet some people's needs more easily or see to the state of health of others. On the other hand, given that the problem stems from equity and affection for blood, it is suitable that the judge should examine each person's wishes thoroughly.[39]

On the maternal side, are only the mother's patrilineal ascendants concerned, or also those in the matrilineal line? It is difficult to decide.[40] Further on, the same author writes: "similarly, the divine Antonius Pius gives to understand that a maternal grandfather ought to provide food."[41] Thus, on the one hand, the text is ambiguous, but on the other, it is quite clear that the two grounds of alimony are, as in the case of *ab intestato* succession of *cognati*, fairness and the bond created by the transmission of *sanguis*, especially between a mother and her children. In the hypercritical days of the "hunt" for post-classical and Byzantine interpolations in the *Digest*, some scholars maintained that the reference to fairness and the affection for blood had been added at a post-classical date, under the influence of Christian thought.[42] The argument (which only concerned chronology) is not convincing, since the literary texts testify both to the widely spread idea that kinship, symbolized by the transmission of *sanguis*, creates bonds and obligations, and to the view that blood is transmitted bilineally: *sanguis* is in no way a specifically Christian notion.

An imperial constitution of 381 CE grants pardon and liberation, on the occasion of the celebration of Easter, to some convicts, but it exempts others, guilty of the most serious crimes, in the verbose and pompous style characteristic of the imperial chancellery at the time:

Emperors Gratian Augustus, Valentinian Augustus and Theodosius Augustus to the most illustrious Antidius, vicar. The day of joy of Easter does not permit to leave in affliction even those who have committed immoral acts. May the horrible prison at last open onto the light they are no longer used to. But We deem that the measures of pardon do not apply to those who have been arrogant enough to commit a sacrilegious crime against sovereign authority, those who, led by a frenzy of parricide, have stained their hands with their own blood, those, too, who have soiled themselves by murdering a human being, whoever he was, those who have slipped into somebody else's marriage bed, those who have deflowered a woman by raping her, those who, in all blindness, have, by sacrilegious incest, breached the blood tie that links them to their *cognati*, which they should have considered sacred. ... Read in public in Rome, on July the twenty-first, under the consulate of Syagrius and Eucherius.[43]

Blood is mentioned twice, in conjunction with parricide and incest. In the former, parricide, the offence to blood affects both the material blood spilled by the culprit and the symbolic *sanguis* that flows in his veins as well as in those of his victim. Incidentally, let us remember that since a *lex Pompeia de parricidiis* from the middle of the first century BCE, such a crime concerned not only the father but also a whole circle of bilateral relatives and even a few close relatives by marriage.[44] In the latter, incest, the offence to blood and to the obligations imposed by its transmission involves a failure to respect the link created by blood, here expressly defined as being common to *cognati*. As a matter of fact, at the time this constitution was written, as probably at all times in Rome, marital prohibitions against incest extended to a large group of bilateral relatives.[45]

Another relevant imperial constitution, also from the late fourth century, concerns the obligation to exercise the functions of *curialis* (a *curialis* being a member of a *curia*, a local city senate). The obligation is hereditary, but in the male line, since only men have to perform these compulsory functions; women, who cannot hold any civic office, cannot transmit the obligation: "Nobody should be bound by the ties of maternal blood [*sanguis materni uinculum*] only, because the incapacity of women transmits no obligation to exercise this kind of functions, from which they are themselves exempted."[46] The expression *sanguis maternus* (maternal blood) speaks for itself, especially when associated with the notion of *uinculum* (link, tie), which expresses the necessary effect of the transmission of symbolic *sanguis*.

We will end with another text, particularly significant since it belongs to the constitution already mentioned several times, by which Justinian abolished the category of *consanguinei*. In a rhetorical question the emperor wonders: "Why, while the rights deriving from the sharing of one and the same blood remain intact when they follow the male sex [*per uirilem sexum*], do we go against nature and away from the right established by the law?"[47]

While Pomata draws from this text the idea that "è solo attraverso il sesso maschile—come ci dice il *Codice* giustinianeo—che i 'diritti di un unico e medesimo sanguine vengono mantenuti incorrotti'" (only through the male sex—as Justinian's *Codex* tell us—"are the rights of the very same blood kept in their purity"), I reckon, on the contrary, that the specification *per uirilem sexum* (through the male sex) logically presupposes another category of *unius sanguinis iura* (rights deriving from sharing one and the same blood), i.e., those that are transmitted along the female line; otherwise this remark would be perfectly superfluous. So in my opinion, there is no paradox in concluding that Emperor Justinian's jurists here faithfully follow the conceptions of their classical predecessors (from Gaius on); it is in the name of a bilineal conception of the transmission of *sanguis* that they have abolished the notion of *consanguinitas* and its successoral consequences.[48]

Further occurrences of *sanguis* could be mentioned, but I think the demonstration is sufficient: classical jurists and imperial constitutions, sharing a conception common in Roman society, considered that *sanguis* was transmitted not only from the father to his children, but also from the mother to her children, and more generally in the matrilineal line.[49] Pomata proposed to explain the opposite conception, which she attributed to Roman jurists, by the influence of medical conceptions, though, in complete intellectual honesty, she wondered how that influence worked from one intellectual circle to another.[50] If one agrees with the present demonstration, the question no longer arises, as Roman jurists did not devise a symbolic pattern of filiation, represented by the transmission of blood, different from that which was widely accepted in the society in which they lived.

## Conclusion: From the Ancient Roman World to the Medieval One

In the case of Rome, one should therefore distinguish, on the one hand, the symbolic notion of *sanguis* transmitted along the two lines, which is used to conceive kinship in a globally cognatic system and implies transmitted identity and compulsory solidarity, but which was never used, in common conceptions, as the basis for a corporate group or for an abstract category of kinship; from, on the other hand, the category of *consanguinitas* devised by jurists to apply in a precise context but certainly not widespread in common thought. If, as seems to be the case, *consanguinitas* plays an important part in medieval structures of kinship, one has to recognize there a break with Roman conceptions, the causes of which remain to be investigated (though the task mainly falls to medievalists, of course). As a mere suggestion, I would mention two directions of reflection: first, new conceptions of the symbolic value of blood may have been introduced by "barbarian" peoples, mainly Germanic, as they assumed control over the territories of the empire; and second, Christian thought spread in the West conceptions of filiation specific to the Jewish world and, besides, imposed another substance as the representation of kinship and marriage, namely *caro* (flesh).

# Notes

Preliminary versions of the present study have been presented in seminars held in the Universities of Caen and Nantes and at the École des Hautes Études en Sciences Sociales (Paris). I would like to thank the participants (particularly Jérôme Wilgaux, Françoise Héritier, Anita Guerreau-Jalabert, Gérard Delille) for their comments and suggestions. The names of authors and titles of ancient works are abridged following the usage of the 2nd revised index of the *Thesaurus linguae Latinae* (Leipzig, 1990). As the terms *a(d)gnatio, cognatio,* and *consanguinitas* (and the corresponding adjectives) do not cover the same meanings as "agnation," "cognation," and "consanguinity" in English, I have kept their Latin form. I am greatly indebted to my colleague and friend Mme Josette Florent and to Ms. Ellen Wilson for their English translation of my admittedly austere French text.

1.  In France, the essential influences have been those of two works by Françoise Héritier, *Les deux sœurs et leur mère* (Paris, 1994), and *Masculin/féminin. La pensée de la différence* (Paris, 1996); also Florence Dupont, "Le lait du père romain," in *Corps romains*, ed. Philippe Moreau (Grenoble, 2002), 115–37; Philippe Moreau, "Sangs romains. Taxinomie du sang dans la Rome ancienne," in *Penser et représenter le corps dans l'Antiquité. Actes du colloque international de Rennes, 14 septembre 2004*, ed. F. Prost and J. Wilgaux (Rennes, 2006), 319–32. Of the various Latin terms referring to blood *(sanguis, cruor, tabum, sanies)*, only *sanguis* was used metaphorically to represent filiation.
2.  F. Vattioni, ed., *Sangue e antropologia biblica* (Rome, 1981); F. Vattioni, ed., *Sangue e antropologia biblica nella patristica* (Rome, 1982); F. Vattioni, ed., *Sangue e antropologia nella letteratura cristiana* (Rome, 1983). Other collections about blood in Christian liturgy, cult, and theology were published by the same scholar between 1984 and 1989. See also Gianni Guastella, "La rete del sangue. Simbologia delle relazioni e modelli dell'identità nella cultura romana," *Materiali e discussioni per l'analisi dei testi classici* 15 (1985): 49–124; Jane Fair Bestor, "Ideas about Procreation and their Influence on Ancient and Medieval Views of Kinship," in *The Family in Italy from Antiquity to the Present*, ed. D. I. Kertzer and R. P. Saller (New Haven and London, 1991), 150–67.
3.  See Guastella's remarks in "La rete del sangue," 65–66.
4.  Guastella, "La rete del sangue," 80: "entrambi i genitori trasmettono ai figli il sangue," based among others on Hor. *Carm. saec.* 50; Ov. *Fast.* 471–72; *met.* 14.588–89; Bestor, "Ideas about Procreation," 155: "classical sources ... suggest that blood ... symbolized the bonds to both paternal and maternal kin." See Philippe Moreau, "La *domus Augusta* et les formations de parenté à Rome," *Cahiers Glotz* 16 (2005): 17–20. To put Rome into perspective among the cognatic systems, see Laurent Barry's admirable synthesis, *La Parenté* (Paris, 2008), 481–87.
5.  Cic. *P. red. in sen.* 15: "cognoram enim propter Pisonum adfinitatem quam longe hunc ab hoc genere cognatio materna Transalpini sanguinis abtulisset."
6.  Cic. *Sest.* 130: "conlacrumauit uir egregius ac uere Metellus, totumque se P. Seruilio dicenti etiam tum tradidit, nec illam grauitatem plenam antiquitatis diutius homo

eiusdem sanguinis potuit sustinere"; the same event is reported by Cicero in *P. red. in sen.* 25: "quem P. Seruilius ... et auctoritatis et orationis suae diuina quadam graui- tate ad sui generis communisque sanguinis facta uirtutesque reuocauit" (P. Seruilius ... managed, by the almost divine ascendancy of his authority and his eloquence, to call him back to the exploits and virtues of their common lineage and blood). On this kinship, see Robert A. Kaster, *Cicero, Speech on Behalf of Publius Sestius* (Oxford, 2006), 369; Kaster, incidentally, translates *homo eiusdem sanguinis* as "his kinsman," which unfortunately erases the metaphor of *sanguis* (ibid., 98). See also Friedrich Münzer's genealogical chart, *Römische Adelsparteien und Adelsfamilien* (Stuttgart, 1920), 304.

7.  Lucr. 4.1212–14: "Sed quos utriusque figurae / esse uides, iuxtim miscentes uolta parentum, / corpore de patrio et materno sanguine crescunt."

8.  Sen. *Apoc.* 9.4: "cum diuus Claudius et diuum Augustum sanguine contingat nec minus diuam Augustam, auiam suam." For the analysis of *sanguine contingere*, which literally means "to touch by blood," see Guastella, who, in "La rete del sangue" (90n111) indicates, wrongly though, that Claudius was not "parente di sangue" of Augustus.

9.  Gianna Pomata, "Legami di sangue, legami di seme. Consanguineità e agnazione nel diritto romano," *Quaderni storici* 86 (1994): 299–334; Gianna Pomata, "Blood Ties and Semen Ties: Consanguinity and Agnation in Roman Law," in *Gender, Kinship, Power: A Comparative and Interdisciplinary History*, ed. Mary Jo Maynes et al. (New York, 1996), 43–64. Only the first article will be quoted here.

10. Pomata, "Legami," 307–8, and nn30–36.

11. Pomata, "Legami," 312–20.

12. See the etymological explanation given by the jurist C. Cassius Longinus, toward the middle of the first century CE, quoted in Ulp. *12 ad Sabinum, Dig.* 38.16.1.10: "consanguineos autem Cassius definit eos qui sanguine inter se conexi sunt" (Cassius defines *consanguinei* as persons linked together by blood). The beginning of the text was questioned by Theodor Mommsen, in his edition of Justinian's *Digest* (Berlin, 1868), *ad l.*, because it gives too wide a definition of *consanguinei* by not mentioning the brothers and sisters, but Mommsen does not question the authenticity of the etymology.

13. Pomata, "Legami," 300: "cosa significava *sanguis* nella definizione legale di *consanguinitas*?"

14. For the exceptions, see endnote 23 in this chapter.

15. Explanations of this system and the categories of those liable to inherit will be found in Pasquale Voci's general survey, *Diritto ereditario romano*, vol. 2., *Parte speciale. Successione ab intestato. Successione testamentaria* (Milan, 1963), 6–8; Alan Watson, *The Law of Succession in the Late Roman Republic* (Oxford, 1971), 176–78; Bernardo Albanese, *Le persone nel diritto romano* (Palermo, 1979), 291–92; Gilbert Hanard, "Observations sur l'*adgnatio*," *Revue internationale des droits de l'Antiquité* 27 (1980): 191–96. The basic text is Twelve Tables V.4; see Michael H. Crawford, *Roman Statutes*, vol. 2, statute no. 40 (London, 1966), 641.

16. Justinian expresses himself in 533 CE, two years after the abolition of the rule of *consanguinitas* by the constitution of *Cod. Iust.* 6.58.14; cf. endnote 21 in the present chapter. *Inst. Iust.* 3.2.3a (533): "et haec quidem lex duodecim tabularum nullo modo introduxit, sed, simplicitatem legibus amicam amplexa, simili modo omnes adgnatos siue masculos siue feminas cuiuscumque gradus, ad similitudinem suorum, inuicem ad successionem uocabat. Media autem iurisprudentia, quae erat lege qui- dem duodecim tabularum iunior, imperiali autem dispositione anterior, subtilitate

quadam excogitata praefatam differentiam inducebat et penitus eas a successione adgnatorum repellebat" (and, as to this rule, it has in no way been introduced by the law of the Twelve Tables, which, adopting on the contrary the simplicity suitable to laws, called all the *adgnati*, men and women, of any degree, to succeed to each other, as in the case of *sui*. But the jurisprudence of the intermediate period, after the law of the Twelve Tables but before Imperial legislation, inventing a rather subtle measure, introduced the above difference and entirely ruled women out of the succession of their *adgnati*).

17. For Paul, see Paul *Sent.* 4.8.20: "feminae ad hereditates legitimas ultra consanguineo-rum successiones non admittuntur: id quoque iure ciuili Voconiana ratione uidetur effectum: ceterum lex duodecim tabularum sine ulla discretione sexus admittit" (women are not entitled to succeed beyond the successions of *consanguinei* accord-ing to civil law. This rule seems to have been established by civil law following the logic of the Voconian law. As a matter of fact, the law of the Twelve Tables permits succession without any discrimination based on sex). See also Paul *Sent.* 4.8.3: "sane consanguinei, quos lex non apprehenderat, interpretatione prudentium primum inter agnatos locum acceperunt" (it is a fact that *consanguinei*, whom the law [of the Twelve Tables] had not taken into account, were granted the first rank among *agnati* because of the jurists' interpretation). The *Sententiae* ascribed to the jurist Paul (early third century CE) were revised until about 450 and so they describe positive law before Justinian's reform. On the connections between *lex Voconia* and the creation of the category of *consanguinitas*, see among many articles, Uwe Wesel, *Rhetorische Statuslehre und Gesetzesauslegung der römischen Juristen* (Cologne, 1970), 90–91, and M. Balestri Fumagalli, "L'incapacità successorale delle *adgnatae* non con-sanguinee e la *lex Voconia*," chap. 2 in *Riflessioni sulla "lex Voconia"* (Milan, 2008), 39–65, 39n1, and bibliography. Cassius *ap.* Ulp. *Dig.* 38.16.1.10, quoted in endnote 12 above.

18. Gaius 3.14: "nam feminarum hereditates proinde ad nos agnationis iure redeunt atque masculorum, nostrae uero hereditates ad feminas ultra consanguineorum gra-dum non pertinent. Itaque soror fratri sororiue legitima heres est, amita uero et fratris filia legitima heres esse non potest; sororis autem nobis loco est etiam mater aut nouerca, quae per in manum conuentionem apud patrem nostrum iura filiae nacta est" (the successions of women fall to us on the legal ground of *agnatio* just as those of men, whereas our successions only concern women up to the degree of *consanguinei*. This is why, according to civil law, a sister inherits from her brother or her sister, while a paternal aunt and the daughter of a brother cannot inherit accord-ing to civil law; besides, our mother or stepmother who, as a result of their passing under marital authority, have acquired the rights of a daughter are also assimilated to a sister). Gaius, around 170 CE, describes the law in force. When he says "we," he refers to men, of course, by an unconscious bias. Other sources in Albanese, *Le per-sone*, 291n377.

19. See Justinian's historical excursus, *Inst. Iust.* 3.2.3 (see also endnote 16 above): "ce-terum inter masculos quidem adgnationis iure hereditas etiam longissimo gradu ul-tro citroque capitur. Quod ad feminas uero, ita placebat ut ipsae consanguinitatis iure tantum capiant hereditatem si sorores sint, ulterius non capiant. Masculi uero ad earum hereditates, etiam si longissimo gradu sint, admittantur. Qua de causa, fra-tris tui aut patrui tui filiae uel amitae tuae hereditas ad te pertinet, tua uero ad illas non pertinebat. Quod ideo ita constitutum erat quia commodius uidebatur ita iura constitui ut plerumque hereditates ad masculos confluerent. Sed quia sane iniquum erat in uniuersum eas quasi extraneas repelli, praetor eas ad bonorum possessio-

nem admittit ea parte qua proximitatis nomine bonorum possessionem pollicetur: ex qua parte scilicet admittuntur si neque adgnatus ullus nec proximior cognatus interueniat" (besides, one receives a succession, between men, in any case on the legal ground of *agnatio*, even to a very distant degree in both ways. But in the case of women, the rule was that they only received succession on the legal ground of *consanguinitas*, if they were sisters, whereas to a more distant degree they did not. That rule had been established because it seemed more advantageous, in general, that successions fall into the hands of men. But given that it was truly unfair that women should be totally excluded, as if they were alien to the family, the praetor allows them to inherit property in the part [of his edict] which warrants possession of property on the legal ground of closeness of kinship. But women are in fact admitted only if there is no closer *adgnatus* or *cognatus* between her and the deceased). The end of the text no longer concerns the system of "civil law," initially based on the Twelve Tables and strictly patrilineal, but the "praetorian system," which corrected the former and admitted parents of both lines *(cognati)* to succession.

20. See the texts (Cicero, Gaius, Justinian) collected and commented upon by Fumagalli, in his *Riflessioni*, chap. 2n18. The dissymmetry introduced in this reform, considered as unequal and unfair to women, raised numerous criticisms from antiquity onward and eventually justified the abolition of the category *consanguinitas* and the successoral mechanisms linked to it.

21. *Cod. Iust.* 6.58.14.1, in a historical synthesis: "sed posteritas, dum nimia utitur subtilitate, non piam induxit differentiam" (but the following generations, out of excessive minuteness, introduced a difference which did not take family links into consideration). See, two years later, the same insistence on *differentia* and the same criticism of the jurists' *subtilitas*, in the passage of *Inst. Iust.* (3.2.3a), quoted in endnote 16 above. The clearest text is *Inst. Iust.* 3.5.4: "consanguinitatis ius species est adgnationis (the right of *consanguinitas* is a category of the right of *adgnatio*). See also the *Tituli ex corpore Vlpiani 26.1* (between 320 and 342 CE), for a useful synthetic presentation of the civil system corrected: "intestatorum ingenuorum hereditates pertinent primum ad suos heredes, id est liberos qui in potestate sunt, ceterosque qui in liberum loco sunt. Si sui heredes non sunt, ad consanguineos, id est fratres et sorores ex eodem patre. Si nec hi sunt, ad reliquos agnatos proximos, id est cognatos uirilis sexus per mares descendentes, eiusdem familiae: id enim cautum est lege duodecim tabularum hac: "'si intestato moritur, cui suus heres nec escit, agnatus proximus familiam habeto'" (intestate successions of persons free by birth firstly regard their internal [direct] heirs, that is their legitimate descendants being under the paternal power, and all those who are assimilated to legitimate descendants. If there are no internal heirs, the succession falls to *consanguinei*, that is the brothers and sisters from the same father. In case there are none of the latter, the succession falls to the closest *agnati*, that is the *cognati*, the male descendants in male line, belonging to the same family. The system was established by the following clause of the law of the Twelve Tables: "If someone with no heir in direct dies intestate, let his closest *agnatus* inherit his property"). Obviously, for the author, *consanguinei* are only a sub-category of *agnati*. Similarly, according to the collector of *Sententiae* 4.8.3, the *consanguinei* only constitute "the first rank among *agnati*" (see endnote 17 above).

22. See endnotes 16, 19, 21 above. *Cod. Iust.* 6.58.14.4: "huius modi itaque legis antiquae reuerentiam et nos anteponi nouitati legis censemus et sancimus omnes legitimas personas, id est per uirilem sexum descendentes, siue masculini siue feminini generis sint, simili modo ad iura successionis legitimae ad successionis intestatorum uocari, secundum gradus sui praerogatiuam, non ideo excludendas quia consan-

guinitatis iura secundum germanae obseruationem non habent" (so, we consider, on the one hand, that the respect of the old law as it is prevails over legal innovation, and, on the other hand, we decide that all those designated by the law, that is the descendants in the patrilineal line, either male or female, are equally entitled to the right of succession according to the law, to the succession of persons who have died intestate, according to their degree of kinship, without their having to be excluded on the grounds that they do not possess the right of *consanguinitas* in accordance with the taking into account of the patrilineal sister). *Inst. Iust.* 1.3.2.3b states the same principles and the same decision. See Fumagalli, *Riflessioni*, 49–50. On the importance of the reference to *sanguis* in this constitution, see endnote 49 below.

23. One can suggest the following evaluation, work by work, of the uses of *consanguineus* or *consanguinitas* conforming to the specific meaning that the jurists had determined (doubles due to multiple quotations of the same passage in two works or more have been taken into account): Gaius, 5 out of 5 occurrences; *Tituli e corpore Vlpiani*, 5 out of 5; *Collatio*, 14 out of 15; Paul *Sent.*, 7 out of 7; *Cod. Theod.*, 8 out of 13; *Dig.*, 38 out of 39; *Inst. Iust.*, 13 out of 14; *Cod. Iust.*, 15 out of 19. Even considering that a few cases are questionable, the general picture remains significant. Pomata, "Legami," 309nn38–39.

24. See Clémence Dupont, *Les constitutions de Constantin et le droit privé au début du IV^e siècle. Les personnes* (Lille, 1937), 197–200: people argue whether this constitution ruled the guardianship of women in general or only that of wards, but the agnatic character of the guardianship in question is not questioned. For the same reasons, Clyde Pharr's translation, *The Theodosian Code* (Princeton, 1952), 78: "a consanguineous paternal uncle," seems rather unsatisfactory to me.

25. *Cod. Iust.* 5.30.3: "manente agnationis iure, tam consanguineus (id est frater), quam patruus ceterique legitimi ad pupillarum feminarum tutelam uocantur" (the right based on *agnatio* being still in force, the *consanguineus* [i.e., the brother] as well as the paternal uncle and all the other relatives designated by civil law can exercise guardianship over female wards).

26. See Jean-Pierre Waltzing, *Etude historique sur les corporations professionnelles des Romains* (Louvain, 1895), 2:297–303. On this meaning of *originalis*, see Waltzing, *Etude*, 303. *Cod. Theod.* 14.4.5: "consanguineos quoque eorum uel originales ut memoratorum nomini functionique iubeas adiungi, plenum et aequitatis et iuris est." See the translation of Pharr, *Theodosian Code*, 411 (which adopts the disjunctive meaning). The translation adopted here is deliberately ambiguous.

27. *Cod. Theod.* 14.4.8 (408 CE): "tam qui paterno quam materno genere inueniuntur obnoxii" (those who are subjected to the obligation due to their paternal filiation as well as to their maternal one); see Waltzing, *Etude*, 303.

28. For example, matrimonial prohibitions, family solidarity in justice, the rules of mourning, alimony, and so on. It is in a different system, that which the praetors devised to remedy the patrilineal bias of the civil law, that matrilineal relatives gradually received, under the name of *cognati*, successoral rights *ab intestato* (*Inst. Iust.* 3.2.3, which is quoted in endnote 19 above, alludes to it); see Voci, *Diritto*, 10–17.

29. See Guastella's excellent analysis, "La rete del sangue," 86, distinguishing *consanguinitas*, a "horizontal" relation, from the "vertical" link between father and son. Pomata's gloss, "Legami," 311, "la *consanguinitas* deve riferirsi al legame di parentela naturale fra un padre et i suoi figli" (*consanguinitas* must refer to the natural kinship tie between a father and his children), does not seem quite appropriate to me.

30. Ulp. *12 ad Sabinum, Dig.* 38.16.1.11: "non solum autem naturales, uerum etiam adoptiui quoque iura consanguinitatis habebunt cum his qui sunt in familia uel in

utero uel post mortem patris nati" (it is not only the natural children [in the sense of "the result of begetting"], but also adoptive children, who will have the right of *consanguinitas* with those belonging to the family, or else the children to be born or the father's posthumous children). Other texts in Albanese, *Le persone*, 229n108. *Pace* Pomata, "Legami," 311, one cannot draw from Ulp. *12 ad Sabinum, Dig.* 38.16.1.10, the idea that *consanguinitas* was independent from *patria potestas*. In fact, in her note 3, Pomata quotes, in all honesty, texts that clearly indicate the contrary: Ulp. *Inst., Coll. Mos.* 16.6.1, and Constantine, *Cod. Theod.* 5.1.1 (between 317 and 319 CE; *emancipatio*, that is an act performed by virtue of *patria potestas*, abolishes *consanguinitas*). See Albanese, *Le persone*, 291n377, and Guastella, "La rete del sangue," 84n95. See Gaius 3.14, quoted above in endnote 18. Other texts in Albanese, *Le persone*, 291n377.

31. We will see a particularly clear example of this in *Cod. Theod.* 9.38.6; see endnote 43 below.

32. Gaius's main work, *Commentarii iuris civilis*, dates back to circa 170 CE. Some of Ulpian's works (Ulpian was a jurist in the days of the Severi, in the early third century CE) were transmitted to us in a post-classical compilation, *Mosaicarum et Romanarum legum collatio* (written in 315 CE, then revised at the end of the fourth century); his works are also presented in Justinian's *Digest* (533 CE). The Code of Theodosius dates from 438 CE, that of Justinian, from 534 CE.

33. We will simply quote, in the present study, the text by Gaius (3.14), quoted in endnote 18 above.

34. The praetor promised succession (see Voci, *Diritto*, 10–16), by order of priority, to the *liberi* (legitimate descendants), to the *legitimi* (patrilineal relatives), lastly, to the *cognati*, the definition of which is given in the immediately preceding passage, by Ulpian, in the *Digest* (38.8.1.1–3): relatives with a common ascendant with the deceased, up to the sixth degree, and even the seventh for the children of second cousins (*sobrino et sobrina natus et nata*).

35. Gaius 16 *ad edictum prouinciale, Dig.* 38.8.2: "hac parte proconsul, naturali aequitate motus, omnibus cognatis promittit bonorum possessionem, quos sanguinis ratio uocat ad hereditatem, licet iure ciuili deficiant. Itaque etiam uulgo quaesiti liberi matris et mater talium liberorum, item ipsi fratres inter se ex hac parte bonorum possessionem petere possunt, quia sunt inuicem sibi cognati." The sentences mentioning the *naturalis aequitas* and the *sanguinis ratio* have been suspected of interpolation by Gerhardt Beseler, "Aequitas," *Zeitschrift der Savigny-Stiftung für Rechtsgeschichte* 45 (1925): 454. That hypercritical attitude is no longer accepted, as far as *aequitas* is concerned, according to Herbert Wagner, *Studien zur allgemeinen Rechtslehre des Gaius (ius gentium und ius naturale in ihrem Verhältnis zum ius ciuile)* (Zutphen, 1978), 153, 166–67n1, 184, who also refutes Beseler's critique as far as *sanguis* is concerned: according to Wagner, taking *sanguis* into account materializes, in the field of kinship, the taking into account of nature.

36. Pomata, "Legami," 328n26, claims that it is the only passage in the *Digest* mentioning the *ratio sanguinis* when talking about a mother and her children, and adds "significativamente, si tratta di figli illegitimi. Laddove il padre non è identificabile, a quanto pare, il sangue materno può in qualche modo avere riconoscimento, anche se non dà origine a diritti legali" (significantly, the point is about illegitimate children. When the father's identity cannot be established, it seems that, to a certain extent, the mother's blood can be taken into consideration, even though no legal right can proceed from it). The end of the sentence, unclear to me, perhaps means that the origin of the successoral vocation granted to illegitimate children is a praetorian and

proconsular norm, not the law. In any case, in the logic of the compilation, the first sentence of Gaius does not comment on the second, but of course on Ulpian's preceding fragment (Gaius's words *hac parte* of course refer, for the reader of the *Digest*, to Ulpian's words) which is about all the *cognati*.

37. On the civil system and the praetorian system of *ab intestato* succession to the property of the emancipated, see Voci, *Diritto*, 24 and 27–28. Ulp. *Inst.*, *Coll. Mos.* 16.9.2: "quod si is qui decessit liber fuit nec ex remancipatione manumissus, lex quidem duodecim tabularum manumissori legitimam hereditatem detulit, sed praetor aequitate motus decem personas cognatorum ei praetulit has: patrem matrem, filium filiam, auum auiam, nepotem neptem, fratrem sororem, ne quis occasione iuris sanguinis necessitudinem uinceret."

38. *Inst. Iust.* 3.9.3: "tertio, decem personis quas extraneo manumissori praeferebat (sunt autem decem personae hae: pater mater, auus auia tam paterni quam materni, item filius filia, nepos neptis tam ex filio quam ex filia, frater soror siure consanguinei siue uterini)."

39. See Erich Sachers, "Das Recht auf Unterhalt in der römischen Familie der klassischen Zeit," in *Festschrift F. Schulz* (Weimar, 1951), 1:310–63; Maria Gabriella Zoz, "In tema di obbligazioni alimentari," *Bollettino dell'Istituto di diritto romano* 73 (1970): 323–55. Ulp. *2 de officio proconsulis, Dig.* 25.3.5.2: "utrum autem tantum patrem auumue paternum proauumue paterni aui patrem ceterosque uirilis sexus parentes alere cogamur, an uero etiam matrem ceterosque parentes et per illum sexum contingentes cogamur alere, uidendum. Et magis est ut utrubique se iudex interponat, quorumdam necessitatibus facilius succursurus, quorumdam aegritudini; et cum ex aequitate haec res descendat caritateque sanguinis, singulorum desideria perpendere iudicem oportet."

40. Sachers, "Das Recht," 355, and Zoz, "Obbligazioni," 34, do not decide and speak about ascendants in general.

41. Ulp. *2 de officio proconsulis, Dig.* 25.3.5.5: "itam diuus Pius significat quasi auus quoque maternus alere compellamur."

42. See Pietro Bonfante, *Corso di diritto romano*, vol. 1, *Diritto di famiglia* (Rome, 1925), 380n3, and again Sachers, "Das Recht," 352n2. Biondo Biondi, in *Il diritto romano cristiano*, vol. 2, *La giustizia. Le persone* (Milan, 1952), 214, saw a Christian idea in the invocation of *natura*, but wrote nothing of the kind about *sanguis*. For another suspicion of interpolation, see endnote 35 above.

43. *Cod. Theod.* 9.38.6: "Imppp. Gratianus, Valentinianus et Theodosius AAA. ad Antidium u. c. uicarium. Paschalis laetitiae dies ne illa quidem gemere sinit ingenia quae flagitia fecerunt: pateat insuetis horridus carcer aliquando luminibus. Alienum autem censemus ab indulgentia qui nefariam criminum conscientiam in maiestatem superbe animauerit, qui parricidali furore raptus sanguine proprio manum tinxit, qui cuiusque praeterea hominis caede maculatus est, qui genialis tori ac lectuli fuit inuasor alieni, qui uerecundiae uirginalis raptor extitit, qui uenerandum cognati sanguinis uinculum profano caecus uiolauit incestu. ... Recitata XII Kal. Aug. Romae, Syagrio et Eucherio conss." The constitution also excepts poisoners and sacrilegious persons.

44. List of *cognati* in Marcianus *14 institutionum, Dig.* 48.9.1 and 3. See Duncan Cloud, "*Parricidium:* From the *lex Numae* to the *lex Pompeia de parricidiis*," *Zeitschrift der Savigny-Stiftung für Rechtsgeschichte* 88 (1971): 1–66; Lucia Fanizza, "Il parricidio nel sistema della *lex Pompeia*," *Labeo* 25 (1979): 266–89; Yan Thomas, "*Parricidium* I. Le père, la famille et la cité," *Mélanges de l'Ecole Française de Rome. Antiquité* 83 (1981): 643–713, here 651–54. The forms of repression may have concerned those various

relatives in different ways, but the definition of crime in terms of bilateral parent-hood is still present in the *Digest*.

45. See Salvatore Puliatti's *Incesti crimina. Regime giuridico da Augusto a Giustiniano* (Milan, 2001), tables 13 and 14, very telling lists; and, for the bilateral character of matrimonial interdicts, Philippe Moreau, *Incestus et prohibitae nuptiae. Conception romaine de l'inceste et histoire des prohibitions matrimoniales pour cause de parenté dans la Rome antique* (Paris, 2002), esp. 289–91.

46. *Cod. Theod.* 10.32.44: "nullus solius materni sanguinis uinculis illigetur, quia muli-erum infirmitas nunquam huius modi functionibus reddit obnoxios, a quibus ipsa habetur immunis." On the hereditary obligation for certain people to sit in their city's *curia*, see François Jacques, "*Obnoxius curiae.* Origines et formes de l'astreinte à la cité au IV$^e$ s. de notre ère," *Revue historique de droit français et étranger* 63 (1985): 303–85 (obligation transmitted by patrilineal filiation, 317–20).

47. This rhetorical figure is also used in a parallel passage in *Inst. Iust.* 3.2.3b, where it has been clearly identified by Balestri Fumagalli: see Fumagalli, *Riflessioni*, 48. *Cod. Iust.* 6.58.14.5: "cum enim unius sanguinis iura remanent per uirilem sexum incor-rupta, quare naturae offendimus et legitimo iuri derogamus?" See also endnote 22.

48. Pomata, "Legami," 311n45.

49. Pomponius 5 *ad Sabinum*, *Dig.* 50.17.8: the *iura sanguinis* cannot be countered by civil law; Paul 35 *ad edictum*, *Dig.* 1.7.23.pr, about the effects of adoption, associat-ing the *ius sanguinis* with *cognatio* and opposing it to *ius agnationis*; Ulp. 6 *de officio proconsulis*, *Dig.* 40.2.12.pr, about the law Aelia Sentia, links *sanguine contingere* (to be linked by blood) to *cognatio*; Papinian 36 *quaestionum*, *Dig.* 48.5.39.1, about in-cest with the daughter of a sister, speaks of *sanguinis contumelia* (an offence com-mitted against blood); *Cod. Iust.* 2.21.7 (294 CE), referring to *proximitas sanguinis* between an *auunculus* and his sister's daughter; *Nouell. Maior.* 7.2 (458 CE): the son of a *curialis* and an *ancilla* cannot sit in the *curia*, *ne materni sanguinis uilitate splen-dor ordinum polluatur* (to prevent the splendor of city senates from being soiled by low maternal blood). Legal texts offer forty-six occurrences of *sanguis*, thirty-eight of which concern filiation: the six texts commented upon above, plus the six simply mentioned in this note, constitute, in my view, a representative sample.

50. Pomata, "Legami," 320: "è chiaro che possiamo dirlo solo in via ipotetica." Com-pare ibid., 321. Besides, the author notes (a further difficulty) that the medical the-ory of hemogenesis did not completely deny the role of maternal blood in sexual reproduction.

# Chapter 3

# Flesh and Blood in Medieval Language about Kinship

## Anita Guerreau-Jalabert

The reference to blood as a symbolic support for the link between certain categories of kin is currently of common usage, at least in some European languages, and historians generally employ it without further reflection. With regard to the language of anthropology, both English and French have retained the terms *consanguinity/consanguinité*, which come from the Latin *consanguinitas*, to designate the tie that unites individuals who recognize a common ancestor. One fact has become clear: in Western Europe, at least since Roman times, filiation was transmitted and described by blood.

Yet a somewhat careful observation of medieval data reveals a more complex situation, one that is not easy to interpret. But the very task of describing it imposes methodological constraints on historical enquiry since, turning on a question of terminology, it falls primarily within the domain of linguistics. If we need to draw attention briefly to the main aspects of such terminology, this is because the results depend on it.

We need to take into account the fact of medieval multilingualism and the status of the written languages. Throughout the entire medieval period Latin was certainly the common written language of clerics (in the wide sense of the term) and for long centuries was even the only language; in that milieu it could also serve as a vehicle of spoken communication among a very limited number of individuals. But it was an exclusively scholarly language and had a composite nature. Heir to Classical Latin, it was built upon the language of the Church Fathers, which was also the language of the Bible. The latter not only introduced lexical transformations, of which we are generally aware, but also, and most importantly, gave new contents to old words—thus translating a profound change in the social structures. Finally, Medieval Latin was continuously marked by the vernacular languages and their evolution, notably in its lexical and semantic aspects, and this process occurred even during periods when the vernaculars were not written down. So over the thousand years of the Middle Ages, Latin mutated, while always remaining subject to synchronous geographic or individual variations. Within a language that was more or less fixed by writing, these variations corresponded to a form of structural instability. We must be careful, when faced with lexical differences and discrepancies, to avoid confusing variations or idiosyncrasies with structural features. That is why it is absolutely necessary to take into consideration the vernacular languages, which, in the forms they have come down to us, were also scholarly languages and tend to provide a more accurate image than Latin does of linguistic usages in the Middle Ages. A comparison between Latin and the vernacular is indispensable, for beyond the apparent continuity of form, the lexicon of Medieval Latin, in its semantic structure, is always much closer to the vernaculars than to Classical Latin.

Another difficulty lies in the nature of the texts, and this is a problem that also arises when dealing with other periods. There is no question that different registers of language existed, in which the same words did not have exactly the same values. The technical language of jurists is a particular case in point, or that of physicians and theologians, as well as that which is probably closest of all to "common sense," the language used by "literary authors" (though poets themselves often had a particular language of their own). Ideally, we would need to examine and compare all these registers, while accounting for the chronological and geographic divisions of the data; in this case, however, experience has shown that the variations are more of the lexical order than the semantic.

Finally, we should point out that the phenomenon being studied—reference to a bodily substance as a metaphor for the tie of kinship—has a very limited frequency compared with other modes of expression. The research, therefore, requires consulting large corpora of data; otherwise the results will not be significant. For lexical or semantic studies of this kind, the emergence of digitalized texts has led to extraordinary progress. However, for the time being, all we can obtain are clues, not precise results based on statistical measures, and there are several reasons for this: Latin is overrepresented compared to the vernacular; in Latin itself, texts of a practical nature are dangerously underrepresented compared to theological and hagiographical texts along with texts from the last two centuries of the Middle Ages. Moreover, the search engines used in the digitalized corpora are notoriously insufficient for the purpose of performing fine and detailed analyses. These corpora, then, provide information that dictionaries alone could not; they make it possible now to sift through extensive groups of texts, though these texts are only partly representative.[1]

# The Terminology of Medieval Latin

## *Sanguis, Consanguinitas, Consanguineus*

As Philippe Moreau has shown in his contribution to this volume, the Romans definitely conferred symbolic value on blood in the area of kinship, in particular as an image of filiation, of the continuity of a descent line.[2] This phenomenon is illustrated as much by the uses of the word *sanguis* as by the notions of *consanguineus* and *consanguinitas*.

The classical language used phrases such as *patrius/maternus sanguis, communis/idem sanguis, (ex)* or *(de) sanguine ortus/natus, sanguine conjuncti*, which were partly taken up by Medieval Latin and supplemented by other formulas (for example, *propinquus sanguine*). *Sanguis* in this sense began to compete with other terms, particularly *genus*, which were probably more frequent.

Medieval Latin received the terms *consanguineus* and *consanguinitas*, also conveying the idea of a substance being shared by individuals who recognized the fact of belonging to the same group by filiation. Operating within the framework of rules on succession, jurists of the second century BCE had used these terms to designate a particular category of *agnati* (abolished in Justinian's Code). In literary language the terms corresponded to a cognatic terminology.

Both *consanguineus* and, even more so, *consanguinitas*, present low levels of frequency in Classical Latin.[3] According to the current tools of investigation both words appeared much more frequently in Medieval Latin. This phenomenon is associated with an important reorganization of the terminology of kinship at the time of the Church Fathers, which was marked by the disappearance of the patrilineal inflexion contained in *agnatio* and a transition to an Eskimo-type terminology; added to this was a simplification that tended to reduce the use of *consobrinus* and *sobrinus* in favor of more generic terms. In this context, *consanguineus* entered into a body of terminology where it became completely or partly interchangeable with *cognatus, propinquus, parens, affinis,* and even *amicus;* while as early as the Carolingian era, *consanguinitas,* taken as the equivalent of *cognatio,* came to designate a group of kin and no longer a tie of kinship, although *cognatio,* in this sense, appears more often. More detailed and complete observations than the ones currently available would allow us to shed light on the usages that were preferred and to estimate the different relative weights of these terms in various periods, geographic areas, types of text, and authors. The variations in usage are not very open to question, for the simple reasons mentioned above; but it is absolutely vital that we do not confuse simple variants with structural trends in terminology.[4] What the medieval system of terminology shows is that *consanguineus* and *consanguinitas* continued to translate an undifferentiated conception of kinship.

In this register, Medieval Latin clearly depended upon the heritage of the classical language. The Latin Bible generally used the image of *semen* (also known in Classical Latin) when talking about filiation and descent—for example, in phrases such as *ex, de,* and *a semine David* (which may also be found in medieval authors), whose productivity outside this context, however, does not appear to have been very highly developed. *Sanguis* in this sense is almost entirely absent from the biblical vocabulary, due to the fact that blood had no place in conceptions about kinship in the Jewish world.[5] The formula used in John 1:13, "qui non ex sanguinibus ... nati sunt," which belongs to the New Testament, appears to be a rather isolated example; and we may observe that Alain de Lille, in his *Distinctiones,* ascribed a series of figurative meanings to *sanguis* but illustrated the value of *parentela* by quoting from Virgil: "Sanguis proprie ... Dicitur parentela, unde Virgilius dicit: Alto de sanguine Teucri."[6] However, whatever the seeming ties of the medieval vocabulary with the classical and biblical heritage, patristic and medieval authors did innovate strongly with the introduction of two new substances into the discourse about kinship: *caro* (flesh) and *spiritus* (spirit).

## Caro

With the Church Fathers, a new conception of man developed, and a new vocabulary to deal with it. Thus *caro* made an impressive entry into the Latin lexicon through translations from the Bible—where it rendered the Hebrew *basar*—and in Christian writers as early as Tertullian.[7] The presence of this word is characterized by very high frequencies and by an important diversification in semantic values. The classical language used *caro* to designate only one part of the body of living beings, the muscles, as opposed to the bones, or blood, or skin (the term especially referred to meat for consumption). This sense was not unknown in Medieval Latin, but here, the principal importance of *caro* resided in the following three designations:

(1) The totality of human nature, as assumed by Christ (hence the term sometimes is applied to designate both kinds—body/blood—of the Eucharist, and not just one of the two kinds—body).
(2) Man, as a living being, as a creature.
(3) Flesh, as one of the two main components of the human being (spirit being the other component).

This last is a numerically and semantically very weighty element because of the multiplied number of meanings that dovetailed into it and the moral/symbolic charge now carried by *caro*: everything that designated the human compared to the divine, the terrestrial as opposed to the celestial, evil as opposed to good, was susceptible of being designated by *caro*. Finally, the importance of the notion *caro* may also be seen in its fertility, in the numerous derivatives and neologisms that it spawned, *carnalis* and *carnaliter* being among the most frequent.[8]

## A Conception of Man: "*Caro*" and "*Spiritus*"

Christian Latin innovated not only by attributing an entirely new value to *caro*, but also by conferring within the context of the same movement an equally new sense to *spiritus*, and by generating the pair *spiritus/caro* for the purpose of thinking about human beings. In Classical Latin *spiritus* essentially had designated breath (figuratively, pride, or a state of mind). Henceforth, *spiritus* (enriched by the neologisms *spiritualis, spiritualiter*) would be used in a general sense to designate the plane of the divine, the celestial, the good. Thus it underwent a metamorphosis as marked as the one that affected its sister term in the new pair.[9]

The pair *spiritus/caro* came to overlap and interact with the ancient pair *animus/corpus*; in fact, the latter pair also underwent a formal reorganization in the Christian context, since *anima* tended to replace *animus*, as well as a semantic reinterpretation, which corresponded to the reinterpretation of the system of conceptions about man, society, and the world that came in with the advent of Western Christianity.[10] What is of crucial importance in these transformations is precisely that *caro* and *spiritus* not only served to define the substantial properties of the human being, something that *corpus* and *animus* already did, but also provided, through an expansion of their contents, a homological conception for social relationships—the relationship between man/woman, clerics/laymen, and relationships among kin—which amounted to the presentation of social structure as natural.

## Kinship of the Flesh, Kinship of the Spirit

Christian society was characterized by the generalization of a ritual form of kinship relations, accepted as superior to other forms, the engendering of which commenced in the baptismal rite. As lexical usages clearly indicate, baptism was thought to be a second birth, one whose operator was the Holy Spirit. This spiritual engendering of the Christian as a son of God and the Church made it possible to abolish the negative effects of the carnal engendering that transmitted original sin; at the same time it sealed the entry of the child into society (membership in the *ecclesia*) and into his kin group (attribution of a name).[11]

Beginning with Saint Ambrose and above all with Saint Augustine, and in line with the general system of conceptions about man and the world, the Western system of kinship thus recognized two main forms of relations: *cognatio carnalis* (or *secundum carnem*)—covering consanguinity and marriage, and associated with the exercise of sexuality—and *cognatio spiritualis* (or *secundum spiritum*)—produced by baptism and secondarily by confirmation. It is to this model that the passage quoted above from John 1:13 refers: "qui non ex sanguinibus neque ex voluntate carnis neque ex voluntate viri sed ex Deo nati sunt."

In the first of these two registers, the reference to flesh was commonly used to evoke ties of consanguinity and marriage—the use of the term *flesh* to designate kinship already being in the Latin Bible; however, the reference to blood, which had been received from Classical Latin, was not abandoned by patristic and medieval authors. Nevertheless, given the current state of research, it appears impossible to arrive at any estimate of the relative weight of these usages and their likely observable variations based on periods, places, and authors: for example, we need to test the hypothesis that the High Middle Ages were more faithful at conserving inheritances from Classical Latin, a formal conservation that was also accompanied, however, by a shift in meaning. What can be stated with some confidence is that *sanguis* now appeared to be a simple variation of register for *caro*, in opposition to *spiritus* and without any real semantic autonomy.

This is made apparent in the principle formulations in the texts. The content of generic terms such as *cognatio/cognatus*, *affinitas/affinis*, and *propinquitas/propinquus* could be specified by mentioning a substance, either blood or flesh. Thus, we see *affinitas, propinquitas, proximitas sanguinis, or carnis* (or even *consanguinitatis*); *cognatio carnis, carnalis,* or *sanguinis;* for adjectives there are phrases such as *affinis, propinquus, proximus sanguine,* or *carne, juxta, secundum carnem.* But we also find redundant combinations of a type that was common in Medieval Latin, in which the reference bunches the two substances together. For example, *cognatio carnis et sanguinis* or *propinquitas carnis et sanguinis.* And also less simple formulas: *consanguinea et carnis cognatione propinqua* (Hincmar of Reims); *hic carnis propinquitate consanguineus* (Thietmar of Merseburg).[12] This latter case may be identified with phrases in which the reference to blood contained in *consanguinitas/consanguineus* appears to have been, in some sense, canceled out: *secundum carnem consanguinei, consanguinitas carnis,* which are by no means very common, but which occur from Hilary of Poitiers to Gratian, passing through Augustine, Alcuin, and Anselm, who were not minor authors. Finally we have some indication that *consanguinitas* was almost exclusively associated with the register of *caro:* there being apparent almost no trace of its connection with the spiritual register—unlike what happened with other terms, which could be used in the register of *spiritus.*[13]

In conclusion, I would like to insist on two essential points: first, that the usages listed above are in the minority; and second, that the illustration of combinations and commutations among terms representing the two substances indicates that in Medieval Latin, *sanguis* was no more than a variant of *caro,* referring to what the men of the Middle Ages designated as flesh kinship. Like the entire body of terms that had come down from Classical Latin, *sanguis* received its meaning from the general terminological system of which it was now a part; for it is structure that defines sense through the relation of the terms with each other. Only a lack of knowledge of the structural approach to linguistic questions—an approach indispensable here—could lead to an attempt to give such terms a value independent from their context, a context on which we now aim to shed light by looking at the French language.

# The Data from French

## Old French

The main digitalized corpus of literary works, *Corpus de la littérature médiévale,* shows that in Old French (twelfth to the early fourteenth centuries), blood was not ordinarily associated with kinship, which is confirmed by Tobler-Lommatzsch's *Altfranzösisches Wörterbuch.*[14] Nevertheless, blood often flows copiously through these texts, and other symbolic values are attributed to it, especially for describing psychological states: as in *sanc bouillant* (impetuous, angry), *sanc rassis* (calm, tranquil), *sanc muez* (troubled, frightened), and *sanc meslez* (troubled, overwhelmed), phrases that also gave rise to the creation of verbs, nouns, and adjectives (*sancmesler, sancmesleüre, sancmué*).

In the register of kinship, it is flesh that constituted the substantial referent, when there was one: essentially, *amis de char* or *amis charnels, père, frère* or *seur charnel* (also possibly *un carnel,* for a relative); a relation of kinship could be designated by *carnalité.* There is no word in Old French that derives from *consanguinitas* or *consanguineus.* This phenomenon can be considered as an indicator of the deletion of the reference to blood as early as the High Middle Ages; were this not the case, Old French, which had its roots in the spoken language of northern Gaul between the end of the Roman Empire and the High Middle Ages, would have kept a trace one way or another.

One text provides a good illustration of the distance between Latin and French: the French version of Gratian's *Decretum* produced in the Anglo-Norman area, probably around 1170 according to its latest editor.[15] Because of its faithfulness to the Latin text this French version resembles a translation. Clause XXXV of the *Decretum,* devoted to marriage prohibitions, makes abundant use of the words *consanguineus* and *consanguinitas,* but we also find *cognatio, propinquitas, parentela.* All these are translated by the single term *lignage. Genus humanum* is translated by *l'humain lignage. Consanguinei* has its equivalent in the terms *parents* and *cousins,* and the latter is also used to translate one of the rare instances of *consobrinus* in this text. *Cognatio* is rendered on one occasion by *lignée.* The translator's choices confirm that the different Latin terms were semantically equivalent to each other, and a reading of Gratian's text, which is completely unoriginal in this respect, makes this clear. We can also see an equivalent meaning for different vernacular terms and, above all, we find the wide and plastic content that the word *lignage* had—in keeping with its etymology and quite far from what too many historians have said.[16]

But above all, it is remarkable that nowhere is any mention made of blood, even when the Latin text indirectly alludes to it with *consanguinitas* and *consanguineus*—while the reference to flesh is retained in the translation of *consanguinitas carnis* by *lignage de char.* We may consider that the translator's lexical usages are particularly reliable since they agree with what can be found in other texts. Neither was blood introduced by the copyists of the manuscript that has come down to us and which is dated in the 1280s (the editor, Leena Löfstedt, did manage to detect a number of interventions in the text by the copyists).[17]

Thus, neither this technical text (in the form of a translation), nor literary works, which, we should remember, were connected with the dominant and especially aristocratic milieus, associated blood with kinship. The situation for Old French is, therefore, much simpler than for Latin during the same period: there was a tendency toward use of a reduced terminology, and the single substantial referent was flesh.

## Middle French

This situation remained stable until around the middle of the fourteenth century, when we can observe the beginning of an evolution whose effects need to be studied beyond 1500. References to flesh appear to have remained not only common, but the majority in every type of text, even in the technical language of the practitioners of law at the Parlement of Paris and of the *rédacteurs de coutumes*.[18] Likewise, *lignage* remained a major term, endowed with the same semantic breadth it had in Old French (kindred and tie of kindred); other terms were used with certainly less frequency, especially *lignée*, which designated in particular ancestors and descendents. Nevertheless, references to blood do begin to appear, becoming perhaps more frequent over the course of the fifteenth century, and this in narrative, normative, and documentary texts. The current state of the digitalized corpora prevents us from measuring the extent of the phenomenon, which, moreover, has received almost no scholarly attention, with the exception of the very recent study by Charles de Miramon.[19] It seems to me that these references show up as essentially two types of occurrences: on the one hand, the *princes* or *seigneurs du sanc*, the *sanc roial*, the *sanc de France*, to designate relatives of the king; on the other, the phrase *sanc et lignage* (on occasion *sanc et lignée*).[20]

For the first group, usages date back to the middle of the fourteenth century. It was without doubt within this group that the greatest innovation took place. Miramon has found a number of instances of blood, which he has qualified as "sporadic," in the area of kinship (four occurrences between 1317 and 1330), in France and England, in royal milieus: he dates the appearance of *sanc roial*, and *princes* or *seigneurs du sanc* to the middle of the century.[21] It would be necessary to follow up the numeric development of these formulas (while above all avoiding mixing Latin and the vernacular), but also to determine the precise content of *sanc roial*; that is, to ascertain which of the king's relatives belonged to this category.

In the second group, the semantic value of *sanc* was supported by that of *lignage*. The field of application of *sanc et lignage* remains to be identified, as well as the referent of *sanc* in this phrase, which shows up among the terms that were used to designate royal kinship (for example in the *Ordonnances* of the kings of France in the fifteenth century) but seems to have had a wider extension, particularly in the registers of Parlement.[22]

The particular characteristics of language in the Middle Ages suggest that in this type of synonymic phrase *sanc* and *lignage* were equivalent, and we find this in the analogous constructs *être de haut, grand, noble sang* and *être de grand, haut,* and *noble lignage*. In this case, both terms (to which we should add *ligniée*) referred to the different forms of kinship, and in particular to the kinship of descent to which an individual belongs, either to his ancestors (the most frequent case) or, sometimes, to his own descendents. In some rare examples, *sanc noble* also appears to have been a way of referring to nobles as a group, beyond any explicit reference to kinship: "iceux menuz gens et vers de terre susserent tout le noble sang de France et furent tuez plusieurs gentilz hommes en leurs litz."[23]

On the whole, blood is clearly evident in the Middle French lexicon about kinship. Its range of meaning, however, remained more limited than that of flesh; moreover, the two terms did not overlap: blood was used to designate a group of kin and flesh to signify a relationship. For the moment, it is not clear to me how to interpret this difference. It is, however, significant that the image of blood is present in the work of certain authors (Christine de Pizan, Georges Chastellain, Simon de Phares), while elsewhere it is absent, a reminder that we ought not to draw general conclusions from too small a number of examples.

Other romance languages appear to have had evolutions comparable to French, at around the same time, if one is to believe what can be gathered from the very scanty lexicographic data, which need to be checked and completed. In German, a few pieces of information provided by William Jervis Jones indicate nothing like this at all: here reference is to birth (*geborn, erborn*), possibly also to *sippe*, which distinguishes kin from within the group of *frunde*. But Simon Teuscher cites examples where blood appears: *mit blut frundschaft ... gesipt* and *mit blut verwandt*.[24]

## Possible Interpretations and Open Questions

The situation is thus more complicated than common discourse, which often pays too little attention to the vocabulary being used, would have it. An example of this is the article *Jus sanguinis* by Ernest Champeaux, cited everywhere despite its limited interest, in which the author comments without reflection on a text that mentions *caro* as if it were speaking of blood.[25] This prevents him from enquiring into the fact that, in the texts he is examining, the principle of *una caro* is applied to the registers of both consanguinity—father and son—and marriage—spouses. It is essential, however, that we take into account the sense and weight of this operator when analyzing Christian conceptions about kinship.

The evolution that can be perceived at the end of the Middle Ages brought into play both terminological usages and a body of representations at the same time. The question that arises is whether we can see in this an indication that changes were also occurring in the organization of kinship. Medievalists can only reasonably claim to advance interpretative hypotheses, given the all too fragmentary state of the linguistic data and our knowledge about the medieval system of kinship, as well as the fact that the Middle Ages experienced only the initial stage of a phenomenon that developed over subsequent centuries.[26]

## Evolving Representations

If we may take the evolving use of language as a sign that representations were changing, still, in my view, it is necessary to avoid any sort of "naturalization" of ideal elements that is premised on contemporary conceptions, and not on those of the Middle Ages. I feel this caveat also holds true for the notion that because blood is a fluid, it is better suited than flesh to express filiation. For centuries, and still at the end of the Middle Ages, flesh perfectly expressed ties of descent, the transmission and sharing of certain properties between certain categories of kin (consanguineal). But the debates about the Immaculate Conception, explored by David Warren Sabean in this volume, identified flesh as the instrument that propagates original sin from generation to generation; and this was consonant with the conceptions underlying the discussions on original sin and its transmission, which had their origins in the patristic era.

The medieval system of ideas concerning substances seems to me to have been structured by a double binary system—*caro* and *spiritus*, *caro* and *sanguis*—in which the sense of each term was defined by a relation and not by an essential value.

The choice of the term *caro* primarily reflected a relationship between the spiritual and the carnal. In the area of kinship, the idea of *caro* referred at once to the generation of matter produced by sexual intercourse and to a model of matrimonial union, that of the *unitas carnis* which was manifested in the sexual union between the marriage partners but was not limited to that.[27] In effect, the model referred to a fundamental idea in Christian society, that of unity, of which it was but one expression. The unity of spouses was based chiefly on the agreement of their wills, that is, of their minds; but it was also realized (and even more perfectly so) in the relationship between Christ and the Church, between God and the Soul, and possibly between Christ and human nature. It thus brought into play elements hierarchically arranged and articulated by the concept of spiritual love (this is why in the couple, the man is on the side of *spiritus* and lawfully dominates the woman, who is equated with *caro*). Even if the theory of marriage acknowledged the part that sexual conjunction played in the production of a new being, a unique entity, the sense of *caro* cannot be reduced to the modern notion of sexuality; for *caro* inscribed the marriage relationship into a much wider system of homological relations that made it sacred and gave it meaning. We see that this ideal system was very complex and its deployment based on different values for *caro*, which we have mentioned above. The model of *unitas carnis* did have the effect, nevertheless, of putting together relationships of consanguinity and affinity, which was consistent with the fact that marriage interdictions concerned both consanguineal and affinal kin. Over this register of *caro*, that of *spiritus* was superimposed: in the human being, we encounter the *anima*, which is outside the order of carnal reproduction because it is blown in by God; and in the order of society we have the ties created by the baptism ritual, as well as by less ritualized forms of relations that rested on the idea of the *copula* or *copulatio animarum*—that is to say different aspects of what I call "spiritual kinship," whose cement is spiritual love. In this setting, anything that was not thought of as *spiritus*, even blood when it expressed a relation of filiation, was relegated to *caro*.

However, the register of *caro* could be further subdivided into *caro* and *sanguis*, flesh and blood.[28] This subdivision, found at the heart of Christian representations, was influenced by the discourse on Christ, the common setting for thought about mankind (and society) in the Middle Ages.[29] If Christ was incarnated, that is, if he assumed human nature in its totality (recall that this is one of *caro's* meanings), then the rite of the Eucharist introduced the issue of redundancy between *caro* (or *corpus*) and *sanguis*. Beginning with Saint Ambrose, and then with Saint Augustine, exegetes and theologians grappled with two thorny questions: on the one hand, how to interpret certain passages from the Old Testament (Gen. 9:4–6; Lev. 17:11 and 17:14), which associated *anima* with *sanguis*; on the other hand, the existence of the two kinds of the Eucharist. In the debate these two problems sometimes intersected. In the case of the first, it appears to have been accepted that the *anima* was the vital principle and by no means the rational soul that had been infused by God (Augustine was careful to warn against mistaking the vital principle as the conveyor or support of the immortal soul).[30] And this vital principle did have a relationship with blood, according to common conceptions about physiology inherited from Antiquity. In the second case, it was said that the bread/flesh of Christ brought health to the Christian's flesh and the wine/blood did the same for his *anima* (and here the ambiguity was greater, for *anima* also referred to the rational soul, but the blood in question was Christ's, which changed everything).[31] Overall,

blood did, therefore, have something to do with *spiritus*, a fact that established its higher value in the pair *caro/sanguis*. As a logical outcome,
the communion in two kinds tended to disappear in the thirteenth century for laymen, who were the fleshly part of the *ecclesia*, blood being
reserved for its spiritual part, the priests, in a practice that the Utraquists
contested.

If we attempt to decipher the lexical evolution under examination
as being a phenomenon related to the order of ideals, then references
to *sanc roial* and to *grand, noble, haut et noble sanc,* first used in royal or
aristocratic milieus, could be interpreted as a new formulation of an old
claim to spiritual properties, expressed by the dominant lay groups. For
this is how we can understand the great themes of courtly literature:
the *fin'amors,* the *grail,* chivalry as a model of spiritual relations.[32] This
claim, of course, had its origin in an ideological configuration in which
the laity was placed, by definition, on the side of the flesh, in opposition
to clerics, while social legitimacy was based only on the spiritual side.
Only a detailed enquiry would enable us to verify how the reference to
blood spread, while depending ideologically (and perhaps practically)
on the *sanc roial* (that is, on royal kindred), which seems to have been
the first form to appear.

The question of chronology—why do we have to wait until the middle
of the fourteenth century before the kinship of flesh could be expressed,
under certain circumstances, by the substance of blood—still remains
to be settled. I would be tempted to look for a solution in the general
evolution of Western societies: beginning in the fifth century these societies were slowly transformed by the intrusion of spiritual principles
as the foundation for the organization of social relations, particularly
relations of kinship. This movement ended up by incorporating consanguinity and marriage into the much vaster and much more highly sacralized system of ties cemented by *spiritus* and *caritas*. A number of clues
suggest that by the end of almost a thousand years of evolution this
model had generally come to be accepted. I would cite the considerable
development of baptismal kinship, the establishment of confraternities
and pious foundations in the last two centuries of the Middle Ages, the
consolidation of the parish as a form of localized community. As may
be seen in the literature from the beginning of the twelfth century, the
adherence of dominant lay groups to these models is strikingly evident,
even if it is expressed in the apparently subversive search for distinctive differences. With regard to theological conceptions of man, the idea
of a being composed of two hierarchically distinguished components,
*spiritus* and *caro*, joined by a "mystery" (Augustine), gave way to the
substantial hylomorphism of Saint Thomas Aquinas, in which spirit is

the form of body; which is as much to say that the latter was engulfed
by the former, another step in the process of spiritualizing the carnal. At
the same time, however, these conceptions are a way of speaking about
social relations.[33] The universal priesthood established by the Reformation was in effect the logical outcome of this process, as was the generalization of marriage rites performed in church. In a certain sense, the
role assigned to consanguinity and marriage in the workings of society
no longer aroused any debate: the fact that they now could be associated with blood would appear to reflect not so much a promotion but
another step along the way to "spiritualizing" the "flesh," a process also
shown by the success of the Immaculate Conception or the new representations of the Holy Kinship.

### An Evolution of the Kinship System?

Can we pursue the interpretation even further by postulating transformation, not only in how kinship was conceived, but in how kinship
functioned? Miramon advances the hypothesis that a "biological" or "hereditary" conception of "nobility" emerged. There is not enough space
here for a critical commentary on these notions. But, once again, this
idea was conveyed quite aptly by the reference to "flesh," which remained the most widely used term until the end of the Middle Ages
(even among "nobles" who had *amis charnels* for example), and equally
by the terms *hors substance* and especially *lignage* (but also *ligniée, affins,
amis, parents*). Moreover, birth alone did not suffice in the Middle Ages
to determine legitimate membership in dominant groups: numerous
studies have shown that belonging to a group of "nobles" depended just
as much on the fact of "living nobly" as on birth; additionally, in the register of discourses, a tension existed between social origin and individual
qualities. The problem was inherent to a society that knew neither caste
nor order, nor impermeable boundaries between different social levels;
to a society with a dominant institution (the Church), which did not
reproduce itself through kinship and which thus radically undermined
the legitimacy of the hereditary principle. Inherent in the relationship
*caro/spiritus* (both in Latin and in French, reference may be found to a
nobility of the flesh, as opposed to a nobility manifested by virtue), the
tension between origins and qualities was often resolved in dominant lay
thinking by combining the two elements (birth and virtue) together.[34] It
was a common strategy in the *Vitae* of saints as early as the Merovingian
period and one that also came through in courtly literature beginning
from the twelfth century. Quite remarkably, however, the hereditary
principle was understated in these writings, in line with a project by the
dominant lay groups to construct a spiritual identity for themselves. It

is possible that, beginning in the thirteenth century, and even more in the fourteenth century, an evolving medieval society tackled the problems of defining groups and of establishing criteria for delimiting their contours (with the illusion of being able to "close" groups) with renewed vigor; but the causal link between such activities and the appearance of kinship blood discourses in the course of the fourteenth century needs to be demonstrated, especially since, once again, the term is new, but the problem is not.

Can we detect a relationship between an evolution in the terminology and the way kinship functioned? Different analytical leads have been suggested to me, both by Miramon's text and by certain authors in this volume:

(1) Reference to blood would have made it possible, when necessary, to demarcate a category of consanguine kin from within the indistinct group of "flesh" relatives (who might also be affines), and the need to do this may have increased at the end of the Middle Ages.
(2) The blood reference was a tool ideally suited for the construction of male lineages in a cognatic system (somewhat analogous to the *agnatio* in Rome).
(3) The new image of blood may have accompanied the transition at the end of the Middle Ages from a system centered on the marriage alliance to a system preponderantly organized by filiation—the latter having been restructured by patrilineal transmission practices.

Given the current state of our knowledge, any attempt to answer these questions, in my opinion, is very risky, since we are far short of having broad and precise data. We thus run into a difficulty with regard to the link between filiation and blood: the common usage at the end of the Middle Ages of the phrase *hoir* [heir] *de sa char* (or *de son corps*) has no equivalent for blood.

We would need to verify to what extent the reference to blood corresponded to a masculine inflexion. The equivalence in French between *sanc* and *lignage* at first sight does not suggest any such correspondence. Even the contours of *sanc roial* do not appear clear for the moment: Miramon considers that it stood for a group of relatives who were connected to the king by a proximity based on loyalty and from which certain people were excluded: among the cousins of Charles VI, Bernard Guenée includes relatives of the female line: yet in his view, the presence of lily flowers on the coat of arms is the distinctive sign of a relation passing through men—the lords of the lily flowers. In his stress on the importance of real proximity to the king, not just genealogical proxim-

ity, Guenée's position is very close to Miramon's.[35] In view of his observations, along with the scanty textual data from the *DMF*, one cannot
help thinking that there existed no precise definition of *sanc roial* at the
end of the Middle Ages (while in the seventeenth century the princes of
the blood were defined by a clear genealogical principle); as in the case
of *lignage* the composition of the group depended on context. Nonetheless, the fundamentally cognatic value of *lignage* did not prevent the
ideological valorization of male lineages.

For the fact is that these societies were sharply marked by male dominance—which, for example, justified the preferential transfer of family
estates, the foundation of powers and status, to a male rather than female
heir. Was blood the ideal construct to express a quality that was by and
large male, but that could also pass through women (since we also find
mention of women *de sanc roial* or *de noble sanc*)? This would need to
be examined closely. Whatever the case, we must absolutely avoid confusing the weight of masculinity in a society with a patrilineal organization of kinship—in which social membership, and what pertained to it,
rested on a principle of exclusiveness based on the distinction between
the sexes. This exclusiveness was absent in European societies, but it
is possible to detect a reinforcement of male domination at the end of
the Middle Ages and the beginning of the early modern age, which in
France, for example, translated into an increase in patriarchal power.[36]

Primogeniture and unigeniture were practiced in France (and certainly elsewhere) from the beginning of the eleventh century for the
same reasons as later: the systemic need to transmit the core properties
to a single heir in order to avoid fragmenting the powers and status associated with those lands, with other claimants inheriting more or less
richly according to the size of the estate. This is what led Georges Duby
to go back to Karl Schmid's model (an erroneous one) on the transition
from a "horizontal" to a "vertical" organization of kinship.[37] This need
resulted from the wide-ranging functions assigned to kinship in societies
otherwise lacking highly structured, autonomous, political, or economic
institutions. However, the choice of a primary heir/successor produced
numerous conflicts precisely because it ran counter to the principle of
cognatism (where all children of a couple were equal heirs). This is perhaps why we observe, at the very end of the Middle Ages, the first attempts to formalize and regulate male transmission, in keeping with
the principle of social domination by men: *majorats, fideicommis*, entails,
all were aimed at controlling a mode of preferential transmission to a
single heir, if possible male (but not always); why also, as J. Morsel has
shown, the transformation of lands into fiefs, defined as being transmissible only to men, went hand in hand in some German-speaking regions

with the emergence of the ideological construct *Geschlecht*.[38] But these practices developed within a system of kinship that remained cognatic (no changes in the terminology occurred and transmission by women continued through the early modern era).[39]

Finally, the changeover from alliance to filiation would need to be demonstrated. A solid anthropological theory of the medieval kinship system might lead us to consider that the principle of *unitas carnis*, marriage interdictions, and the indissolubility of the matrimonial tie provided a more marked level of structural reinforcement to marriage than in other systems. But this mechanism is not really transformed until the end of the early modern age—and certainly not at the end of the Middle Ages.[40] Historians need to avoid being led astray by indigenous discourses: those that deal with filiation and that follow especially from the systemic mechanisms mentioned above cannot conceal the vital role that marriage played in the functioning of social relations throughout the entire medieval and early modern periods: assets of considerable importance transited through women, and these might be material (dowries and inheritances) or symbolic (social position). This essential point still requires serious research and not superficial consideration.

The problem before us is one of undeniable complexity and it demands a profound effort of reflection that will focus simultaneously on languages, their properties, and usages; on kinship, its terminology, structural principles, and practical modes of functioning; on the link between kinship and social structures; on representations of the human being and the organization of society, structured by the Christian model; all through a collection of dense documents whose language needs to be interpreted and cannot be reduced to our own modes of thinking. Faced with such complexity, we must not settle for methodological approximations. For my part, I think that only the structural approach to linguistic, ideological, and social phenomena, which of course need not prevent us from reflecting on the dynamics of evolution (itself generated by structure), will ultimately enable us to see things a little more clearly. In any case, the enquiry appears to me one we should pursue for both the Middle Ages and the early modern era.

# Notes

1. For Latin I used the two corpora accessible online at http://www.brepolis.net/: *Library of Latin Texts* (ancient texts; and patristic and medieval texts, essentially theological in nature, very rich until the twelfth century, a good deal less so for the thirteenth and fourteenth centuries) and *Monumenta Germaniae Historica* (texts of a various types, mainly from the Merovingian period to the twelfth century).

For Old and Middle French, the *Corpus de la littérature médiévale* (http://www
.championelectronique.net) was created for commercial, not scholarly, purposes
(texts free of copyright); but because of its size, it is still the main resource. Dictionaries, in some cases, provide very useful information, especially Alfred Tobler
and Ernst Lommatzsch, *Altfranzösisches Wörterbuch* (Wiesbaden 1925–2002), essentially until the thirteenth century; Frédéric Godefroy, *Dictionnaire de l'ancienne
langue française, IX<sup>e</sup>–XV<sup>e</sup> siècles* (Paris, 1881–1902); and Robert Martin, ed., *Dictionnaire du Moyen Français* (hereafter *DMF*), currently under preparation at the ATILF
[Analyse et traitement informatique de la langue française] laboratory of the CNRS,
accessible free of charge online, and without equal for Middle French (http://www
.atilf.fr/dmf).

2.  I refer to the chapter in this volume by Philippe Moreau. I am most grateful to him
    for having allowed me to see an initial version of his work at the very beginning of
    my research.

3.  The frequency levels in Classical Latin may be observed in the *Thesaurus linguae
    latinae* (Munich, 1900–).

4.  The most recent attempt to analyze Latin terminology was done by Gerhard Lu-
    bich, *Verwandtsein: Lesarten einer politisch-sozialer Beziehung im Frühmittelalter (6–
    11. Jahrhundert)* (Cologne, 2008). Drawing on digitalized corpora (*Patrologia Latina
    Database, Mgh digital*), the author examined the usage of a certain number of terms
    having to do with relations between kin in the Frankish area during the High Middle
    Ages. I shall not comment on the numerous methodological biases that mar this
    work (particularly the elimination of the terms *parentes* and *amici*, which were very
    important both numerically and semantically, an ignorance of the linkages between
    Latin and the vernacular, and a lack of knowledge of the problems of structural
    linguistics and of the anthropology of kinship). The study ends up by highlighting
    variations connected to the chronology and nature of the texts, and also the clearly
    undifferentiated character of the terminology, as well as the common use of generic
    terms translating a structural mechanism in which indistinctiveness is the rule, not
    only between paternal and maternal kin, or between consanguineal and affinal kin,
    but also with spiritual kin and those we would consider as non-relatives (the *proches*,
    the *amis*). On this point, see also Anita Guerreau-Jalabert, "La désignation des rela-
    tions et des groupes de parenté en latin médiéval," *Archivum Latinitatis Medii Aevi*
    46–47 (1988): 65–108.

5.  David Biale, *Blood and Belief: The Circulation of a Symbol between Jews and Christians*
    (Berkeley, 2007).

6.  *Patrologia Latina* 201, col. 934A.

7.  For an outline of these usages, see especially Albert Blaise, *Dictionnaire latin-français
    des auteurs chrétiens* (Strasbourg, 1954), also available on the platform *Brepolis* (no.
    1). On this point, and in general, it would be interesting to follow the creation of the
    Bible's Latin vocabulary from Hebrew and Greek. However, Christianity formulated
    a specific set of conceptions about the human being that were different from those
    of the Jewish world; thus, the link with *basar* is not enough to define fully the con-
    tents of *caro*.

8.  The various meanings of *caro* may be found in the Old French word *char.*

9.  We are hampered by the absence of details from the *Thesaurus linguae latinae*,
    which has not yet reached the letter *S*. The idea of a "soul" pointed out by Blaise, in
    the *Dictionnaire latin-français*, should be treated with caution and is at best rare and
    poetic.

10. In this usage the four terms gave rise to different combinations, for example *anima/ caro* or *spiritus/corpus;* however, *caro* and *corpus* are not interchangeable in all their values (the former having a wider range of meaning), while *spiritus* and *anima* are more broadly equivalent; furthermore, there is only one adjective and one adverb to designate this register, as a result of the sense of *animalis* and *animaliter.* The shift from *animus* to *anima* may be explained by the sense of the "breath" contained in the latter, which corresponded to that in the *spiritus.* Certain authors continued to use *animus* but within a system that semantically unified a series of terms, *spiritus, anima, animus, cor, mens, intellectus.*

11. Anita Guerreau-Jalabert, "*Spiritus et caritas.* Le baptême dans la société médiévale," in *La parenté spirituelle,* ed. Françoise Héritier and Elisabeth Copet-Rougier (Paris, 1995), 133–203.

12. Hincmar de Reims, "Epistula 22," in *Patrologia Latina* 126, col. 136A; Thietmar of Merseburg, "Chronicon," in *Patrologia Latina* 139, col. 1409D.

13. Nonetheless, any exception being possible in any language, and especially in Medieval Latin for reasons already indicated above, the *Mittellateinisches Wörterbuch* (Munich, 1959–) provides an example of *consanguinitas fidei,* s.v. *consanguinitas.*

14. Evidently this is a statistical trend, which does not rule out that we might find some examples in a very vast corpus. The *Corpus de la littérature médiévale* shows, in a branch of the *Roman de Renart,* a single reference to *sanc et char* used to express common origin; but this is a set phrase introduced to take the place of *char* alone, in a text of verse, which may be a factor; Middle French also provides several occurrences of it.

15. *Gratiani decretum,* ed. Leena Löfstedt (Societas Scientiarum Fennica, 1993–2001).

16. Etymologically derived from the Latin *linea, lignage* designated the group of lines (of kinship) to which Ego was attached, thus cognatic kinship; the word also designated the kinship relationship. As is the case for other terms and also in other languages, further precision could be added when necessary: *lignage de par père* or *de par mère.* See also for the subsequent period, in the registers of Parlement and in wills, the coexistence of a precise designation for a particular relative and of an encompassing formula, *tous parens, amis et affins,* or *tous parens et amis,* reported by Françoise Autrand, "Tous parens, amis et affins: Le groupe familial dans le milieu de robe parisien au XVᵉ siècle," in *Commerce, finances et société,* ed. Philippe Contamine, Thierry Dutour, and Bertrand Schnerb (Paris, 1993), 347–57. In view of the tendency to structural indistinctiveness that characterizes medieval kinship terminologies, *lignage,* taken as the equivalent of *parens, parenté,* or *parentage,* may possibly have included spouses in certain cases.

17. See *Gratiani decretum,* 5:46–52.

18. In addition to the various *coutumiers* composed at the end of the Middle Ages, for the language of the Parlement, see Juliette Turlan, "Amis et amis charnels d'après les actes du Parlement au XIVᵉ siècle," *Revue historique de droit français et étranger* 47 (1969): 645–98. One can only regret historians' lack of interest in the terminology of kinship; some studies dealing with the very rich series of the Parlement, which are by the way still unpublished, do not provide an even slightly precise idea of the chronology and extension of the reference to blood in these texts: see especially Françoise Autrand, *Naissance d'un grand corps de l'Etat. Les gens du Parlement de Paris, 1345–1454* (Paris, 1981); and Claude Gauvard, "*De grace especial.*" *Crime, Etat et société en France à la fin du Moyen Age* (Paris, 1991). Significant attention is devoted to the *amis* and *amis charnels,* already mentioned by Marc Bloch, probably

because of the exoticness of the term compared to contemporary French; but for the
Middle Ages the term was completely normal, and it would have been more useful
to know something more about blood, which marked a notable evolution in terminology. Gauvard makes a certain number of observations on *amis* but says nothing
precise about the phrase *sanc et lignage*, which she mentions in passing.

19. Charles de Miramon, "Aux origines de la noblesse et des princes du sang. France et
    Angleterre au XIVᵉ siècle," in *L'hérédité entre Moyen âge et Epoque moderne. Perspec-
    tives historiques*, ed. Maiike van der Lugt and Charles de Miramon (Florence, 2008),
    157–210. Special acknowledgement is owed to this highly interesting volume and to
    the work of Miramon, who is the first to have made a close study of medieval lexi-
    cal usages. On the chronology of French his conclusions and my own coincide. Our
    interpretations of the phenomenon are more divergent.
20. DMF, "Sang" et "Lignage," which also shows an important usage for *ligniée* in this
    type of phrase—*noble ligniée* or less frequently, *noble de ligniée.*
21. Miramon, "Aux origines," 177–88. The *DMF*, in the entry "Sang," cites a document of
    the Parlement of Paris, dated 1345, dealing with the king of England and *aucun de
    son sanc.*
22. See Gauvard, "*De grace especial.*" Besides the imprecision of the references in this
    volume, we should also point out that this language reflected the scholarly habits
    specific to the *rédacteurs du Parlement.*
23. Simon de Phares, *Recueil des plus célèbres astrologues*, end of the fifteenth century, in
    *DMF*, "Sang."
24. William Jervis Jones, *German Kinship Terms (750–1500)* (Berlin and New York,
    1990). The same precision can be applied to *mâc*: Simon Teuscher, *Bekannte-Kliente-
    Verwandte. Soziabilität und Politik in der Stadt Bern um 1500* (Cologne, 1997), 76, 79.
25. Ernest Champeaux, "*Jus sanguinis*, trois façons de calculer la parenté au Moyen Age,"
    *Revue historique de droit français et étranger* 4, no. 12 (1933): 241–90, here 247–48.
    But this criticism can be extended to the majority of recent works, as Miramon re-
    minds us in "Aux origines," 159–61.
26. We see the appearance of other phenomena at around the same period, with dispari-
    ties from region to region, as in the case of blood: in the register of representations,
    genealogical trees (see Christiane Klapisch-Zuber, *L'ombre des ancêtres. Essai sur
    l'imaginaire médiéval de la parenté* [Paris, 2000]); and in inheritance practices, *majo-
    rats* and *fideicommis*, which attempted to predetermine the lines of heirs, preferably
    male but not always, as opposed to more random rationales. As regards terminology,
    we also notice the appearance of the term *race* (toward 1490 according to Miramon
    and two examples from the *DMF*), or *maison*, a little earlier (fifteenth century ac-
    cording to the *DMF*).
27. In Medieval Latin *coitus* remained one of the most ordinary ways for designating the
    sexual act, but we also find *commixtio, permixtio carnis, carnalis*, and, rarely, *sanguinis.*
    *Commixtio*, which had classical origins, was used alone without a qualifier. Old and
    Middle French only knew the idea of flesh—this was one of the common usages
    for the adjective *charnel* in Middle French: *conjunction, compagnie, copule, copulance
    charnelle, connoistre charnellement.*
28. *Caro et sanguis* is a common phrase in the Bible and among Latin authors. It can be
    found in French and was commonly used when speaking of Christ, but also for men.
    In a few cases it designated kinship, for example in the *Ménagier de Paris* (c.1392–
    94): "Je n'ay porté honneur et reverence a mes amis qui sont de mon sang et de ma
    char, especialment a mes pere et mere et leurs successeurs dont je suis venu, a mes

freres et seurs naturelz, a mon mary et autres bien faicteurs et souverains, ne a mes autres freres et seurs d'Eve et d'Adam" (*DMF*).

29. Any study of blood in the Middle Ages ought therefore to include the blood of Christ; but given the social sense of discourses dealing with the latter, the field before us is immense and still very little explored.

30. Augustin, *Quaestionum in Heptateuchon libri VII*, I.3, q. 57. See also Alain of Lille, *Distinctiones:* "Anima. Dicitur vita corporis, unde Levit.: Omnis anima in sanguine est, id est omnis vita." This was, in fact, quite a common idea.

31. See for example Peter Lombard, *Sententiae* IV, 11.4; the same chapter also takes up the previous idea, as does Saint Thomas Aquinas, in *Summa theologica* 3.74.1. In several works, Honorius Augustodunensis deals with the idea of Christ's double sacrifice for the redemption of our flesh and our soul; see, for example, "Eucharistion," in *Patrologia Latina* 172, col. 1257A. He complicates the answer a little by recalling the two values of *anima* and proposing the idea that the wine redeems the *anima*, the lower part of the soul, while the water, which is mixed with it, redeems the *spiritus*, the higher part of the soul, following a completely unoriginal mechanism that associated water with the spirit.

32. Developed in the twelfth century, the *fin'amors* corresponded to a reorganization of the spirit/flesh relationship in the laic imagination, a sort of "spiritual fornication," which was the lay equivalent of ecclesiastical models of the spiritualization of the flesh; the grail provides a more manageable tool for making distinctions by attributing, after 1200, the possession of Christ's blood to the institution of chivalry. See Anita Guerreau-Jalabert, in collaboration with Michel Sot and Jean-Patrice Boudet, *Histoire culturelle de la France*, vol. 1, *Le Moyen Age* (Paris, 1997), here 201–21; Anita Guerreau-Jalabert, "Aimer de fin cuer. Le coeur dans la thématique courtoise," in *Il cuore. Micrologus* XI (2003): 343–71; Anita Guerreau-Jalabert, "Le graal, le Christ et la chevalerie," in *Pratiques de l'eucharistie dans les Eglises d'Orient et d'Occident (Antiquité et Moyen Age)*, ed. Nicole Bériou, Béatrice Caseau, and Dominique Rigaux (Paris, 2009), 1057–72.

33. The Christian construct derived its compactness and force from a system of homological registers that naturalized a social organization and sacralized it at the same time. If we remember that the register of *caro* was the province of laymen, clerics being on the side of *spiritus*, hylomorphism translated a vision that made the *ecclesia* into the basic form of society. Now, contrary to what is too often asserted, this theological vision was taken up and reworked as an echo in the imagination of the dominant lay groups, who until the end of the Middle Ages made every effort to define themselves as spiritual. The vitality of themes related to *fin'amors* all the way until the end of the fifteenth century provides ample witness of this.

34. Miramon, "Aux origines"; Guido Castelnuovo, "Revisiter un classique: Noblesse, hérédité et vertu d'Aristote à Dante et à Bartole (Italie communale, début XIIIᵉ–milieu XIVᵉ siècle)," in Van der Lugt and Miramon, eds., *L'hérédité*, 105–55. This dichotomy found two ways to be expressed—in the predominance of either *nature* or *nourriture*, having two possible outcomes, and in the expressions that Miramon identified: *nobilis carne, nobilitas carnis*, as opposed to (explicitly or implicitly) nobility of spirit. The *DMF* indicates the phrases *noblesse charnelle* or *noblesse qui de char viengne* (Christine de Pizan, who, moreover, resorts to the image of blood). For the modern period, Robert Descimon, "Chercher de nouvelles voies pour interpréter les phénomènes nobiliaires dans la France moderne. La noblesse, 'essence' ou rapport social?" *Revue d'histoire moderne et contemporaine* 46, no. 1 (1999): 5–21.

35. Bernard Guenée, "Le roi, ses parents et son royaume en France au XIV<sup>e</sup> siècle," in *Un roi et son historien* (Paris, 1999), 301–24, also reports that numerous consanguine loops complicated relations with royal kindred, but that their precise aim was to recreate proximity; he also mentions that Louis the Bavarian, brother of the queen and brother-in-law to Charles VI, was sometimes counted among the "seigneurs du sanc roial."

36. Sarah Hanley, "Engendering the State: Family Formation and State Building in Early Modern France," *French Historical Studies* 16, no. 1 (1989): 4–27.

37. Georges Duby, *Hommes et structures du Moyen Age* (Paris and La Haye, 1973); Karl Schmid, *Gebetsgedenken und adliges Selbstverständnis im Mittelalter* (Sigmaringen, 1983).

38. Joseph Morsel, "Le médiéviste, le lignage et l'effet de réel. La construction du *Geschlecht* par l'archive en Haute Allemagne à partir de la fin du Moyen Age," *Revue de Synthèse* 125 (2004): 83–110. What the author draws attention to is the ideological construction of male kindred, which went hand in hand with an ideal of the construction of male lineages for the transmission of fiefs, but which coexisted with cognatic kinship practices (we would need to verify if this usage of the term *Geschlecht* may be generalized). For his part, Karl Heinz Spiess found no cases of single female heiresses being excluded in favor of agnates before the very end of the fifteenth century (*Familie und Verwandschaft im deutschen Hochadel des Spätmittelalters* [Stuttgart, 1993], 337–43).

39. On the modern period in France see, Elie Haddad, *Fondation et ruine d'une "maison." Histoire sociale des comtes de Belin (1582–1706)* (Limoges, 2009). See also Anna Bellavitis, Laurence Croq, and Monica Martinat, eds., *Mobilité et transmission dans les sociétés de l'Europe moderne* (Rennes, 2009); Fanny Cosandey, "La maîtresse de nos biens. Pouvoir féminin et puissance dynastique dans la monarchie française d'Ancien Régime," *Historical Reflections/Réflexions historiques* 32, no. 2 (2006): 381–401; Robert Descimon and Elie Haddad, eds., *Epreuves de noblesse* (Paris, 2010). Haddad resorts to the notion of *maison*, borrowed from Claude Lévi-Strauss, precisely in order to account for the absence of a unilineal system of transmission. However, this observation in no way excludes the hypothesis formulated by Gérard Delille (in particular, see his contribution to this volume): the institution of a more rigorous usage of the patronym, associated with the reference to blood, provided a tool for the construction of male lineages, which played a special part in the functioning of marriage and which corresponds to the "ideology of race" (Arlette Jouanna, *L'idée de race en France au XVI<sup>e</sup> siècle et au début du XVII<sup>e</sup>* [Lille, 1976]).

40. In spite of too many approximations in the presentation of European kinship systems, anthropologist Laurent Barry's *La parenté* (Paris, 2008) is worth reading. In the chapter devoted to the *principe de parenté cognatique* (481–635), he reaches, by means of other pathways, the panorama proposed by David Warren Sabean and Simon Teuscher in David Warren Sabean, Simon Teuscher, and Jon Mathieu, eds., *Kinship in Europe: Approaches in Long-Term Development* (Oxford and New York, 2007), 1–32.

# Chapter 4

# Flesh and Blood in the Treatises on the *Arbor Consanguinitatis*
## *(Thirteenth to Sixteenth Centuries)*

## Simon Teuscher

One might think that kinship in pre-modern Europe, despite its importance in practice, has never become a prominent subject of philosophical
thought. While there is an ancient—and to this day uninterrupted—
Western tradition of writing books with titles such as *De amicitia* or
*De amore*, *On Friendship* or *On Love*, there are no comparable classics
called *De cognatione*, *On Kinship*. Since the High Middle Ages, there
has been, however, a tradition of systematic reflection on kinship in the
context of the Catholic prohibitions of sexual intercourse among kin. I
am thinking of commentaries on the kinship diagrams that lawyers used
to determine whether a kin-connection fell under incest prohibitions
(fig. 4.1). These diagrams, often referred to as *arbores consanguinitatis*,
first emerged in manuscripts of the *Etymologiae* by Isidor of Seville.[1] In
the late twelfth century, the *arbores* became a standard supplement to
canon law manuscripts. Consequently, they were, much like textual passages of canon law, time and again commented on, whether in the form
of a few paragraphs in comprehensive scholastic *Summae*, or, from the
fourteenth century onward, also in short specialized treatises devoted
exclusively to the kinship diagrams. Although such commentaries have

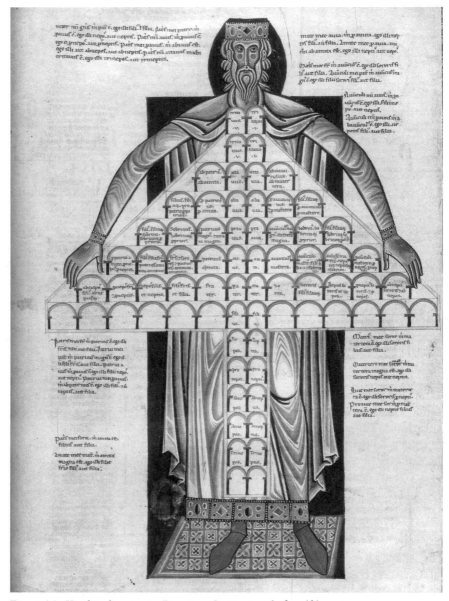

Figure 4.1. Kinship diagram, in *Decretum Gratiani,* end of twelfth century.

come down to us in large numbers, they have received little attention by modern historians. They stand in an intellectual tradition that was legal rather than philosophical, operational rather than conceptual, and that relied as much on visual as on verbal means of expression. The commentaries assumed different functions. Most described the individual parts of the diagram and explained what these stood for. Some, moreover, gave instructions as to how to draw such diagrams and how to use them in reckoning kinship. But the commentaries also addressed more fundamental problems. Most provided definitions of consanguinity and affinity, discussed why incest was prohibited, and explained how this prohibition derived from the nature of kinship ties. Some went even further, relating kinship to a larger cosmology. Throughout the later Middle Ages the commentaries appeared at short intervals. New ones often simply incorporated a few novel sentences or paragraphs into older texts, copied more or less literally. Authors frequently engaged in dialogues, quoting, glossing, correcting, or contradicting each other. The content of the treatises changed between the thirteenth and early sixteenth centuries, in small steps that would nevertheless add up over time to quite dramatic changes in kinship conceptualization.

Among the things that changed radically are the ways the treatises addressed questions about the bodily substances shared by kin. The very name of the kinship diagram, *arbor consanguinitatis*, could lead one to believe that blood at all times had been the principal shared substance. But this is not the case. Christiane Klapisch-Zuber has shown that this name was a legacy from ancient Rome that had lost most of its original semantic context by the High Middle Ages.[2] In texts written around 1200, comments on blood are largely absent, a silence that confirms arguments that blood metaphors actually played a subordinate role in discourses about kinship during the early and central Middle Ages.[3] Only toward the passage to the early modern period did references to blood begin to multiply. It is perhaps no coincidence that the topic of *arbor*, tree, went through a similar development. Klapisch-Zuber has also demonstrated that it was not before the end of the Middle Ages that the *arbor* diagrams were drawn to resemble trees. Nor, I can add, did commentaries before then make more than passing reference to this resemblance.[4] This, in and of itself, indicates that the emergence of a discussion about blood in the treatises needs to be related to other changes in the interpretation of the diagram—and of the kin-relations it represented.

Flesh and blood in the scholarly tradition of the Middle Ages can neither be equated with metaphor nor with biological facts in the modern sense. The concepts arose from and functioned within a system of knowledge radically different from ours, in which descriptions of natural entities (such as animals, plants, flesh, or, for that matter, blood) were not separated from descriptions of the symbolic meanings attributed to them.[5] Despite such differences, however, some lines of continuity going back to the Middle Ages can be said to persist in Western academic thinking about kinship. One is the stress on the immutability of the substances shared by kin. This stands in contrast to examples of Melanesian and other people pointed out by Janet Carsten, who attribute great convertibility and mutability to the substances that related people share: for instance, that people who eat together come to have similar blood.[6] Comparable views were probably expressed in the Middle Ages, since they were rigorously refuted by academics such as Thomas Aquinas. His (or his students') *Supplementum* argued against the doctrine that since blood (as Aristotle thought) is made from the surplus of food, our blood might have more in common with things we eat than with the blood of the parents who engendered us. This, Thomas says, would hold only according to the false opinion that all forms are accidents, and therefore changeable. For Thomas substance is quite the opposite, an immutable essence.[7] The immutability of substance, however, can play many different roles in the conceptualization of relationships, and such roles certainly also depend on whether the substance in question is flesh, blood, or, for that matter, biogenetic material.[8]

Altogether several dozen different treatises on kinship diagrams are known to have been written in the period between the thirteenth and the early sixteenth centuries, but any attempt to establish their exact number faces major difficulties. First, many of the treatises share large amounts of identical text, which complicates any attempt to determine when a redaction can be seen as a separate text. Second, only a few of the texts are easily accessible. Apart from the prominent treatise written by the Bolognese lawyer Johannes Andreae at the beginning of the fourteenth century, almost none are available in proper modern editions.[9] A good handful of treatises found their way early into print, but a great many are accessible in manuscript form only. Quite generally, the diagrams contained in these manuscripts have been examined far more thoroughly than the texts that comment upon them.[10] The latter remain a largely unexplored territory, and what follows will be no more than a first glimpse inside the boundaries of a rich intellectual tradition.

For the purpose of this chapter, I have only been able to analyze a small sample of easily accessible texts from different corners of Europe. These include the relevant passages of some well-known comprehensive commentaries on topics of canon law, such as the *Summa de Matrimonio* by the Bolognese lawyer Tancred (c.1210), the *Summa de Poenitentia et Matrimonio* (c.1235) by the Catalan Raymundus de Pennaforte, the *Summa super Titulis Decretalium* (1243), by Goffredus Tranensis, as well as the *Summa* (1253) by the Piedmontese Henricus de Segusio, or Hostiensis, the *Summa Theologica* of Thomas Aquinas, in particular its posthumous

*Supplementum* (last third of the thirteenth century), and the *Summa Confessorum* (1298) by Johannes de Friburgo from the German South-west. More typical of the younger generation of commentaries are the specialized treatises dealing exclusively with the diagrams, such as the *Lectura arborum consanguinitatis et affinitatis* by Johannes Hispanicus Egitanensis, and the treatises with similar names by Johannes Andreae (1308), Prosdocimus de Comitibus (fifteenth century), and Henricus Greve and Johannes Lintholtz (both early sixteenth century).[11] This sample allows putting forward initial, tentative hypotheses on changes that, though they occurred in a discourse that was highly specialized and restricted to a narrow circle of lawyers, may nevertheless point to some broader shifts in the understanding of kinship.[12]

In what follows, I approach major trends in the development of these commentaries in two steps. First, I examine changes in notions of what the *arbor consanguinitatis* represented. Then I trace the slow, gradual emergence of the topic of blood in the treatises. Toward the end of the chapter, I try to relate these changes to a few general developments in the social organization and cultural perception of kinship at the passage to the modern period.

Before I proceed, I would like simply to mention another shift in the treatises that this chapter cannot discuss at length, the ever-increasing reliance in the commentaries on the visual explanatory power of the diagram. Authors writing in the early thirteenth century still explained how to reckon kinship degrees without ever referring to the actual diagram or to the support it could provide for this purpose.[13] Johannes Hispanicus Egitanensis, writing in the mid thirteenth century, was among the first to explicitly praise the diagrams for facilitating kinship reckoning. He underlines his point by quoting a passage from Horace saying that people believe more easily what they see than what they hear. Johannes also gives instructions on how to draw the diagrams and on how, in their absence, to reckon kin by using one's fingers and their joints.[14] Finally Hostiensis, in his *Summa* from 1253, reminds future doctors of canon law that when they have to teach incest prohibitions, they should sit down in front of their students, open their books at the page with the diagram, point to the pertinent cells and branches, and take care to address topics in the order of their appearance in the diagram.[15] The growing reliance on the interplay of text, or speech, and pictorial diagrams might even have affected the contents of the treatises. One is tempted to ask whether some of the new ideas in the more recent treatises emerged because preconceptions inherent to the diagrams eventually unfolded their potential. It will take an additional essay to further explore how attempts to visualize kinship affected its understanding.

# From Relation to Group

A first set of changes in the treatises has to do with what the commentators think the *arbores consanguinitatis* and *affinitatis* represent. All authors treated the diagram primarily as a representation of the numerous possible dyadic kin-relationships, but only the later authors saw additionally in the diagram a model of an actual group of interrelated kin. The latter perception also suggests itself to our own eyes, because we are accustomed to reading modern family trees and thus tend to associate the interlinked cells to members of an actual kin-group, expanding out from a core formed by a father, a mother, and their children. Nevertheless, even though kinship diagrams probably served as the model for modern family trees from the fifteenth century onward, they were very far from operating like such to begin with. The early commentaries suggest that they were used more as gauges for measuring the closeness of a connection between two kinsmen, or as field guides that helped identify the category under which a given connection could be subsumed.

The proper use of the *arbores consanguinitatis* required specific skills in what could be called "kinship calculus" or "kinship combinatorics." It was a principle goal of almost all treatises on the *arbores* to teach such skills. This is made very clear in the *enigmata*, the riddles, or, more appropriately, exercises, contained in the manuscripts of some fifteenth-century commentaries (fig. 4.2). These exercises taught students to use kinship diagrams to make transparent constellations that are opaque and overly convoluted when expressed in words. A comparatively easy example is this: Two fathers and two sons go hunting. They catch three rabbits, and each carries one home. In the chart it becomes immediately evident how the seeming paradox in this state-

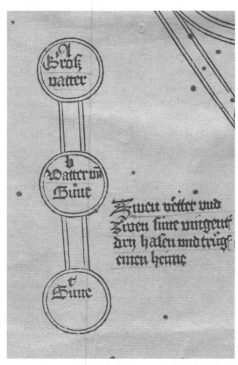

Figure 4.2. Detail from a kinship enigma, in Johannes Andreae, *De arbore consanguinitatis affinitatis et cognationis spiritualis*, before 1482.

ment can be resolved.[16] In kinship calculus, two fathers and two sons do not always add up to four people, but might as well be no more than three, with the one in the middle being a father as well as a son. Or, to take a slightly more complicated example: A count had twelve knights, four of which were his sons, four his brothers-in-law, and the remaining four his sons-in-law, but all were born from one woman. Here, it takes two charts to give a hint as to how to solve the riddle (fig. 4.3). The

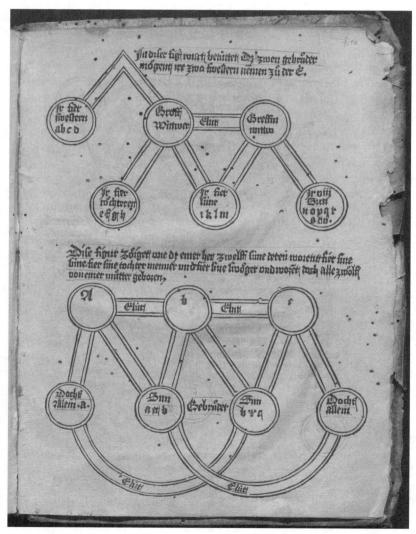

Figure 4.3. Kinship enigma, in Johannes Andreae, *De arbore consanguinitatis affinitatis et cognationis spiritualis,* before 1482.

count has four sisters and four daughters. After his wife's death he marries a widow with eight sons. These marry his four sisters and his four daughters, and in addition he has four sons with his second wife. Riddles such as these do not seem to emerge in manuscripts before the fifteenth century. But they may have been around in the practice of teaching for some time and are characteristic of what had been a main concern of the treatises all along, namely, conveying the requisite skills for identifying and discerning types of kin-relationships, and for kinship reckoning.

Between the thirteenth and the fifteenth century, the diagrams were no longer read solely as a mapping of individual kinship types and their combinatorics, but also as the representation of a coherent group as a vast extended family. I see at least three different indicators of such a change. The first one is a debate about what to call the central cell in the diagram; the second, the emergence of comparisons between the diagram and an organically grown tree; and the third, the rise of new debates about the outer limits of kinship.

First, there is likely a connection between incipient uncertainty over how to read the *arbores* and the emergence of a debate over naming the middle cell of the diagram (fig. 4.4). The old commentaries, up to those by Tancred and Pennaforte, did not address this question at all. By the middle of the thirteenth century, however, Johannes Egitanensis mentions three different names for the middle cell: truncus, which is Latin for stem, as well as two male first names, Proteus and Joachim.[17]

Johannes explains each of these names. Some call the cell stem because the entire tree rests on it—or as we might add: ramifies out from

Fiugre 4.4. Middle cell, in Johannes Andreae, *De arbore consanguinitatis affinitatis et cognationis spiritualis,* before 1482.

(the stem was here not thought of as the representation of the older generation such as in a modern genealogical tree). Others, Johannes continues, call the cell Proteus, after the herdsman of the sea beasts in ancient Greek mythology who can change his face. Unlike the other cells in the diagram that unambiguously stand for one single denomination, say, "father," "grandfather," and so on, the middle cell has no stable denomination. It becomes "son" when related to "father," but "nephew" when related to "uncle." Calling the cell "Proteus" thus corresponds to the perception of the diagram as the representation of the panoply of possible kinship constellations.

Johannes Egitanensis goes on to explain that some scholars call the middle cell "Joachim"—i.e., the name of the husband of Ann, the mother of the Holy Virgin. Ann and Joachim stand at the center of the so-called Holy Kinship, a genealogical network that is complicated, given the fact that Ann, according to legend, had been married three times and was ancestress not only of Christ, but also of Simon, Judas, John the Evangelist, and others.[18] Calling the middle cell "Joachim" suggested that the *arbor consanguinitatis* represents an actual kin-group, namely, the one of Christ, which in turn could stand as a model for any kin-group. This appellation probably had additional symbolic implications. The fourteenth and fifteenth centuries witnessed a spread of devotional images of the Holy Kinship intended as tools in the meditative practice of imagining oneself becoming a member of the Holy Kinship, of Joachim's family, so to speak. An *arbor* diagram also required an act of imagination, in this case the one of identifying with the middle cell, of "becoming Joachim," an operation that can hardly have failed to call forth reminiscences of the pious practice, and of the doctrine about the Christian community as the family of Christ.

Perhaps to avoid such suggestive symbolism, Johannes Andreae, who was arguably the fourteenth century's most famous teacher of Roman Law, suggested yet another denomination. He called the middle cell "Petruccio," after his beadle—probably to make it clear that the middle cell could be just anybody.[19] Most authors writing after Andreae embraced this proposal. One joked that he would call the cell simply "beadle," given that he, unlike the great professor Andreae, had no beadle of his own to name it after.[20] But this innovation did not deter later authors from continuing the tradition of calling the cell "Joachim" to make explicit the reference to the Holy Kinship.[21]

Second, there probably is a connection between the trend to read the *arbor consanguinitatis* as the representation of a coherent kin-group and its novel interpretation as a tree. As Christiane Klapisch-Zuber has demonstrated, the *arbores* were conceived of as actual trees only at the passage to the modern period. Early treatises had referred to the diagrams' stems and branches, but only the late ones went further: comparing the whole to an actual tree, sometimes even a specific species of tree, and also referring to its leaves, roots, and fruits, as well as addressing ways to make the whole grow or thrive.[22] That the kinship diagram no longer was seen as a mere assemblage of conceivable constellations, but as an entity, an organically grown living being, indicates that something new is being represented, a group organized such that every cell in the diagram is related to every other.

Diagrams that looked like actual trees did not become common until the fifteenth century (fig. 4.5). Previously, many diagrams were simply abstract networks of related cells. Others, however, were projected onto a human body, such that the middle cell was located at the pelvis and the descending-generation cells at each joint of the legs, while the ascending ones, the ancestors, were positioned at the joints from the shoulders down the arm to the fingertips. At the end of the Middle Ages these bodies were successively replaced by tree-shaped forms. An additional step was the introduction of the so-called *arbores conversae*, where the traditional diagram was turned on its head, so that the part below no longer represented the middle cell's descendants, but its ancestors. Such a representation made it even easier to equate the diagram with a kin-group in which each new generation grows out of an older one. This is the form that was to become constitutive for the modern genealogical tree. Here, the organic growth of the tree could be juxtaposed with the succession of interrelated generations. Some diagrams from around 1500 borrow heavily from the iconography of the tree from which the Christ's cross was made. Like that tree, some *arbores* were shown as growing out of Adam's skull or as watered and cared for by God the Father and Mary. In these instances the tree seems to stand for the successive generations of Christianity at large.[23]

Third and finally, there is evidence in the treatises of growing concern about the location of the outer limits of kinship. The old treatises I have examined, such as the ones of Tancred and Pennaforte, quite simply stated that all kinship ends in the seventh degree—i.e., in the degree to which incest prohibitions in canon law had extended before the reform of 1215. From the middle of the thirteenth century onward, some authors declared that this only applied to the collateral line, whereas they held kinship to be unlimited in the direct line of descent. As a consequence, Johannes Egitanensis wrote that Adam, were he still alive today, could marry no woman at all, because all women descend from him in direct line. A great number of succeeding authors repeated this sentence, but it seems to have worried no one until Prosdocimus de Comitibus in the fifteenth century. He inferred that were this true, all human beings would be kin. This, he wrote, would be ridiculous, because it would imply that there was kinship between Christians, Muslims, and Jews as well.[24] Early sixteenth-century authors such as Heinrich Greve and Johannes Lintholtz repeated that all men are kin and seem less worried about this than their predecessors—probably because they were thinking of kinship in a new way, namely, in terms of a shared blood that was rapidly diluted with growing genealogical distance.

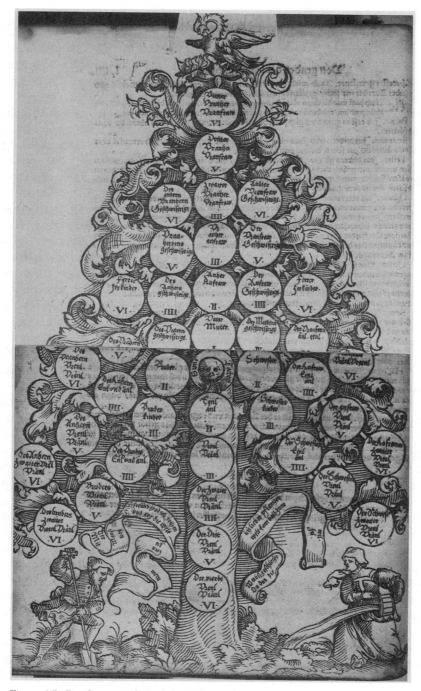

Figure 4.5. Family tree with God the Father and Mary, 1536.

# From Flesh to Blood

A second major transition affected the manner in which the treatises described the bodily dimensions of kinship. Here, roughly speaking, an interest in flesh was successively overlaid by one in blood. Of course, even the oldest treatises I have examined made at least passing reference to the connection between consanguinity, Latin *consanguinitas*, and the word *sanguis*, blood. Hardly any author failed to use the etymology of consanguinity as one of several approaches to its meaning. Consanguines, wrote Tancred, already at the beginning of the thirteenth century, are "quasi communem habentes sanguinem vel de una sanguine producentes" (consanguines are so to say those who have common blood or those who have come from one blood).[25] Variations of this sentence that can be traced back to Isidor of Seville, writing in the seventh century, recur in almost all subsequent treatises on the *arbor consanguinitatis*. But most treatises written before the fifteenth century left it at that. They neither asked what was meant by blood in this context and how it could be shared with others or passed on to the next generation, nor explored the metaphorical potential of an equation of blood and kinship. This is all the more surprising as the medical and physiological discourse since antiquity had been highlighting blood as the substance merged during sexual intercourse and from which embryos were built. This ultimately applied to theories of generation in both the Galenic and Aristotelian traditions.[26] But the medical discourse stressing blood seems at first to have had very little impact on legal reflections about kinship, incest, and impediments to marriage.

Quite generally, the early treatises were dominated by a discourse that was less concerned with blood than with flesh. Another definition of consanguinity that almost all authors repeated is that consanguinity is the bond between people who descend from the same person by *propagatio carnalis*—i.e., by fleshly reproduction.[27] Similarly, the foremost concern of passages that discussed how affinity comes into existence talked, not about mixing blood but about unifying flesh, using expressions such as *carnali copula* or *carnalis commixtio*.[28] The *Supplementum* to Thomas Aquinas even feels compelled to explain why it is appropriate to talk about consanguinity rather than about carnality, *carnalitas*.

Also the famous constitution passed by the Fourth Lateran Council (1215) that reduced marriage prohibitions from the seventh to the fourth degree of consanguinity highlighted not primarily blood, but several different components of the body. The constitution says it is appropriate to prohibit bodily intercourse up to the fourth degree of consanguinity because there are four different fluids (*humores*) in the body, which itself consists of four elements.[29] The council thus ties the prohibitions of intercourse into a cosmology in which the number four plays a prominent role. Johannes Andreae, who commented on the constitution about a hundred years later, admitted that the argument was based on similarity, rather than cogent logic. But he nevertheless added even more analogies. The prohibition until the fourth degree, he wrote, corresponds also to the four seasons, the four evangelists, the four rivers of paradise, and the four doctors of the church.[30] Only Thomas Aquinas made an attempt at explaining the text of the constitution in terms of blood that loses ever more of its identity as it is mixed with other blood in each generation.[31] But this thought was not, as far as I can see up to this point, taken up by any of the treatises on the *arbores* written before the fifteenth century.

For the most part, blood loomed larger in the newer texts. Where old texts had written about *copula carnalis*, the new ones wrote about *commixtio sanguinis*, the mixing of blood. A telling detail is the emergence of new interpretations of the kinship diagram, in which the authors now actually saw symbols of blood. The diagram, it should be noted, normally contained cells, each with two sets of dots signifying degrees of kinship as treated in the two forms of law, canon and Roman, governing that subject: red dots represented canon law; black or dark ones, Roman law (fig. 4.6). From the thirteenth century, most authors who explained the diagram and the relationship of canon to Roman law focused on these dots. Many repeated that the choice of red dots for canon law indicated the greater excellence of that law. Implicitly, this argument probably refers to the political symbolism of purple as the color of majesty. Prosdocimus de Comitibus in the early fifteenth century, however, takes the symbolism further, explaining that red as a color is superior to black because the latter contains less light.[32] In contrast, later treatises, such as the one of Lintholtz written at the beginning of the sixteenth century, associate red with blood, as if this were a natural pairing: because, explains Lintholtz, "the

Figure 4.6. Red dots indicating degree of kinship according to Canon Law, in Johannes Andreae, *Liber Sextus Decretalium,* fourteenth century.

canon law dots indicate consanguinity that comes from blood that by its nature is red, but Roman law cares about nothing but inheritance, which occurs after death, hence it is appropriate to refer to the latter by black or dark dots."[33]

The more the treatises accentuated blood as the constitutive substance of consanguinity, the greater their interest in the details of when and how substances merge during sexual intercourse. The treatises had always made passing reference to sex, primarily as the act that constitutes affinity—according to canon law—even if it was illicit. But before the fifteenth century, only a few authors had discussed sexual practices in detail. Among them were Raymundus de Pennaforte in 1235, and his glossator Johannes de Friburgo, writing from 1270 onward. Pennaforte simply stated that in order to constitute affinity, a man had to ejaculate inside, not outside a woman's vagina, and that it was not sufficient that he penetrated her, but that he also had to "complete the act." De Friburgo was more graphic. "Completing the act," he specified in his glossa, must mean that semen has been released. He discussed whether it was necessary for the woman as well as the man to release semen.[34] De Friburgo probably assumed that semen was blood.[35] But it is worth noting that neither he nor any other of the early authors explicitly set ejaculation into the context either of mixing blood or of generating "common blood." Instead de Friburgo still says that the release of semen is necessary for man and woman to become *una caro*, one flesh.

In contrast, the authors of the fifteenth century often explicitly equate semen with blood, and they stress that the ejaculation of both woman and man is necessary so that a *commixtio sanguinis* might take place. These authors also engage in ever more graphic discussions of sexual intercourse, in order to assess under what condition blood actually is mixed. Certainly an *oscullum*, a kiss, said Henricus Greve, will not do, because it does not entail the physical mixing of two bloods.[36] Greve here is articulating one of the new elements in fifteenth-century treatises—the stress on the purely material character of this merger, independent from consciousness. Affinity, consequently, can be constituted even if one partner is violated, asleep, or unconscious at the moment of the intercourse. Affinity, said Greve, "is made by blood, not by words."[37]

The stress on blood sharpened distinctions between affinity and consanguinity, as well as among different lines of descent. From the thirteenth century to the fifteenth, the taxonomy of types of kinship (*cognatio*) common to most older treatises was overthrown. Authors writing up to the middle of the fourteenth century had distinguished three basic kinds of kinship; namely, *cognatio legalis* that resulted from adoption, *cognatio spiritualis* that resulted from godparent relationships declared at baptism and confirmation, and *cognatio carnalis*. The last type was subdivided into consanguinity and affinity. All authors of the period seem to have considered the distinction between spiritual and carnal kinship as fundamental, but several of them blurred the line between affinity and consanguinity. Thomas Aquinas treated them as similar in that they both rested on relations of the flesh: "Husband and wife are made one flesh. Therefore if the husband is related in the flesh to all his kindred, for the same reason his wife will be related to them all."[38] And Raymundus Pennaforte used the word *consanguinitas* to designate a broad range of kin-relationships, which later authors found objectionably unspecific. Thus, giving an example of how intercourse constitutes kinship, Pennaforte wrote: "when my sister sleeps with P, P becomes my consanguine." Pennaforte's glossator Johannes de Friburgo, writing at the end of the thirteenth century, felt he had to rectify this statement: "he [P] is not becoming my *consanguineus*," he wrote, "such as my sister is, but my *affinis*."[39]

Treatises written from 1400 onward no longer used the term *cognatio carnalis* and forwent any category that would have comprehended affinity as well as consanguinity. It would probably be an exaggeration to say that affinity and consanguinity now became opposites as radical as carnal and spiritual kinship had been before. But spiritual, legal, affinal, and consanguineal kinship were now all appearing on the same hierarchical level, indicating that each of them was equally different from all the others. Some authors writing around 1500 further dramatized the distinction between affinity and consanguinity. Lintholtz explains that persons related to us by descent, such as our children, belong to the same root and blood as we do, while those we marry, or to whom we are related through marriage, are "quasi extrinsecus adiuncta" (as if pinned on from the outside).[40] This sentence was an unacknowledged quote from Thomas Aquinas. Lintholz, however, omitted Thomas's preceding sentences (which I have rendered in the last paragraph) on the similarity between affinity and consanguinity arising from their relation to flesh. Thus, while Thomas described a small difference among relationships all primarily carnal, Lintholtz used Aristotle to establish a radical difference between consanguinity, seen as the tight form of kinship, and affinity and other less essential forms of belonging. Accordingly, Lintholtz's remarks introduce an *arbor consanguinitatis* that operates with completely novel categories. Here, only a person's descendants are referred to as *consanguinei*, while his or her predecessors belong either to the category of *agnates* or to the one of *cognates*.[41] This is a consistent extension of the thought that kinship is based on shared blood: Strictly speaking, my blood (i.e., the exact mix of parental bloods running in my veins) is contained only in the blood of my descendants. In my ancestors' veins, in contrast, there is running none of my blood, as a unique mixture, but rather only its components, as separate bloods, and the components coming from mother's side and from father's side have nothing in common. It can therefore seem to be appropriate to keep the two strictly apart.

The new preference for metaphors alluding to sex as the process of mixing blood, rather than of uniting flesh, facilitated thinking descent in terms of a substance that is not simply shared or not shared, but that is diluted a little more with each generation. Lintholtz, from just after 1500, was the first to take up the interpretation that Thomas Aquinas had given to the statute of the Fourth Lateran Council. What authors around 1500 quoted was Thomas saying that each generation comes about as the result of a mixture of one blood with a different blood, and that the more often one mixes, the greater the difference between the subsequent bloods and the original one. Thus, Thomas went on, with an argument that is not easy to comprehend, in the first generation the identity of blood disappears as to the first element, in the second generation as to the second element, and so on, until the identity has entirely vanished after four generations so that the original conjunction could be made again. Thomas had originally made this statement to contribute to a discussion of the cosmological foundations of the revised incest prohibitions of 1215.[42] Authors from around 1500 quoted the passage to solve a problem that had only become urgent against the background of a new understanding of kin as an actual group of people with mutual obligations. Authors of this period were worried that there had to be kinship among all people in the world, given that they all shared a portion, however small, of Adam's blood. Thomas's notion that shared blood is thinned when mixed with other blood allowed Lintholtz to understand that love and friendship between kin decrease with each generation "and after some generations were not much larger than between complete strangers."[43]

Whence this new interest in blood? So far, I find the explanations about a growing appreciation of kinship offered by Anita Guerreau-Jalabert most convincing. In the symbolism of Christianity and in particular in the Eucharist, in the couple blood/flesh, blood was the superior of the substances, the one standing for the more spiritual part of the body.[44] The argument could be strengthened if it were related to the increased importance of blood in the pious practices of the fifteenth century. As Caroline Bynum has pointed out, this was the period when blood moved to the core of Christian concerns with holy matter, with the possibility of God being inherent in matter, and with thinking body in categories different from flesh, doomed to decay.[45] Against this contemporary backdrop, talking about kinship in terms of blood rather than flesh almost certainly indicated a higher valorization of kinship, even though there was nothing directly divine about the blood shared by kin.

Both substances of kinship, flesh and blood, had been thought of as immutable. But while "flesh" tended to be seen in opposition to "soul" and thus to be associated with the mortal, the corruptible, sin, and decay, blood allowed combining immutability with stability over time. In this respect it certainly matters that the Latin word *sanguis* referred to running blood only, while there was a different term, *cruor,* for clotted or dried blood. *Sanguis* thus had stronger associations with the concept *alive* than the modern English word *blood*—which possibly paved the way for imagining that the blood of deceased ancestors is still alive in their descendants.[46] At any rate, the language of blood facilitated attributing to kinship the ability to constitute groups that last over generations and thus reinforced the turn away from the inclusive kinship of the Middle Ages, wherein affines counted as kin as much as consanguines, toward a more restrictive form that gave preeminence to descent and shared blood passed down over the generations. Moreover, blood—in contrast to flesh—could be thought of as pure or tainted.

At the end of the Middle Ages, even canon law specialists wrote about kinship, no longer solely as a profane structure one had to know about in order to avoid incest, but as a dignified principle of social order. A higher valorization of kinship is also reflected in the purposes the *arbores* diagrams had to answer. Reference to kinship in terms of flesh coincided with the almost exclusive use of the diagrams to measure the closeness of kin in order to prevent incest—i.e., ultimately in order to avoid marriage among kin. The emphasis on blood, in contrast, came with a new understanding of the diagram as a description of coherent kin-groups, able at once to keep kin-groups together and to separate them from others.

The two concepts of flesh and blood were each prone to particular visions of kinship. To put it simply, the language of flesh tended to highlight sex and marriage, while that of blood placed more emphasis on descent. Speaking of flesh and its unification provoked associations to the act of sex and the merger of a man and a woman. Speaking of blood and of mixing blood suggested, in contrast, that the significance of sex rests less in the union of partners' bodies than in the mixture of their bloods—in their offspring. While the stark opposition of the High Middle Ages, between an exalted spiritual kinship and a depreciated carnal kinship, was whittled away, a new, also slightly hierarchic discrepancy made itself felt: the one between kinship by descent and kinship by alliance.

The shifts that emerge from treatises on the *arbores* can—with due precaution—be related to some general developments in the social organization and the cultural perception of kinship in the course of the later Middle Ages.[47] It is certainly too simple to describe these developments as a passage from cognatic to agnatic forms of kinship, as was suggested by Karl Schmid and Georges Duby in the 1960s and 70s.[48] But a series of recent studies suggest that kinship in the central Middle Ages—and in many domains still in the late Middle Ages too—was primarily conceptualized as an extended network of living people connected by marriage alliances as well as by sibling and cousin relationships.[49] Such networks had little generational depth and their definition was not particularly concerned with keeping agnates and cognates or consanguines and affines apart; in the vernaculars these were often all indistinctively referred to as *amis* or *fründe*.[50]

At the passage to the early modern period, novel conceptions emerged that primarily mattered in political representation, in the devolution of noble or patrician estates, and in determining the succession to offices. By and large, these new conceptions gave more weight to descent, generational depth, and the continuity of families over generations (that is, to lineages) and marked distinctions between affinity and consanguinity as well as between agnatic and cognatic ties.[51] We can associate the metaphors of flesh and of the unification of flesh through sex and marriage with the older system and its stress on marriages as central hitches in an extended network of kin related by a variety of different dyadic relationships. Metaphors of blood, in contrast, are adjusted to conceptions of kinship that attached greater importance to lineage and descent, the constitution of kin-relationships around a patrimony that should be "kept within the family" over generations. Concepts of the bodily substances that kin are believed to share may be quite closely related to a completely different but no less fundamental kind of "substances of kinship," namely, the material privileges and property that circulate within and between families.

## Conclusion

*Arbores consanguinitatis* have not always been family trees, and even less trees of blood relations. Both the comparisons of kinship diagrams with naturally grown trees and the association of kinship with blood were topics that became prominent in the commentaries on the *arbores* only shortly before the passage to the early modern period. This was the result of several, closely related shifts in the way these treatises conceptualized kinship. The treatises from around 1200 were primarily interested in the *arbores* as instruments of categorizing individual kin-relationships and of determining their closeness. This function remained important later on, but both the blood and the tree metaphors seem to have emerged in the context of a new use of kinship and kinship diagrams to define coherent groups, stable across generations.

The new concepts of kinship based on shared blood largely replaced an older set of ideas highlighting flesh and its unification. The two concepts did not exclude but rather limited each other. While the language of flesh laid emphasis on sex and marriage as the focal point of kinship organization, the language of blood gave more weight to descent and lines of descent that outlast generations. Speaking of blood rather than of flesh appears to liquidize the bodily substances of kinship and to facilitate processes of mixing and dilution. Nevertheless, the notion of being of the same blood paved the way for very exclusive conceptions of belonging. Thus being of one blood, or of the right blood, became a precondition of belonging to the nobilities and patriciates at the passage to the early modern period, and the transmission of blood also played an important role in the emergence of concepts of ethnicity, race, and, more recently, genetic identity. All of these concepts owe a great deal to developments in medieval theoretical thinking about kinship—a field that remains largely unexplored.

# Notes

1. Hermann Schadt, *Die Darstellungen der Arbores Consanguinitatis und der Arbores Affinitati. Bildschemata in juristischen Handschriften* (Tübingen, 1982), 61.
2. Christiane Klapisch-Zuber, *L'ombre des ancêtres. Essai sur l'imaginaire médiéval de la parenté* (Paris, 2000); Klapisch-Zuber, "La genèse de l'arbre généalogique," in *L'arbre. Histoire naturelle et symbolique de l'arbre, du bois et du fruit au Moyen Âge*, ed. Michel Pastoureau (Paris, 1993), 41–81.
3. Caroline Walker Bynum, *Wonderful Blood: Theology and Practice in Late Medieval Northern Germany and Beyond* (Philadelphia, 2007); Charles de Miramon, "Aux origines de la noblesse et des princes de sang. France et Angleterre au XIV<sup>e</sup> siècle," in *L'hérédité entre Moyen Âge et Époque Moderne. Perspectives historiques*, ed. Charles de Miramon and Maaike van der Lugt (Florence, 2008), 157–210.
4. Cf. above, note 2.
5. Michel Foucault, *Les mots et les choses. Une archéologie des sciences humaines* (Paris, 1966), 170–76.
6. Janet Carsten, "Substantivism, Antisubstantivism, and Anti-Antisubstantivism," in *Relative Values, Reconfiguring Kinship Studies*, ed. Sarah Franklin and Susan McKinnon (Durham, NC, 2001), 29–53; Françoise Héritier-Augé, "Semen and Blood: Some Ancient Theories Concerning their Genesis and Relationship," in *Fragments for a History of the Human Body*, ed. Michel Feher, Ramona Nadaff, and Nadia Tazi, 3 vols. (New York, 1989), 3:158–75.
7. Thomas Aquinas, Quaestio LIV, "De impedimento consanguinitatis," in *"Summa theologica" diligenter emendata Nicolai et al., notis ornata*, 8 vols. (Luxemburg, 1870), 7:502–12.
8. Conceptually important: Gianna Pomata, "Blood Ties and Semen Ties: Consanguinity and Agnation in Roman Law," in *Gender, Kinship, Power: A Comparative and Interdisciplinary History*, ed. Mary Jo Maynes et al. (New York and London, 1996),

43–64; Sarah Franklin, *Dolly Mixtures: The Remaking of Genealogy* (Durham, NC, and London, 2007); Brigitta Hauser-Schäublin, "Blutsverwandtschaft," in *Mythen des Blutes*, ed. Christina Braun and Christoph Wulf (Frankfurt am Main and New York, 2007), 171–83.

9. Ioannes Andreae, "Consanguinitas per tres regulas declaratur," in *Corpus iuris canonici*, ed. Emil Friedberg (Leipzig, 1879), pt. 1: Decretum Magistri Gratiani, col. 1427–36.
10. Klapisch-Zuber, *L'ombre*; Schadt, *Darstellungen*.
11. Johannes Lintholtz is also known as Ioannes Cyntholtz. I use Lintholtz in my text, but preserve the alternative spelling, where applicable, in note references.
12. The treatises referenced in this paragraph are Tancredus Bononiensis [Tancredus de Bologna], *Tancredi summa de matrimonio*, ed. Agathon Wunderlich (Göttingen, 1841), 27–32; Raymundus de Pennaforte, *Summa Sancti Raymundi de Peniafort Barcinonensis de poenitentia et matrimonio cum glossis Ioannis de Friburgo* (Rome, 1603), 533–34; Goffredus Tranensis, *Summa super titulis decretalium. Novissime cum repertorio et numeris principalium et emergentium questionum impressa* ([Lyon, 1519]; 2nd repr. Aalen, 1992); Henricus de Segusio [cardinalis Hostiensis], *Summa. Una cum summariis et adnotationibus Nicolai Superantii* (Lyon, 1537; repr. Aalen, 1962), fol. 211v.; Thomas Aquinas, *"Summa theologiae," Questions on God*, ed. Brian Davies and Brian Leftow, Cambridge Texts in the History of Philosophy (Cambridge, 2006), Supplementum Q 54–55; Ioannes Egitanensis, *Lectura arborum consanguinitatis et affinitatis magistri Ioannis Egitanensis*, ed. Isaias da Rosa Pereira, *Studia Gratiana* 14 (1967): 155–82; Ioannes Andreae, *Arbor consanguinitatis, mit Kommentar von Heinrich Greve* (Leipzig, [not before 1492]), fol. 144v; Prosdocimus de Comitibus, "Tractatus de arbore consanguinitatis et affinitatis," in *Tractatus universi iuris, duce, et auspice Gregorio XIII in unum congesti*, vol. 9 (Venice, 1584–86), fols. 141r–44v, cited hereafter as *Tractatus universi iuris*; Ioannes Cyntholtz [Lintholtz], "Tractatus seu commentaria in arborem consanguinitatis, affinitatis, cognationis spiritualis atque legalis," in *Tractatus universi iuris*, vol. 9, fols. 145r–58r.
13. Tancredus, *Summa*; Raymundus, *Summa*.
14. Ioannes Egitanensis, *Lectura arborum consanguinitatis et affinitatis*, 167.
15. Henricus de Segusio, *Summa*, fol. 211v.
16. The riddles are to be found in a German language edition of Andreae, Ioannes Andreae, *Super arboribus consanguinitatis, affinitatis et cognationis spiritualis* (Strasbourg, before 1482), fols. 11–12.
17. Ioannes Egitanensis, *Lectura arborum consanguinitatis et affinitatis*, 167.
18. Ioannes Egitanensis, *Lectura arborum consanguinitatis et affinitatis*, 167–68.
19. Ioannes Andreae, "Consanguinitas," col. 1428.
20. Prosdocimus, "Tractatus," fols. 140v–44v, here 142r.
21. Prosdocimus, "Tractatus," fol. 142; Cyntholtz, "Tractatus," fols. 145r–58r, here 145r.
22. Schadt, *Darstellungen*, 350.
23. Schadt, *Darstellungen*, 328, plates 155, 167.
24. Prosdocimus, "Tractatus," fol. 141r.
25. Tancredus, *Summa*, 26; cf. Karl Borchardt, "Tancred v. Bologna," in *Lexikon des Mittelalters*, vol. 8, ed. Robert-Henri Bautier et al. (Munich, 1997), col. 458.
26. Thomas Laqueur, "Destiny is Anatomy," chap. 2 in *Making Sex: Body and Gender from the Greeks to Freud* (Cambridge, MA, 1990), 25–62; Caroline Walker Bynum, "Der weibliche Körper und religiöse Praxis im Spätmittelalter," in *Fragmentierung und Erlösung. Geschlecht und Körper im Glauben des Mittelalters*, ed. Caroline Walker Bynum (Frankfurt am Main, 1996), 148–225; Gianna Pomata, "Blood Ties and Se-

men Ties," 43–64; Gotthard Strohmaier, "Blut und Blutbewegung im arabischen Galenismus," in *Blood in History and Blood Histories,* ed. Mariacarla Gadebusch Bondio (Florence, 2005), 39–47; Alberto Jori, "Blut und Leben bei Aristoteles," in Bondio, ed., *Blood,* 19–38; Walter Burkert, "'Blutsverwandtschaft.' Mythos, Natur und Jurisprudenz," in Braun and Wulf, *Mythen des Blutes,* 245–56.

27. See, for example, Henricus de Segusio, *Summa,* fol. 210r.
28. The term *carnali copula* can be found in Raymundus, *Summa,* 556; Gottfredus Tranensis, *Summa,* 371; Ioannes Andreae, "Consanguinitas," col. 1435. Cf. Maurice Gilbert, "Une seule chair," *Nouvelle révue théologique* 100 (1979): 66–89. *Carnalis commixtio* occurs in Ioannes Egitanensis, *Lectura arborum consanguinitatis et affinitatis,* 176.
29. Antonius Garcia y Garcia, *Constitutiones concilii quarti Lateranensis una cum commentariis glossatorum* (Vatican City, 1981), 91; cf. Schadt, *Darstellungen,* 196n4: "Quaternarius vero numerus bene congruit prohibitioni coniugii corporalis, de quo dicit Apostolus, quod vir non habet potestatem sui corporis, sed mulier, neque mulier habet potestatem sui corporius, sed vir [1 Cor.7:4], quia quatuor sunt humores in corpore, qui constant ex quatuor elementis."
30. Johannes Andreae, "Commentarium in quartum decretalium librum Novella. De cons. et affinitate cap. VIII," in *In quinque decretalium libros novella commentaria* ([Venice, 1581]; repr. Torino, 1963), fol. 45v; cf. Schadt, *Darstellungen,* 198n19.
31. Thomas Aquinas, *Summa Theologica,* Supplementum Q 54, Art. 4.
32. Prosdocimus, "Tractatus," fol. 142r.
33. Cyntholtz [Lintholtz], "Tractatus," fol. 146v: "nam punctuatio canonica querit de consanguinitate quid dicitur a sanguine qui est rubeae naturae, seu rubei coloris, sed ius civile non curat nisi de successione, quod habet locum post mortem, quare esseent per nigra puncta et obscura recte designatur."
34. Raymundus, *Summa,* 557–58.
35. Cf. Gianna Pomata, "Legami di sangue, legami di seme. Consanguineità e agnazione nel diritto romano," *Quaderni storici* 86 (1994): 299–334.
36. See Greve's gloss in Ioannes Andreae, *Arbor consanguinitatis,* fol. 144v.
37. See Greve's gloss in Ioannes Andreae, *Arbor consanguinitatis,* fol. 144r.
38. Thomas Aquinas, *Summa theologiae,* Supplementum Q 55, Art. 1.
39. Raymundus, *Summa,* 556.
40. Cyntholtz [Lintholtz], "Tractatus," fol. 150v.
41. Cyntholtz [Lintholtz], "Tractatus," fol. 150r.
42. Thomas Aquinas, *Summa Theologiae,* Supplementum Q 54, Art. 4.
43. Cyntholtz [Lintholtz], "Tractatus," fol. 145r.
44. See the chapter by Anita Guerreau-Jalabert in this volume.
45. Bynum, *Wonderful Blood,* 1–21.
46. Bynum, *Wonderful Blood,* 17, 168–72, 187, 214.
47. David Warren Sabean and Simon Teuscher, "Kinship in Europe: A New Approach to Long Term Development," in *Kinship in Europe: Approaches to Long-Term Development (1300–1900),* ed. David Warren Sabean, Simon Teuscher, and Jon Mathieu (Oxford, 2007), 1–32.
48. Anita Guerreau-Jalabert, Régine LeJan, and Joseph Morsel, "Familles et parentes. De l'histoire de la famille à l'anthropologie de la parenté," in *Les tendances actuelles de l'histoire du Moyen Âge en France et en Allemagne,* ed. Jean-Claude Schmitt and Otto Gerhard Oexle (Paris, 2002), 433–46.
49. Michael Mitterauer, *Warum Europa? Mittelalterliche Grundlagen eines Sonderwegs* (Munich, 2003), 70–87.

50. Simon Teuscher, *Bekannte—Klienten—Verwandte. Soziabilität und Politik in der Stadt Bern um 1500* (Cologne, 1998), 75–80; Juliette M. Turlan, "Amis et amis charnels. D'après les actes du parlement au XIV$^e$ siècle," *Revue historique du droit français et étranger* 47 (1969): 645–98.

51. Sabean and Teuscher, "Kinship," 1–32; Joseph Morsel, "Geschlecht als Repräsentation. Beobachtungen zur Verwandtschaftskonstruktion im fränkischen Adel des späten Mittelalters," in *Die Repräsentation der Gruppen. Texte—Bilder—Objekte*, ed. Otto Gerhard Oexle and Andrea v. Hülsen-Esch (Göttingen, 1998), 259–325.

# Chapter 5

# Discourses of Blood and Kinship in Late Medieval and Early Modern Castile

## Teofilo F. Ruiz

Among the many definitions of the word *sangre* (blood) found in the influential *Diccionario de autoridades* (1737), one of them is *sangre* as synonymous with *alcuña* (*alcurnia* in modern Spanish, meaning ancestry or lineage). The entry cites both a Latin life of the Emperor Julian and a medieval *cancionero* (collection of lyrical poetry) of the mid fifteenth century as testimony for equating blood with lineage or kinship.[1] More to the point, the discussion of blood glosses a well-known phrase in Spanish (Castilian) literature, "la sangre se hereda y el vicio se apega" (blood is inherited and vice is acquired), stating that it is "a phrase addressed to nobles of well-known families (blood) who do not wish to correct or avoid their vices or right their wrongs."[2] Composed under the auspices of the Real Academia Española in the first half of the eighteenth century, the *Diccionario de autoridades*'s exploration of the Castilian language reflected late medieval usage, as is obvious in the examples deployed throughout the text. It also echoed the taxonomic and classifying systems that, as Foucault has argued in *The Order of Things*, were at the center of the transition to new forms of knowledge.[3] In the case of *sangre*, the meaning was deeply imbedded in Castilian medieval and early modern ideas about descent and family: blood was passed from generation to generation, binding individuals into lineages.

There were of course other meanings. One of the earliest appearances of the word in Castilian was in the *Poema del Cid*, written around the first decade of the thirteenth century. There blood is deployed in terms of the shedding of Moorish blood (to one's elbow), as promised to be done by one of the Cid's faithful followers, Minaya, in homage to his lord. The *Poema* ends with a reference that, although not explicitly using the word *blood*, nevertheless implies descent. After the disastrous wedding of the Cid's daughters to the "infantes de Carrión," they are married once again to the kings of Navarre and Aragón. The *Poema* explains how through marriage (through the mixing of blood) the Cid became related (*parientes son*) to kings.[4] Predating these usages was, of course, the enduring concern with blood and its redeeming qualities found throughout the medieval West. The blood of Christ assumed a unique role in mystical discourse during the twelfth century as its charismatic and redemptive power was associated with the Host and female piety.[5] The influential Fourth Lateran Council (1215) reified the importance of blood by stating categorically that the blood of Christ is present in the Eucharist.[6] More significantly for our discussion, the council issued the well-known injunction against marriage within the fourth degree of consanguinity (with the implications about inherited blood) and restrictions on the clothing of Jews and Muslims, both directly aimed at preventing sexual exchanges between a Jew or Muslim and a Christian.[7]

As early as the twelfth century, and continuing throughout the Castilian late Middle Ages well into the sixteenth century, *blood*, *lineage*, and their many synonyms were part of the same semantic field and formed key semantic markers in an evolving discourse.[8] First and foremost, these words were deployed to describe membership in the upper ranks of the nobility. Such a sense of the power of blood, or, to use David Warren Sabean's felicitous title, "power in the blood," is most evident in some of the excerpts cited from the *Poema del Cid*, and in the Cid's resistance to marrying his daughters to nobles far above him; or in the stanza of Jorge Manrique's (d. 1479) greatest poem, *Coplas a la muerte de mi padre ...* (*Ode on the Death of My Father*), which conflates Visigothic descent with exalted lineage and nobility.[9] Although Manrique's aim in that particular stanza was to lament the decline of Gothic blood with the passing of time and sinful (or ignoble) behavior, his association of blood, lineage, nobility, and Gothic descent is crucial to my remarks on the topic below. Effectively, the words *blood*, *lineage*, and *nobility* serve as a verbal map for tracing the different discourses of blood during the transition between the Middle Ages and the early modern period.

# Discourses of Blood, Lineage, and Nobility

If I have gone to such painstaking detail in attempting to define the contours of the semantic field in which the meanings of blood and lineage
were deployed in late medieval and early modern Castile, it is because
concerns with blood in Spanish historiography over the last decades have
been focused, almost exclusively, on the connections between discourses
of blood and religion: specifically, the bloods of Jews and Muslims, and
the fear that these bloods would contaminate Christian blood through
sexual exchanges. The enactment of edicts of cleanliness or purity of
blood from the mid fifteenth century onward and their continued en-
forcement in the sixteenth century (though this was less strict than has
been argued) have obscured the continued vitality in the Spanish realms
during the early modern period of different, older discourses of blood,
some dating back as early as the eighth century. Yet all these discourses,
old and new, sectarian and noble, actually intertwined and fed upon
each other. Ideas about the relationship between religious beliefs, kinship, race (*raza*, rare until the sixteenth century, when it also came to
encompass natives in the New World), and blood could not be imagined
by those engaged in disputations about purity of blood in late medieval
and early modern Spain, without reference to parallel concerns in the
blood, lineage, and nobility discourse of an earlier period.[10] During the
crucial fifteenth and sixteenth centuries the latter discourse influenced
and shaped the former, constructing boundaries of difference and hierarchical distinction not just between dominant Christians and other
religious groups but also between lower and higher social orders, or
rural and urban groups. In a process most vividly seen in the dichotomy
between the blood of the Visigoths and the blood of the Jews, these
blood discourses would slowly and inexorably shift in the sixteenth
century, until not being a descendant of a Jew or a Muslim would ipso
facto confer some modicum of nobility or, at least, claim to nobility.
Such a shift was most ironically rendered by Sancho Panza's famous
utterance that because he was an Old Christian (by which he meant
a Castilian peasant, thus not connected to either Jews or Muslims), he
could be a count.[11]

Cervantes was of course engaged in a witty critique of such vain pre-
tenses, and he was part of a long-standing literary tradition of questioning pride in one's blood in the absence of virtue. Dorotea, another of
his wonderful characters, though a rich peasant, is nonetheless worthy
of marriage to a duke's son because of her honesty and virtue (and her
clean blood, one may add). The key words in Dorotea's story are *lab-
radores* (farmers), *cristianos viejos ranciosos* (Old Christians of ancient

rank).[12] Manrique had already emphasized deeds over descent, reminding his readers also that death privileges no one, that fortune is mutable,
that in Christ, all are equal. Cervantes would reiterate such themes by
assigning greater importance to deeds and honor than to lineage. In one
of his most mordant moments, he also pointed to the role of money in
establishing lineages more influential than those created by descent or
blood: he had Sancho solemnly expound on the two great lineages of the
world—those who have and those who have not.[13]

As shall be seen in greater detail later, variants of these blood discourses were advanced in late medieval and early modern Castile, but
all reflected the following basic assumptions: Pure blood, meaning Visigothic descent, privileged the claims of nobles' houses and lineages.
Pure blood granted superiority over persons of tainted blood, even if the
purity claims came from uncouth peasants like Sancho Panza. Conversion to Christianity did not cleanse the blood of Muslims, Jews, and heretics, or of their descendants, arguments to the contrary notwithstanding;
their stained blood was retained eternally. These ideas were certainly not
unique to Castile. Many traditional societies and fundamentalist religious groups still adhere today to the belief that transgressive tenden-
cies, above all in the sexual realm, are inherited through the blood. The
Nazis codified the difference between pure blood or racially pure mixed
blood, and the utterly impure. J. K. Rowlings's wonderful volumes on
Harry Potter are all about blood classification. The last volume of the
series is propelled by the conflict between pure bloods and half bloods,
i.e., Mudbloods, who though lacking any blood connection to wizards or
witches could nevertheless perform magic, and their opposite, Muggles,
unable to do so at all. All these observations, however, serve only as a
preface for my argument that these ideas about blood (and lineage or
kinship) operated together and represented different facets of one discursive reality; and that legal procedures, ancestry, and place of origin
could actually shape and determine one's location within these varied
discourses. Here it may be useful to provide a brief account of the rise of
lineages and kinship groups in Castile in the central Middle Ages and to
explore the mechanisms that led to the construction of these concepts
among nobles and urban oligarchs.

Exploring these themes opens up a world of complex theoretical issues
without which it would be impossible to articulate or to understand the
long and intertwining history of these conflicting discourses on blood.
Here I follow David Nirenberg's numerous and luminous interventions
into these methodological and interpretational problems. His critical reflections linking Jews, Muslims, and Christians within a particular social
setting—first presented in his rightly influential book, *Communities of*

*Violence*—have been finely honed in further articles and papers over the last decade. Over the years, his work has turned more and more from the actual history of events, now displayed mostly as examples, to the critical assessment of how we do such a history, of what the theoretical approaches should be that inform our scholarly work on blood, race, and, to a lesser extent, kinship. This is certainly the case in one of his recent articles, "Race and the Middle Ages: The Case of Spain and its Jews." After offering a brilliant summary of diverse scholarly treatments of race and blood as they affected the Jews, Nirenberg proceeds to explore discourses of blood in the polemical anti-Jewish literature of the fifteenth century, paying special attention to comparisons of Jews to animals.[14] This enquiry leads him to a stunning insight into the overlapping of "race" (by which we could also read "blood" or "lineage"), "culture," and "natural histories." His observation refocuses our attention onto discourses of blood (or race) that are centered around ways of defining Jews as essentially different from others, as maintaining their inherited "Jewishness" even after conversion. This Jewishness, this "tainted blood" in the language of the day, fixed the place of Jews within Spanish Christian society. And animal husbandry, with its roots in rural Spain, seems to have provided the practice-based knowledge about blood purity and taint that supported this particular hierarchical framing of society.[15] Yet, though such explanations for impure blood and inherited traits became central to the decrees of blood "purity" and to the establishment of the Spanish Inquisition (often charged with enforcing these edicts), the focus on these often complex debates, which did not necessarily reflect the reality of lived lives, has often obscured other important aspects in the long-term construction and imagining of lineages.[16]

My aim, therefore, is to decenter the role played in Iberian historiography by discussions on Jewish blood or purity of blood. To restate my earlier argument, any study of blood, as it relates to Jews, Conversos, Muslims, and Moriscos must move beyond the immediate concern with religious filiation to consider the contributions of the underlying discourse of descent. In other words, a far more prominent and older concern with Christian descent (and blood) shaped the contours of late medieval and early modern fixation on Jewish blood. One discourse cannot be understood without the other. Moreover, the social and political realities of the formation of noble and bourgeois lineages, the emergence of extensive kin networks—what Jacques Heers has described for urban settings as the "familiar clan"—and the easy flow between these different categories shaped the making of peculiar cultural constructs in late medieval Castile.[17] In the end, the purity of blood decrees emerged from a more generalized discourse on lineage that had been constantly deployed in literature and social practice among Christians from the eighth century onward.

## The Visigothic Inheritance and the Birth of the Nobility in Castile

Much has been written about the symbolic importance of Visigothic descent and its impact over the course of Spanish history. The Visigoths' humiliating defeat at the hands of Muslim invaders in 711 would come in time to be explained either as God's punishment for their many sins, or as the outcome of a perfidious betrayal orchestrated by the Jews. Within a century of the defeat, small Christian polities rose in the regions of Asturias and León and made claims to links with the Visigothic past. Although clearly a political construction, this Gothic revival narrative—that is, the conscious claim that an uninterrupted link existed between the last Visigothic rulers in Toledo and the newly self-appointed Christian kings in the northwestern part of the Iberian peninsula—was a carefully laid out ideological program that in time succeeded beyond the wildest dreams of its early architects.[18] Several important components went into establishing a continuous link between these fledgling kingdoms and the Visigothic past. The claims to the charismatic relics of Saint Isidore of Seville (the great Visigothic polymath) in León, the convenient discovery of the tomb of the Apostle Saint James near Compostela in the late ninth century, the beginnings of the royally sanctioned pilgrimage to his shrine by thousands of the faithful from all over Europe, the removal, whether by voluntary migration or by forceful removal to the North during Christian raids into the Toledo area, of numerous Mozarabs in the late ninth and tenth centuries—all of this fostered the use of Visigothic administrative practices and helped cement the northern realms' claims to a Visigothic legacy.

Although there are no references to blood, implicit in the Gothic revival is the idea of an enduring kinship with the Visigoths. The chroniclers wasted no opportunity to emphasize that such-and-such an Asturian king was related to such-and-such a Visigothic ruler or Visigothic noble family.[19] This mythic ethnogenesis was not less compelling for being false. The argument posited a North denuded of people (it was not!) and the transplant of Visigoths there, as they fled the bitter defeat of 711. Like the actual Visigoths, who mixed freely with the Roman-Celtic-Iberian population of Roman Hispania before 711, the few survivors who made it to the North intermarried with the native populations of the mountainous areas of Asturias, Cantabria, the Basque homeland,

and elsewhere. Nevertheless, because these mountains were never con-quered by the Romans, Visigoths, or Muslims, they would become in time a trope for pure blood lines. That it had little to do with Visigothic blood (if there ever was such a thing) did not matter at all.

Underlying appeals to Gothic blood in the purity discourses of later periods were two themes drawn from interpretations of the Visigothic past. First was the narrative of difference, distinguishing between the Visigoths' sixth-century conversion from heretical Arian Christianity to what might be called Catholic Christianity and the later conversions of Jews and Muslims. For the Visigoths, unlike for Jews and Muslims, there was no presumption that a residue of stained blood would persist after their conversion to be passed along to descendants, no suspicion as to the authenticity of, or motivations for, their embrace of Catholic Chris-tianity. Second was the insistence that Visigothic history, both in Arian and Christian eras, included an enduring antagonism toward the Jews. These two themes would sound whenever appeals to Visigothic inheri-tance and blood purity were made and would aid in the construction of the discourses of exclusion and inclusion. This filiation is nowhere more evident than in the ordinances of the Cortes against the Jews in the mid thirteenth century, which replicated almost verbatim Visigothic legisla-tion of the late seventh century.[20]

## Christians on Top

The changing nature of the relations between Christians and Muslims in Castile, conferring advantage to the former to the detriment of the latter, became evident after the breakdown of the Córdoba Caliphate and its fragmentation into warring small Muslim kingdoms in the 1030s. Chris-tian advantage was confirmed by a series of signal victories—the taking of Toledo in 1085, the great victory at Las Navas de Tolosa in 1212, and the occupation of most of western Andalucía by the mid thirteenth century. Christian hegemony in the peninsula paralleled and probably shaped the emergence of great noble clans in most of Spain. Certainly this was the case in Castile. But unlike in the lands of the former Caro-lingian Empire, where important aristocratic houses had created elabo-rate genealogies and associated themselves with monastic institutions, establishing necrologies and other forms of legitimating distinctiveness, in Castile a warrior nobility derived most of its privileges and benefits from the king, as rewards for military service.[21] As Marie-Claude Ger-bet, Simon Barton, Simon Doubleday, and others have shown, Christian gains allowed for the emergence during the eleventh and twelfth centuries of a territorial nobility, in which royal service led to ownership of large landed estates—as allodial property, not as fiefs. From this period dates the emergence of some of the most influential aristocratic families or lineages in Castile, a process in which, as Gerbet has pointed out, the linking of property with ancestry and endogamy played a fundamental role.[22] Since the concept of lineages (*linajes*) also began to be deployed in this period by noble kin groups, the period witnessed also a further refinement of the Asturian tradition of claiming descent from Visigothic blood, in the attempt to reserve Visigothic descent to just the nobility.

It is the fluctuation of the application of Visigothic blood connection from a rarefied group in society to anyone not "tainted" by Jewish, Muslim, or heretical blood, that lies at the heart of the dynamics of Castilian discursive practices on blood: hence Manrique's identification of Visigothic blood with the high nobility (the grandees), or the practice—emerging in the late fifteenth century and sixteenth century as a reaction to Jewish conversion—of attributing such a Visigothic link to almost everyone, as, for example, in Sancho Panza's famous dictum, or in the legal processes of the Chirinos family, to be discussed below. Although the claim to Visigothic "pure" blood (or lineage) was quite malleable, there was, nonetheless, a distinct noble discourse, conflating both descent and power into claims to privilege. Moreover, in Castile, unlike elsewhere in western medieval Europe, the great twelfth-century lineages became almost extinct by the mid fourteenth century.[23] The civil wars around the middle of that century then led to the emergence of a new high nobility that, although related to the old great houses Lara and Castro, represented either lesser branches or the pressure of lesser men now made immensely wealthy and privileged by the vicissitudes of war. That these "arrivistes" sought to emphasize their Visigothic blood, as fictitious as this was, is not surprising.

Beginning in the late twelfth century, urban elites also organized themselves into lineages that mirrored, though at a lower social rung, those of the nobility. Members of these urban lineages, although not yet nobles, often married either endogamously or with the lesser nobility, frequently adopted a common last name (for example, the Dávilas in Avila, Sarrazín and Bonifaz in Burgos), invented and wore heraldic coats of arms, lived close to each other in the privileged areas of their respective cities, and monopolized municipal and ecclesiastical offices in their towns. Thus, we witness the rise of an alternate strategy for advancing status and power, also based on blood or lineage. This discourse, easily detectable in royal privileges, in the ordinances of the Cortes or representative assemblies, and in daily praxis, articulated the uniqueness of certain powerful groups within urban Castilian society.[24]

# The Blood of Others

Concurrent with and connected to the formalizing of extended noble kin networks and familiar clans in Castile's cities, were increases in pejorative representations of Jews and Muslims throughout the realm. There were of course other factors at work. For one, the reception of the edicts of the Fourth Lateran Council in Spain provided a doctrinal backdrop for the discourses of difference that were emerging not just in the Iberian peninsula but also throughout European society in this period.[25] The shift in the nature of the relationship between Christians and Muslims from 1212 onward also hardened the attitude of the now dominant Christian majority toward other religious minorities. What is important to emphasize here is that, although anti-Jewish and anti-Muslim propaganda already had a long history in the medieval West, the articulation of antagonisms against these groups in early- and mid-thirteenth-century Castile and Spain grew to new, sharper, and highly confrontational levels. The archeology of these trends shows that the new propaganda was formulated by those on top and quickly appropriated by those below. Its foundations rested on new representations of self and others. The slow construction of regional and realm-wide identities and the conflation of religious beliefs with a new awareness of Castile as a territorial entity (*tierra*) led inexorably to the emergence of novel forms of inclusion and exclusion.[26]

Literary works, legal codes, the ordinances of the Cortes or representative assemblies, and polemical works against Jews and Muslims from the mid thirteenth century onward tell us in no uncertain terms that Christians in Castile sought to segregate Jews and Muslims from Christian society, despite the reality of continuous contact and cohabitation (but not *convivencia*) with these religious minorities in cities and villages. Difference was inscribed on the very bodies of members of both religious minorities in the form of identifying marks on their vestments, specific types of clothing, and haircuts.[27] In the *Poema de Fernán González* (circa 1250), invading Muslims in 711 are accused of killing mothers and children in their mother's arms and, worse, of cannibalism.[28] In *Milagros de Nuestra Señora* (*Miracle XVI*), also an influential mid-thirteenth-century literary work, the author, Gonzalo de Berceo, tells the story of a Jewish child who had gone to mass and taken the Host. His father, enraged by his actions, throws him into a burning oven. The Virgin of course protects him, and the Jewish father is burned alive instead. *Miracle XVIII* tells of Jews in Toledo who crucified and tortured a wax image of Jesus. The text describes Jews with words ranging from "false" to "traitors" to "blind" to "deaf," while perpetuating the charge of Jewish guilt in Christ's death.[29]

From the mid thirteenth century onward, the place of religious minorities in Castile became much more difficult overall, despite interludes
in which relations approached normalcy.[30] While following Nirenberg
in rejecting a teleological interpretation of Christian-Jewish relations in
this period (in the sense that attacks against Jews in this period did not
lead to such things as the Holocaust later on), I nevertheless must argue
that it is clear that a double-edged discourse, however fictive, already
had been formulated and internalized. In rough outline, the Christian
perspective on non-Christians rested on a bedrock of literary and legal
representations and traditions (think of the vitriolic edicts against Jews
and Muslims found in the *Siete partidas*).[31] In simple terms, this perspective went more or less like this: We (Christians) are superior to you Jews
and Muslims because (a) we *are* Christians; (b) we descend from pure
Visigothic blood, untainted by miscegenation with infidels; (c) we are
warriors, and our unqualified success in the battlefield (the reconquest
and repopulation of most of Iberia after 1085) testifies to the righteous-
ness of our cause and to God's favor. You are inferior to us because (a)
you have rejected Christianity; (b) you descend from a cursed and guilty
race, and the traits and weaknesses of your origins are encoded in your
blood (an argument that opened the door for the exclusion of converts);
(c) you have proven yourselves incapable of withstanding our might.
Of course there were numerous variations on these lines of thought, as
there were movements back and forth, but this general outline represents
prevalent beliefs among the Christian population, above all at the lower
social levels of society. Thus, as ahistorical as these general assertions
may have been, and as denuded of the nuances necessary for any serious historical analysis, they are not too far removed from the dominant
discourse developed against Jews and Muslims from the mid thirteenth
century onward. Christian apologists (even recently converted Jews
such as Abner of Burgos [Alfonso of Valladolid] or Jerónimo de Santa
Fe) did not hesitate to add other faults to the endless list of errors associated with Jewish and Muslim descent.[32] By the late fifteenth century,
representations of Jews and Conversos could turn quite vitriolic, as, for
example, in the references to "their peculiar smell," sexual habits, prolific
progeny, greed, and urban residence in Andrés Bernáldez's chronicle of
the Catholic Monarchs. Here and in other such descriptions, chroniclers
and polemicists also engaged in relentlessly feminizing the Other and in
piling up stereotypes.[33] It is not surprising that Bernáldez even faulted
Jews and Conversos for living in cities, a sign of their wickedness; that is,
they engaged in trade and artisanal activities. Their urban vocation stood
in sharp contrast with the idealization of rural life and rural occupations.
And this ideal world for Bernáldez and others, not coincidentally, was
untainted by proximity to or miscegenation with Jews and Muslims.

# Internalizing a Discourse

Ironically, the great waves of violence against Jews in 1391, and the Disputation of Tortosa in 1413, which impelled massive conversions to Christianity, actually opened up new opportunities in Christian society to persons of Jewish descent, as Conversos rapidly accessed positions of power in municipal government, the Church, and the royal court. Their success was fiercely resisted by many Old Christians on precisely the grounds of descent, blood, and suspected orthodoxy, leading to the first cleanliness-of-blood statutes in 1449.[34] As Albert Sicroff shows, many voices were raised to oppose these new measures. Some advocated the redemptive nature of conversion and the equality of Old and New Christians within the Church, while others, Fernán Díaz de Toledo among them, pointed to the many noble and even royal families with Jewish blood in their lines. Nevertheless, the edicts led to the internalizing of a discourse on blood by those on both sides of the question. "*Pureza de sangre*" functioned at a variety of levels. The various Church, municipal, and royal edicts that formalized the contrast between pure and impure blood actually produced statutes with two faces, concerned not so much about purity of blood as about impurity and pollution. On the one hand they branded the descendants of Jews (albeit not all), and eventually the descendants of Muslims, as impure and stained by those impurities forevermore; on the other hand, they posited pure blood for the rest of society—quite an ambitious program. This category included not just people of noble birth, wealth, or claimed Visigothic descent, but even those of low social rank so long as they came from places not traditionally known as Jewish or Muslim enclaves—hence Sancho Panza.

# In the Real World: The Workings of Discourses of Blood in Late Medieval and Early Modern Castile

The history of how the statutes of cleanliness of blood worked in Spanish society is a story well known. Although these edicts essentially simply barred access to benefices in certain ecclesiastical establishments and military orders, and to fellowships to the main university colleges (*colegios mayores*), their humiliating nature had a nefarious impact on Castilian culture by creating an ideal of blood purity inaccessible to most of the descendants of recent Jewish and Muslim converts. As always, the gulf between legal proscriptions and the reality at ground level was wide indeed. The examples that show the difference between legal injunctions and praxis are many, and here it will suffice to mention the ways in which Conversos circumvented these laws and, far more important, to indicate what these strategies for refashioning oneself into an Old Christian of pure blood tell us about the structure and nature of these discourses.

By the late Middle Ages, questions about who was a nobleman or how to become one had become intertwined with issues of lineage and, of course, blood. Wealth transformed the social landscape, allowing for a continuous self-fashioning by Conversos, non-nobles, and even Moriscos. In Francisco de Quevedo y Villegas's satirical poem, *Letrilla* (early seventeenth century), money makes nobility, but it can also make Christians and Moors equal. As the author, writing ironically, points out, the wealth that flows from the Orient into Spain renders "all blood royal, making rich and humble alike."[35] It may be useful to part from these generalizations and literary examples, and to look at a specific legal case. The case, an almost Castilian *Bleak House*, was litigated in the courts from the late fifteenth century to the second half of the sixteenth century. The kind of evidence marshaled in the arguments on behalf of the litigants sought to secure noble status for the family and determine what material advantages, if any, pertained to such a position. But underlining the legal arguments are clear traces of a discourse on lineage, purity of blood, and descent.

## Hernando Mexía de Cherinos (or Chirinos)

A beautiful sixteenth-century illuminated manuscript extant in the Bibliothèque nationale in Paris (ms. espagnol 435) summarizes the long, expensive, and trying litigation that the Mexía de Chirinos family initiated in the fifteenth century to prove the nobility of its members and, therefore, the validity of their claims to exemption from municipal taxes.[36] The black, leather-bound manuscript, written in an impeccable, very readable hand and illuminated by a genealogical tree that glorifies the Chirinos line and links it with the Virgin and Saint George, is hardly unique. Spanish archives contain numerous examples of similar litigation, undertaken by individuals and families seeking to assert their noble status and privileges. In many of them, as in the Chirinos brief, we can trace the history of a particular family (or at least the history the family wished the court and others to believe) over a period of almost a century; and far more important, we can see what kinds of arguments were advanced to sustain claims to nobility and how these arguments changed over time to fit the shifting social and cultural context in which these cases were being argued. In this way, the briefs provide a road map to the importance of descent and of discourses of blood.

What gave an argument for pure blood—or a claim to nobility—credibility and legal standing? In the Mexía de Chirinos case, litigation to prove nobility was prompted by the insistence of the municipal councils of Úbeda and Jaén that family members pay taxes. Municipal officials refused to accept their claims either to nobility or to tax-exempt status. The actual process began during the reign of the Catholic Monarchs in the late fifteenth century—though appeals were made to events that had taken place earlier, in the middle of that century—but the final decision on the case was not reached until much later, shortly before 7 February 1567, when the manuscript was originally drawn up. Through the narrative of the document, we follow the peripatetic careers and lives of the Chirinos family: first Pedro Alminial (or Almirante, or Almíndez) de Chirinos, a citizen of the town of Guadalajara; then his son, Alonso de Guadalajara, and his grandson, Hernando Alonso de Guadalajara. The list continues with the great-grandson of Pedro Alminial and one Hernán Mexía Cherinos and ends with Hernán's daughter, Doña María de Narváez. Altogether six generations of the family are invoked (including deceased ancestors), plus a good number of collateral branches and other relations by marriage. In the century covered by the litigation, the family moved from Guadalajara (a small town northeast of Madrid and the main holding of the great noble family of the dukes of Infantado), to Cuenca (in southern New Castile-La Mancha), to Úbeda (near Jaén), and finally, to Jaén itself (north of Granada), which was, by comparison with Úbeda, a larger town. While shedding light on the possibilities of geographical and social mobility in late medieval and early modern Spain, this summary suggests that the perambulations of the Chirinos family may have been prompted by other, more unpleasant circumstances. It is this last possibility that I shall now examine.

Numerous witnesses were called to testify, either to support Chirinos claims or to back the municipal councils of Úbeda and Jaén. Most of the witnesses were old: Alonso de la Mula was seventy years of age; Diego de Arriaga, around seventy-five; and Gil Núñez, canon of the cathedral of Cuenca, seventy-three. The witnesses were clearly middling sorts—an archpriest and a canon—but provincial lower-middling sorts, pointing to the lesser status of the Chirinos and their clients. The testimonies of supporters were fairly uniform, except that, as the family kept failing to win its case in court, the witnesses advanced new and stronger claims for nobility, until finally, the litigants succeeded in 1567.

The reason most often given to justify the Chirinos claim to noble status was that they had never, in their history as a family, paid taxes. Neither the great-grandfather, nor the grandfather, nor the father of any of the claimants (which claimant is speaking depends on which stage of the litigation we are examining) had ever paid taxes. They had, in fact, been exempted from them, had never been inscribed in the tax rolls in either Guadalajara or Cuenca. Therefore, the claimants argued, they themselves ought to be exempted in Úbeda and Jaén. This was a very Castilian argument: a family that was exempted from paying taxes for three generations in a row achieved the privileges of nobility.[37]

The second most often deployed argument for noble status in the depositions turned on the claim of belonging to a lineage that had originated in the mountains. Though not fully deployed in the fifteenth-century testimonies, by the sixteenth century it was fully developed, with the Chirinos arguing (and the witnesses corroborating) that the family had come originally from the mountainous areas in northern Castile and the Basque country where there had never been Jews or Moors—an assertion that was, of course, also false. The northern mountains here functioned as code for a heritage untarnished by Jewish or Moorish connections. But those born "in the mountains" also supposedly came from the fountain of *hidalguía* (knighthood) in Castile. Thus this common and widespread strategy, of tracing family roots to a region never conquered by Islam and supposedly never or only sparsely populated by Jews, was in fact a replay of the arguments about Gothic blood and purity-of-descent that had been deployed by other families, centuries earlier.

The third most common reason given by the witnesses to explain why they believed that the Chirinos were noble is that the family had owned great houses in Guadalajara and Cuenca. Alonso Hernández, an archpriest in Cuenca, swore that Pedro Almíndez de Chirino "was a generous and principal inhabitant of Guadalajara." He stated that he had known Hernando Alonso Chirino in Cuenca as "a knight" (an *ome hijo-dalgo* "who carried a sword") and that his wife, he added, as if to denote her wealth and importance, wore a gold ring. The couple's residence in Cuenca, the witness testified, was an important house, with an extensive retinue of servants. Moreover, Hernando had been a *regidor* (a city official) for life. Wealth, social prominence, and municipal service—the legal and material markers of urban nobility—were all here conjured to confirm noble blood.

To these points were added reports of military deeds and references to the legitimacy of all the family descendants. According to one witness, Hernando Alonso de Guadalajara Cherino had fought in the wars against Granada during the reign of John II (1406–54). Hernando's brother, another witness testified, had been one of the defenders of Cuenca during the civil wars before the ascent of Isabella the Catholic. Other members of the family had also served the crown or their respective municipalities, which attested to their martial history. Finally, several witnesses who, the uniformity of their statements suggests, had been well prepared by lawyers or by the Chirinos themselves, proclaimed that there was no illegitimacy in the family. All of the Chirinos had been married in the Church; thus their children were all legitimate.

In the sixteenth century, a final proof of nobility was offered. The octogenarian Francisco Tebaeca, a citizen of Úbeda, taxpayer, and neighbor in the parish of San Pablo, testified that the male line of the Chirinos family descended neither from "plain men (*hombres llanos*, taxpayers), nor from Jews, nor Moors, nor Conversos; nor had they or any of their ancestors … ever been prisoners of, or punished by, the Holy Office of the Inquisition."[38] Their main claim to nobility, as Tebaeca argued, was that they came from a lineage of *fijosdalgo* (lower nobility), thus, implicitly, from a line of pure blood. It should be noted that the financial stakes in this long legal process were not significant, the original tax in dispute having amounted to only five hundred *sueldos*, a meager sum in late fifteenth-century Spain. The costs of litigation for over a century would have far exceeded that amount: consider not only the great expense of carrying out a lawsuit for such a long time, but also the high cost of drawing up a document as elaborate as the one Hernando Mexía de Cherinos and his daughter commissioned to certify their noble status. But then, we should not be surprised. This suit about a disputed tax bill was actually primarily about status and about refashioning a former Converso connection into a pristine Old Christian one. And, in that sense, the stakes were high indeed. For the fact is that the Chirinos were Conversos, seeking to overcome the social barriers that Converso blood entailed. (Some of the members of the family were well-known doctors at the royal court but their Converso identity hampered their further rise.) Their frequent moves—from Guadalajara to Cuenca to Úbeda to Jaén (the latter a stronghold of Converso artisans and shopkeepers)—provide strong support for a Converso origin. Such peripatetic lives bespeak of attempts to carve a new life, a new identity, in different towns, where old connections and familial ties may not have been known or at least may have been less known. Saint Teresa of Avila's family had engaged in the same sort of self-fashioning, moving from Toledo to Avila, marrying into the patrician elite, and forging a new identity cleansed of Jewish ancestry. So too had the Bernuy family. Important Converso textile merchants, originally from Avila's hinterland, some members of this family became Protestants in Toulouse. Others returned to Judaism in Amsterdam, while those who remained in Spain rose to the rank of grandees, providing just one example of commercial success parlayed to overcome blood and propel a family into the highest rank in Christian society.[39]

There is additional evidence for the Chirinos family's Jewish origins and Converso filiation. A relative named Diego de Valera (son of Alonso Chirino de Guadalajara) was a well-known (Converso) intellectual in the court of the Catholic Monarchs and, as shown by Rodríguez Velasco, among the most prolific authors on questions of knighthood. And, although some members of the family, often females, seem to have married into the "pure" nobility, others did not. Among them was none other than one of the founders of the Chirinos lineage at the center of this court case, the Hernán Mexía de Cherino whom we have already met. His wife, Doña Isabel of Murcia (daughter of a *bachiller,* a university-trained commoner of Murcia), bore a name indicating probable, if not completely certain, Converso origins.

# Conclusion

As I have argued early in these pages, the almost obsessive association of studies of blood with policies hostile to Jews and Conversos in late medieval and early modern Spain has obscured the presence of intertwining discourses on lineage, nobility, and kinship. To an extent, an earlier construct, that of Visigothic lineage and blood, served as the foundation for new ways of defining difference and establishing blood hierarchies. In Castile, blood, lineage, kinship, and descent functioned as a discursive shorthand for the singular preoccupation with establishing a hegemonic identity in a pluralistic society. Sweeping changes in European culture in the early to middle thirteenth century and hardened attitudes toward religious minorities led to antagonistic representations of these groups. Yet the harsh edicts of the late Middle Ages and beyond were not always translated into reality. People with money, connections, patrons, and cunning were able to fashion new identities. In doing so, above all in carving a noble identity, several categories of argument became almost obligatory. One was to deny any relation to Jews, Muslims, or heretics, unless, like the family of the illustrious Converso descendants of Pablo de Santa María, one could claim a Jewish lineage of such prestige (descendants of King David) as to be exempted altogether from the purity-of-blood statutes. Another was to trace one's origin to the region that had escaped Muslim control and had lacked Jewish presence: the mountains. Implicitly, these arguments reinvigorated claims to a Visigothic inheritance. Clearly, family ancestry, place of origin, wealth, purity of blood (after the mid fifteenth century), military and municipal service, and a history of tax exemption were essential components in the making of a noble identity, which meant, of course, one untainted by miscegenation with religious minorities. Being a noble was of utmost importance if one wished to overcome Converso ancestry and to attain social distinction. Although the Chirinos had a hard time obtaining their noble patent from the royal court, they, and others like them, ultimately achieved their goal. Then and now, social mobility and a self-fashioning of one's lineage were possible, if one had wealth, determination, and a good lawyer.

# Notes

1. "*Sangre*," in *Diccionario de la lengua castellana en que se explica el verdadero sentido de las voces...* , 6 vols. ([Madrid, 1737]; facsimile ed., Madrid, 1979), 3:39.
2. "*Sangre*." The entire phrase is "la sangre se hereda, el vicio se apega." Although I use the terms *Spain* or *Spanish* throughout the chapter, I focus mostly on Castile. Since Spain does not become a centralized kingdom until the eighteenth century and consisted of diverse linguistic communities (Catalan, Galician, Hebrew, Arabic), what may have been true in Castile was not necessarily so elsewhere.
3. See Michel Foucault, *The Order of Things: An Archaeology of the Human Sciences* (New York, 1970).
4. See these references in the bilingual edition of *Poem of the Cid*, trans. W. S. Merwin (New York, 1959), 72, 300.
5. See Caroline Walker Bynum, *Holy Feast and Holy Fast: The Religious Significance of Food to Medieval Women* (Berkeley, CA, 1987), 55–56, 161–80, et passim. See also her *Wonderful Blood: Theology and Practice in Late Medieval Northern Germany and Beyond* (Philadelphia, PA, 2007).
6. Fourth Lateran Council (1215), Constitutions 1, Statement of Faith, http://www .ewtn.com/library/councils/lateran4.htm: "His body and blood are truly contained in the sacrament of the altar under the forms of bread and wine, the bread and wine having been changed in substance, by God's power, into his body and blood, so that in order to achieve this mystery of unity we receive from God what he received from us."
7. Fourth Lateran Council (1215), Constitutions 50, 68, at http://www.ewtn.com/ library/councils/lateran4.htm: "Moreover the prohibition against marriage shall not in future go beyond the fourth degree of consanguinity and of affinity, since the prohibition cannot now generally be observed to further degrees without grave harm." And: "Whence it sometimes happens that by mistake Christians join with Jewish or Saracen women, and Jews or Saracens with Christian women. In order that the offence of such a damnable mixing may not spread further, under the excuse of a mistake of this kind, we decree that such persons of either sex, in every Christian province and at all times, are to be distinguished in public from other people by the character of their dress—seeing moreover that this was enjoined upon them by Moses himself, as we read."
8. For the dating of the first usage of Castilian words, see Joan Corominas, *Diccionario crítico etimológico de la lengua castellana*, 4 vols. (Madrid, 1954–57). He traces *sangre* to 1140, *lindo* (literally, pretty or beautiful, but meaning good or pure lineage and synonymous with lineage) to about 1280, *puro* (pure) to 1330, *linaje* (lineage) to 1209, perhaps as early as 1107, but *raza* (race) only to the fifteenth century.

9. Jorge Manrique, "Coplas por la muerte de su padre," in *Ten Centuries of Spanish Poetry*, ed. Eleanor L. Turnbull (Baltimore, MD, 1955), 52–53: Pues la sangre de los godos, / y el linage y la nobleza / tan crescida, / por cuantas vías y modos / se sume su gran alteza / en esta vida! (The noble blood of Gothic name / heroes emblazoned high to fame / In long array, / How, in the onward course of time, / The Landmarks of that race sublime / Were swept away!) The translation by Henry W. Longfellow is, of course, horrible, neglecting to preserve the conflation of blood and lineage conveyed by the poem.

10. For a brilliant discussion of these topics and of the emergence of racial discourses, see Margaret R. Greer, Walter D. Mignolo, and Maureen Quilligan, eds., *Rereading the Black Legend: The Discourses of Religious and Racial Difference in the Renaissance Empires* (Chicago, IL, 2007), 1–24, 71–98, 188–202.

11. "Sea par Dios—dijo Sancho—; que yo cristiano viejo soy, y para ser conde esto me basta"; Miguel de Cervantes, *Don Quijote de la Mancha*, ed. Martín de Riquer, 12th ed., 2 vols. (Barcelona, 1995), 1:201.

12. Cervantes, *Don Quijote*, 1:278–88.

13. Cervantes, *Don Quijote*, 2:chap. 20.

14. David Nirenberg, "Race and the Middle Ages: The Case of Spain and its Jews," in Greer, Mignolo, and Quilligan, eds., *Rereading the Black Legend: The Discourses of Religious and Racial Difference in the Renaissance Empires*, 71–87.

15. Nirenberg, "Race and the Middle Ages," 83: "We have seen that fifteenth-century Spaniards utilized a vocabulary of race grounded in theories of animal husbandry that posited the biological reproduction of somatic and behavioral traits. We have also seen how this vocabulary underwrote a series of strategies that explained and legitimated the creation and perpetuation of certain hierarchies and discriminations through the language of reproduction. We cannot, however, therefore conclude that we are justified in speaking of modern 'race' and 'racism' in fifteenth-century Spain. All we have shown is that one influential family of arguments for dismissing the relevance of 'race' to medieval Spain, that of Américo Castro and his disciples, makes inadequate sense of the 'natural histories' available to residents of the Iberian peninsula in the fifteenth and sixteenth centuries." On the issues of race see also the *Journal of Medieval and Early Modern Studies* 31 (2001), a special issue on race; in particular, Robert Bartlett's essay, "Medieval and Modern Concepts of Race and Identity," 39–56.

16. In this context it may be useful to note that decrees on purity of blood emerged simultaneously with certain important linguistic developments. The emergence of Castilian as a formal language, codified in Antonio de Nebrija's *Gramática de la lengua castellana* of 1492 (the first vernacular grammar printed in western Europe), was not a coincidence. Castilian was seen as the instrument of empire and of dominance over other languages: Arabic and Hebrew. Purity of blood meant also purity of language. On this subject, see Peter Burke, *Languages and Communities in Early Modern Europe* (Cambridge, 2004), 142–44.

17. On the emergence of kin groups in late medieval cities, see Jacques Heers, *Le clan familial au Moyen Age. Etude sur les structures politiques et sociales des milieux urbains* (Paris, 1974).

18. On the construction of a Visigothic past, see *Crónica de Alfonso III*, ed. Antonio Ubieto Arteta (Valencia, 1971). See also Claudio Sánchez Albornoz, *Estudios sobre las instituciones medievales españolas* (México, 1965); Joseph F. O'Callaghan, *A History of Medieval Spain* (Ithaca, NY, 1975), 137–90; Luis García de Valdeavellano, *Historia de España antigua y medieval*, 2 vols. (Madrid, 1988), 2:25–56 and 1:bk. 4.

19. O'Callaghan, *A History of Medieval Spain*, 100.

20. I owe a debt of gratitude to my colleague Ra'anan Boustan for his comments on this topic at a recent meeting.

21. On the Carolingian and post-Carolingian aristocracy, see Barbara H. Rosenwein, *To Be the Neighbor of Saint Peter: The Social Meaning of Cluny's Property* (Ithaca, NY, 1989); for lineages and power, see Teofilo F. Ruiz, *From Heaven to Earth: The Reordering of Castilian Society, 1150–1350* (Princeton, NJ, 2004), chap. 5.

22. See the pioneering work by Marie-Claude Gerbet, *Les noblesses espagnoles au Moyen Âge. XI–XV siècles* (Paris, 1994), chap. 1; and her broad discussion of lineage-formation in ibid., chap. 2. See also the wonderful books by Simon Barton, *The Aristocracy in Twelfth-Century León and Castile* (Cambridge, 1997); Simon R. Doubleday, *The Lara Family: Crown and Nobility in Medieval Spain* (Cambridge, MA, 2001), 9–43; and Margarita Torres Sevilla, *Linajes nobiliarios de León y Castilla, siglos IX–XIII* (Salamanca, 1999), 25–41.

23. See David Warren Sabean, Simon Teuscher, and Jon Mathieu, eds. *Kinship in Europe: Approaches to Long-Term Development (1300–1900)* (New York, 2007), 2–24; Salvador de Moxó, "De la nobleza vieja a la nobleza nueva. La transformación nobiliaria castellana en la baja edad media," *Cuadernos de historia: Anexos de Hispania* 3 (1969): 1–210.

24. On these topics, see Teofilo F. Ruiz, "Two Patrician Families in Late Medieval Burgos: The Sarracín and the Bonifaz," chap. 6 in *The City and the Realm: Burgos and Castile 1080–1492* (Aldershot, Hampshire, 1992). Also see Teofilo F. Ruiz, *Crisis and Continuity: Land and Town in Late Medieval Castile* (Philadelphia, PA, 1994), 196–261; María Asenjo González, *Segovia. La ciudad y su tierra a fines del medievo* (Segovia, 1986), 82–85; María Asenjo González, *Espacio y sociedad en la Soria medieval. Siglos XIII–XV* (Soria, 1999), 437–91; Adeline Rucquoi, *Valladolid en la Edad Media*, 2 vols. (Valladolid, 1987), 1:116–267.

25. This is a much-debated topic. After Robert I. Moore's influential book, *The Formation of a Persecuting Society: Authority and Deviance in Western Europe, 950–1250*, 2nd ed. (Malden, MA, 2007), see also Carlo Ginzburg, *Ecstasies: Deciphering the Witches' Sabbath*, trans. Raymond Rosenthal (Chicago, IL, 2004), and Nirenberg's critique of this position in his *Communities of Violence*, 3–40 et passim. See also Ruiz, *From Heaven to Earth*, 1–36.

26. On territoriality, see Ariel Guiance, "To Die for Country, Land, or Faith in Castilian Medieval Thought," *Journal of Medieval History* 24 (1998): 313–32. For anti-Judaism see José Monsalvo Antón, *Teoría y evolución de un conflicto social. El antisemitismo en la corona de Castilla en la baja Edad Media* (Madrid, 1985); see also my discussion of the position of Jewish and Muslim minorities in northern Castile in *Crisis and Continuity*, 272–82. For a synthetic treatment of Jewish and Muslim life in this period see my "Jews, Muslims, and Christians," in *A People's History of Christianity*, vol. 4, *Medieval Christianity*, ed. Daniel E. Bornstein (Minneapolis, MN, 2009), 265–99.

27. In Castile, sumptuary laws also sought to distinguish between the kings and the nobility, between noble and bourgeois, but the ones aimed at Jews and Muslims preceded these by almost forty years.

28. *Poema de Fernán González*, ed. John Lihani (East Lansing, MI, 1991), 15: "Dezían y afirmavan que los vieron cozer,/cozían e asavan omnes para comer … matavan a las madres, en braços a sus fijos." These charges followed from the "official" royal history of the mid thirteenth century, *Primera crónica general. Estoria de España que mando componer Alfonso el Sabio y se continuaba…* , 2 vols., 3rd repr. (Madrid, 1977), 1:310–13.

29.  Gonzalo de Berceo, *Milagros de Nuestra Señora* (Madrid, 1982), 72–75, 81–83.

30.  A word of caution is due here. As Mark Meyerson and others have shown, it is incorrect to look at the long history of Christian-Jewish relations as one in which the conditions deteriorated inexorably, though most of the examples for fluctuation come from the Crown of Aragon. See, for example, Jonathan Ray, *The Sephardic Frontier: The Reconquista and the Jewish Community in Medieval Iberia* (Ithaca, NY, 2005); two books by Mark D. Meyerson, *Jews in an Iberian Frontier Kingdom: Society, Economy and Politics in Morvedre, 1248–1391* (Leiden, 2004), and its sequel to this work, *A Jewish Renaissance in Fifteenth-Century Spain* (Princeton, NJ, 2005); also Teófilo F. Ruiz, *Spain's Centuries of Crisis: 1300–1474* (Oxford, 2007), 139–63.

31.  Based on Roman law, the *Siete partidas* was a great legal compilation issued in Castile (although it was not formally adopted until 1348) under the sponsorship of Alfonso X between the 1250s and 1270s.

32.  On Abner of Burgos (a fourteenth-century Jewish Converso, who wrote a vitriolic treatise against his former coreligionists entitled *The Wars of the Lord*, and on Jerónimo de Santa Fe see Yitzhak Baer, *A History of the Jews in Christian Spain*, 2 vols. (Philadelphia, PA, 1966), 1:327–54, 2:170–210.

33.  Andrés Bernáldez, *Historia de los Reyes Católicos*, in *Biblioteca de autores españoles*, vol. 70 (Madrid, 1953), 599–699: "Habeis de saber, que las constumbres de la gente común de ellos [conversos] ante la Inquisición, ni mas ni menos que era de los propios hediondos [smelly] judios, ... ansi eran tragones y comilones ... y ansi sus casas y puertas hedian muy mal a aquellos manjares y de no ser baptizados, mortificado el carácter del bautismo en ellos por la credulidad, é por judaizar."

34.  The classical study of the genesis of the statutes of purity or cleanliness of blood is the book by Albert A. Sicroff, *Les controverses des statuts de "pureté de sang" en Espagne du XV^e au XVII^e siècle* (Paris, 1960), 32–36 et passim.

35.  Francisco de Quevedo y Villegas, *Letrilla*, in Turnbull, ed., *Ten Centuries of Spanish Poetry*, 304–8.

36.  All the references and descriptions below are to ms. espagnol 435, at the Bibliotheque nationale, Paris. I have already used this document in my monograph *Spanish Society, 1400–1600* (Harlow, 2001), 75–79, for the purposes of establishing the criteria for nobility. Here I shift my arguments slightly to examine this case for what it tells us about blood. The document uses the spellings *Chirino, Cherinos*, or *de Cherinos*. This was not actually the family name. The names of grandparents and fathers differed from those of their descendants. Last names were only beginning to be established for the "middling sorts" in the late Middle Ages and the onset of the early modern period. Here I will use *Chirino*, except in cases where I am citing a name directly from the manuscript.

37.  See Teófilo F. Ruiz, "The Transformation of the Castilian Municipalities: The Case of Burgos," *Past & Present* 77 (1977): 3–33.

38.  Paris, Bibliotheque nationale, ms. espagnol 435, fol. 34.

39.  Hilario Casado Alonso, "Una familia de mercaderes castellanos extendida por toda Europa: Los Bernuy," in *El triunfo de Mercurio. La presencia castellana en Europa (siglos XV y XVI)* (Burgos: Cajacírculo, 2003), 136–62.

# Chapter 6

# The Shed Blood of Christ

## *From Blood as Metaphor to*
## *Blood as Bearer of Identity*

## Gérard Delille

In the numerous crucifixions, depositions, and entombments he painted between the second half of the fifteenth and the first decade of the sixteenth centuries, Giovanni Bellini at times used the color red to represent the blood of Christ spilt on the ground (*Dead Christ*, Milan, Poldi Pezzoli Museum), and at other times, a whitish gray (*Dead Christ Supported by Angels*, Venice, Correr Museum). This different treatment was not the result of any desire on his part for artistic experimentation, but rather, more simply, was an attempt to meet the contrasting demands of the clients who had commissioned the paintings: "those who believe in blood" ask for red, "those who do not believe in it" ask for gray.[1]

In Italy during the second half of the fifteenth century, debate raged over the question of blood. Dominicans and Franciscans were bitterly opposed over the cult of the Blood of Christ (as over the cult of the Immaculate Conception, which itself turned on a question of blood defilement) during the celebration of Corpus Christi or the Eucharist and, more generally, over the cult that surrounded the relics of the Precious Blood—all cults of popular origin that had spread from the middle of the twelfth to the beginning of the thirteenth centuries. In 1462, the controversy finally came before the pope. The question put to him was the following: did the blood that Christ shed during his passion remain united with the Word and was it, therefore, still worthy of adoration? This question was related to more general issues such as the hypostatic union of Christ's human and divine natures, transubstantiation (in the Eucharist the wine is the real blood of Christ), and the unity of the body's substantial form. The development (*déroulement*) of the debate and the different texts that were submitted are well known thanks to the subsequent publication of these very texts.[2] All of this is set out in the *Dictionnaire de théologie catholique* in the article "Sang du Christ," which describes both the political and doctrinal context of the affair, and I need not go into any more detail on this point.[3] The Franciscans held that the shed blood, once it had been separated from the body, was also severed from the Divinity, from the Word, just as in mortal man the blood is separated from the soul or the "breath" given by God. In the Greek and Jewish traditions, the internal blood circulating within the body is the bearer of that breath, of that soul. Here we may see the traditional dichotomy between *cruor*, or blood that has been shed, and *sanguis*, internal blood. Spokesman for the Dominicans, Domenico Domenici, whose text was published later, mobilized the entire traditional and cultural arsenal around blood as the bearer of life (*sanguis*), from Leviticus ("anima omnis carnis in sanguine est" [the spirit of all flesh is in the blood]) to Saint Augustine, but he also drew on Hippocrates and Galen. He concluded: "et quibus inseparabilita sanguinis a deitate clarus deduceretur" (therefore it is clearly to be concluded that blood is inseparable from the divinity).[4] So in the case of the Divinity the distinction between *cruor* and *sanguis* no longer existed. Might one therefore not conclude, if the same were true at the human level, that blood was not simply the bearer of "breath" but that, in part, it was the source of that breath, or more prosaically, that it contained, produced, and transmitted qualities? As we shall see below, debate in Italy at this time, apparently for other reasons, centered precisely over this latter question with its considerable implications. And a little later, in France, theories of *race* transformed this ideology of blood that had been shed on the battlefield, blood that continued to retain all its virtues, into one of the pillars of the definition of nobility and the "hereditary" transmission of its qualities.[5] For the time being, however, Pius II not only refrained from taking an official position but also prohibited any further debate on these questions (see the papal bull *Ineffabilis summi providentia*, 1464), leaving the field open to civil society. There were a number of reasons for the pope's considerable prudence. The first stemmed unquestionably from the deep rifts that existed both within the bosom of the Church and among the Christian fold over the subject. In fact, sitting on the commission for the Franciscan side, besides the bishop of Ferrara, was none other than Francesco della Rovere, the future Sixtus IV, who, after becoming pope in 1471, would have his own treatise from 1462 published.

In Florence, where an oligarchy put an end to the regime of the guilds in 1382, the problem of redefining the concept of nobility was one of keen importance.[6] Yet in 1400, Coluccio Salutati, author of *De nobilitate legum et medicine*, was still distinguishing precisely between having famous ancestors and ancient blood, the latter of which cannot be used to differentiate among men, since we all descend from Adam ("inolevit illos appellare nobiles, qui maiorum quorum claritate cospicui sunt; non quidam antiquitate sanguinis, quoniam omnes unico descendimus ab Adam"), and was reaffirming the relationship between virtue and nobility, arguing that nobility consists of virtues, not reputation or blood ("vera tamen nobilitas, non in cognizione vel sanguine, sed in virtutibus est")[7] A few years later, however, Salutati did not hesitate to nuance these views, and even to contradict them: nobility certainly must be virtuous, but it does not derive from virtue, nor is it the same thing as virtue. It is the result of a *dispositio nature*, not of an external *qualitas*. Salutati aptly conveyed (*traduit*), a distinction that today we might indicate with the "nature or nurture" dichotomy. In 1429, Buonaccorso da Montemagno composed one of those philosophical dialogues between two imaginary characters, each of whom expounds on his own concept of nobility. This type of presentation became a veritable "literary genre" in the sixteenth and seventeenth centuries. No matter which of the theses was chosen to prevail, the sharp, polemical character of these dialogues had the advantage of clearly exposing the themes and arguments advanced by each participant. Here the first character takes a resolutely "naturalist" position: sons are part of the bodies of fathers who pass on their glory to their sons and then to their descendents. In the medieval tradition, Buonaccorso employs words like *body* or *flesh, transmission, heritage*, but a heritage that is conferred by nature, which is something new. The second character has a different view of the matter: nobility is in the human soul; it is not passed on by human parents but is infused into the body by the gods.[8]

This idea was an ancient one that had been much elaborated during the thirteenth century, when the mercantile and financial "bourgeoisie" had used discriminatory measures to establish the collective responsibility of the lineage and remove the old families of the *magnats* from power.[9] The spokesman for these emerging groups was Dante himself: nobility, he said in the *Convivio*, is nothing more than a "seme de felicitade, messo da Dio ne l'anima ben posta" (a seed of happiness put there by God in the well-placed soul) and may be recognized by its effects, the moral virtues.[10] One cannot reason in terms of antiquity since we all descend from only one ancestor, Adam: if he was noble, we are all noble, if he was vile, then we are all vile. Nobility, inasmuch as it is a gift from God, "non cade in ischiatta, cioè in stirpe, ma cade ne le singolari persone" (it does not attach to a descendancy, to a family, but to single persons), and it is false to say that "because I am from such a family I am noble." A little later, Bartolo da Sassoferrato, an enlightened and pragmatic jurist, expressed this in no uncertain terms: neither God, nor virtue, nor glorious ancestors—what ennobles is service to the city or the prince, "politica et civilis nobilitas."[11] The result was a diversity of situations and definitions of nobility offered up to the view of all. Bartolo's "realist" vision exerted considerable influence and long remained one of the sturdiest bulwarks against the theory of blood. Yet already in the first half of the fifteenth century, the central idea, which was expressed by Dante and by Buonaccorso's second character—that of the unity of the human race, or of the universality and permanence of the transmission of original sin, which prevents thinking of transmission as a process that reserves certain qualities to a particular social group—had fissured in the philosophical and political thought of Italy.[12]

The debate, always extremely polarized, continued, and this is not the place for a detailed analysis; let us simply note that numerous texts from the second half of the fifteenth century tended either to dissociate notions of virtue and nobility (one can have one without the other), or to fuse them all together (virtue is transmitted simultaneously with nobility and a nobleman is necessarily virtuous). In 1528, Baldassar Castiglione stresses the importance of being born noble, since nobility ignites virtue "because in everything nature has placed this hidden seed that extends a force and a property from its beginnings to everything that derives from it, and makes that resemble itself, as we see not only in breeds of horses and other animals, but also in trees where new shoots almost always resemble the trunk" (perché la natura in ogni cosa ha insito questo occulto seme, che porge une certa forza e proprietà del suo principio a tutto quello che da essa deriva, ed a sé lo fa simile, come non solamente vedemo nelle razze di cavalli e d'altri animali, ma ancor ne gli alberi, i rampolli dei quali quasi sempre s'assimigliano al tronco).[13] Natural filiation and filiation by virtue converged. The allusion to breeds of horses was possibly influenced by a French theory of races. In 1537, Giambattista Nenna, a jurist from Bari, has a character in one of his dialogues say that true nobility is that which "has been bequeathed over a very long time as a hereditary gift by ancestors to their successors" (che per lungo tempo da' maggiori a' suoi successori sì come ereditario dono è lasciata); furthermore, that if two brothers present different characters, they probably descend from different fathers, since ultimately everything depends on a "noble or ignoble seed" (da nobile o ignobile seme) without forgetting to specify that nobility depends on the condition and nobility of the father and not of the mother.[14] And in 1548, Marco della Fratta et Mont'Albano, in another philosophical dialogue, has one of the interlocutors launch into a veritable hymn of praise on the *natural* inequality of men: there is no nobility outside of birth and, while nobles may suffer the accidents of fortune, "they never become plebeians, but some of that splendor always shines through in them of those virtues that are born of nobility" (non però giamai divengono plebei, ma sempre in loro traluce alcuno spendore di quelle virtù, che nascono della nobiltà).[15] Alessandro Sardi, in 1586, observes that nobility cannot be taken away from the family; it does not come to an end, unless with the end of the family itself.[16] And Paola Paruta, in 1579, notes that even if the nobleman is excluded from the city's honors, he never ceases to be noble.[17] A few years earlier, in 1574, Stefano Guazzo, reflecting naturalist doctrine, rejects unequal marriages, which abase the blood and produce less courageous children.[18] Finally, in 1588, the published collection *Coutûmes generales du Duché d'Aoste* repeats the traditional classification of the population into nobles and commoners but makes it clear that these conditions are transmitted from generation to generation through the male line. The barrier posed by "heredity" cannot be overcome without obtaining a privilege of nobility from the duke.[19]

In the 1570s, finding himself in the thick of the debate over the reform of the system of the *alberghi*, Leonardo Lomellini, a Genoese who had been heavily influenced by the French theory of race and by the Spanish *limpieza de sangre*, put forward an extreme version of the definition of social groups, one that was redolent of racism: "natural things cannot be changed with inventions … ; being patrician or plebeian, ancient or new proceeds from nature and from the blood"; "distinctions" are not merely civil, but "come from nature itself, which cannot be changed" (le cose naturali non possono con le inventioni scambiarsi … ; et perché l'essere patricio o plebeio, vecchio o nuovo procede dalla natura e dal sangue … le distinzioni … vengono da la natura istessa, la quale non si può mutare). Confusion between those who are naturally noble and others is inadmissible and repugnant.[20]

The die had been cast: naturalist theory, which rested on the idea that qualities are transmitted through "inheritance" and so describe, classify, and perpetuate particular and definite human groups, began to assert its position vigorously in a debate that blended the definition of nobility with social orders, social mobility, the place and function of kinship, the nature and role of blood. Even so, the theory remained only one among several; many continued to defend notions of individual virtue, of divine endowment, of nobility acquired by service to the city or the prince, often over a spectrum of minutely nuanced values and combinations.

In naturalist theory, blood was identified as the substance that transmitted qualities from one generation to the next. Toward the middle of the seventeenth century the great Neapolitan genealogist C. De Lellis summed up the cultural developments I have just sketched in precise and lapidary fashion: "the nobility of families being nothing other than an ancient splendor acquired through virtuous acts and transmitted by the blood to the descendents" (non essendo altro la nobiltà delle famiglie ch'un antico splendore con le virtuose operationi acquistato, e per mezzo del sangue tramandato ne' posteri); such a nobility cannot be lost anywhere or under any circumstances.[21]

In naturalist theory, blood is not the only substance capable of transmitting; semen and also milk were sometimes regarded as having this property. Certain texts urge care in the choice of wet nurses: "let no Moorish woman or descendent of Jews suckle a child of old Christians, since their blood still has the taste of attachment to the old beliefs of their ancestors, and even if they are blameless, the children might acquire some vice in this domain" (Juan de Pineda, 1589); "good or ill morals come essentially from the milk ... which engenders their [the newborns'] blood and their humors which then greatly resemble that of their nurses" (Gutiérrez de Godoy, 1629).[22] The Aristotelian cycle blood/milk/semen engenders the cycle of good or bad morals, of nobility and virtue.

In Venice, from the early years of the sixteenth century, "purity of blood" became the deciding criteria for admittance to the Great Council. The Golden Book of Venetian nobility, which first appeared in 1427, involved the editing and updating of genealogical trees for legal purposes. It was used to verify filiations and to confirm recognized and legitimate blood ties for the purpose of accessing Venetian office. Women played a fundamental role in preserving the purity of blood, and a law of 1414 obliged noblewomen to declare their "immaculate purity," which in essence meant having noble Venetian ancestors. Control over the legitimacy of blood ties, "biological" lineages, and marriages was completed by 1506, with the creation of the Book of Births of All Nobles, followed in 1526, by the Book of Marriages.[23] The "closing" process (chiusura) was now accomplished. In its wake, further closings would be imposed in other Italian states, often much later, after the end of the sixteenth century.

But the social, political, and cultural problems in the case of Italy were not specific to the peninsula. In 1449, the leaders of the anti-tax and anti-monarchy revolt gripping the city of Toledo entrusted the *bachiller* Marcos García de Mora, called "Marquillos," with the task of editing the *Sentencia-Estatuto*, which was intended to be used against "past, present and future" Conversos, and which, by means of a systematic mechanism that excluded lineages, had the effect of keeping these people out of public office. The text, which had some precedents in fourteenth-century Andalusia, was the template for the numerous statutes concerning *limpieza de sangre* that proliferated between the sixteenth and seventeenth centuries. It is worth noting that the *Sentencia* of Toledo did not explicitly mention blood, but spoke rather of the transmission of impurity (religious) and the social and administrative consequences that would result therefrom. The idea of blood was "tagged on" later to this line of reasoning in order to justify the impossibility of wiping away the Jewish or Moorish taint. Arce de Otolora, and later Escobar del Corro, compiled and summarized all the recommendations that had been made with regard to Jews and New Christians in a set of unified doctrinal theories that were founded entirely on anatomic or characterological premises: the seed of the Jew is bad and contains within it a hatred for Christians, his blood bears depraved morals. Nothing, not even the great power of the king, through the possibility of ennoblement that he might accord, can cure this infection.[24] All these aspects connected to *limpieza de sangre* have been widely studied and I shall not dwell on them here. It is worth noting, however, that this doctrine met with strong opposition, not only from the Jesuits (who later yielded to it), but also from a part of the episcopate, which understood the profound religious and doctrinal implications of these statutes. As early as 1449, the Toledo *Sentencia* was condemned by the pope, Nicholas V, in the bull *Humanis generis inimicus*, and in the *Defensorium unitatis Christiana* by the bishop of Burgos, Alonso de Cartagena (himself a Converso): a right of blood as outlined in the *Sentencia*, which determines the social inclusion or exclusion of individuals, is incompatible with the universalism of Christian doctrine and the saving force of baptism, which takes away every impurity and gives birth to a new man.[25] But the Church itself did not take long to give way, for in 1531, Pope Clement VII approved the statutes of Capilla de Reyes Nuevos established in 1530 by the Empress Isabella, which denied access to candidates descended from converts. In 1547, the archbishop of Toledo drew inspiration from the statutes when he banned all New Christians from Spain's leading church, a decision that the pope ratified in 1555, and the king in 1556.

In France, too, the concept of nobility continued to veer away from that of virtue.[26] The term *race* appeared at the beginning of the fifteenth century and "contributed to the development of the idea of a biological and hereditary dimension of nobility, the clearest sign of which was the emergence of the concept of noble blood."[27] We know how the concept and word *race* came to be accepted in the sixteenth and seventeenth centuries; here I refer the reader to the older but still relevant work of Arlette Jouanna.[28] *Race* was used to denote the "family," the "lineage," or in more general terms, the "species." Families or lineages were natural beings whose social personality rested on a foundation which today we would term biological. In fact, noble or common qualities were "hereditary," and hence social inequality went hand in hand with natural inequality. Race is transmitted by blood, which itself is transmitted by men. For Saint-Simon and Boulainvilliers in the second half of the seventeenth century, "blood as the receptacle of virtues became the chain that linked one generation with another, and the guarantor that the past would perpetuate itself in the present."[29] The ideology of race was also the terminus point for the profound transformations of the medieval ideal of shed blood and the gift of blood: in the sixteenth century the nobility claimed to be prodigal with its blood, which it shed in battles or in duels fought to the first blood or to the death, common events in France at that time—expiatory blood that washes away stains, the blood of vengeance, but also the blood of alliances and brotherhood.[30] Blood was the source of political legitimization. In the French context, blood rights were also responsible for setting off a symbolic competition between royal blood and noble blood: the latter claiming to be similar and equal to the former. Nobles had a duty to rebel against a power that destroys blood, a power that was increasingly centralized and absolute, and which tended to rely on competent administrators and no longer to use offices or honors to reward "shed blood."[31]

Here we touch on an essential problem. Within this dialectic/polemic over blood and the transmission of natural differences among human groups that shook Europe from the fifteenth to the seventeenth centuries, the naturalist theory ran up against two fundamental poles of opposition: the Church with its notion of the unity of the human species, which we have already seen, and the State with its notion of "politica et civilis nobilitas." Although the nobilities in both France and Spain never ceased challenging the sovereign's right to ennoble, the outcome of the conflict was rather different in each country. Having put down the revolts, the French monarchy, while appearing to recognize and regulate blood rights through revisions of nobility, continued the practice of ennobling and rewarding the "vile bourgeoisie" in its service. Instead of the ideal of aristocratic prodigality and gift of blood, it offered up an alternative ethic of sacrifice in the service of the state. In Spain, pressed by the Cortes, the Catholic Kings limited ennoblements at the end of their reign. In 1523, Charles V abolished the bestowal of *hidalguía* and so deprived himself of the right to ennoble. Thereafter, access to nobility, as well as challenges or confirmations of nobility were dealt with in proceedings held by the Salas de los Hijosdalgo of the chancelleries of Valladolid and Grenada.[32] The task of defining and conferring nobility was thus abandoned to civil society, which raised the bar for notions of honor, blood purity, and the hereditary transmission of qualities. The monarchy's renunciation of its power to ennoble, no doubt, partly explains why the ideology of blood purity was constructed and expressed in extreme terms, defining social groups on religious bases and rigidly partitioning these groups on the basis of blood. In Italy, the same debates never led to a unified "racist" theory, since the relationship between access to office and ennoblement continued to be a practical reality and the notion of a civil nobility in the service of the prince was never entirely abandoned.

The political usage that was made of theories of *race* or *limpieza de sangre* may be clearly seen in a little-known but illustrative episode in the history of the League of Paris. The assassination of Henry III de Valois on 1 August 1589 paved the way for a possible seizure of the French throne by Phillip II. In 1590, an anti-Spanish pamphlet appeared that was destined to have great success: *Coppie de l'Anti-Espagnol faict à Paris par un catholique françois.* The arguments advanced are of an extreme violence and are purely and simply "racist."[33] Spain is described not as a nation but as a race, "the black race of Africa," irremediably corrupted by the intermingling of ethnic groups and the Jewish and Islamic religions, even if it was fighting against these. There was nothing new about this depiction of Spain: Louis Turquet de Mayerne in his *Histoire d'Espagne*, published in Lyon (1587), had already declared that "over time the noble families of Spain, in allying themselves by marriage with this race [Jews] have been completely contaminated and polluted in their blood and beliefs."[34] In *L'Anti-Espagnol* Phillip II is defined as a barbarian king, an incestuous tyrant, half Jew, half Moor: "Why, what an indignity, what a shame to France that this new arrival, this new Christian whom we have lifted up out of the Koran and the Synagogue, who without us would still be a Saracen or Jew, that he would so much as dare to think of marching against our most-Christian Majesties, successors of the greatest and most ancients Kings in the world."[35]

The order of racial prejudice has been completely overturned: Spain, which preached and practiced ethnic and religious exclusion, is itself, in effect, a corrupted race and its king nothing but an upstart Christian who cannot be compared to the most-Christian and racially pure kings of France. In the case of Phillip II, the allusion refers to the presence of

Jews among his ancestors: Giovanna Henriquez, mother of Ferdinand the Catholic, in fact had Jewish ancestry. This "return to sender" of racial prejudice was in itself not new. In the sixteenth century the citizens of Naples, upon whom the viceroy Don Pedro de Toledo wished to let loose the Spanish Inquisition, were shocked at the methods deployed by the Spanish Inquisition and Spain against its own "peoples" (specifically Jews and Moors, and their religions), whose traits still permeated the Spanish population. In 1547, a popular uprising forced the viceroy to abandon his project, and Torquato Tasso has one of his characters say that the "complexion" and the "humors" of the Neapolitans were not apt to be cured by a remedy (the Inquisition) that was suitable for a body like the Spanish nation infected by "semi de l'opinione moresche de l'ebraiche" (the seeds of Moorish and Jewish beliefs and customs). The accusation leveled against the Spanish royal family of having Jewish or Moorish blood in its veins was one of the bases for the "Black Legend" of the monarchy.

   *L'Anti-Espagnol* was successful in its aims and no doubt contributed to the decision by the Parlement of Paris on 28 June 1593 to reconfirm the validity of the Salic law, thus excluding the Infanta of Spain, Isabella Clara Eugenia, daughter of Elisabeth of Valois, from the French throne. All this would have merely anecdotal value were it not for the identity of the text's author: Antoine Arnauld (1560–1619), advocate in the Parlement of Paris, prosecutor-general, auditor and comptroller of Catherine de Medici's revenues, celebrated orator, Catholic adversary of the League, and most importantly, father of "Le Grand Arnauld," and of Angélique and Agnès Arnauld, the founders of Port Royal. It is clear what current of thought we are dealing with here: Jansenism, Pascal and *Les provinciales*, and Pierre Nicole, co-author with "Le Grand Arnauld" of "La perpétuité de la foi de l'Église catholique touchant l'Eucharistie," an anti-Calvinist work reaffirming the religious and symbolic value of the precious blood of Jesus.

   As Diego Venturino has stressed, we should certainly avoid being excessively judgmental.[36] The assimilation between blood, race, and the hereditary transmission of values, one that was always contested, had no scientific foundation; it derived from a usage and manipulation of representations, symbols, and metaphors. The medieval and early modern eras knew nothing about a notion of "biological heredity," such as would be constructed in the nineteenth and twentieth centuries around the new scientific discoveries, and in this sense we would be mistaken "to attribute to references about blood that were made by the contemporaries of Montaigne and Racine the same meaning that we would to those made in the age of Pasteur," or to rashly dismiss Jansenism and the sum total of noble culture as merely "racist." The use of the term *race* to denote not social class or family but "ethnic" groups did not become generalized until the end of the seventeenth century and during the eighteenth century.[37] After that, things moved very quickly; paradoxically, in his *Essai sur l'inégalité des races humaines* (1853), Gobineau no longer needed to provide a definition of the word *race*.[38] It is true that the aristocratic theory of "the heredity of virtues and privileges is part of an inegalitarian universe of thought that is alien to the paradigm of biological and essentialist racism" as constructed during the nineteenth and twentieth centuries.[39] But the charges against this theory cannot all be cleared, for by imposing a naturalist ideology based on the idea that blood was the origin of and hereditary justification for social, religious, and now even ethnic differences, the foundations for racism were laid.

* * *

The evolution I have attempted to describe and the conclusions I have drawn still do not answer every question. We might well wonder why blood was given the role of fundamental agent in the transmission of hereditary qualities? How it was that in the social and collective imagination, and also to some extent in the scientific imagination, blood replaced the medieval notion that generation was the result of contact between flesh? And why no one came up with an explanation for the transmission of qualities that was based on blood as Peter Lombard had begun to do in the twelfth century when he affirmed the existence of a specific part of the body, inherited from our parents, which transmitted original sin?

In Italy, in the theological, religious, and ideological debates on the problem of human nature, the transmission of original sin, the relationship between the body and the soul, and the use of the term *blood* did not become particularly frequent or systematic until the fourteenth century. Blood was often synonymous with *ischiatta* or *stirpe* (descendancy/lineage/family). In this sense it remained what it had been for a very long time: a metaphor for kinship. In its Indo-European etymology, the word *blood* indicates patrilineal procreation and enters directly into the construction of words having to do with kinship—SW-[E]SŌR, sister, in Proto-Indo-European appears to have meant "the blood internal to a group" and UK-[E]SŌR, wife, "the blood internal to a group, acquired or captured."[40] In the Homeric poems the term for *blood* (*haima*) was used to designate kinship: the *omaimos* were consanguineal relations. The same usage may be found in Latin in *sanguis*: *consanguinei* (which includes natural kin but also adopted family members) and *sanguine coniuncti* (but *cruor*, shed blood, was never used in this sense). The metaphoric use of the word *blood* for kinship does not imply that blood "transmitted" any particular qualities from one generation to another.

In Indo-European traditions blood is connected to the mythologies surrounding the cycle of the seasons; the internal blood of life is likened to the spring (the relationship expands to the trinomen blood/Spring/semen). Ancient Greek could use the same word, *ear*, for blood or spring. In Galen's theory of humors, in which the entire period of the Middle Ages and the sixteenth and seventeenth centuries all were steeped, blood corresponded to spring, to the warm and moist, to air, and so to the breath, to the *pneuma* (phlegm corresponded to winter and to water; yellow bile to summer and fire; black bile/melancholy to autumn and earth). The four humors upon which depended the harmony and health of the body corresponded to the four elements that regulated the harmony of the universe. According to the Fourth Lateran Council of 1215, which conclusively prohibited alliances within the fourth degree of kinship and ratified the doctrine of the transubstantiation: "Quaternarius enim numerus bene congruit prohibitioni coniugii corporalis … : quia quatuor sunt humores in corpore, quod constat ex quatuor elementis." There is a correspondence between the four prohibited generations, the four humors, and the four fundamental elements of nature; to respect the interdiction of four generations was to respect the harmony of the universe.

The contrast is striking between these ever-present Indo-European traditions and those inherited from the Chaldean-Semitic world where the concept of blood was absent from thinking about kinship. When the Old Testament deals with questions of generation or places restrictions on kinship and alliances, it does not use the term *blood*, but rather *flesh*, and also *nakedness* and *shame*—"you will not uncover the nakedness of your father's sister: it is the flesh of your father," or "the two will be one flesh." The same is true for other ancient texts such as the Damascus Document: "If the daughter of a brother uncover the nakedness of her father's brother, when she is the flesh"; or the Temple Scroll: "A man shall not take the wife of his father; he shall not withdraw from her the cloth (of the coat) of his father."[41]

However, the Greco-Roman and Jewish cultural/religious currents converged at another level, one that viewed blood not as the cause but as the support, the vehicle of life, of breath, of the *pneuma* that God or Nature has infused. In Greek, *pneuma* stands for breath and *psycho* (giving us *psyche*, soul) for to breathe. In Hebrew, *rouakh* designates the wind, breath, but also spirit; whence derives an interpretation of the blood sacrifice (the life bestowed by God must be given back to him), an idea which was present everywhere, but particularly pronounced in the Jewish world, and whose survival was prolonged by the well-known dietary restrictions. This sacrificial interpretation was kept by Christianity, which, however, completely reversed the roles: no longer did men offer the blood-soul to God. Now God sacrificed himself and shed his blood, once and for all, for the salvation of men.

Medieval Christianity was the heir to these two traditions, the Jewish and the Greco-Roman, which attributed to blood—on the semantic level, as well as on the level of the interpretations of carnal relations, of procreation, of sacrifices—roles that might be similar or different depending on the case. Nonetheless, until the end of the Middle Ages, blood remained, above all, the blood of sacrifice (as it had been in the Jewish tradition), the blood of Christ's sacrifice as represented in the Mass. Other blood, that is, the blood of men and animals, which no longer had to be sacrificed, gradually lost its importance and its role. Confirmed by the Acts of the Apostles, the prohibition to consume blood or meat from strangled animals continued through the High Middle Ages[42] only to disappear in the wake of other dietary restrictions.[43]

At a political level, with the disappearance of the barbarian dynasties, blood lost its function of legitimizing power. Both Merovingians and Lombards, whose mythological genealogies Paul the Deacon traced in detail, attributed a magic power to the blood of their royal families. In the Carolingians this role devolved on the pope, who, by means of a rite, conferred upon the sovereign the capacity to guarantee God's order on the earth. Blood would "recover" its political functions only gradually.

In Christian thought, the blood of the sacrifice explains and justifies the redemptive water of baptism, which washes away every impurity and ensures the salvation of all. In northern Germany during the last two centuries of the Middle Ages, as Anita Guerreau-Jalabert has emphasized and Caroline Walker Bynum has shown, blood returned again to the center of religious and political debates, and also to the center of exhibitions of popular piety.[44] All segments of medieval society were affected by this interest in blood. In a recent and fascinating book, David Biale shows to what extent theological and philosophical debates in medieval Christian and Jewish communities ran along parallel lines, often turning around the same questions, and how mutual influences, both positive and negative, were strong and persistent.[45] The works of Moses Maimonides, to cite just one example, influenced Abertus Magnus, Duns Scotus, and Thomas Aquinas. In fact, Maimonides was one of the first great thinkers of the Middle Ages to introduce the idea of filiation, of a "hereditary" pathway for the transmission of sociological characteristics. Gradually, in "both medieval Christianity and in Judaism blood came to occupy a central place in conceptions of God and, hence, in the way the

divine ought be venerated."[46] For Catherine of Siena, ingesting the blood
of Christ—the blood that sprang from the wounds, the spilt blood that
was the symbol of death—went far beyond a simple mystical communion. It permitted the body of the disciple to become the body of Christ.
Blood *transmitted* the body of Christ and its divinity.

Jewish thought proceeded along parallel lines, and debate concentrated around problems about the definitions and qualities of substances, in particular, around water and blood. In thirteenth-century
France, Joseph Official held that the redemptive power in the blood of
circumcision (which is drunk by the *mohel*) was stronger than the water
of baptism. Jews and Christians—or rather, we should say, currents of
Jewish and Christian thought that were often in the majority—found
themselves in agreement in asserting that blood surpassed water, which
for Christians meant that the universal redemptive power of baptism
did not completely wipe away the stains and impurities that had been
transmitted by blood. This was the very position that had been condemned by Alonso de Cartagena. From the Jewish standpoint it meant
that conversion or baptism did not really cancel Jewish blood. It was
society as a whole, not a single group or religion, that imposed the ideology of blood—blood that forged and defined identities and maintained
them over the course of generations.

Above all, the new conception of blood also expressed a new conception of kinship. Christianity had imposed an idea of kinship based on
the notion of flesh and carnal relations, and in this it had followed the
Jewish tradition. But it had also inherited the Roman terminology for
kinship. As Anita Guerreau-Jalabert and Bettina Bildhauer have shown,
beginning mainly from the twelfth and thirteenth centuries, Christianity
began adopting the terms *consanguinity* and *consanguineal* in law, while
continuing to think in terms of flesh and the body.[47] Moreover, the sense
of this Roman terminology had itself evolved considerably: as regards
consanguineal relations, the original meaning of *patrilineality* had weakened, indeed disappeared, or had converged with other meanings. Being
consanguineal, a blood relation or of the same blood, now denoted close
or distant kin indiscriminately, through men or women or both, according to circumstances and customs. This is precisely what the contribution by Philippe Moreau on imperial Rome in this volume has shown,
notwithstanding the controversy with Gianna Pomata. Christianity accentuated this transformation, and beginning from the eighth century
the term *consanguinitas* gradually is substituted for *agnatio* and *cognatio*
to indicate a "blood" relationship that prohibited marriage. This was in
effect a cognatic relationship that could be transmitted by men as well
as women. From the second half of the twelfth century the term passed

into civil law where it acts as a substitute for the old Roman notion
of agnation; it was with the "rediscovery" of Roman law that the term
*consanguineal* in civil law again came to be used to designate children
born to the same father, as opposed to uterine children born of the same
mother, or *germain* born of the same mother and to the same father.[48]
Starting from the beginning of the thirteenth century family law centered primarily on questions of filiation and biological reproduction with
important consequences for the interpretation of canonical restrictions.
For Luther, the justification for the prohibitions resided in the hereditary link between parents and children; we are far from the explanations of 1215. The naturalization of family law constituted a pillar upon
which the naturalization of sociological facts would develop and later be
affirmed over the course of the fifteenth and sixteenth centuries.

Starting from the thirteenth century, "the great Tuscan merchant and
banking families asserted their lineal solidarity by endowing themselves
with a family name that was transmissible through the male line."[49] It
was between the fourteenth and sixteenth centuries that the system of
family name and given name became prevalent everywhere. Name and
blood were now linked and the cognatic system of kinship and alliances
waned sharply. The patronym defined groups of continuous and non-
segmentary patrilineal descent, an essential characteristic of which was
to be exogamous. As a general rule, in the fifteenth, sixteenth, and seventeenth centuries one did not marry into the same name—that is, with
one's patrilineal kin. In Burgundy as in Hesse-Saxony (the families of
the Hohenlohe, Solms, Ysenbourg), marriages among patrilineal cousins
without consideration as to degree (these marriages often united distant kin), still numerous in the thirteenth and fourteenth centuries, disappeared almost completely in the fifteenth and sixteenth centuries.[50]
Within the ideology of race, the conjunction of blood and patrilineality
was now complete: "race" was in effect transmitted by blood—in other
words, by men—and it was defined by a name. In a celebrated passage
Montaigne could hardly be clearer about the relationship between race
and patronym: "I have no name which is quite my own: of the two that
I have, one [Montaigne] is common to my entire race, that is to others.
There is a family in Paris and in Montpellier which is surnamed Montaigne ... , as for my name [Michel], anyone who wishes is free to bear
it."[51] Race, as referring to lineage (*stirps generis*) or to a group of people
with the same kin (*familia*), was automatically explained by blood, symbol of filiation. In 1583, François Ragueau defined *race* as "gens, sanguis,
stirps generis, familia quae ab ejusdem ultimi genitori sanguine."[52]

Both in the nobility as well as among commoners, race and patronym
became confused, unless phenomena of segmentation, resulting from

the multiplication of branches or internal splits marking departures or changes of residence (for example, the "upper" Vigilante and "lower" Vigilante of Solofra in Campania in the sixteenth and seventeenth centuries), introduced an internal differentiation within the descendancy by adding a surname or sobriquet (in seventeenth-century Limoges, Cibot-Malinveau and Cibot-Bureau are different races). At the end of the Middle Ages and in the sixteenth century such segmentation was residual, but it was the rule from the tenth to thirteenth centuries: a nobleman, upon taking possession of land that carried titles and functions more important than those he already possessed, would assume the new name and abandon the previous one. Thus, through a series of inheritances the House of Toulouse gave rise to the families Rouergue (late ninth century), Comborn (tenth century), Turenne (late tenth, early eleventh century), Ventadour (late eleventh), and Limoges (early twelfth century).[53] In this case, the groups named, delimited, and identified were segments of descendancy which themselves came to be changed later on. We are worlds away from an idea of race that groups together an ensemble of patrilineal descendents, especially since the segmentations were, more often than not, the result of inheritances brought by women.

The patronymic revolution put an end to these regular fragmentations and imposed a rule of patrilineal continuity. The idea of race, of hereditary transmission of qualities through blood is concomitant to it. The *sanguis* of the fifteenth to sixteenth centuries is no longer that of the Middle Ages: blood transmitted qualities and values that previously had depended upon the relation with God and once again performed a patrilineal classificatory function. The process of naturalizing the world—and many other factors need to be considered—was marked by these new usages, the new symbolic and metaphoric constructs for blood: shed blood, that is, sacrificial and redemptive blood, was now being challenged or supplanted by internal blood, the blood that classified kin, that defined and separated races, the blood that transmitted and in its most extreme representations denied the very notion of redemption. The entire symbolic, cultural, and religious edifice of medieval Christianity was in the process of fracturing.

# Notes

1.  Dominique Rigaux, "Autour de la dispute De Sanguine Christi. Une relecture de quelques peintures italiennes de la seconde moitié du XVᵉ siècle," in *Le sang au Moyen Age. Actes du quatrième colloque international de Montpellier, Université Paul-Valéry, 27–29 novembre 1997* (Montpellier, 1999), 393–403. It should be noted that

flowing blood is sometimes replaced by milk in depictions of executed martyrs by other Renaissance painters.

2. Paris, Bibliothèque nationale, ms. lat. 12,390.

3. Marie-Dominique Chenu, "Sang du Christ," in *Dictionnaire de théologie catholique*, vol. 4 (1939), cols. 1094–97.

4. Domenico Dominici, *De sanguine Christi tractatus reueren. D.d. Dominici de Dominicis veneti, episcopi Torcellani & Brixiensis theologi praestantissimi. Accessit Tractatus eiusdem de filiazione Ioannis Evangelistae ad b. Virginem pulcherrimus. Indicem quaesitorum quarta pagina explicabit* (Venice, 1557).

5. Arlette Jouanna, *L'idée de race en France au XVIᵉ siècle et au début du XVIIᵉ siècle (1498–1614)* (Montpellier, 1981; first ed., Lille, 1976).

6. Claudio Donati, *L'idea di nobiltà in Italia. Secoli XIV–XVIII* (Rome and Bari, 1988).

7. Colucci Salutati, *De nobilitate legum et medicine. De verecondia*, ed. E. Garin (Florence, 1542), 8. The manuscript, dated 1399–1400, was published for the first time in 1542.

8. Buonaccorso da Montemagno, "De nobilitate tractatus," in *Prose e rime de' due Buonaccorsi da Montemagno* (Florence, 1718), 2–97. The manuscript is dated 1429, the year of Buonaccorso's death.

9. Christiane Klapisch-Zuber, *Retour à la cité. Les magnats de Florence, 1340–1440* (Paris, 2006).

10. Dante Alighieri, *Convivio*, ed. Giorgio Inglese (Milan, 1997). The probable date is 1307.

11. Bartolo da Sassoferrato, "Tractatus de dignitatibus," in *In secundam Codicis partem … Novissime accesserunt Additiones Iacobi Menochii* (Venice, 1585). The *tractatus* is a commentary written between 1342 and 1355, on Book XII, "De dignitatibus," of Justinian's Code.

12. Alain Boureau, "Hérédité, erreurs et vérité de la nature humaine (XIIᵉ–XIIIᵉ siècles), in *L'hérédité entre Moyen Age et Epoque moderne*, ed. Maaike van der Lugt and Charles de Miramon (Florence, 2008), 67–82.

13. Baldassar Castiglione, *Il libro del cortegiano*, ed. Amedeo Quondam and Nicola Longo (Milan, 2009; first ed., 1528), 38–39.

14. Giovanni Battista Nenna, *Il Nennio. Nel quale si ragiona di nobilta* (Venice, 1542).

15. Marco de la Fratta et Mont'Albano, *Il nobile. Ragionamenti di nobiltà partiti in cinque libri* (Florence, 1548), 14–20.

16. Alessandro Sardi, *Discorsi del S. Alessandro Sard. Della bellezza. Della nobilità. … Di novo posti in luce* (Venice, 1586), 38–65.

17. Paolo Paruta, "Della perfezione della vita politica libri tre," in *Opere politiche*, ed. C. Monzani (Florence,1852), 35–413. The text dates from 1579.

18. Stefano Guazzo, *La civil conversatione del sig. Stefano Guazzo gentiluomo di Casale di Monferrato. Divisa in quattro libri … i modi, che s'hanno a serbare nella domestica conue* (Brescia, 1574).

19. *Coûtumes générales du Duché d'Aoste, proposées et rédigées par écrit en l'Assemblée des trois États: gens d'église, nobles, patriciens et coûtumiers […] confirmé et approuvé par Son Altesse* (Aoste, 1684; first ed., 1588).

20. See Leonardo Lomellini, *Risposta a Marco Antonio Sauli* (n.p., c. 1575), in Rodolfo Savelli, "La pubblicistica politica genovese durante le guerre civili del 1575," *Atti della società ligure di storia patria* 20 (1979): 82–105.

21. For the quotation, see Carlo De Lellis, *Discorsi delle famiglie nobili del Regno di Napoli*, 3 vols. (Naples, 1654–1671; ed. anast., Bologna, 1968), 3:202.

22.  Sarah Pech, "L'influence des nourrices sur la formation physique et morale des enfants qu'elles allaitent selon les médecins et moralistes espagnols des XVI^ème et XVII^ème siècles," *Paedagogica Historica* 43, no. 4 (2007): 493–507 (with texts of Juan de Pineda and Gutiérrez de Godoy).

23.  Bernard Doumerc, "'De lignée antique et consanguine.' L'idéologie nobiliaire à Venise (fin XV^e–début XVI^e siècle)," in *Le sang au Moyen Age*, 87–108.

24.  See Juan Arce de Otalora, *Summa nobilitatis hispanicae et immunitatis Regiorum … recognita* (Salamanca, 1559); also Juan Escobar del Corro, *Tractatus bipartitus de puritate et nobilitate probanda … Philippo IV latae, Matriti, 10. februarii … 1623* (Lyon, 1637).

25.  Michel Jonin, "De la pureté de la foi vers la pureté de sang: les ambiguïtés bien orthodoxes d'un discours chrétien de défense des *conversos*," in *L'hérédité*, ed. Van der Lugt and Miramon, 83–104. See Alonso de Cartagena, *Defensorium Unitatis Christiana: tratado en favor de los judios conversos*, ed. Manuel Alonso (Madrid, 1943). The manuscript is dated 1449.

26.  Ellery Schalk, *L'épée et le sang. Une histoire du concept de noblesse (vers 1500–vers 1650)* (Paris, 1996; first American ed., Princeton, NJ, 1986).

27.  Maaike van der Lugt and Charles de Miramon, "Penser l'hérédité au Moyen Âge: une introduction," in *L'hérédité*, ed. Van der Lugt and Miramon, 3–40.

28.  Jouanna, *L'idée de race en France*.

29.  André Devyver, *Le sang épuré. Les préjugés de race chez les gentilhommes français de l'Ancien Régime (1560–1720)* (Brussels, 1973), 324.

30.  François Billacois, *Le duel dans la société française des XVI^e–XVII^e siècles. Essai de psychologie historique* (Paris, 1986).

31.  Arlette Jouanna, *Le devoir de révolte. La noblesse française et la gestation de l'État moderne* (Paris, 1989).

32.  Janine Fayard and Marie Claude Gerbet, "Fermeture de la noblesse et pureté de sang en Castille à travers les procès de *hidalguía* au XVI^e siècle," *Histoire, économie et société* 1, no. 1 (1982): 51–75, here 51–52.

33.  Maria AntoniettaVisceglia, "Gli 'humori' delle nazioni. La rappresentazione della Spagna nella Francia del primo Seicento (1590–1635), *Dimensioni e problemi della ricerca storica* 2 (1995): 39–68, here 39–41.

34.  Louis de Mayerne-Turquet, *Histoire générale d'Espagne* (Lyon, 1587), 1298.

35.  Quoted in Visceglia, "Gli 'humori.'"

36.  Diego Venturino, "Race et histoire. Le paradigme nobiliaire de la distinction sociale au début du XVIII^e siècle," in *L'idée de "race" dans les sciences humaines et la littérature (XVIII^e–XIX^e siècles)*, Proceedings from the International Conference held in Lyon (November 16–18, 2000), ed. Sarga Moussa (Paris, 2003), 19–39.

37.  Danièle Lochak, "La race: une catégorie juridique?" *Mots* no. 33 (1992): 291–303.

38.  Colette Guillaumin, "Usages théoriques et usages banals du terme race," *Mots* no. 33 (1992): 59–65.

39.  Venturino, "Race et histoire," 20.

40.  Umberto Rapallo, "Linguistica e antropologia del sangue: convergenze macroreali," in *Sangue e antropologia nel Medioevo: atti della VII settimana, Roma, 25–30 novembre 1990*, Centro Studi Sanguis Christi (Rome, 1993). The publications of the Centro Studi Sanguis Christi were fundamental as a point of departure for this study. I have drawn on them extensively.

41.  *La Bible. Ecrits intertestamentaires*, ed. André Dupont-Sommer and Marc Philonenko (Paris, 1987). See, in particular, Rouleau du Temple, 65–132, here 132; and Écrit de Damas, 141–83, here 152.

42. Jacques Voisinet, "Le tabou du sang dans les pénitentiels du Haut Moyen Age," in *Le sang au Moyen Age*, 111–25.

43. Pierre Bonnassie, *Les sociétés de l'an Mil. Un monde entre deux âges* (Brussels, 2001), in particular chap. 5, "Consommation d'aliments immondes et cannibalisme de survie dans l'Occident du Haut Moyen Age," 143–52. Vanessa Rousseau, *Le goût du sang. Croyances et polémiques dans la chrétienté occidentale* (Paris, 2005).

44. See the chapter by Anita Guerreau-Jalabert in this volume. See also two works by Caroline Walker Bynum, *Wonderful Blood: Theology and Practice in Late Medieval Northern Germany and Beyond* (Philadelphia, PA, 2007) and *The Resurrection of the Body in Western Christianity: 200–1336* (New York, 1995).

45. David Biale, *Blood and Belief: The Circulation of a Symbol between Jews and Christians* (Berkeley, CA, 2007). The book, which is fascinating, deals at length with the medieval period and then goes on directly to the contemporary period, curiously skipping the centuries in between.

46. Biale, *Blood and Belief*, 148.

47. Bettina Bildhauer, *Medieval Blood* (Cardiff, 2006). For Anita Guerreau-Jalabert, see chapter 3 in this volume.

48. On consanguinity substituting for agnation, see Franck Roumy, "La naissance de la notion canonique de *consanguinitas* et sa réception dans le droit civil," in *L'hérédité*, ed. Van der Lugt and Miramon, 41–66.

49. Christiane Klapisch, "Le nom refait," *L'Homme* 20, no. 4 (1980): 77–104, here 78.

50. Gérard Delille, "Parenté et alliance en Europe occidentale. Un essai d'interprétation générale," *L'Homme* no. 193 (2010): 75–136, here 89–90.

51. André Burguière, 1980, "Un nom pour soi. Le choix du nom de baptême en France sous l'Ancien Régime (XVIe–XVIIIe siècles)," *L'Homme* 20, no.4 (1980): 25–42, esp. 25 for the quotation from the *Essais* by Montaigne.

52. François Ragueau, *Indice des droits royaux et seigneuriaux des plus notables dictions, termes et phrases de l'estat et de la justice et practique de France* (Paris, 1583).

53. "Généalogies de la Maison de Toulouse," in *Europäische Stammtafeln*, vol. 3, pt. 4 (Marburg, 1989), tables 763–72.

# Chapter 7

# Descent and Alliance
## *Cultural Meanings of Blood in the Baroque*

### David Warren Sabean

Alliance and descent are the two axes around which I want to think through the different configurations of kinship during the seventeenth century, as evidenced for the most part in literary texts from both the sacred and secular sides of French society. An examination of many such texts suggests that the treatment of blood theologically resonated with models of social circulation and with how people were or could be connected with each other. On the one hand, there is the question of descent, and its corollaries heredity, inheritance, and succession, the axis of relations that works downward from parents to children and over generations; on the other hand, the axis of connections set up through exchange, alliance, and affinity, which tend to configure relations within a generation or abstracted from time. While considerations of how blood works, both metaphorically and in reality, are part of thinking about relationships that we can broadly conceptualize as vertical or horizontal, each of these in turn is subject to a series of different ways of drawing connection: generation, engenderment, conception, substantiation, replication, incarnation, exchange, contagion, and incorporation. The images depended very much on what happens in sexual intercourse and on how generation, or conception, takes place. Blood could be thought of in the generic sense as a link between parents and their children, or in the specific sense, as the connection of children to *one* of the parents. And it could be communicated through lactation as well as through gestation.[1] It could connect the generations, providing particular privileges, obligations, and rights, and it could connect allies in friendship, exchanging the substance of a line, lineage, or *race* with other similar entities. In any genealogy, each consanguineal link could be a conduit of blood, and each alliance, a sharing of blood. It was possible to think of maternal blood as in some way the intermediary or instrument for creating alliance, while conceiving the paternal principle as the agent for the direct sharing of substance, the replication of the line, the incarnation of the father in the son, the self incorporated, as both differentiated in person and substantially the same.[2] In such a model, the maternal principle is nourishing, caritative, cooperative, and indispensable to male continuity, and it can be grasped as a vector for solidarity between allies, a channel for social circulation. As we will see in many texts from the seventeenth century, a group of males, an agnatic line, a house, a *race* could express the marriage of one member with another house as a mingling of blood: an alliance could only be thought of (or could best be thought of) through a language of flows, channels, conduits, coursings, and circulations.[3]

# Kinship in Seventeenth-Century Europe

Before I turn to the texts, I would like to adumbrate a broad argument about the dynamics of kinship in seventeenth-century Europe and suggest that a general and persistent trend toward an ever greater emphasis on lineal thinking, patrilineal practices, and vertical representations set in during the late Middle Ages.[4] Although the movement toward stronger agnatic relationships was *initiated* during the Middle Ages, recent scholarship is finding that thoroughgoing patrilineal systems of property devolution developed only at the passage to early modernity, crucially between 1400 and 1700. In many, but not all regions and social groups, daughters, and then younger sons, came to be excluded from succession in favor of transmission of property and/or status from fathers to one (usually the eldest) son.[5] And in both partible and impartible systems alike, the devolution of property came to be modeled as a downward movement, unaffected by marriage alliances.[6] This shaped perceptions of property as something that belongs to lines of descent and entails lasting legal obligations to members of the family of origin.[7] We find an ever-increasing organization of kinship relations structured vertically and hierarchically around restricted succession to office, rank, and privilege, and around ever more clearly regulated—and often more narrowly defined—inheritance practices.[8]

As verticality, lineality, hierarchy, and familial particularity became distilled from social and political processes, newly constituted agnatic groups reconfigured relationships among neighborhoods, circles of friends, and marriage partners, which themselves invited new kinds of social dynamics and systems of representation. *No family could reproduce itself without creating allies.* Thus while property and office increasingly came to be thought of as a vertical flow, still, complex patterns of circulation among different political and corporate groups and wealth strata also took place in practice.[9] Marriage had to be with "strangers," given the ever more narrowly defined understanding of the line or lineage and the wide circle of prohibited marriages.[10]

# Biblical and Classical Sources for Flesh and Blood

In the seventeenth century, the understanding of how people might be connected to each other was informed by a series of Bible passages: Genesis 2:24, Matthew 19:5–6, 1. Corinthians 6:16, Ephesians 5:31. In Genesis and the New Testament texts, the basic principle is that a husband and wife become "one flesh."[11] More or less explicitly paralleling, underpinning, or overlaying biblical passages were ancient texts by Hippocrates, Galen, and Aristotle on generation, widely discussed during the period, which encouraged a semantic slippage from "flesh" to "blood." In the Galenic understanding of generation, both the male and the female generated sperm—a concoction of blood—that mixed to produce a child, and that model could lead to a description of marriage as a *commixtio sanguinis* or, as in Corneille's *Andromède*, a *mélange* of two bloods.[12] In the Aristotelian account, however, the male and female produce different things altogether—the female provides the matter, or blood, while the male provides form, or sperm.[13] Sperm acts upon blood as a carpenter acts on wood, giving it form, shaping according to idea, acting as a causal principle.[14] Neither of these ways of viewing generation suggests that a child is more apt to be a blood relative of the father than of the mother, and yet—as we shall see—there are writers who maintained precisely this notion.[15]

# Bishop Bossuet and the Blood of Kinship

### The Immaculate Conception and the origins of salvific blood

The writings of Jacques Bénigne Bossuet (1627–1704), the prominent court preacher and ecclesiastical administrator during the reign of Louis

XIV, offer an example of the way particular theological doctrines were reconfigured in the context of new social practices and discourses about family and kin. He represents nicely the recourse to a new language of blood, superseding the older language of flesh, for construing descent and alliance, the former subsumed in expounding the relationship of Christ to Mary, and the latter in explaining the nature of the Eucharist.

Bossuet was a strong champion of the doctrine of the Immaculate Conception, a central tenet of baroque Catholicism, erected as a bulwark against Protestant understandings of the faith. It had been adopted by the Council of Basel in 1439 after three centuries of development and had won over the majority of the Catholic establishment by the end of the fifteenth century, but, at Bossuet's time, had yet to be proclaimed an incontrovertible principle of the Catholic faith.[16] The central issue had to do with the physical relationship between the Virgin Mary and her son, that is, with the connection between her blood and His, between her flesh and His. The problem, of course, could only be imagined within the available frame of ideas of descent, consanguinity, generation, and the unity of the flesh, adapted to fit the constraints of the established theological doctrine of Original Sin. At the heart of the theological debate lay the notion that the conception and birth of a sinless Christ necessitated not just the miracle of a virgin birth but the purity of the flesh He assumed. His conception/birth also had to be a unique occurrence, meaning that His mother's had to have taken place in the normal way, through human sexual intercourse—otherwise there would have had to have been an infinite regression of miraculous conceptions. The "traditional" answer to the conundrum was to understand Mary's flesh to have been purified or sanctified sometime after her conception (the best idea being at the Annunciation, with the Holy Spirit as the vehicle), so that while subject to original sin like all humans she was actually sinless at the time of her son's conception. But, beginning in the twelfth century, the purification of Mary was slowly pushed back to the time of her conception, and with the debates over how to understand all of this, theologians and preachers had to discuss the nature of human sexuality, the physiology of generation, the unity of the human race, the implications of the Fall, the heritability of substance and sin, the dynamics of lineage, and the characteristics of both paternity and maternity.

Theologians following Augustine thought of the union of male and female seed as producing a matter that was itself sinful, *caro peccati*, subject to an *infectio carnis* or *qualitas morbida*, "imprinted quasi physically by the disorderly pleasure from the parents."[17] When God infused a not-yet-corrupted soul, they argued, it was contaminated at the precise moment of its union with the flesh.[18] In a very real way, the most visible expression of the corruption of spirit by unruly appetites, communicated over and over again in each subsequent generation, lies in the human sexual act, with each link in the chain recapitulating or transferring the original defect. In Bossuet's account, the language is of palpable materiality, a semantics of disease, illness, and contagion, and Bossuet's choice of words suggests flows, channels, the natural coursing of fluids: "By the channels of original sin, venom and plague (*peste*) circulate in our nature."[19]

Because Mary was conceived like all other humans, she by that very fact needs the salvation bought for all humans with the blood of her son. Yet she also has to be sinless to pass pure flesh on to her son. But how can she be both sinless (although conceived in the ordinary way) and needing salvation (the universal task of Christ), a gratuitous act where there is no sin? Duns Scotus—among other theologians—seems to have solved the issue for Catholic theology by developing the notion of "extraordinary grace," exercised at the moment of conception, which freed Mary from sin. Christ's sacrificial act is here inscribed backward, so to speak: He acts as a "prevenient Mediator."[20]

In the seventeenth century, blood enters the equation as the specific substance involved in the double miracle of sinless conception—both Mary's and her son's. But how does this framing of blood work? In two different ways: Christ's blood is necessary for the prevenient action that makes Mary pure, and the blood that Mary carries and gives to her son (from which He is made, that which makes Him man) has to be pure, in turn.[21] The purity is circular, like the flowing of blood itself, and this circulation is the essential communicating element between mother and Son, Son and mother. As Bossuet puts it, that blood of the Son that saves Mary is the very blood that was taken from her chaste body.[22] Jesus gives His blood to all the faithful, but He acquired it from her. In fact, the conception of Mary is the first source of the blood of Christ.[23] Bossuet uses the analogy of a fountain that sprays water into the air, which then falls back to rejoin its source. He also thinks of this blood as a running stream (the French verb is *couler*), which flows through our veins through the ingestion of the Eucharist. In fact, Bossuet considers that the blood that circulates among members of the Church and the flesh that unites its members, that embodies it, is in some essential way Mary's flesh and blood.[24] "Her blood flows [*est coulé*] in our veins through the sacraments."[25]

In this understanding of generation and alliance, it is blood that transmits the essential properties from parent to child and the same blood that links people together in alliance. In fact, Bossuet sees a parallel between ingesting the eucharistic sacrifice and sexual intercourse, which derives from his understanding of the circulation of blood.[26] It is also closely tied up with the idea of a woman as the necessary instrument for the male strategy of transmission: in incarnation, uniting the substance of God with the substance of man, God's paternity is at heart an alliance through a particular woman that, in turn, is the center of a larger, more encompassing alliance. The central idea of circularity—whereby the blood of Jesus intervenes preveniently to purify Mary's blood at the moment of her conception—is similar to the Aristotelian notion that in the generative act male form acts in such a way on female matter that the blood of the child can be said to be that of the father. Jesus (the son) as God (the father) secures His own blood and determines His own succession.

### From a language of flesh to a language of blood

A key problem in understanding the centrality of blood in Bossuet's representation of the descent and alliance problematics lies in a central shift in language, from flesh to blood, subsequent to the fifteenth century.[27] My hypothesis is that the ever-greater stress on lineage in the social and political lives of Europeans from the Renaissance onward paralleled the development of a semantics of blood both in cultural and theological discourses.[28] According to the detailed account by Marielle Lamy of the development of the doctrine of the Immaculate Conception from the twelfth century onward, it appears that all the way into the fifteenth century the terms of discourse were of "flesh" not "blood."[29] There is almost a strictly *biological* necessity for the Word to assume an innocent flesh. And the fleshly unity of Mary and Jesus, mother and son, is modeled on the unity of spousal flesh—always already implicitly a sexual union: Jesus is "bone of her bone and flesh of her flesh"—the same language to be found in Gen. 2:24, when Adam claims Eve.[30]

It appears that well into the sixteenth century, flesh remained the central conceptual tool, giving way primarily to blood during the seventeenth century.[31] The interesting anonymous text from 1515, *Le Defensoire de la conception de la glorieuse Vierge Marie*, still considers the doctrine of the Immaculate Conception and the relationship of Mary to Jesus in terms of "body" and "flesh," with practically no reference to blood.[32] The problem elucidated concerns the precise way in which original sin is transmitted from generation to generation and the relationship of parents to progeny. The emphasis on lineage and line that seems to motivate Bossuet's adoption of a language of blood is missing here. In fact, this Mary marks an abrupt break with the sinful *masse* of Adam and all those of his generation: she and her son have only one flesh, while her parents are not one flesh with her.[33] Here the key concepts are flesh, body, *masse*, and seed. And seed is associated with *masse*—that is, with a substance that one can think of as solid or "doughy," not with blood, a fluid coursing down through the generations.[34] The accent is on the sexual act. The author imagines the body to be like a "whore," which corrupts the pure soul provided by God.[35] All flesh generated by male seed is corrupt, morbid, and susceptible to the *fomes peccati* once joined with a soul.[36] So Christ is excepted because he was not generated by seed, and Mary excepted through divine intervention and a disaggregation of her flesh from the seed (*masse*) of her parents.[37]

A slightly later consideration, a dialogue by Nicole Grenier, a canon regular of Saint Victor, published in 1549, dealt with many of the same issues, and here again, the discussion centers completely around flesh and shows no interest in blood. The late medieval notion of prevenient grace is central to the argument, but so also is a stress on the role of male seed in the propagation of original sin.[38] According to the law of human propagation, writes Grenier, a blot or stain (*macule*) is communicated to the newly constituted body.[39] This process is grasped in terms of a "contagion," which communicates to the newly generated human body a fetid quality, an inevitable stain (*tache*). This blemish (*souillure*) and corruption dwells in the flesh and infects the soul too when it is joined to the body, just as a pure liquid is corrupted by a soiled vessel.[40] In a sense, there are two conceptions, the first through the mixing of parental seed and the generation of a body, and the second when the rational soul is infused into the body.[41] Christ is unique in that he is not conceived through *male* seed—and the stress throughout the treatise is on male seed—but he is also not conceived through the action of female seed. The same point about male seed or the seed of Adam is part of orthodox Christian argument but reiterated in discussion of the Immaculate Conception doctrine; for example, the seventeenth-century saint, François de Sales, explained that Christ was of the *masse* of Adam but not of his seed.[42] And Grenier explains the action of the Holy Spirit on Mary as like the action of a dye on pure, white wool.[43] Mary, of course, was conceived in the ordinary way, but *her flesh* was preveniently preserved by the *flesh* of Jesus Christ, because His flesh was her flesh.[44] Once again, the spousal passage of Genesis 2:24 is brought to bear to explain the relation of Mary's flesh to that of her son.[45] The mother was destined as spouse.[46] Our redemption begins with the Immaculate Conception, the corporeal substance of Christ. [47]

## Bishop Bossuet on descent and salvific blood

In a sermon on the Nativity, Bossuet quoted Saint Bernard to the effect that the finger of God composed the flesh of the Son from the pure blood of Mary.[48] Here, it seems to me that Aristotelian categories work well, since in ordinary intercourse, according to them, the male sperm is thought of as producing form, as something spiritual, as mental, while the female provides the material substrate necessary for the formation of a child, the blood.[49] Form and matter together produce substance. Here Mary offers the same material conditions as other women, but the conception takes place outside the normal conditions of physical intercourse. In the process of fixing the maternal blood, the Holy Spirit drew into her chaste womb (*flancs*) that blood that washed away our sins. Once again, the blood that Christ sacrificed was Mary's blood—the pure distillate, given form and direction through the divine "germ," idea, or spirit, was actuated, made efficacious, by a male principle.[50]

At this point Bossuet went on to the issue of Mary's genealogy. Again it is a matter of blood. Mary is the conduit of royal blood but has the particularity of being the immediate source for Jesus. "She has the blood of kings and patriarchs in herself with a particular dignity, because she has it in order to pour (*verser*) it directly into the person of Jesus Christ."[51] Precisely the notion of channel is used here—Mary is the sacred channel through which the blood of kings and patriarchs reaches Christ.

## Did Bossuet have some doubts?

In a late work, published only after his death, Bossuet discussed the relationship of the Son to the Father. God can only be *named* "Father," even though he carries the Son in His womb (*sein*) eternally. God conceives in Himself and carries in Himself His fruit, who is coeternal. "While He is uniquely father, and the name of mother, which is attached to a degenerate [*dégenérant*] sex, imperfect in itself, is not suitable for Him, still He has always a maternal-like womb [*un sein comme maternal*] where he carries His Son."[52] In this account, Bossuet seems to be following classic Aristotelian ideas.[53] The stronger the formative male principle, the more the offspring resemble the father. In the act of eternal generation, Christ is the same substance as God: "immaterial, incorporeal, pure, spiritual."[54] So when Christ is born in time, the act of the celestial father is to extend His eternal generation in Mary.[55] The Son receives from the Father the same substance, without any division. In fact, whenever we speak of a son and father, we understand the former to be another self (*lui-même*) of the latter. By the act of engendering, the child is made to be what its father is.[56] This account fits readily into contemporary representations of male lineage constructs that treated women as problematic intrusions, as deficient and "degenerate," but also mediate and instrumental, as vessels for the reproduction of male *soi-mêmes*. In this text, at least, Mary (as woman) is an ambivalent figure.

## Bishop Bossuet, the Eucharist, and models of alliance

Bossuet's account of the Eucharist draws on material metaphors of marriage. The Eucharist celebration is a "consummation of sacred marriage," an act of incorporation, in which the celebrant becomes bone of Christ's bone and flesh of His flesh. Once again, as we have seen above, the blood that we receive is that of the Virgin: "Her blood flows (*est coulé*) in our veins through the sacraments."[57]

Bossuet's theological arguments resonate continuously with contemporary understandings of lineage and the transmission of paternal substance. The central problem in the management of property was to construe the line as the channel along which rights and obligations flowed. Bossuet finds the language of conduits and circulation useful to model the relationship of the *humanation* of the Son Jesus to the eternal paternity of God. The properties of the heir cannot be abstracted from the materiality of the actual flow of blood from parent to child. And that blood in the vessel of a woman could only be actualized, given form, or purified through agnatic intervention. In Bossuet's final thoughts on the subject, God Himself supersedes Mary as mother, since just as for a male lineage, the instrument by which the line is reproduced is of secondary importance, a threat to paternal transmission, a problem for continuous agnatic purity. The stronger the male power in the act of conception the more the image of the father is to be found in the son. And yet it is the blood of a woman that is essential to the construction of alliance. Without mediation, no line could reproduce itself, and without the wider set of allies connected through the blood of the spouse, no line could overcome its isolation.

# Corneille and the Blood of Heredity and Alliance

## Lines of blood: The question of legitimacy

In the Middle Ages, lineage and line, and kinship relations in general, were not modeled on and did not derive their metaphors from blood. The blood language is absent from both religious and civil discourses, except in the term *sang royal*, which is known from the fourteenth century.[58] But, by the seventeenth century, such a discourse was fully available, as we have already seen in our exploration of the logic of the Immaculate Conception doctrine. André Devyver has provided a great deal of evidence to show that a shift in vocabulary and in the symbolics of self-understanding within the French nobility took place in the decades after 1560, precisely around a notion of purity of blood.[59] And with that went a refusal by noble families of alliance by marriage with those bourgeois families considered desirable during the fifteenth and early sixteenth centuries. Both nobles themselves and their self-conscious defenders began to talk about the blood of ancestors running in their veins, and about that blood being the receptacle for psychic and moral virtues.[60] Other key expressions of baroque noble culture made their appearance in the second half of the sixteenth century: "noble de race" by 1550, "lignage" in 1549, and by the end of the century "sang clair," "sang épuré," "sang ancien et illustre, "sang bleu."[61] And by the time one gets to Madame de Sévigné, we find an expression like "good blood does not lie" actually in use.[62] Devyver cites one writer, J. B. Nenna, who, writing on the nobility of race, explicitly tied the purity of noble blood and the purity of Christ's blood together as a conceptual pair.[63] What is important to understand in this new discourse of blood is that it stressed the male principle of devolution. After 1560, the primacy of the paternal line was no longer contested. And a memoirist like Gaspard de Saulx-Tavannes simply assumed male transmission of seed/blood, citing Aristotle about the degeneracy of the female. Taking the primacy of paternal principles for granted, he expressed the key idea that like engenders like.[64]

The argument here is that a consideration of kinship in terms of blood developed with the rise of lineal thinking and the adoption of ever-stricter agnatic forms of property devolution, restricted processes of inheritance or succession, such as found with primogeniture and genealogical constructs favoring male lineages. Blood became a metaphor for handling issues of purity and legitimacy but was also palpable matter; real blood flowing through the veins of fathers and sons distributed both privileges and moral obligations and formed the basis for political and social practices. There are many texts that I could take to explore these issues and to compare with the theological representations to be found in Bossuet and many of his fellow clerics. A good place to begin to examine secular texts is with the dramatic literature of Bossuet's contemporaries, precisely those plays staged for the entertainment of the nobles gathered around the French court. What follows is a systematic reading of the dramas of Pierre Corneille, a writer who continuously focused on the problematics of descent and alliance, more often adumbrating social dilemmas than providing particular solutions.[65]

In Le Cid, the conflict that will be explored through the action of the play begins when the royal counselor Diègue (a father) charges Rodrigue, le Cid (his son), with the task of avenging an insult that just happens to have been delivered by Rodrigue's father-in-law-to-be.[66] In obligating Rodrigue, Diègue uses the language of shared substance: "my blood." That people could actually talk this way is attested by a letter of Madame de Sévigné to her cousin, addressing him as "my blood," and talking about the mutual blood circulating in their veins.[67] Chimène, Rodrigue's betrothed, uses the same construct when she remarks that her blood is her father's blood: indeed the blood on Rodrigue's sword that killed her father is hers. The construction resembles Bossuet's understanding of Christ's sacrificial blood being that of Mary. In both cases, the parent's blood is substantially the same as the child's.[68] Rodrigue makes the same point: as son, he is blood of his father.[69]

In *Horace*, Corneille uses an account of war between Rome and the city of Alba to intertwine issues of descent and alliance with patriotism, filial duty, allegiance to the state, and attachment to family. Each of the dramatic roles provides an occasion to think through different positions. Both Horace and his father see blood strictly in terms of agnatic succession and the in-marrying wife as incorporated into their family. Sabine, Horace's Alba-born wife, counters that marriage does not erase earlier ties and responsibilities; it does not abolish the profound character of attachment to origins. Nature establishes such ties as a matter of first right. Indeed, while anyone can choose a spouse, no one can choose siblings, and they continue to provide an essential identity—they are *nous-mêmes*.[70] The blood ties arising from common descent are ascribed, derived from the incontrovertible natural facts of procreation. One cannot choose one's family of origin.

Throughout the Cornelian oeuvre, having the same blood explains the action. Descent provides an identity of material substance to parents and children, siblings, and even members of the same nation, all considered as engendered, embodied, and incorporated through material sanguinary channels. The resemblance to Bossuet's arguments is marked: blood transmits essential properties from parent to child and constructs a material identity among individuals of the same lineage.

The material flows of blood are part of a complex transmission of material substance. Thus descent through proper bloodlines distributes rights and legitimizes claims to the possessions of the lineage. Corneille explores this theme frequently as it touches on matters of royal legitimacy and rights of succession. But blood even binds together people unconnected by direct descent. We will deal later with notions of marriage as the mixing of blood of two families or lineages. Here, it will suffice to note the presence of a sense of blood "passing" from a father to his sons-in-law. Agésilas, the eponymous hero of another of Corneille's dramas, for example, confronting his brother Lysander over the proposed marriages of the latter's daughters, says that Lysander's blood will pass entirely from him to his sons-in-law.[71] Thus while marriage, which involves contract, decision, and choice, is not inherently "natural," there is a sense in the argument that the passage of blood it entails, just like that in descent, mediates ascribed obligations.

## Sequence of birth and succession

In the mechanics of inheritance or succession, blood is key but not in itself sufficient to establish particular rights or claims; sequence of birth and gender also come into play.[72] In *Nicomède*, Queen Laodice of Armenia, who is living at the court of her guardian, King Prusias of Bithynia, is being courted by two of Prusias's sons—Nicomède, eldest and heir to the throne, and Attale, the younger half-brother, who has been raised in Rome, having been taken there as a hostage. Laodice treats the younger suitor with contempt, calling him a "mere bourgeois" and "subject" because he is not the first-born and presumed successor.[73] As a queen she will only contemplate marrying an equal, namely Nicomède, the royal heir: blood is one thing and rank another. Rank order of birth determines deference and life chances. Attale should be looking to lower ranks for an alliance—to the daughter of a tribune. The sequence of birth determines the order of respect, master and subject.[74] In a conversation with King Prusias and the Roman ambassador Flaminius, who is seeking to prevent any expansion of Bithynian power, Nicomède champions the notion of nature, namely that generation *and* birth order together determine claims and rights. He puts the political issue this way: "I have enlarged the realm of Bithynia, but Rome wants to divide up the power, and in this project, the prince [his half-brother Attale] is too well born to be my subject. And I ought to give up the goods of my ancestors or the price of my blood to put him in my rank."[75] When the ambassador says that Rome would be satisfied if Attale married Laodice, thereby preventing Bithynia and Armenia from being united under one crown, and urges King Prusias to command her to marry Attale, Nicomède protests that she has full freedom as queen. Prusias makes the point that love has nothing to do with alliances among princes, which must be concluded according to reason of state. Having been persuaded that Bithynian state interest is best sustained by accepting the Roman position, he goes on to threaten Laodice, telling her to decide between destruction of her country and deposition from her throne on the one hand, and marriage to Attale on the other.[76] To the Roman ambassador, Laodice insists that Attale is not of sufficiently high status: "I regard him as a common soul and a man better born for another fortune, more my subject than my spouse, and the conjugal knot would not be able to overcome the unequal rank."[77] Later, in a pique, Nicomède leaves everything to his brother, hoping this will persuade Attale to drop his suit of Laodice, but repeats that Laodice is free to make her own decision. Prusias is incensed that his son Nicomède would abandon his estate for a woman, but Nicomède tells him that this act will not jeopardize his accession to the throne; that he will be recalled to the kingdom to assume the throne when Prusias dies: "The old right of the eldest is so strong that to fill a throne, it would recall the absent one. I will do for myself what I have done for you [reconquer rightful possessions]."[78]

## Linking "houses," political groups, cultures, alliance, and circles of kin

A central aspect of the rhetoric in Corneille's representation of the dynamics of kinship has to do with blood as a vector of alliance. Although sometimes this can be understood metaphorically, the widespread assumptions about the exchange of fluids in intercourse always point to a substantial, carnal, physical link that carries moral weight. Blood binds together "houses," political and ethnic groups, circles of kin, lineages, clans, nations, and cultures through the strategic marriage of "strangers." Just as much as descent is understood as a passage of blood along generations, alliance is represented as a coursing of blood among horizontally positioned groups. The former implies the idea of an apical ancestor, whose substance is communicated through progeny, whose proximity and obligation to each other in turn are determined by the degree to which they share in that substance, while the latter involves the image of a nodal pair, whose substantial union also determines relationships of nearness and distance within the field of relationships.

Corneille also organizes dramatic action around such nodal pairs. In *Le Cid*, Don Rodrigue (the Cid) and Chimène are engaged to be married, the point being to link their houses by "sacred bonds" through a marriage arranged by their fathers.[79] Similarly, Lysander in *Agésilas* wants to unite his blood with that of a Persian nobleman by making the latter his son-in-law.[80] In *Polyeucte*, Félix, the Roman governor of Armenia, arranges a political marriage between his daughter, Pauline, and the high Armenian noble, Polyeucte. The alliance Félix aims at is meant to bring together two different nations, states, social orders, and cultures.[81] One marriage, of course, can be followed by many more. In yet another setting, Corneille has the Roman general Sertorius, in the tragedy bearing his name, consider marriage with the Spanish Queen Viriate. That would begin a series of marriages between the two nations—thousands would follow and "would chain one to the other, mixing so well blood and common interest that they would soon reduce two people to one."[82]

## Blood exchanged or mingled between families, lineages, houses, and cities

Up to now, we have been looking at marriage as an exchange moment between different kinds of groups. Now the issue is to look at the way the texts reveal concerns about blood, mixed, exchanged, mingled. In a confrontation with her father, the Roman governor, Félix, who is caught in the dilemma between imperial law condemning Christians and paternal sentiment, Pauline, the wife of the convert Polyeucte, says that by marrying her Polyeucte *has become Félix's blood*.[83] Pauline's argument is a classic statement of alliance. Her marriage has made the two men so close that they are to be considered to be of the same blood: the daughter/wife conveys the father's blood to the son-in-law. She is the conduit or channel for the coursing of blood both between generations and between allies. In the last act, Pauline uses the terms *nature* and *love* to refer to her relationships with her father and her husband, respectively.[84] In this construction, nature, blood, and birth are ascribed characteristics, creating primary loyalties and duties crucial to the moral order. Love, in contrast, is negotiable, derivative, created, and dependent. It too is part of the moral order, but it is situational and follows from primary obligations. Still, it has two aspects, one related to the senses and passions, suspect, transient, creating no permanent attachment, and the other part of the rational order, derived from social facts or the consequences of primary allegiances, assumed and permanent. Alliance, in turn, can be viewed from different angles: the exchange relationship set up between two families, lineages, or houses, with all of its different in-law connections, hierarchies, intimacies, and distances; and the particular couple, the nodal point in the wider system of reciprocities, the individuals who are exchanged, whose marriage provides the structural permanency, and who are charged with the reproduction of the system through the bearing of children. All of the images of becoming one blood assume the exchange of fluids in intercourse. At the end of *Polyeucte*, in which both father and daughter are converted to Christianity following the martyrdom of the son-in-law/spouse, the blood of the spouse falls upon his wife with salvific effect: thus proclaims Pauline, "by the beneficial blood you see me baptized."[85]

## Place of women in alliance

In almost all of Corneille's plays, alliance is a matter of agnatic lineages, royal houses, or parents arranging for the marriages of their children, with a strong sense that it is women who are exchanged between lines. Nonetheless, women are actors in their own right. They may have to obey in the end, but when they consider a marriage problematic, they try to negotiate. In many situations, especially in the comedies, the trick is to get the parents to come around to support their children's inclinations. Nonetheless, without exception, the young women maintain that the ultimate decision is in the hands of their fathers (or failing them, their mothers or brothers charged with paternal responsibilities and powers). A clear distinction is made between love that is based on mutual attraction and the kind of love that makes for a settled marriage. The latter always is accompanied by reason—and, frequently, "reason" is understood to be what proceeds from paternal authority. Love based on sexual attraction is too unsteady and impermanent to be the foundation of a long-lasting marriage, and in the context of infrequent divorce, the decision is too important to leave to sentiment. Given these exigencies, it is still the case that women have claims (an expectation to a marriage of suitable status, for example) as well as obligations, and they are actors in their own right. They are frequently the key players in keeping an alliance alive and mediating between agnatic groups.

The factors that place women in mediating positions between different groups are explored in *Horace*. Sabine opens the play by observing that by virtue of her marriage to Horace, she has become Roman.[86] This suggests rules of patrilocality and the assumption of a new status through marriage. There is never any hint that Horace has become Alban through marriage. Sabine, as befitting the position of woman-as-connecting link, as the person who gets uprooted yet maintains sentiments, passions, and desires connected to her family of origin and her country of birth, is caught in the dilemma of loyalty to warring families and warring fatherlands. She is Roman because her husband, Horace, is Roman, but she nevertheless retains her sentimental attachments to the place of her birth. Birth matters and blood matters. By distinguishing her position from that of a slave, Sabine suggests that, marriage notwithstanding, she continues to have the rights and claims of a free person; her position, poised between two cities and two families, is an active one, one of mediation. She points out that Romulus came from Alba, and that Rome originated in Alba; that Roman blood stems from the Alban kings, and—with a shift in metaphor—that Rome now points its weapons at the breast of its mother. In any event, she finds herself suspended, hating whichever side wins and weeping for whichever one loses. Horace actually kills her three brothers in battle and then also his sister, who has dared suggest that *her* own sentiments are less tied to her Roman blood, and to Horace's glory, than to her hope for marriage, love of Curiace, and expected incorporation into another state. Sabine cannot cease lamenting her brothers. Horace, however, expects her to stop mourning, observing that "if the absolute power of a chaste passion allows us both only one thought and only one soul, it is for you to raise your sentiments to mine and not for me to descend to the shame of yours."[87] While he expects her to be more a wife than a sister, her response is to make a distinction between the public and the domestic realms. In public, it is all right to celebrate Horace's victory, but at home she should be capable of mourning her brothers, though they were fighting on the losing side; she is not willing to forget the loss of her brothers. Corneille has the city of Alba play the female to Rome's male. It is the Alban king, not the Roman Horace, who stops the battle; and he does so on grounds that the two cities are allied, one blood. No Roman hesitates to pursue the conquest. Alba is sometimes portrayed as "mother" of Rome, at other times as the origin of its wives. Horace will not tolerate divided loyalties; he demands absolute loyalty and power. He even kills his sister over her suggestion that the alliance between the two cities is one of balanced reciprocity. Sabine is not prepared to give up the ties that come from her family of origin, which are rooted in nature and provide precisely the identity that distinguishes a wife from a slave. She continues to argue that she is responsible to both necessary ties (of birth) and voluntary ties (of marriage). In the end, however, she is clear that the blood of lineage trumps alliance.

The obligation of women to defend the family is crucial to the argument in *Pompée*, where the action is driven by the civil war that made enemies of the former triumvirs Pompée and Julius Caesar. Cornélie, the widow of Pompée, is destined forever to identify with her deceased spouse.[88] In fact, because he is not alive to release her from her obligations toward him, there is no possibility for her to act according to her own free will and make peace with Caesar. A chasm divides Cornélie and Caesar forever, she declares. Throughout, her interests and positions vis-à-vis other people are strictly tied to her husband. She has two stories to tell about herself—descent from a Roman hero and two marriages, both to Roman heroes. Her motivations are sorted out in such a way as to have the precepts of cultural Romanness dictate the solution to her conflicting loyalties. She acts most Roman when she acts in tandem with the house into which she married, where she can carry out her duty. Thus she must ally against Caesar, with Pompée's sons, as well as with the sons of Cato and other kin.[89] In some ways, the play suggests, the split in interests between Caesar and Pompée could have been overcome if the latter had lived to submit to Caesar and to be pardoned by him. But his death precludes forever submission by the wife. Cornélie can admire Caesar, find him honorable, and even support him against some of his enemies. There is a proper way to oppose him and an improper one—the former Roman, the latter un-Roman.

The transfer of loyalties to the family into which one has married is developed also in *Polyeucte*, with the further complication introduced by conflicting religious loyalties. When a confidante tells Pauline that by his conversion Polyeucte has become an enemy of the state and thus someone she must revile, Pauline replies that her love is from duty, and that her duty and virtue are not at all dependent on her husband's beliefs or actions.[90] Pauline embodies the ambiguous position of a married woman. She obeyed her father blindly and immediately when he commanded her to marry Polyeucte, in the act extinguishing a great love, in accord with the "laws of birth." Now married, her duty is to her husband, whose embrace of a proscribed religion has placed him, and her with him, in conflict with her father and the state. As the mediate character, the daughter/wife, she is not free, except to fulfill the duties of both offices, but being both daughter and wife, she can act as go between. Her marriage has made her father and husband so close that they are to be considered of the same blood. She has to balance between nature (attachment to father) and love (attachment to husband).[91] Unlike her first love, this love is based on "reason," as conveyed by paternal command.

This obviously pre-Kantian understanding of morality accepts that the "ought" can be derived from what "is," all of which, of course, is believed to have been ordained by God. But morality in seventeenth-century understanding cannot be detached from will. Corneille's voluntarism fits very well within the theological argument of the period, especially with the wide-ranging debate over the nature of law and of morality—whether law, and therefore moral action, proceed from the will of God or the king or the state, or whether there is a good in itself; that is, that God does the good, rather than that the good is what God wills. In a sense, this debate spills over into the one about the nature of the aristocracy or royalty, with the idea that blood carries inherent qualities, the blood of the highborn incarnating the most prized moral qualities. This debate, with its many ramifications, is carried on between Cleopatre and her brother, Ptolomée, in *Pompée*.[92] The king is of the opinion that the exercise of will governs moral and legal action and, furthermore, that the will of the king determines the justice or injustice of a specific act. His sister essentially argues against the voluntarist ethical position that establishes law as an expression of the will of God (the "gods" here) or the will of the prince. She clearly thinks that there is honorable or moral action as such and that it is beneath the highborn to act otherwise. Therefore, by implication, if a king acts unjustly, it is because of the counsel of base advisors. Ptolomée says explicitly that anything a king orders for the good of the state is just. Asked why she had supported Pompée when Caesar is in love with her and she can get everything from him, Cléopatre answers: "Princes have something from their high birth; their soul receives impressions in their blood, which orders their passions under their virtue; their generosity submits everything to their glory."[93]

## Ascriptive vs. negotiated obligations

Earlier I alluded to the distinction between ascriptive obligations that are established by nature and negotiated duties worked out in exchanges of friendship and alliance. *Le Cid* relates a story in which inherited blood has ascriptive power and takes priority over relationships based on negotiation and choice. The plot moves toward an aporia, where members of two families are honor bound to kill each other despite conflicting desires, and Chimène, finding no resolution for her ambivalent motives, plans to kill herself right after her lover's death.[94] In *Polyeucte*, Pauline distinguishes between "nature" and "love."[95] Nature, a matter of blood and birth, determines primary loyalties, obedience, and ascribed duties. And nature is the foundation of the moral order. For her, love is a derivative concept, a result of fulfilling primary obligations. When love is based on attraction or passion alone, it is transient and cannot be the foundation for permanent relationships. But when it is rooted in nature, in the natural order, in the facts of birth, or secondarily derived from an alliance based on the wishes of paternal authority, it also is fundamental for the moral order. In this Christian drama, the only challenge to the blood of families is Christ's salvific blood, the model for the blood of martyrs as the seed of the Church, a point made categorically by Polyeucte.[96] In this case, it is the specific blood of the martyr/husband that explicitly and suddenly leads to Pauline's conversion, and hence salvation—the image is at once drawn from the office of the lover/husband and the Christ/martyr. It is subsequent to this that Pauline announces her disobedience to her father, to the laws of birth. The rights over her have been transferred to the new alliance—to the husband/martyr and to the Christian faith.[97]

Even in a situation of moral failure, such as found in *Rodogune*, the mother expects the sons implicitly to share her rage—for them not to do so is to violate nature. In the debate between mother and son, Antiochus maintains that love and nature have separate, compatible rights, while the mother fears that love can snuff out nature. Among other aspects of the conflict within this family, the debate circles around duties transmitted by descent (nature) and obligations of contract (love).[98]

Recognition of a blood attachment—cousins, for example—evokes both claims to support and a moral obligation. In *Théodore*, a key figure in the plot is Cléobule, a blood relative of Théodore, who speaks of their

closeness as derived from "rights of blood."[99] Marcelle expects that he
will support Théodore just because she is his kin.[100] In *Héraclius*, marriage, once accomplished, brings in its train the same kinds of sentiment
one finds through blood: Pulchérie fears that if the marriage to the tyrant Phocas's son takes place while Phocas is alive, then she will inevitably shift her affective stance toward the father-in-law/tyrant. She would
be united to his family; he would be her father and she his daughter. She
would owe love, respect, and fidelity merely by such a connection: "My
hate would no longer be impetuous and all my wishes for you [Martian]
would be timid and weak when my wishes against him would be of parricide"[101]—thus her wish to see Phocas dead before the wedding. *Medée*,
of course, portrays a tragedy that turns on love and passion breaking the
power of primary loyalties, manifested as betrayal of father and country.
Medée does not find any mediating position between ascribed loyalties
and negotiated ones. She thinks her betrayal of all her duties to family
and kin should bind Jason to her all the more securely.[102] But passions,
especially Jason's, are a weak cement, unable to reproduce structure. In
the *Toison d'or*, which looks at the Medée/Jason connection in an earlier
phase, the same issues of choice (love) and nature (blood) are dealt with.
The king, Aaete, after his daughter, Medée, has betrayed him and helped
Jason get the fleece, says to his son: "you know too little how a wild
love surpasses tyranny. It does not spare rank, country, father, modesty.
Maybe you yourself are the enemy of your father. All my blood revolts
and betrays my hopes. Everything becomes suspect. I do not know what
to believe, only what to fear. Love keeps little respect for the rights
of blood. Everyone can be innocent or culpable."[103] In the end, when
Medée has helped Jason steal the fleece, she proclaims that "from the
country of blood, love breaks the ties, and the gods of Jason are stronger
than mine."[104]

## Reproducing the Lineage

Images of blood in the seventeenth century offer models of social circulation. The relationship of a man to his progeny, the circulation of blood
down the generations, follows the same conduits as property, status, and
privilege. The coursing of blood derives from nature, and the connections it makes among those whose veins flow with the same juice are
ascriptive, not subject to negotiation, choice, or contract. The key terms
for grasping the group whose substance is shared constantly reappear in
belles-lettres, legal discourse, and theology: *Geschlechter, lineages, cogna-
tionum, Freundschaften, races*. Such groups of kin are internally differen-

tiated and subject to hierarchies based on principles of age, gender, and birth order, but they are characterized by moral demands, sentimental attachments, and orientations of identity.[105] In baroque culture there was a palpability, substantiality, and corporality to the lineage. And the family was perceived on a vertical axis in terms of legitimate descent and succession, all emphasizing agnatic ties, the flow of vital substance through male lines, and an extreme egoism of familial identity.

It is just because each agnatic line could not reproduce itself without help from strangers that it had to enter into dangerous alliances with other groups, each, in turn, with their own sense of identity. Women were brought in to care for the line, and their "blood" was crucial for the success of father/son continuity. Maternal blood only becomes actuated by a male spark, concept, idea, or form, such that the blood of the children is, ironically, essentially paternal. The blood that ends up transmitted to the son is the father's blood even in this Aristotelian understanding of generation where sperm is robbed of its materiality and works its magic through spirit.

The link between two clans or lineages or descent groups or families had to be substantial enough to provide a foundation for continuous exchange. The alliance was so important that women of an allied family could no longer be available either as objects of sexual desire or for reproduction. The thesis I am trying to explore is that behind the force of this idea lay the many services that close allies provided. They could be guardians for children, gender tutors for sisters- and mothers-in-law, administrators of estates, curators for widows, legal representatives for married and single women, executors of wills, or underwriters and guardians of liens and contracts. Protecting property and reproducing the line made allied kin all the more necessary and all the more useful, precisely because they had no expectation to the property of an allied line. Commentators found the mutual exchanges between allied families and their responsibilities for each other to be so intimate that marriage back into the same family overlaid substance with substance, flesh with flesh.[106] The Jansenist theologian Antoine Arnauld maintained that conjugal love would degenerate into brutal passion and excessive ardor if close kin already linked by blood and familiarity added conjugal tenderness to such strong ties.[107] This seems to me to be a way of suggesting that obligation requires the right degree of distance and a systematically constructed set of roles with carefully maintained boundaries. In this construction, the set of rights, duties, obligations, and claims, the circulation of goods, the patterns of exchange, and the tensions between vertical and horizontal relationships, between consanguineal and affinal kin, between structure and change, and between identity and difference created considerable unease in baroque culture about repeated marriage into the same family, symbolized through a set of scriptural and medical metaphors of flesh and blood—the subject for another essay.

# Notes

For the plays by Corneille, I have consulted *Théatre complet de Corneille*, ed. Maurice Rat, 3 vols. (Paris, n.d. [1942]). In references to individual plays, the format I am using is 1.2.3:4 indicating volume, act, scene, page number in that order. All translations into English are mine.

1.  On the fungibility of blood, see Thomas Laqueur, *Making Sex: Body and Gender from the Greeks to Freud* (Cambridge, MA, 1990), 35–43; Barbara Duden, *The Woman Beneath the Skin*, trans. Thomas Dunlap (Cambridge, MA, 1991), 124–26; see also Gianna Pomata, "Blood Ties and Semen Ties: Consanguinity and Agnation in Roman Law," in *Gender, Kinship, Power: A Comparative and Interdisciplinary History*, ed. Mary Jo Maynes et al. (New York and London, 1996), 43–64, here 56–57.

2.  In *Idomenée*, P. J. Crébillon père has the son say to the father that he recognizes the blood that made him; see *Idomenée* (1706), in *Oeuvres* (Paris, 1831), 1:68. Molière lets a character speak of his father as the source of his blood and author of his being; see Molière, *L'etourdi* (1663), in *Oeuvres complètes*, ed. E. Despois (Paris, 1873), 235. And H. Racan has a man conceived of the *same blood* as his father *in the womb* of his mother; see H. Racan, *Les psaumes* (1660), in *Oeuvres complètes*, ed. P. Jannet (Paris, 1857), 2:181.

3.  The image of mixing the blood of two lineages or families through the agency of a son or daughter is a recurring theme in the seventeenth century. I explore this theme both in Bossuet and Corneille in the present chapter. In Corneille's plays, a son-in-law becomes the same blood with his father-in-law (*Polyeucte*, 2.3.3:46); two noblemen become linked through the blood of their children (*Andromède*, 2.1.1:550); the union of a husband and wife is a union of blood (*Toison d'or*, 3.3.1:118); the union of husband and wife also becomes a union of two nations (*Sertorius*, 3.1.2:170); and a political marriage links the blood of two leaders (*Agésilas*, 3.1.2:367). Note that there is a more elaborate discussion of blood in the Corneille plays later in this chapter. Bossuet, in a funeral sermon for a noble woman, spoke of her uniting the blood of the Gonzagas, Cleves, Lorraine, and France; *Oraison funèbre de très haute et très puissante princesse Anne de Gonzague de Clèves* (1685), in *Oeuvres oratoires* (Paris, 1922), 6:291. And, finally, Jean de Routrou writes that a man gave his own blood to his son-in-law through his daughter; see Jean de Routrou, *Le veritable St-Genest* (1647), ed. E. T. Dubois (Droz, 1972), 62.

4.  The core of familial ties was the set of vertical, descending relationships: those people who shared the same blood, diluted according to their distance from the stem. For blood to touch blood—killing, feud, intercourse—meant defilement and pollution. In fact the phrase "parricide and incest" is one that frequently occurs, and not just in the Orestes and Oedipus stories that saw a resurgence around the early eighteenth century. On this, see Christian Biet, *Oedipe en monarchie: Tragédie et théorie juridique à l'âge classique* (Paris, 1994). D'Aubigné in *Les tragiques* polemicizes against Philip II of Spain, who after marrying his son's fiancée had his son killed, as "incestueux & meurtrier" and as "parricide inceste"; see Théodore Agrippa d'Aubigné, *Les tragiques*, ed. A. Garnier and J. Plattard, vol. 3, bks. 4/5 (Paris, 1932), 53. I am drawing on

the introduction to *Kinship in Europe: Approaches to Long-Term Development (1300–1900)*, ed. David Warren Sabean, Simon Teuscher, and Jon Mathieu (New York and Oxford, 2007), by Simon Teuscher and myself. I have developed my understanding of the transition from the Middle Ages to the early modern period through discussions with Teuscher.

5. I discuss these issues in "From Clan to Kindred: Thoughts on Kinship and the Circulation of Property in Premodern and Modern Europe," in *Heredity Produced: At the Crossroad of Biology, Politics and Culture, 1500–1870*, ed. Staffan Müller-Wille and Hans-Jörg Rheinberger (Cambridge, MA, 2006). See Eileen Spring, *Law, Land, and Family: Aristocratic Inheritance in England, 1300–1800* (Chapel Hill, NC, and London, 1993), 144; Ute Essegern, "Kursächsische Eheverträge in der ersten Hälfte des 17. Jahrhunderts," in *Witwenschaft in der frühen Neuzeit: Fürstliche und adlige Witwen zwischen Fremd- und Selbstbestimmung*, ed. Martina Schattkowsky (Leipzig, 2003), 116–34, here 123–25.

6. Bernard Derouet, "Territoire et parenté. Pour une mise en perspective de la communauté rurale et des formes de reproduction familiale," *Annales HSS* (1995): 645–86, here 675–76, 678, 685–86; Bernard Derouet, "Le partage des frères. Héritage masculin et reproduction sociale en Franche-Comté aux XVIII$^e$ et XIX$^e$ siècles," *Annales ESC* (1993): 453–74, here 467; Bernard Derouet, "Pratiques de l'alliance en milieu de communautes [sic] familiales (Bourbonnais, 1600–1750)," in *Le choix du conjoint*, ed. G. Brunet, A. Fauve-Chamoux, and M. Oris (Lyon, 1998), 227–51, here 228–29. See the discussions of changes in inheritance during the sixteenth century in rural southern Germany in David Warren Sabean, *Landbesitz und Gesellschaft am Vorabend des Bauernkriegs* (Stuttgart, 1972); and most recently in Govind P. Sreenivasan, *The Peasants of Ottobeuren, 1487–1726: A Rural Society in Early Modern Europe* (Cambridge, 2004). Bossuet, in *De la connaissance de Dieu et de soi-même* (1704), speaks of rights being transmitted with blood, meaning transmission through the father; for this work see Bossuet, *Oeuvres complètes* (Paris, 1864), 23:201.

7. On the older synthesis see Karl Schmid, "Zur Problematik von Familie, Sippe und Geschlecht, Haus und Dynastie beim mittelalterlichen Adel. Vorfragen zum Thema 'Adel und Herrschaft im Mittelalter,'" *Zeitschrift für Geschichte des Oberrheins* 105 (1957): 1–62; Gerd Tellenbach, "Vom karolingischen Reichsadel zum deutschen Reichsfürstenstand," in *Herrschaft und Staat im Mittelalter*, ed. Hellmut Kämpf (Darmstadt, 1956), 190–242; Georges Duby, "La noblesse dans la France médiévale: une enquête à poursuivre," *Revue historique* 226 (1961): 1–22; Georges Duby, "Lignage, noblesse et chevallerie au XII$^e$ siècle dans la région maconnaise. Une révision," *Annales ESC* 27 (1972): 803–23. For overviews of recent contributions to the debate, see Martin Aurell, "La parenté en l'an mil," *Cahiers de civilisation médiévale* 43 (2000): 125–42; Dieter Mertens and Thomas Zotz, "Einleitung der Herausgeber," in *Karl Schmid. Geblüt, Herrschaft, Geschlechterbewusstsein: Grundfragen zum Verständnis des Adels im Mittelalter. Aus dem Nachlass herausgegeben*, ed. Dieter Mertens and Thomas Zotz (Sigmaringen, 1998), ix–xxxiii, here xviii–xxviii; Janet Nelson, "Family, Gender and Sexuality in the Middle Ages," in *Companion to Historiography*, ed. Michael Bentley (London and New York, 1997) 153–76, here 160–64. For recent critiques: Anita Guerreau-Jalabert, Régine Le Jean, and Joseph Morsel, "Familles et parents. De l'histoire de la famille à l'anthropologie de la parenté," in *Les tendances actuelles de l'histoire du Moyen Age en France et en Allemagne*, ed. Jean-Claude Schmitt and Otto Gerhard Oexle (Paris, 2002), 433–46; Anita Guerreau-Jalabert, "La designation des relations et des groupes de parenté en latin médiéval," *Archivum Latinitatis Medii Aevii* 46/7 (1988): 92f; Anita Guerreau-Jalabert, "Sur les structures

de parenté dans l'Europe médiévale (Note critique)," *Annales ESC* (1981): 1028–49, here 1030–31, 1043–44; Simon Teuscher, *Bekannte—Klienten—Verwandte. Soziabilität und Politik in der Stadt Bern um 1500* (Cologne, Weimar, and Vienna, 1998) 75–84; Joseph Morsel, "Geschlecht Repräsentation. Beobachtungen zur Verwandtschaftskonstruktion im fränkischen Adel des späten Mittelalters," in *Die Repräsentation der Gruppen. Texte—Bilder —Objekte*, ed. Otto Gerhard Oexle and Andrea von Hülsen-Esch (Göttingen, 1998), 263–70, 308–10; Juliette M. Turlan, "Amis et amis charnels. D'après les actes du parlement au XIVᵉ siècle," *Revue historique du droit français et etranger* 47 (1969): 645–98.

8.  See for example Heinz Reif, *Westfälischer Adel 1770–1860. Vom herrschaftsstand zur regionalen Elite* (Göttingen, 1979); Christophe Duhamelle, *L'heritage collectif. La noblesse d'Eglise rhénane, 17ᵉ et 18ᵉ siècles* (Paris, 1998); Gérard Delille, "Kinship, Marriage, and Politics," in *Kinship in Europe*, ed. Sabean, Teuscher, and Mathieu 163–83.

9.  A good example is offered by Pierre Lamaison and Elisabeth Claverie, *L'impossible mariage. Violence et parenté en Gevaudan, XVIIᵉ, XVIIIᵉ, et XIXᵉ siècles* (Paris, 1982). There is a detailed review of this book in David Warren Sabean, *Kinship in Neckarhausen, 1700–1870* (Cambridge, 1998), 407–16.

10. This is discussed in detail in Sabean, *Kinship in Neckarhausen*, 64–72.

11. Genesis 2:23–4: "And Adam said, This is now bone of my bones, and flesh of my flesh: she shall be called Woman, because she was taken out of Man. Therefore shall a man leave his father and his mother, and shall cleave unto his wife: and they shall be one flesh." Matthew 19:4–6: "And he answered and said unto them, Have ye not read, that he which made them at the beginning made them male and female, And said, For this cause shall a man leave father and mother, and shall cleave to his wife: and they twain shall be one flesh? Wherefore they are no more twain, but one flesh. What therefore God hath joined together, let no man put asunder." These passages clearly refer to marriage, but biblical interpreters throughout the seventeenth century understood them to refer to any act of completed sexual intercourse.

12. In the seventeenth century, William Harvey would summarize the point this way: "But that neither the *Hen* doth emit any Seed in *Coition*, nor poure forth any blood at that time into the cavity of the Vterus; as also that the egge is not formed after *Aristoteles* way; nor yet (as *Physitians* suppose) by the commixture of Seeds, and likewise that the *Cocks* seed doth not penetrate into the hollow of the *womb*, nor yet is attracted thither, is most manifest from this one observation, namely, *that after coition there is nothing at all to be found in the Uterus, more than there was before*"; William Harvey, *Anatomical Exercitations Concerning the Generation of Living Creatures: To which are added Particular Discourses of Births, and of Conceptions*, &c. (London, 1653), 199. Compare the discussion in Pomata, "Blood Ties and Semen Ties," 51–57. In 1615, Benedict Wincler gave a Galenist interpretation of marriage as a *commixtio sanguinis*, i.e., explicitly a mixing of blood, and also spoke of a *reverentiam sanguinis*; see Benedict Wincler, *Principiorum iuris* (Leipzig, 1615), 267, 333. Johann Karl Naevius as late as 1709 saw sex with in-laws as a commixture of blood; see Johann Karl Naevius, *Jus conjugum, Oder das Ehe-Recht* (Chemnitz, 1709), 256–58. Not just consanguines come from one blood but also affines. Not just participation in the flesh as with blood relatives but also *commixtio sanguinis* as with in-laws; see Jean Pontas (Dr. en droit-canon, Fac. de Paris), *Dictionnaire de cas de conscience ou decisions des plus considerables difficultez touchant la morale et la discipline ecclesiastique, tirées de l'ecriture, des conciles, des decretales des papes, des peres, et des plus célebres théologiens et canonistes*, 2 vols. with supp. (Paris, 1715; with supp., 1718), in which the article on "empêchement de l'affinité," case 8, stresses the need for *commixtio seminum* to

establish affinity, and affinity once established does not end with death of either spouse. Breaking the hymen and withdrawing does not count as consummation and as establishing affinity. There actually has to be a mixture of seed. In criminal law, semen had to flow into the vagina to establish intercourse as mixing flesh. In 1752–53, Pierre Collett, writing on a case of conscience where a man wanted to marry the sister of a girl with whom he had had relations when he was twelve, notes that the flow of semen into the girl was necessary to create an impediment on grounds of incest to the proposed marriage; see Pierre Collett, *Traité des dispenses en général et en particulier, dans lequel on résout les principales difficultés, qui regardent cette matiere*, 3 vols. (Paris, 1752–53), 3:143–44. In J. Bertaut, *Les oeuvres poetiques* (Paris, 1611), a man refers to the strict tie of blood that unites him and his wife. In *Andromède* (1650), one of the characters talks about a man and woman linking their blood in a *mélange*; see Pierre Corneille, *Andromède*, 2.4.6:389.

13. Harvey describes the position thus: "For some conceive the *Seed* and *Blood* to be the *Matter* which doth *constitute* the *chicken*: Others conceive the *Seed* to be the *Efficient* and *producing cause*, or Artificer that *builds* the *fabrick* of it: when yet upon deliberate consideration it appears most infallible, that there is *no matter at hand at all, nor no menstruous blood*, which the *Seed* of the *Male* can fall to work upon, or coagulate: (as Aristotle would have it) *nor is the Foetus made of the Seed of the Male or Female, or any Commixture of them both*"; Harvey, *Anatomical Exercitations*, 79–80.

14. See the important account on Aristotle by Giulia Sissa, "Subtle Bodies," in *Fragments for a History of the Human Body*, ed. M. Féher (New York, 1989), 3:133–41. One of the writers in the Oettingen *Colloquy*—see *Hochangelegene / und bißhero vielfältig bestrittenen Gewissens-Frage / Nemlich: Ob Jemand seines verstorbenen Weibes Schwester / sonder Ubertrettung Göttlicher und Natürlicher Gesetze / in wiederholter Ehe zu heuraten berechtiget? Durch auff dem in der Fürstliche Residentz zu Oettingen den 10. Octobr. Anno 1681 gehaltenen* COLLOQUIO *Ergangene Wechsel-Schrifften / Responsa und hochvernünfftige Judicia; Nach höchstes Fleisses überlegten beyderseitigen Rationibus, und hierüber gefaßten Grund-Schlüssen Erörtert: Und als ein Curiöses und ungemeines Zweiffel-Werck / Zu eines jeden genugsamen Unterricht in offentlichem Truck ausfertiget* (Frankfurt and Leipzig, 1682), 293–94—arguing *for* the wife's sister and *against* the brother's wife, maintained that God did not sanction the confluence of seed in one vessel but did allow the communication of seed in different vessels. The wife does not cause blood to flow in the husband. How is one to understand the position in a juridical *consilium* reported in Brückner, which argued that *a man becomes one flesh with his brother* when his blood flows into the flesh into which his deceased brother's blood has flowed? Clearly here the man contacts something through intercourse and the ejaculation of semen is seen as a flow of blood. The flow of blood into a woman leaves something permanent, so that the next man who causes his blood to flow into the woman contracts something from the first man. For a brother to do so seems to redouble a substance in an illegitimate way: Hieronymus Bruckner [J.U.D., Consil. Saxo-Gothani aulici et consistorialis], *Decisiones iuris matrimonialis controversi* (Frankfurt and Leipzig, 1692), 279. The great French court preacher Jean-Pierre Camus, in one of his homilies at the beginning of the seventeenth century, explained the generation of Christ in purely Aristotelian terms. The Virgin Mary provided the pure blood, while God provided the spirit for the conception: Jean-Pierre Camus, *Homélies des Etats Généraux (1614–1615)*, ed. Jean Descrains (Geneva, 1970), 259.

15. Molière, in *L'etourdi*, has a man speak of his father as the source of his blood and the author of his being, while in *Malade imaginaire*, he has a man refer to his daughter as

"his blood." In 1626, Johann Bechstad, a lawyer and consistory judge in Saxe-Coburg, revives the Roman law notion of consanguines being agnatic relatives and cognates being uterine ones; Johann Bechstad, *Collatio jurium connubalium, tam universorum et communium, quam municipalium quorundam, inter congnatos et affines* ... (Coburg, 1626), 1–30. Brückner, in *Decisiones iuris matrimonialis controversi*, at page 312, distinguishes between blood siblings and uterine siblings: "German" sisters (progeny of a father) are blood relatives, with the same name and legal position, while uterine sisters (through the mother) are not the same. Marrying the father's brother's wife is marrying into the same family, but the mother's brother's wife involves a different family and a different name. All of this is thought through in terms of agnatic lineage assumptions. Compare Pomata, "Blood Ties and Semen Ties," 45–51.

16. The papal bull *Ineffabilis Deus*, which proclaimed the Immaculate Conception a dogma, was issued only in 1854. The best introduction to the medieval discussions and debates is the study of the texts by Marielle Lamy, *L'immaculée conception. Etapes et enjeux d'une controverse au moyen-âge (XIIᵉ–XVᵉ siècles)*, Collection des Études Augustiniennes, Série Moyen Age et Temps modernes 35 (Paris, 2000).

17. Lamy, *L'immaculée conception*, 41.

18. See Peter Lombard, *Sentences*, 1.II, d. 31, c. 4 (1981 ed.): "In concupiscentia igitur et libidine concipitur caro formanda in corpus prolis. Unde caro ipsa, quae concipitur in vitiosa concupiscentia, polluitur et corrumpitur; ex cuius contactu anima, cum infunditur, maculam trahit qua polluitur et fit rea, id est vitium concupiscentiae, quod est originale peccatum" (cited in Lamy, *L'immaculée conception*, 42).

19. Bossuet, "Premier sermon pour la Fête de la conception de la Sainte Vierge," in *Oeuvres complètes de Bossuet* (Paris, 1862), 11:1–20, here 11:4; this work cited hereafter as Bossuet, *Oeuvres complètes* (1862). See Lamy, *L'immaculée conception*. The basic theological problem facing the medieval theologians was how to understand the divine maternity of Mary. As Lamy puts it, Mary "is situated at the articulation of two categories of human nature, *natura vitiata* of the sons of Adam and innocent nature assumed by the Word. In her, one goes from the one to the other" (152). "The implication of divine maternity rests on the greatest equality between mother and infant, since the fleshes are linked organically up to birth" (154). What was implied here was that Mary needed purification or sanctification in order for her/Christ's flesh to be unsullied. For the earlier theologians this purification took place at the Annunciation, and the key figure in this act was the Holy Spirit (155). Even as late as the second half of the twelfth century, this was the position of the majority of theologians (156). The immaculist standpoint erased the period in which Mary was subject to original sin, positing an equality between mother and Son. In this later position, there is special attention to the flesh (158). Mary is the one in whom the Word acquires a human nature true and intact. Human nature is transmitted completely by flesh, in a theological and philosophical construction that refuses traducianism (the doctrine that some kernel of purity remained intact from Adam onward, which communicated purity directly to Mary). Rejecting traducianism has great consequences: it is flesh alone that carries the unity of the human race in linking the diverse generations and that makes of humanity a single human, identified with Adam. And at the same time, flesh is seen as the sole vehicle of sin, since the soul is created by God and good in itself. The rejection of traducianism was completed by the doctrine of the *infectio carnis*, which furnishes an explication of the transmission of original sin, without resolving in a satisfactory way the problem of culpability of the descendants of Adam for a hereditary fault. There is thus in the Augustinian tradition a tendency to assimilate, from the point of view of transmission, human

nature to flesh and flesh to sin. For the Incarnation, it is necessary to break the linkage of nature and sin in the flesh, the place where the tie is established. Virginal conception associated with a purification of Mary offered the condition of a generation without the propagation of original sin, generation which is a gift to the Word, his soul coming from God directly. The immaculists find this unsatisfactory (159). Pure flesh is not flesh cleansed of pollution but that which remains intact. Also, the idea that the flesh of the Word exists before the Incarnation suggests that Mary herself has to have never known sin.

20. For a standard view, see the *New Catholic Encyclopedia*, 7:381. Lamy, *L'immaculée conception*, 345–78, looks at all the evidence for Duns Scotus being the "hero" of the doctrine of the Immaculate Conception and comes to the conclusion that his texts are at best ambivalent, even though they were soon received for the most part with an immaculist reading. The doctrine of "prevenient mediator" had been around for a while before Duns Scotus developed it at the beginning of the fourteenth century.

21. See the recent discussion by Caroline Walker Bynum, *Wonderful Blood: Theology and Practice in Late Medieval Northern Germany and Beyond* (Philadelphia, PA, 2007), for late medieval discussions of Mary's blood and Christ's body, 117–18, 158–59, 161.

22. Bossuet, "Second sermon pour la Fête de la conception de la Sainte Vierge," in *Oeuvres complètes* (1862), 11:20–42, here 28.

23. Bossuet, "Second sermon de la conception," 29. John of Capistrano in his treatise of 1440–42, *De sanguine*, argued that Christ's body was composed completely from Mary's blood. In the medieval theory of generation, the body was composed of menstrual blood. See Bynum, *Wonderful Blood*, 117–18.

24. Bossuet's contemporary, the influential Jesuit preacher Louis Bourdaloue, in a sermon on the Annunciation made a similar point: Louis Bourdaloue, "Second sermon sur l'annonciation de la Vierge," in *Oeuvres complètes de Bourdaloue de la compagnie de Jésus*, new ed., 6 vols. (Paris, 1905), 5:265–84, here, 5:268, 5:275. Mary is a cooptrice in human salvation, since she formed the Savior and gave the blood that was the price of redemption. He goes on to say that when the Word took on human flesh, that in itself constituted an alliance, and the flesh of man became the flesh of God. At the moment when the virginal flesh of Christ was conceived, all human flesh was penetrated by the unction of God. In this formulation, the alliance constituted by the united flesh of the Virgin and the son is a general alliance of divinity and humanity, and Mary's flesh and blood have cosmic significance. Bynum argues that in the fifteenth-century representation typical around Weingarten in South Germany, Christ's body almost becomes Mary's blood; see Bynum, *Wonderful Blood*, 158–59, 161. The hesitation is gone for Bossuet. See, for example, Bossuet, "Troisième sermon pour la fête de l'annonciation," in *Oeuvres complètes* (1862), 11:164–176, here 172; and Bossuet, "Troisième sermon pour la fête de la nativité de la Sainte Vierge," in *Oeuvres complètes* (1862), 11:100–21, here 119.

25. Jacques Bénigne Bossuet, "IIIe sermon pour la fête de la nativité de la sainte vierge," in *Sermons*, in *Oeuvres complètes de Bossuet* (Paris, 1846), 4:152–58, here 4:158.

26. Jacques Bénigne Bossuet, *Méditations sur l'évangile*, ed. critique M. Dreano, Études de théologie et d'histoire de la spiritualité (Paris, 1966), 184, 370–71, 376, 420, 431.

27. Bossuet, "Second sermon de la conception," 28.

28. Bynum, *Wonderful Blood*, 157, 256, suggests that older literature overemphasized lineage in the later Middle Ages. If she is right, the use of blood as a symbol of lineage and line postdates the fifteenth century.

29. See Lamy, *L'immaculée conception*. Of all of the writers that Lamy deals with, the only one who speaks of blood rather than flesh is Pope Benedict XII (Jacques Fournier), but he is concerned with blood, not in terms of inheritance or substance that connects families, lineages, or descent groups together, but rather as something equated with sin: "by blood one understands sins or inclination to sin derived from first sin or the corruption of the human body from the fault of sin" (447). All sin can be called blood, but it more properly means original sin. "Et sic per sanguinem peccata intelliguntur, vel inclinatio ad peccandum ex peccato precendenti causata, vel corruptio corporis humani introducta merito peccati. ... Quamvis autem omne peccatum etiam actuale sanguis dici possit supradicto modo, tamen magis proprie peccatum originale et fomes vel inclinatio ad malum sequens ipsum et mors carnis que ex peccato originali in omnes homines venit. ... Et sic emundari id est perfecte mundari sanguis id est originale peccatum dicitur, cum et ipsum tollitur et inclinatio eius absciditur et mors que ipsum consequitur in incorruptionem transmutatur, quod non potest fieri nisi per Deum" (447–48).
30. Lamy, *L'immaculée conception*, 164, 196. Bossuet, "Second sermon de la conception," 28. In the Genesis account of the creation of man, just after Eve has been formed from Adam's rib, Adam enunciates the first marriage compact: "And Adam said, This *is* now bone of my bones, and flesh of my flesh: she shall be called Woman, because she was taken out of men. Therefore shall a man leave his father and his mother, and shall cleave unto his wife: and they shall be one flesh" (Genesis 2:23–24). The text clearly posits this union of flesh as the foundation of marriage.
31. For a time, the semantics of "flesh" and "blood" will run along parallel tracks. For example a predecessor of Bossuet, the French theologian, mystic, and cardinal, founder of the French Oratory, Pierre de Bérulle (1575–1629) remained totally with a semantics of flesh and rarely utilized the word *blood*. See his "Discours de l'estat et des grandeurs de Jesus," in *Oeuvres complètes de Cardinal Bérulle*, 2 vols. (Paris, 1644; repr. Montsoult, 1960), 1:364–66, 498–99. See also *Oeuvres complètes*, texte établi et annoté by Michel Dupuy, vol. 1 ( [Paris], 1995–), pt. 1:219, and pt. 2:76, 385, 387. On the other hand, his contemporary, the court preacher Jean-Pierre Camus, in his *Homélies des Etats Généraux*, 259, put the relationship between Jesus and Mary as one of blood: "La Saincte Vierge est un autre calice et patente de ce Verbe incarné, car n'est-ce pas dans ses entrailles, et de son plus pur sang, que ce precieux corps a esté formé?"
32. Anon., *Le Defensoire de la conception de la glorieuse Vierge Marie, en forme de dialogue a Rouen chez Maistre Martin Morin, l'An de grace 1515*, in *Monumenta Italo-Gallica ex tribus auctoribus maternâ linguâ scribentibus pro Immaculata Virginis Mariae Conceptione. Scilicèt, P. Domenico de Carpane, Nicolao Grenier, et anonymo colloquio inter sodalem et amicum. Pars secunda*, 3 vols. in 2, ed. Pedro de Alva y Astorga (Louvain, 1666; repr. Bruxelles, 1967) ; cited hereafter as *Defensoire*.
33. *Defensoire*, 196.
34. *Defensoire*, 87, 90.
35. *Defensoire*, 35.
36. *Defensoire*, 8, 35, 39, 101.
37. *Defensoire*, 196, 200, 217.
38. Nicole Grenier, *Tome second du Bouclier de la foy contenant l'antidote contre les adversaires de la pure conception de la mere de Dieu* (Paris, 1549), in *Monumenta Italo-Gallica*, ed. Pedro de Alva y Astorga.
39. Grenier, *Bouclier*, 121.
40. Grenier, *Bouclier*, 121.

41. Grenier, *Bouclier*, 210.
42. Saint François de Sales, "Sermon LXVII, 'Sermon pour la fête de l'immaculée conception de la sainte vierge' (1622)," in *Oeuvres complètes*, ed. J Nièrat (Annecy, 1892–1932), 10:403.
43. Grenier, *Bouclier*, 125.
44. Grenier, *Bouclier*, 33.
45. Grenier, *Bouclier*, 34.
46. Grenier refers in several passages to the sermon on Mary's conception by Jean Gerson, who talks about the son of God taking on human flesh as a marriage of divinity to humanity. Mary was Christ's mother, sister, spouse, and lover (*mie*); see Jean Gerson, "Sermon de la concepcion nostre dame," *Six sermons français inédits*, ed. Louis Mourin (Paris, 1946), 387–429, here 387, 394.
47. Grenier, *Bouclier*, 226.
48. Bossuet, "Troisième sermon de la nativité," 106.
49. Lamy discusses the problem of Aristotelian and Galenic categories for twelfth-century theologians in *L'immaculée conception*, 159–60. Virginal conception supposes that the embryo is produced without male seed. How? The role of mother is different in different schools. For the Aristotelians, there is no female seed, and the role of the mother is purely passive—she provides simply a matter, the menstrual blood, while the male seed acts on this matter and gives it form, and life. In the Galenic tradition, there is a maternal seed, although inferior in quality and importance to the male seed, which unites with the latter to form the embryo, and maternal blood offers nourishment for the embryo (160). As for the virginal birth, in the Aristotelian tradition male seed acts, not as a material principle, but as form and spirit, and possesses *vis generativa*. It was not impossible to see divine power playing this role, unless the *vis generativa* was exceptionally given to the mother. In the Galenic perspective, the mystery seems impenetrable, because the material aspect, with the union of two seeds, does not allow a simple substitution of the divine power as the power carried by paternal seed. In either case, one could think that Mary has taken a part greater than other mothers in the generation of the flesh of her son. The absence of a male seed signifies in a certain way the non-separation between the body of the mother and of the child, between the *caro mariae* and the *caro Verbi*. This non-separation seems to have a decisive consequence—the attributes of the one are those of the other. This ambiguity linked to the idea of the virginal conception predates the discourse on the Immaculate Conception.
50. Note that the male sperm in the Aristotelian understanding is ultimately immaterial (see Sissa, "Subtle Bodies"), much in the way Harvey understood it to be.
51. Bossuet, "Précis d'un sermon pour la fête de la nativité de la Sainte Vierge," in *Oeuvres complètes* (1862), 11:121–29, here 11:125.
52. Bossuet, *Élévations sur les mystères*, ed. M. Dreano (Paris, 1962), 99.
53. Aristotle, *Generation of Animals*, trans. A. L. Peck, Loeb Classical Library 366 (Cambridge, MA, 1942). In Aristotle's account, the male sperm is the active principle that works on the passive, female material (395). If the male sperm "gains the mastery," then a male like itself is produced. If, on the other hand, it gets mastered, it changes over into its opposite and a female is produced. In general, males take more after their fathers and females after their mothers (401). Interestingly, here Aristotle argues that any deviation from the parents is formally a "monstrosity," and the "first beginning of this deviation is when a female is formed instead of a male." He speaks of the *logos* of the movement caused by the sperm: "if this movement gains the mastery it will make a male and not a female, and a male which takes after its father,

not after its mother" (403). It is possible that the sperm will not be able to master
every "faculty" (defined as a particular characteristic of a parent), and where it fails,
in that aspect the resulting child is "deficient." In this way, a male can be produced
that takes after his mother, even though most males take after their fathers (407–9).
"Gaining the mastery at one place but not at another, causes the embryo that is taking shape to turn out diversiform" (411–13). Aristotle clearly thought that form was
superior to matter, male to female (133). In fact, the female is defined in negative
terms, as the one who has an "inability" to "concoct semen" (103), that is, to give
form, to instigate movement, to act as artificer.

54. Bossuet, *Élévations sur les mystères*, 106.
55. Bossuet, *Élévations sur les mystères*, 271.
56. Bossuet, "Sermon sur le mystère de la très-Sainte Trinité," in *Sermons*, 4:1–8, here
    4:3.
57. Bossuet, "III^e sermon de la nativité," in *Sermons*, 4:158.
58. On *sang royal*, see Gaddebusch. See especially Bynum, *Wonderful Blood*, 157–58,
    187, 256. This exhaustive study of blood in religious discourse of the later Middle
    Ages found little interest in using blood as an idiom to grasp the salient features of
    genealogical connection.
59. André Devyver, *Le sang épuré. Les préjugés de race chez les gentilshommes français de
    l'Ancien Régime (1560–1720)*, Editions de l'Université de Bruxelles (Brussels, 1973),
    7–12. See also the article by Guillaume Aubert, "'The Blood of France': Race and
    Purity of Blood in the French Atlantic World," *William and Mary Quarterly*, 3rd ser.,
    61 (2004): 439–78.
60. Devyver, *Le sang épuré*, 31.
61. The semantics of "blood" can be traced in part through the seventeenth- and eigh-
    teenth-century French dictionaries. Significantly, in the early seventeenth century,
    blood as something ascribed to social forms has only to do with the royal family.
    By the end of the century, blood has spread to all social stations, but is particularly
    relevant to the nobility. In Nicot, *Thresor de la langue française* (1606), blood is said
    to be appropriated by antonomasia to the kin of the king. "Accordingly one speaks
    of being the Blood of France, that is, kin to the kings of France." The phrase "princes
    of the blood," then, refers only to kin recognized as able to succeed to the crown. In
    the 1694 first edition of the *Dictionnaire de L'Académie française*, however, *blood* has
    come to signify *race* or extraction in general, and there are various kinds: vile and
    abject, noble, illustrious, royal, the blood of France. One can say, "he is your son, he
    is your blood." Princes of the blood are those who belong to the royal family. Finally,
    the fourth edition, from 1762, of the *Dictionnaire de L'Académie française*, perpetu-
    ates pretty much the definitions and usages from the late seventeenth-century first
    edition but contrasts a little more clearly noble and vile (*vil*) blood. It adds the idea
    of two people being of the same blood and in a more restricted sense the children in
    relation to their *father*. It also adds a new notion about the right of blood, the right
    that birth bestows. Furthermore, one can speak of the "force of blood," the senti-
    ments that one claims nature sometimes gives to people of the same blood. Note
    that Madame de Sévigné used this phrase in this manner; see Marie de Rabutin-
    Chantal, Marquise de Sévigné, *Correspondence*, 3 vols. ([1675–96]; Paris, 1972–8),
    3:356. There is a further extension of meaning tending in the same direction of in-
    herited substance in the phrase "good blood does not disappoint (*mentir*)," meaning
    that children normally retain the good qualities of their fathers and mothers. Again
    this is a usage to be found in Sévigné's seventeenth-century texts (*Correspondence*,
    1:101).

62. Devyver, *Le sang épuré*, 31–37. The author sees the shift in language as an attempt on the part of the nobility to draw boundaries around themselves and to create a new consciousness of themselves as a class. The vocabulary of race became the point around which consciousness could be constructed (88).

63. Devyver, *Sang épuré*, 104, citing J. B. Nenna, *Traicté de la noblesse* (1583).

64. Devyver, *Sang épuré*, 167–71. The *Mémoires* by Gaspard de Saulx-Tavannes (1509–73) were published in 1653.

65. All references to the original plays are, as indicated at the beginning of the endnotes, from Pierre Corneille, *Théatre complet de Corneille*, ed. Maurice Rat, 3 vols. (Paris, n.d. [1942]), hereafter cited as Corneille, *Théatre complet*. The text is based on the edition of Corneille's works from 1682, and contains notes, variants, an introduction, and a glossary.

66. Corneille, *Le Cid*, 1.1.5:600.

67. Sévigné, *Correspondence*, 3:254; 1:459.

68. Corneille, *Le Cid*, 1.3.4:622.

69. Corneille, *Le Cid*, 1.2.2:605. Molière made fun of the notion that a child had the blood of the parent. In *Le médicin volant*, the doctor explains why he is examining the father when the daughter is sick—they are the same blood, so he can look at either one for his diagnosis.

70. Corneille, *Horace*, 1.3.4:691–2.

71. Corneille, *Agésilas*, 3.3.1:391.

72. The lieutenant general of Louis XIII, the comte de Souvigny, wrote: "Notre père et notre mère nous accoutumoient à avoir du respect et de la déférence les uns pour les autres. Mes frères m'obéissoient, et, après moi, mon frère Aignan, ensuite mon frère François, ainsi de l'un à l'autre jusque au dernier."; *Mémoires*, ed. Ludovic de Coutenson, 3 vols (Paris, 1906), 1:7.

73. Corneille, *Nicomède*, 2.1.2:688.

74. Qualities of blood according to station are central to Saint-Simon's picture of the world. In one case, he pointed out that authorities did not look too closely into a particular murder for fear of finding someone of highly respected blood culpable; see Louis de Rouvroy, duc de Saint-Simon, *Mémoires*, 20 vols. (Paris, 1691–1723). Pagination does not correspond to the original edition. Paginated by ARTFL: www.lib.uchicago.edu/efts/ARTFL/databases/TLF/; *Mémoires*, 2:103. In another passage, he attacks one M. Marsan as so low and avid a despoiler of church, widows, and orphans, as to be completely of the blood of the people; see *Mémoires*, 6:167.

75. Corneille, *Nicomède*, 2.2.3:704.

76. Corneille, *Nicomède*, 2.3.1:709.

77. Corneille, *Nicomède*, 2.3.2:711.

78. Corneille, *Nicomède*, 2.4.3:727.

79. Corneille, *Le Cid*, 1.1.3:595.

80. Corneille, *Agésilas*, 3.1.2:367.

81. Corneille, *Polyeucte*, 2.1.3:20.

82. Corneille, *Sertorius*, 3.1.2:170.

83. Corneille, *Polyeucte*, 2.3.3:46. In a passage that deals with the transference of blood to the son-in-law in a somewhat parallel fashion, Saint-Simon deals with the problem of whether inheritance and succession ceded to a sister (of the "second bed") at her marriage ought to revert to the senior line or whether the rights go over to the husband. The woman in question would lose her rank (duchess) and the associated honors upon remarrying. Saint-Simon argues that far from being communicable to her *second* husband, the rank and honors are fixed and transferable only to her son

from the "first bed." This latter argument is based on the idea, reported by Saint-Simon, that the original establishment was attached to the blood of the first husband of the duchess heir and extinguished for her with his death; *Mémoires*, 1:63.

84. Corneille, *Polyeucte*, 2.5.3:69–70.
85. "De ce bienheureux sang tu me vois baptisée"; Corneille, *Polyeucte*, 2.5.5:74.
86. Corneille, *Horace*, 1.1.1:666.
87. Corneille, *Horace*, 1.4.7:706.
88. Corneille, *Pompée*, 2.4.4:129.
89. Corneille, *Pompée*, 2.5.4:139–40.
90. Corneille, *Polyeucte*, 2.3.2:40.
91. Corneille, *Polyeucte*, 2.5.3:69.
92. Corneille, *Pompée*, 2.1.3:96–97; 2.2.3:106.
93. Corneille, *Pompée*, 2.2.1:100.
94. Corneille, *Le Cid*, 1.3.5:627.
95. Corneille, *Polyeucte*, 2.5.3:69–70.
96. Corneille, *Polyeucte*, 2.5.2:67.
97. Corneille, *Polyeucte*, 2.5.5:74.
98. Corneille, *Rodogune*, 2.2.4:345; 2.3.4:352–53; 2.4.1:360; 2.4.2:362; 2.4.3:365.
99. Corneille, *Théodore*, 2.1.1:393.
100. Corneille, *Théodore*, 2.1.2:395.
101. Corneille, *Héraclius*, 2.3.1:491.
102. Corneille, *Médée*, 1.1.4:454.
103. Corneille, *Toison d'or*, 3.5.2:147.
104. Corneille, *Toison d'or*, 3.5.5:153.
105. In his work on Christian morality, Moyse Amyraut, the well-known Huguenot theologian, made a careful distinction between descent and alliance; see Moyse Amyraut, *La morale chrestienne*, 4 pts. in 6 vols. (Saumur, 1652–60), pt. 2:247. No one would doubt that the kinship that comes from consanguinity is closer and more strict than the one that consists in alliance and affinity, which is like a copy and never as strong and clear as the original. The reason here is evident—consanguinity is "dans son propre siège." Affinity, argued Amyraut, arises from communication, while relations from consanguinity are immediate.
106. Johann Jacob Schudt, *Jüdischen Merkwürdigkeiten vorstellende was sich curieuses und denkwürdiges in den neuern Zeiten bey einigen Jahr-hunderten mit denen in all IV.Theile der Welt/ sonderlich durch Teutschland/ zerstreuten Juden zugetragen* (Frankfurt am Main and Leipzig, 1714), pt. 1:240–42; pt. 2:220–21.
107. Antoine Arnauld, *Lettres de Monsieur Antoine Arnauld*, 9 vols. (Nancy, 1727), 7:245.

# Chapter 8

# Kinship, Blood, and the Emergence of the Racial Nation in the French Atlantic World, 1600–1789

Guillaume Aubert

## Sanguinity, Sex, and the Racialized Nation

Some thirty-five years ago, Michel Foucault famously characterized Ancien Régime society as a "society of blood ... of sanguinity." Invoking the centrality of "systems of alliance," the "value of descent lines" and "the differentiation into orders and castes" in structuring "the mechanisms of power," he cast Ancien Régime blood as *a reality with a symbolic function.* For Foucault, seventeenth- and especially eighteenth-century "symbolics of blood" prefigured the emergence of nineteenth- and twentieth-century "racism in its modern biologizing statist form." In this narrative, the "modernity" of racism proceeded from the reinscription of "blood" in a "new technology of sex" when "sex became a police matter [that] required the social body as a whole, and virtually all of its individuals to place themselves under surveillance."[1]

As some followers and critics of Foucault have pointed out, this entangled story of blood, sex, and race might be in need of a revised chronological arc and an expanded spatial framework.[2] Indeed, if, unlike

Foucault, we turn our gaze toward the so-called early modern period of European colonial expansion, we will find that "biologizing forms of state racism" anchored in the policing of sex not only emerged as early as the sixteenth century but found their most explicit manifestations in Atlantic colonial settings before they circulated back to European metropoles. Exploring early modern transatlantic articulations of sanguinity and sexuality might also suggest a similar spatial and chronological reframing of the emergence of racialized conceptions of "nation" and "national belonging"—that is, an understanding of "the nation" as a "community of blood," or, we might say, "of blood relatives."

Taking its cues from colonial and postcolonial scholarship suggesting deep connections between metropolitan and colonial "notions of incorporation and differentiation," and exploring the intersection of constructs of race and gender in metropolitan and colonial discourses, this chapter proposes to examine how the circulation and transformation of ideologies of kinship and blood between France and its Atlantic colonies during the seventeenth and eighteenth centuries shaped the reframing of the French nation as a community of blood.[3] While the arguments developed here do not claim to offer any exhaustive treatment of this complex problem, they suggest how a transatlantic reading of colonial and metropolitan policies and discourses concerned with the management of family formation and the regulating of sex may shed light on the ways in which French national identity became racialized during the seventeenth and eighteenth centuries.

The first section examines the resonance of metropolitan understandings of "blood," kinship, and generation in colonial policies of "assimilation through intermarriage" in seventeenth-century New France. The second section moves to the sometimes haphazard and contradictory apprehensions of cross-cultural sexuality and marriages in eighteenth-century French North American and Caribbean colonies and their contributions to the crystallization of a racial conceptualization of "Frenchness" as ancestry became central to colonial articulations of social and political order. The final section shows how this colonial racializing of French national identity eventually found its way back to France in the second half of the eighteenth century as metropolitan authorities became increasingly anxious about the presence of people of African ancestry on French soil.

## "Un Mesme Peuple et un Mesme Sang": Assimilation and Intermarriage in New France

The early history of French colonial expansion in North America is often remembered for its assimilationist impulses. Indeed, during the first decades of the establishment of New France, the lack of French women as well as the necessity to establish commercial and military alliances with Native populations led to the elaboration of colonial policies encouraging French-Indian marriages. In the 1630s, the founder of Quebec City, Samuel de Champlain, declared to a gathering of Hurons that, following their conversion to Catholicism, "our sons will marry your daughters, and we shall be one people."[4] Few Indian women seemed attracted by such an offer. Almost forty years later, Jean-Baptiste Colbert, Louis XIV's principal minister and chief architect of French colonial policy, lamented that if the Algonquins and Hurons had "long submitted to the authority of the King," they nevertheless continued to live according to "their savage customs." He thus ordered colonial authorities to renew their efforts to encourage Indians not only to convert to Catholicism, but also to settle and marry among the French, "so that after some time, having one law and one master, they may form one people and one blood [un mesme peuple et un mesme sang]."[5] Versailles even established a fund to provide dowries for prospective Indian brides in the hope that the female converts of the Jesuits and Ursulines would soon marry with the numerous single male colonists of New France and thus contribute to the colony's demographic development.[6]

While the failure of Colbertian policies of intermarriage is well documented, less attention has been paid to the peculiar language in which this policy was couched. That French and Indians were to form "one people and one blood" as a result of French-Indian unions seems to imply that they were considered to be of a different "blood." Since historiographical conventional wisdom tells us that biological constructions of race only emerged at the end of the next century, it may be worth exploring how this reference to "blood" could have been understood in the mid-seventeenth century.

In early modern France, the use of *sang* to refer to a group of individuals most often was to be found in texts extolling the "natural" qualities of the nobility, and more particularly, those of noble men.[7] During the Estates General of 1614, for instance, representatives of the nobility expressed dismay at the possibility that those who had purchased royal offices might claim noble status. The only true "French nobility," a group of provincial delegates reminded the king, was composed of this "well purified blood of the most noble and most excellent part of your State," which had been bestowed unto them by "birth" through many generations.[8] Throughout the sixteenth century, the traditional nobility had insisted on their natural superiority over recently ennobled officers. "As nature teaches us and experience confirms," a 1565 pamphlet read, "those extracted from a noble blood ... are commonly more inclined to integrity than others."[9]

Both aristocratic and legal conceptions of filiation and inheritance relied on a particularly gendered understanding of generation. Only those
"men extracted from generous and virtuous races and seeds," nobleman
Pierre Saint Julien de Balleure insisted in 1588, "are the most worthy of
honors and reverence."[10] Ninety years later, Gilles André François de la
Roque's *Traité de la noblesse* stated: "There is in the seed I know not what
force and I know not what principle which transmits and continues the
inclinations of fathers in their descendants."[11] In sixteenth- and seventeenth-century works extolling the political prerogatives of noblemen,
the male heads of aristocratic households were enjoined to preserve the
"illustrious branches" of their family tree by avoiding improper marriages or *mésalliance.*[12] "A generous blood," read a seventeenth-century
treatise on nobility, "must not be mixed with that of a vile and abject
person, and its splendor blackened by the obscurity of a low condition.
… The dignified rank of nobility must not be prostituted by an illicit
conjunction."[13] Aristocratic anxieties about *mésalliances* ran particularly
high in the cases of marriages between male commoners and noble
women.[14] Indeed, early modern French jurists considered that the marriage of a noble man to "a woman of the third estate" entailed no loss of
his status or of its transmissibility to his heirs. In contrast, the union of
a noble woman with "a commoner" constituted a ground for *dérogeance,*
or the temporary suspension of her noble status; only after the death
of her commoner husband could she petition the courts to recover her
nobility, but she could never pass that status on to her *roturier* children.[15]
Similarly, political theorists argued that the children born of the unions
between French queens and foreign princes should have no pretension
to rule since they proceeded from "foreign seed."[16]

The invocation of "seed" and "blood" in the legal and aristocratic articulation of the exclusive right of males to govern and transmit their status
was not simply metaphorical but proceeded directly from contemporary medical and philosophical understandings of generation. According to Aristotelian views of human reproduction, reprised endlessly in
medical treatises since the 1500s, males alone produced the *semence* that
provided the "movement" and "idea" giving the fetus its ultimate form.
From such a perspective, women's bodies were the mere receptacles
of their husbands' *semence de vertus.*[17] Even the proponents of Galenic
and Hippocratic theories attributing the production of an active *semence*
to both men and women conceded that the active virtue of female *semence* was inferior to that of the male seed. Ultimately, most authors and
medical practicioners preferred to embrace a strict Aristotelian seminism
as a "natural" confirmation of women's social and political inferiority.[18]
The idea that the bodies of women were merely passive recipients of

the male *semence* invited agricultural analogies that, implicitly at least, emphasized the exclusive abilities of men, not only to generate life, but also to transform and dominate nature. Royal physician (premier médecin du roy) André Du Laurens, for instance, explained in 1621 that "for generation to occur, fertile and pure [male] seeds must be poured in the matrix as in a field or a garden."[19]

The origin of this *semence*, or of male "seeds," was the object of much speculation and generated a variety of explanations on the part of early modern French authors, who nevertheless all agreed that the *semence* did not constitute a distinct bodily fluid. Following the various opinions of the Ancients, some thought of semen as saliva or sweat while others argued that it proceeded from the brain or the spine.[20] The most widely accepted theory, however, followed Aristotle and Galen who, despite significant disagreements about the respective roles of males and females in generation, both considered that the generative seed emanated from blood. For instance, while Aristotle claimed that "semen is pretty certainly a residue from that nourishment which is in the form of blood," the famous sixteenth-century French surgeon Ambroise Paré, considered the "*semence*," whose production he attributed to both men and women, to be "a whitened blood constituting the material basis to make little creatures of God."[21] Paré's support of the dual seed theory notwithstanding, this hematogenic view of semen was often offered as evidence of the resemblance between fathers and children.[22] For Michel de Montaigne, who like Pythagoras regarded male seed as "the foam of our best blood," "the drop" of this *semence* "from which we are produced bears in itself the impression not only of the bodily form but of the thoughts and inclinations of our fathers."[23]

In early modern France, the resonance of such gendered understandings of generation and filiation extended beyond the realms of medicine, philosophy, and law. Indeed, thanks to the inclusion of the deuterocanonical books in their biblical canon, French Catholics could find a scriptural basis for their embrace of Aristotelian seminism as they read the Wisdom of Solomon: "I myself also am a mortal man, like to all, and the offspring of him that was first made of the earth. And in my mother's womb was fashioned to be flesh in the time of ten months, being compacted in blood, of the seed of man, and the pleasure that came with sleep."[24]

In light of the specific meanings ascribed to *blood* in early modern France, Colbert's use of the term in the context of a plan to promote intermarriage between French men and Indian women conveyed a particularly gendered and essentialist vision of French and Indian identities. In expressing a desire to create "a commonwealth through intermarriage," Colbert's "one blood" policy implied that the all male colonists shared a French blood that would eventually eradicate the feminized blood of Indians.[25]

In seventeenth-century metropolitan context, the use of blood to express a collective identity remained mostly confined to the description of ties within and between families and the naturalization of political and social distinctions between nobles and commoners. References to blood to convey national belonging were rare although some examples can be found in the civil jurisprudence concerning the cases of individuals born abroad of French parents and who returned to France to claim the inheritance rights attached to French citizenship. Peter Sahlins has shown how these cases contributed to "shape a distinctively 'French' nationality law" that increasingly emphasized descent rather than birth in France as a fundamental precondition to citizenship. The idea of "French blood" occasionally surfaced in these legal proceedings. In the 1630s, for instance, barrister Le Maistre successfully argued before the Paris Parlement that "a Frenchman engenders Frenchmen everywhere [since] it is the blood that is French," and not "the air" in which one is born.[26]

## The Colonial "Blood of France"

While such references to "French blood" remained uncommon in the metropole, they quickly became a staple of colonial discourses concerned with the always elusive control of colonial sexualities and the role of filiation in determining social and political boundaries. To be sure, the colonial reinscription of "French blood," whether Frenchmen could indeed engender Frenchmen "everywhere," remained a constant source of debates, disagreements, and new articulations. In matters of race, the discursive landscape of the French Atlantic remained, as it did elsewhere, a complex patchwork of often seemingly contradictory prescriptions and practices predicated on local demographic, cultural, and geopolitical circumstances, and on the ability of people of African and Indian ancestry to contest discriminatory measures and/or to use them to their advantage. Yet, it is through these very tensions that the gendered, racialized, and "nationalized" notion of French blood emerged most vividly.

By the turn of the eighteenth century, the dismal failure of intermarriage as an instrument of assimilation, along with the reluctance of both Indian women and the seemingly ever-growing number of male settlers to embrace colonial agendas of Christian civility and obedience, led a number of colonial officials in New France to question the Aristotelian seminism of Colbert's "one blood" policy. According to these commentators, French-Indian intimacies rarely contributed to the "formation of families" that would conform to the colonial elite's idealized model of patriarchal order. Rather, they insisted, Indian women's "untamable" sexuality had rendered many French male settlers "addicted to vice."[27]

In keeping with French metropolitan moralists' conviction that "the very disorders of men usually come from those of women," some officials decided to rein in those who continued to hold that Indian women, "once instructed in our faith," would provide suitable brides for French settlers and soldiers. In 1709, the new governor of New France, Philippe de Rigaud de Vaudreuil, even took the unprecedented step of prohibiting the celebration of marriages between Frenchmen and Indian women in the Western posts.[28] In a dramatic reversal of the gendered underpinnings of the "one blood" policy elaborated forty years earlier, he explained:

> one should never mix a bad blood with a good one. Our experience ... in this country ought to prevent us from permitting marriages of this kind, for all the Frenchmen who have married savage women have become licentious, lazy, and intolerably independent; and the children they have had have been as lazy as the savages themselves [and] it seems that all the children born of them try to create as many difficulties as possible for the French.[29]

The quasi-biological determinism of Vaudreuil's opposition to French-Indian marriages was arguably the result of a peculiar combination of circumstances. In France the beginning of the eighteenth century was marked by a resurgence of "racist" discourses concerning *mésalliance* (the marriage of people from different social ranks), which emphasized the perils attached to the mixing of "unequal bloods." Sensing that Louis XIV's reign (1643–1715) was drawing to a close, a number of aristocrats had become increasingly outspoken in criticizing absolutist policies that had forced the "best families" of the Kingdom into such marriages. From the perspective of the old nobility, the multiplication of the sales of ennobling venal offices to finance costly wars had not only shattered the natural order but had also destabilized the financial health of many aristocratic families. Because they had been denied the highest paying administrative offices by an absolutist king eager to contain their political claims, some old nobles had been forced into socially undesirable marriages. "It is financial necessity," wrote the Duc de Saint Simon in the early eighteenth century, "which has led the nobility to such a forgetfulness of itself." "So much so," he continued, "that [the nobility] is not ashamed to mix its blood with that of the vilest commoners or to make it flow in its veins."[30]

As a member of the old aristocracy, Vaudreuil may have been inclined to draw on the tendency of his metropolitan counterparts to equate corruption of social order with corruption of blood as he articulated his opposition to French-Indian marriages, but in developing his stance, he actually recast the concept of *mésalliance*. Whereas in the French metropole, the term applied to marriages between persons of unequal social rank and was deemed a threat only to the preservation of the "good blood" of the highest ranks of metropolitan society, in Vaudreuil's hands, the term applied to all French-Indian unions, no matter the social ranks, with the consequence that the threat to "good blood" posed by *mésalliance* now reached all segments of French colonial society.

Yet this recasting of the concept did not always trump practical considerations. Vaudreuil himself was well aware that kinship ties between the French and Indians could occasionally facilitate the forging of alliances upon which the colony relied for military protection against Indian and British enemies. Indeed, at the same time he insisted on the dangers of the "mixing" of bloods in the Western posts, he repeatedly expressed his support for the inheritance claims of Bernard-Anselme de Saint-Castin, the *metis* son of the famous Baron of Saint Castin and of Melchilde, the daughter of a Penobscot leader. While Bernard-Anselme's metropolitan relatives claimed that as the son of a *sauvagesse*, Bernard-Anselme was nothing more than a "bastard," Vaudreuil denounced the argument as a nonsensical "quibble" and urged the minister of the Navy to resolve the matter in Bernard-Anselme's favor.[31] Given Bernard-Anselme's particular usefulness in securing indispensable alliances between New France and his maternal Wabanaki kin, Vaudreuil's contradictions might simply be taken as an expression of realpolitik. Alternatively, Vaudreuil's support of Bernard-Anselme should perhaps be viewed less as a contradiction than as a telling illustration of how, despite their essentializing claims, racial prescriptions remain permanently unstable notions articulating "positional relationships," constantly made and unmade in the always elusive pursuit of a stable and absolute social and political order, and in the very practical pursuit of political, social, and economic interests and power.[32]

Indeed, colonial anxieties about "mixed blood" often emerged during notably tense political and economic junctures. In early eighteenth-century Louisiana, for instance, the first ban against French-Indian marriages occurred in a context of particularly acute concerns for the survival of mostly starving French male settlers and soldiers and of repeated clashes between civil and ecclesiastical authorities. Intent on curtailing regular desertions to Native communities and invoking the need to preserve the integrity of "French blood" in the nascent colony, the commanding officers of the sole settlement, Mobile, attempted to prevent missionaries from celebrating French-Indian unions, both within and outside the settlement. To the vicar of the bishop of Quebec, in residence in Mobile from 1704 to 1710, such an infringement of the sacramental prerogatives of missionaries was unacceptable. Pointing out that those very commanding officers often turned a blind eye to the "scandalous concubinage" imposed by their own subordinates on enslaved *sauvagesses*, the vicar demanded the interference of Versailles in the matter, insisting that, based on his experience, "he did not see the blood of the Savages cause any harm to the blood of the French" since "the whiteness of the children is absolutely equal to that of the French themselves." Confronted with secular authorities' claim that the children of French-Indian couples were "*metifs* [because] they appeared to be of mixed blood," the vicar eventually conceded that the sanctification of marriages between French men and Indian women should perhaps be restricted to the Illinois Country, where "women are whiter, more laborious, cleverer, neater in the household work, and more docile than those of the South."[33] In the end, however, the metropolitan government agreed with the top officials of Louisiana that permitting such unions "would be of no utility for the increase of families" because of the "adulteration to the whiteness and purity of the blood" they engendered.[34]

When both proponents and detractors of the sanctification of French-Indian unions in Louisiana referred to the "whiteness" of "French blood," they reprised an already familiar theme. In French Atlantic colonies, the association between "whiteness" and "Frenchness" had first emerged in the Antilles during the seventeenth century, not only as a means to distinguish the "free" population of the islands from enslaved "Africans," but also and most importantly as a product of protracted debates about the status of people of "mixed" ancestry. While Caribbean regulations adopted as early as the 1640s envisaged that the children of *négresses* (negresses) would inherit the status of their mothers, a number of officials and missionaries nevertheless considered that *mulâtres* (mulattos) born of a "white father" and an enslaved mother should "follow the condition of their fathers." For those eager to see the sexuality of enslaved women circumscribed to the reproduction of enslaved labor, however, such a practice rewarded what they considered both "a crime and a sin." Since "mulattos" were most often the product of the "prostitution" and "disorders of the negresses," who "easily abandoned themselves to artisans, servants, and even the sons of good families," the argument went, they were nothing more than "bastards," thus implying that they could not inherit anything from their fathers. By the 1680s, the legislation of the islands reflected continued tensions on this issue: in Martinique "mulattos" were declared free after they reached their majority while in Guadeloupe they were perpetually enslaved. Even the highest-ranking officials seemed divided on the issue. In 1681, for instance, Governor Charles de Courbon de Blénac (gouverneur général des Isles d'Amérique) explained that since "whites easily form alliances with this blood [black women's]" and "mulattos … easily adopt our manners, our language, and our religion, and are accustomed to the climate," they should all be declared free. The governor also favored intermarriage between French settlers and free *mulâtresses* (mulatresses) as a means of increasing the population of the islands. The Spanish and the Portuguese, he insisted, "have only established their islands through this means." Yet he approvingly explained that they made "blood distinctions" according to the degree of African ancestry.[35] Intendant Jean-Baptiste Patoulet strongly objected to De Blénac's position on French-mulatto intermarriages, which he saw as the source of "scandal and disorders." "It is true," he replied, "that the debauchery of the Spaniards and the Portuguese has brought them to alliances with such an impure blood, but I can also say that their colonies are abodes of abominations, vice, and filth."[36]

Despite their strong disagreements over the status of mulattos and the consequences of their marriages with "whites," both de Blénac and Patoulet seemed to concur that "blood" should serve as a major referent in determining the social order of the islands. Thus when the metropolitan drafters of the famous 1685 Code Noir envisaged compelling unmarried "free men" to wed their enslaved concubines and granted all free people of color the same "rights, privileges, and immunities" as those of "natural subjects," they appeared quite out of sync with the legal culture of the islands. Indeed, the king himself attempted to renege on this last provision just a few years later, after a number of "free blacks and mulattos" invoked it in refusing to pay the royal poll tax, a tax from which "all whites born in the islands" had been exempted since the 1660s.[37]

During the first half of the eighteenth century, colonial legislatures seemed particularly intent on curtailing the aspirations of free people of color to enjoy the benefits of *naturalité*, which, in accordance with French law, the first royal charter of the islands had defined as the ability to receive and transmit property by inheritance, and to be granted "official commissions and honors." As early as 1703, the Superior Council of Martinique refused to register the titles of nobility of two Breton brothers "because they had married mulatto women," thus ensuring that their "mixed" offspring would not inherit their titles.[38] In 1726, a royal declaration excluded all "free Negroes, their children and descendants" from the succession of "whites."[39] In Saint Domingue, where whites were more likely to contract marriages with people of African descent than in the other islands, a 1733 ordinance stated that "any white who will marry a negresse or a mulatress will not be allowed to become an officer, and will be barred from any employment in the colony."[40] According to Saint Domingue officials, such an ordinance would "maintain [whites] in their purity, and there will be no more fear that mulattos may tarnish the blood of France through such alliances in the future."[41]

To be sure, such concerns often varied according to time and place. It is noteworthy, for instance, that the colonial councils of Saint Domingue never registered the 1726 royal declaration on successions and that the actual proscription of marriages between "white subjects of the king" and people of color only became law in Louisiana and the Mascarene Islands of the Indian Ocean.[42] Even the proliferation of discriminatory measures taken against free people of color during the last decades of the Ancien Régime did not prevent the rise of an increasingly wealthy class of so-called *gens de couleur libres*, particularly in the southern province of Saint Domingue. Indeed, complex economic and familial ties between "whites" and "people of color" often allowed the latter to openly protest or discreetly circumvent the letter of the law.[43]

For those who aspired to official or honorific functions, however, being identified as a *sang mêlé* or a *mésallié* often proved insurmountable. By the 1770s, a number of individuals in Saint Domingue and Martinique who had long enjoyed "the status of being White" and had served as militia officers or surgeons found themselves demoted from their posts after ill-intentioned colleagues or neighbors accused them of "being of mixed blood" and prompted the authorities to search their genealogies. A few well-established "white" planters who had obtained letters of nobility and requested their registration met a similar fate.[44]

Remarkably, such cases also signaled a departure from previous colonial hierarchies of blood. When some defendants resorted to the argument that they could not be considered *sang mêlé* since their questionable ancestors were American Indians and not Africans, metropolitan authorities concurred that "those who come from an Indian race should be assimilated to those subjects of the King originally from Europe." Ignoring or feigning to ignore the jurisprudence of the recently lost colonies of New France and Louisiana, the minister of the Navy explained in 1767 that "His Majesty has always admitted ... an essential difference between *les indiens* and *les nègres*" because the former had "always held the advantage of freedom in the colonies" while the latter had been "introduced as slaves" whose descendants carried a "stain" that "even the gift of freedom cannot erase": those who claimed Indian ancestry as means of reincorporation into white subjecthood had first to prove "their genealogy, in such a manner that no doubt remain about their origins."[45]

For most colonial officials, the exclusion of *sang mêlés* and *mésalliés* from public office remained first and foremost a matter of "national" preservation. In 1775, writing in response to metropolitan intellectuals engaged in the emerging antislavery movement, Pierre Victor Malouet, a high-ranking official in Saint Domingue and Guyane, explained that slavery was "essential" to avoid "the incorporation or the mixing of the Races" for "only the ignominy attached to an alliance with a Black slave secures the Nation's own filiation." Seemingly encapsulating decades of colonial discourses connecting sexuality, race, and nationhood, Malouet concluded: "If the Black man among us is assimilated to the Whites, it is more probable that in short order we shall see Mulattos as nobles, financiers, merchants whose wealth would soon procure wives and mothers to all the Orders of the State. It is thus that individuals, families, [and] Nations become altered, debased, & dissolve."[46]

## "Le Sang S'Altère": Racial Anxieties in Eighteenth-Century France

Concerns about "the Black among us" did not long remain confined to colonial discourse and policies. Starting in the late 1730s, the presence of enslaved people of African ancestry in the metropole prompted French government officials and jurists to tap directly into colonial conceptualizations of race and nation.

Prior to the early eighteenth century, metropolitan jurisprudence had long claimed that all enslaved people reaching French soil were to be freed, provided that they had been baptized.[47] In 1698, for instance, the French minister of the Navy informed officials in Martinique that there existed "no ordinance which permits colonists to keep their negro slaves in France when they [the slaves] want to avail themselves of the liberty acquired by all who touch its soil." In this period few slaves apparently did. In 1715, when Pauline Villeneuve, the teenage slave of a Caribbean colonist, invoked this "freedom principle," seeking the protection of the Benedictine Sisters of the Calvary in the premier slave-trading port, Nantes, and refusing to return to her mistress, the admiralty court of Nantes granted her freedom, rejecting the owner's claim and basing their decision upon "common usage," but they reached this conclusion only after debating the case for some time. The case prompted the mayor of Nantes to implore royal authorities to enact some definite legislation on the matter. The following year, the royal government decided to allow colonists to legally keep their slaves on metropolitan soil for a period of one year. Provided that they obtained the authorization of the colonial governor and that they registered them in admiralty courts, the Edict of 1716 stated, they would conserve their slaves. If masters failed to comply with these formalities, however, "the negroes would be free and would not be able to be reclaimed."[48]

By 1738, that loophole was closed. A new royal declaration, noting that too many owners were failing to comply with the formalities outlined in 1716, and fearing that the many negroes who had since come to France had "contracted a spirit of independence ... which may have troublesome results," now stipulated that if masters failed to comply with the directives of the 1716 edict, their slaves would not be freed but confiscated to the profit of the king and returned to the colonies. The ultimate objective of the new law, the ministry explained, was not only to prevent the "multiplicity of manumissions" but also to ensure that the "mixing of black blood in the kingdom" would not occur.[49]

If the 1738 royal declaration made the freedom principle null and void, its implementation was somewhat limited. The Parlement of Paris, whose jurisdiction extended to one third of the kingdom, refused to register the king's decree, mainly for political reasons, thus opening the possibility for slaves residing in Ile-de-France, the Loire valley, and other regions of the interior to obtain their freedom from the admiralty court of Paris. Until the 1760s, only a handful of slaves actually were emancipated in this manner, but still, the situation created by the parlement's action did limit the ability of masters to use the courts to reclaim their slaves.[50]

By the mid eighteenth century, royal officials had become anxious about what they perceived as a growing and uncontrollable black population residing in France. For Guillaume Poncet de la Grave, the king's attorney at the Paris admiralty court, whether blacks were legally free or enslaved while in France seemed to matter less than the fact that they were in France at all. In 1762, he argued that "France, and especially the capital, have become a public market where men are sold to the highest and last bidder; not a bourgeois or a worker is without his black slave. ... Such abuses cannot be tolerated; the introduction of too many blacks in France, whether slaves or of any other sort, has dangerous consequences. Soon, we shall see the French nation disfigured."[51] A year later, the Duc de Choiseul, minister of the Navy, ordered all blacks residing in France out of the country and directed provincial officials to identify and register all blacks residing in their regions. The circular letter he sent along with census forms insisted on the utmost necessity "to put an end to the disorders that they [blacks] have introduced in the kingdom by their communication with the whites, from which has resulted a mixed blood which increases daily."[52]

That these statements were made in metropolitan France following the French military defeat of the Seven Years War is noteworthy. To many commentators, the outcome of the war signified that the French were in need of "regeneration." "The French nation has changed," one typical lament declared; "we are no longer as robust, as strong, as the ancient Gauls from whom we descend."[53] Warnings about the weakness of the French nation were often expressed through the invocation of Gaulish or Frankish ancestry and in a language that equated French political weakness with effeminacy and disease.[54] For a number of philosophes and scientists, the necessity to "regenerate" the French nation, "to meliorate the race," as one member of the Société Royale de Médecine put it, demanded the urgent attention of the state.[55] Partly inspired by the influential vitalist theories developed by the Montpellier medical school, they insisted not only on the causal connection between physical and moral improvement but also on the possibility, and indeed the necessity, to adopt rational policies to achieve national regeneration.[56] First and foremost among the remedies to French degeneration was the management of French sexuality and marriage patterns.[57] According to Charles-Augustin Vandermonde, docteur-régent at the Paris medical faculty, for instance, the implementation of "simple rules and natural principles" already presiding over the breeding of better animal species would forestall "degeneration."[58] For his colleague Louis de Lignac, conjugal hygiene also constituted a cornerstone of socio-political reform. In his voluminous and influential treatise, *De l'homme et de la femme considérés physiquement dans l'état du marriage*, Lignac thus argued for a careful matching of husbands and wives, and for the avoidance of those unions that would further the "temperamental diversity" of Europeans brought on by "luxury, weakness, and debauchery."[59]

Such discourses endured throughout the last decades of the Ancien Régime as the royal government continued to focus on rooting out people of African ancestry from the metropole. In 1777, a new set of regulations known as the Police des Noirs required all "Blacks, Mulattos, and other people of color" residing in the kingdom to register at local admiralty or royal jurisdictions. Those entering France were to be confined to specially created depots or detention centers in French port cities.[60] Disrupting the introduction of blacks into the kingdom, the drafters of the new law explained, would help to prevent the "mixing French blood," and thus curb the transmitting of the "vicious inclinations" of the *nègres* into the French populations "for many generations."[61] For minister of the Navy Antoine de Sartine, the preservation of public health was at stake since blacks now "infected" the public houses, thus accelerating the "mingling" of colors and the "alteration of [French] blood."[62] Although the black population of France never exceeded five thousand in the entire kingdom, some local officials seemed to see the new legislation as a cure-all. Thus the advocate-general at the Bastia Superior Council in Corsica, the first body to register the new law, described it as a "new lease on life" that would help preserve the "purity of French blood." For some, however, the threat to the "white nation" would persist as long as the "monstrous assemblage" of blacks and whites in marriage remained possible. Thus, in April 1778, after consultations with ecclesiastical authorities, Louis XVI issued a decree prohibiting "all his White subjects from contracting marriages with Blacks, Mulattos, and other people of color."[63]

If political and medical discourses shared more or less pronounced anxieties regarding the "mixing of French and Black blood," a few intellectuals seemingly went against the grain of essentialist underpinnings in such discourses. In 1781, for instance, the Baron de Condorcet, future founding member of the then fledgling Société des Amis des Noirs, declared in his "Epitaph to Enslaved Negroes": "Although I am not the same color as you, I have always considered you my brother. Nature has shaped you to have the same spirit, the same reason, and the same virtues as the whites."[64] Yet, what "nature" had done, enslavement had presumably undone as Condorcet estimated that it would take at least seventy years before "all negroes" could enjoy the status of "free man."[65] Whether people of African ancestry residing in the metropole could be considered "free men" and as such be allowed to contract marriages with "whites" did not concern Condorcet, but it apparently did his future fellow "Friend of the Blacks," the famous Abbé Guillaume Raynal. In all editions of the *Histoire des Deux Indes*, a work co-written by Raynal with a number of other Enlightened luminaries, including Denis Diderot, which has long held a reputation as one of the most scathing attacks against colonial slavery in the late eighteenth century, the author(s) enjoined "Young Creoles" to "come into Europe to exercise and practice what we teach you," but to do so unaccompanied by their slaves: "Leave in America your negroes, whose condition distresses us, and whose blood, perhaps, is mingled in all those ferments which alter, corrupt and destroy our population."[66]

Ultimately, direct challenges to metropolitan injunctions against the "mixing of bloods" never came from the quills of the French Enlightenment but from individuals who personally bore the brunt of such measures. Following the 1778 decree against "mixed" marriages, "interracial" couples often had to enlist the support of influential (white) patrons if they wished to circumvent the law.[67] In the summer of 1778, for instance, a "mulatto" named Alexis Brémont and his white bride, Marie Magdeleine Faudon, obtained the authorization of the bishop of Marseille and the Parlement of Provence to have their union celebrated in the town of Cassis. Informed after the fact, the minister of the Navy chastised the provincial intendant, who explained that an exception had been made because Brémont was a rich and "honest man ... generally loved and esteemed" by local notables, including his (white) relatives, "who do not blush to see him bear their name."[68] In 1785, in another instance, Charles Louis Almanzor, a *nègre indien* who resided in Versailles and wished to marry a white laundress named Anne Victoire Dinanceau, obtained an authorization from the king himself, but only after an intervention by the king's sister. The authorization specified that the ceremony would have to take place as discreetly as possible to avoid "any scandal."[69] Until that moment, the king had denied all such requests, even when accompanied by the pleas of some of the most distinguished members of the aristocracy.[70]

# Epilogue

This chapter has attempted to trace the transatlantic filiation between metropolitan and colonial conceptualizations of race and nation during the Ancien Régime, focusing almost exclusively on matters of policy and law. There is much that obviously remains to be uncovered. We still know relatively little about the ways in which the political advent of the racial nation and the racial ascriptions that accompanied it influenced those subjected to them. How, for instance, did people of "mixed blood" conceive of their own relationship to racialized national identity? Two texts written by so-called people of color during the French Revolution may provide the beginning of an answer, while also suggesting the continued resonance of political and social hierarchies based on birth in a period when they supposedly began to unravel. The first is a *cahier de doléances* sent to Paris in 1789, by the "Habitants of Sénégal" (the free people of color residing in Saint Louis du Sénégal and Gorée), requesting the end of the commercial monopoly, including slave trading activities, of the Compagnie de Guyane in Saint Louis and Gorée. Claiming to have always been faithful to "our fathers the French," the petitioners actually invoked both French patrilineal and Wolof matrilineal notions of kinship to articulate their claim to Frenchness: "Negroes or mulattos, we are all French because it is the blood of the French that flows in our veins, or in those of our nephews."[71] The other is a petition of the "Citoyens de couleur des isles françoises" delivered to the National Assembly by the famous mulatto leader Julien Raimond in 1791. Claiming "their rights as active citizens," the petitioners invoked their long-standing kinship ties with colonial "whites," whom they described as "the fathers, the brothers of citizens of color." "It is their blood," they insisted, "French blood, that runs in our veins." Thus, they explained, their "cause had nothing in common with the cause of the slaves."[72]

That same year, however, slaves took matters into their own hands and launched a series of uprisings that would eventually compel the French revolutionary state to abolish slavery and declare all freed slaves French citizens. While state-mandated emancipation was remarkably short-lived (1794–1802) and its implementation anything but "race blind," the struggles of slaves for liberty and citizenship constituted the first real challenge to longstanding ideologies of blood; ideologies that some revolutionary slave leaders themselves did not hesitate to invoke in communicating with those who refused to accept their claims.[73] In July 1792, the "leaders of the negro rebels [chefs des nègres révoltés]" addressed a letter to colonial authorities and all the "citizens" of Saint Domingue. While insisting that both blacks and whites were all "children of the same father" (i.e., God) and as such were all "brothers" and entitled to the same enjoyment of liberty, they reminded slave-owning free people of color whose own struggles had recently afforded them the status of citizen that they owed "this respectable title only to the work of men whose throats you want to slit"; "remember," they concluded, that these men "are your brothers, your parents, and that their blood flows in your veins."[74]

## NOTES

1. Michel Foucault, *The History of Sexuality*, vol. 1, *An Introduction* (New York, 1978), 147–49.
2. Ann Laura Stoler, *Race and the Education of Desire: Foucault's History of Sexuality and the Colonial Order of Things* (Durham, NC, 1995).
3. Frederick Cooper and Ann Laura Stoler, eds., *Tensions of Empire: Colonial Cultures in a Bourgeois World* (Berkeley and Los Angeles, CA, 1997), esp. 10 for the quotation. See also Ann Laura Stoler, *Carnal Knowledge and Imperial Power: Race and the Intimate in Colonial Rule* (Berkeley and Los Angeles, CA, 2002); Kathleen Wilson, *The Island Race: Englishness, Empire and Gender in the Eighteenth Century* (London, 2003).
4. R. G. Thwaites, ed., *The Jesuit Relations and Allied Documents: Travels and Explorations of the Jesuit Missionaries in New France, 1610–1791*, 73 vols. (Cleveland, OH, 1896–1901), 5:211, 20:26.
5. Lettre de Colbert à Talon, 5 April 1667, *Rapport de l'archiviste de la Province de Québec* (1930–31), 72.
6. Cornelius Jaenen, *Friend and Foe: Aspects of French-Amerindian Cultural Contact in the Sixteenth and Seventeenth Centuries* (New York, 1976), 161–85.
7. On this issue, see Arlette Jouanna, *L'idée de race en France au XVI^e siècle et au début du XVII^e siècle (1498–1614)* (Lille, 1976); André Devyver, *Le sang épuré. Les préju-*

gés de race chez les gentilhommes français de l'Ancien Régime (1560–1720) (Brussels, 1973); Ellery Schalk, *From Valor to Pedigree: Ideas of Nobility in France in the Sixteenth and Seventeenth Centuries* (Princeton, NJ, 1986); Jonathan Dewald, *Aristocratic Experience and the Origins of Modern Culture: France, 1570–1715* (Berkeley, CA, 1993).

8. *Harangve faicte par la Noblesse de Champagne & de Brie* (s. l., 1615), 12–13. A digitized copy can be found on the Gallica platform of the Bibliothèque nationale de France at http://gallica.bnf.fr/ark:/12148/bpt6k999621. This text speaks of the nobility as "truly French souls" [les ames vrayement Françoises], at page 6.

9. *Discours sur le congé impétré par Monsieur le Cardinal de Lorraine* (s.l., 1565), 5. See also Pierre de La Primaudaye, *Academie Françoise* (Paris, 1581), fol. 53.

10. Pierre de Saint Julien de Balleure, *Meslanges historiques* (Lyon, 1588), 589.

11. Gilles André François de la Roque, *Traité de la noblesse* (Paris, 1678).

12. Etienne de La Boétie, *Discours de la servitude volontaire* (1550), in *Oeuvres complètes d'Estienne de la Boétie*, ed. Paul Bonnefon (Paris, 1892), 15–16. See also Josse Clichtove, *Le livre et traicté de toute vraye noblesse, nouvellement translaté de latin en françoys* (Lyon, 1533), fol. Aiiii;

13. De la Roque, *Traité de la noblesse*, 326.

14. According to historian François de Belleforest in 1579, such "mixing of the races" would render "the nobility of this Kingdom … completely bastardized": François de Belleforest, *Les grandes annales et histoire générale de France. …* (Paris, 1579), fol. 1620. On the "widespread sense that women threatened the purity of the lineage," see Dewald, *Aristocratic Experience*, 127–28.

15. Gayle K. Brunelle, "Dangerous Liaisons: Mésalliances and Early Modern French Noble Women," *French Historical Studies* 19 (1995): 83, 94, 95.

16. Sarah Hanley, "The Monarchic State in Early Modern France: Marital Regime Government and Male Right," in *Politics, Ideology and the Law in Early Modern Europe*, ed. Adrianna E. Bakos (Rochester, NY, 1994), 116.

17. Jouanna, *L'idée de race*, 149; Devyver, *Le sang*, 164–69.

18. Évelyne Berriot-Salvadore, "Le discours de la médecine et de la science," in *Histoire des femmes en Occident*, ed. Natalie Zemon Davis and Arlette Farge, vol. 3, *XVIᵉ–XVIIIᵉ siècle* (Paris, 2002), 426–27.

19. André Du Laurens, *Toutes les oeuvres, trad du Latin par Gelée* (Paris, 1621), 392. See also Nicolas Venette, *Tableau de l'amour conjugal* (Paris, 1696), 303; or Jean Liébault, *Trois livres des maladies et infirmitez des femmes* (Rouen, 1649), bk. 3, chap. 5, 525.

20. Pierre Darmon, *Le mythe de la procréation à l'âge baroque* (Paris, 1977), 18–19.

21. Ambroise Paré, "De la Generation," in *Les oeuvres d'Ambroise Paré*, bk. 24 (Paris, 1585), 978.

22. Gianna Pomata, "Blood Ties and Semen Ties: Consanguinity and Agnation in Roman Law," in *Gender, Kinship, Power: A Comparative and Interdisciplinary History*, ed. Mary Jo Maynes et al. (New York, 1996), 52–53.

23. Michel de Montaigne, "Of the Resemblance of Children to Fathers," in *The Complete Essays of Montaigne*, trans. Donald M. Frame (Stanford, CA, 1958), 578. Ninety years later, Nicolas Venette, in *Tableau de l'amour considéré dans l'état du mariage* (Amsterdam, 1687), made a similar point.

24. Wisdom of Solomon 7:1–2. Traditionally excluded from Protestant Bibles, the deuterocanonical books (termed *Apocrypha* by Protestant theologians) were nevertheless included in the King James translation of 1611.

25. And yet we should note that Colbert himself did not seem entirely confident in this outcome. Between the 1660s and the early 1680s, while his ministry allocated

a few thousand livres for the dowries of potential Indian brides, it also spent more than 400,000 livres on transportation and dowries of French girls to be married with French settlers almost as soon as they disembarked. On this, see Guillaume Aubert, "'The Blood of France': Race and Purity of Blood in the French Atlantic World," *William and Mary Quarterly* 61 (July 2004).

26. Peter Sahlins, *Unnaturally French: Foreign Citizens in the Old Regime and After* (Ithaca, NY, 2004), 61–64.

27. La Mothe-Cadillac au ministre, 26 October 1713, Centre des Archives d'Outre-Mer, Aix-en-Provence (hereafter cited as CAOM), C13 A 3, fol. 13

28. Lettre de Lamothe-Cadillac, 1700, CAOM, C11 E, fols. 40–41v; Lettre du Ministre à M. de Vaudreuil, 6 July 1709, CAOM, B30, fols. 159v–160.

29. Lettre du Gouverneur de Vaudreuil au Roi, 17 November 1709, CAOM, C11 A 30, fol. 9.

30. Quoted in Louis Trenard, "Les fondements de l'idée de race au XVIIIᵉ siècles," *L'Information Historique* 43 (1981): 166.

31. Mémoire de Jean de Labaig, 7 October 1709, Bibliothèque nationale, Paris, Nouveau d'Hozier 84, dossier St-Castin.

32. Wilson, *The Island Race*, 11; Stoler, *Carnal Knowledge*, 144.

33. Henri Roulleaux de la Vente to Brisacier, 4 July 1708, Archives du Séminaire de Québec, Lettres R 83, 19–20. See also Mémoire sur l'état présent de la colonie de la Louisiane (1710), CAOM, C13 A 3, fol. 565. On the "whiteness" of Illinois women's blood, see La Vente's 1714 report cited in Arrêt du Conseil de la Marine, 1 September 1716, CAOM, C13 A 4, fol. 255.

34. Arrêt du Conseil de la Marine, 1 September 1716, CAOM, C13 A 4, fol. 255

35. Extrait des avis de Mrs de Blénac et Paoulet sur divers objets d'administration que le Roi avoit fourni à leur discussion par sa lettre du 30 avril 1681, 3 December 1681, CAOM, F3 248, fol. 687.

36. Extrait des avis de Mrs de Blénac et Paoulet, CAOM, F3 248, fol. 687.

37. On the Code Noir, see Guillaume Aubert, "'To Establish One Law and Definite Rules': Race, Religion, and the Transatlantic Origins of the Louisiana Code Noir," in *Louisiana: Crossroads of the Atlantic World*, ed. Cécile Vidal (Philadelphia, PA, 2013). On free people of color and the poll tax, see Léo Elisabeth, *La société martiniquaise au XVIIᵉ et XVIIIᵉ siècles, 1664–1789* (Paris, 2003), 246–52, 297–312.

38. Machault to Pontchartrain, 21 September 1703, CAOM, C8 A 15, fols. 43–44.

39. Déclaration du Roi du 8 février 1726, in *Loix et constitutions des colonies françaises de l'Amérique sous le vent*, ed. *Moreau de Saint-Méry*, 6 vols. (Paris, [1784–90]), 3:159 ; hereafter cited as MSM.

40. Lettre du Gouverneur general de Fayet au Gouverneur du Cap, 7 December 1733, MSM, 3:382.

41. Lettre du ministre aux administrateurs touchant les mésalliances, 18 October 1731, CAOM, F3 91, fols. 96–97.

42. Déclaration du Roi du 8 février 1726, MSM, 3:159.

43. For Saint Domingue, see Dominique Rogers, "On the Road to Citizenship: The Complex Paths of the Integration of Free People of Colour in the Two Capitals of Saint-Domingue," in *The World of the Haitian Revolution*, ed. David Geggus and Norman Fiering (Bloomington, IN, 2009), 65–78; John Garrigus, *Before Haiti: Race and Citizenship in French Saint-Domingue* (New York, 2006). For Martinique and Guadeloupe, see Léo Elisabeth, *La société martiniquaise*, 389–458; Frédéric Régent, *Esclavage, métissage, liberté. La révolution française en Guadeloupe 1789–1802* (Paris, 2004), 143–213.

44. See for instance the following personnel files held at CAOM: "Baldy, Pierre" (1777–84), E 15; "Bayon de Libertat" (1700–85), E 21; "Chapuizet de Guériné, Pierre" (1771–83), E 71; "Gellée, Charles Claude" (1736–67 ), E 201; "Levêque, Charles, et son frère Levêque Guillaume" (1769), E 285.
45. Lettre du Ministre aux Administrateurs contenant une décision aux trois points relatifs aux Races Noires et Indiennes, 7 January 1767, MSM, 5:80–81.
46. Pierre-Victor Malouet, *Mémoire sur l'esclavage des Negres* (Neufchatel, 1788), 53. On the original date of composition, see ibid., 176.
47. By ordering masters to baptize all slaves held in the islands, the 1685 Code Noir had limited this possibility to metropolitan soil.
48. Sue Peabody, *There Are No Slaves in France: The Political Culture of Race and Slavery in the Ancien Régime* (Oxford, 1996), 11–22.
49. Maurepas, 15 February 1739, CAOM, B 18, fol. 95.
50. Peabody, *There Are No Slaves*, 41–56, 72–87.
51. De La Haye, "Sentence de règlement rendue en l'admirauté de la France concernant les declarations a passer pour les nègres et Mulatres," 5 April 1762, Paris, Archives nationales, Z1 D 139.
52. Lettre du Ministre aux Administrateurs, qui défend d'accorder aucun passage pour la France aux esclaves et aux nègres libres, 30 June 1763, MSM, 4:602.
53. Maille Dussaussoy, *Le citoyen désintéressé, ou diverses idées patriotiques* (Paris, 1767), 114.
54. See, in particular, David Bell, *The Cult of the Nation: Inventing Nationalism, 1680–1800* (Cambridge, MA, 2001), 140–54.
55. Sean M. Quinlan, *The Great Nation in Decline: Sex, Modernity and Health Crises in Revolutionary France c. 1750–1850* (Ashgate, 2007), 19–51, esp. 29 for the quotation.
56. Elizabeth Williams, *The Physical and the Moral: Anthropology, Physiology, and Philosophical Medicine in France, 1750–1850* (Cambridge, 1994). See also Anne C. Vila, *Sensibility in the Literature and Medicine of Eighteenth-Century France* (Baltimore, MD, 1998).
57. Michael Winston, "Medicine, Marriage, and Human Degeneration in the French Enlightenment," *Eighteenth-Century Studies* 38 (2005): 263–81.
58. Winston, "Medicine, Marriage, and Human Degeneration," 265–68; Charles-Augustin Vandermonde, *Essai sur la manière de perfectionner l'espèce humaine*, 2 vols. (Paris, 1756), 1:155.
59. Winston, "Medicine, Marriage, and Human Degeneration," 268–70. Winston seems to confuse Joseph-Adrien Lelarge de Lignac, an Oratorian priest, critic of Buffon and close collaborator of Réaumur, with Louis Luc de Lignac, a member of the Collège Royal de Médecine and author of *De l'homme et de la femme*, a two-volume work first published in Lille in 1772, and republished half a dozen times during the 1770s and 1780s. Editions in English, German, and Italian also appeared during the same period.
60. On the Police des Noirs, see Sue Peabody, *There Are No Slaves*, 106–36. The most recent treatment of the legal and social history of blacks in eighteenth-century France is Pierre Boulle, *Race et esclavage dans la France de l'Ancien Régime* (Paris, 2007).
61. *Ordonnances de la Marine* (La Rochelle, 1776), 411.
62. Sartine to Minister of Justice, 6 February 1776, CAOM, F1 B4, no. 334. See also Sartine to Louis XVI, 9 August 1777, Paris, Bibliothèque nationale (Richelieu), Mss. Fonds français, 13,357, fols. 20–21.

63. Arrêt du Conseil d'État du Roi du 5 avril 1778, transcribed in Boulle, *Race et esclavage*, 258.

64. M. Schwartz [Jean-Antoine-Nicolas de Caritat, marquis de Condorcet], *Réflexions sur l'esclavage des Negres* (Neufchastel, 1781), iii–iv.

65. Schwartz [Condorcet], *Réflexions*, 52.

66. Guillaume-Thomas Raynal, *Histoire philosophique et politique, des établissemens & du commerce des Européens dans les deux Indes, Tome quatrieme* (Amsterdam, 1770), 201. Reproduced verbatim in subsequent editions: *Tome quatrieme* (La Haye, 1774), 262; and *Tome troisieme* (Geneve, 1780), 231.

67. Marriages between "whites" and people of color were not unheard of before the 1778 decree. The most comprehensive study of the data collected by metropolitan authorities in 1777, about people of African ancestry residing in France, indicates that out of 2031 identified individuals, 37 had been or were married to a "white" spouse. See Pierre Boulle, *Race et esclavage*, 169, 186–88.

68. Case cited in Boulle, *Race et esclavage*, 183–84.

69. "Almanzor, Charles Louis, noir, autorisation de mariage sollicitée en 1785," CAOM, E 396. The parish priest who celebrated the union simply labeled Almanzor as *indien*. See marriage record (9 May 1785), Archives départementales des Yvelines, Registres paroissiaux de Saint Louis, Versailles.

70. See "Tassime-Didier, Antoine, nègre," CAOM, 395bis and "Frédéric, mulâtre libre," CAOM, E 194.

71. "Très-humbles doléances et remontrances des Habitans du Sénégal, aux Citoyens Français tenant les Etats-Généraux (15 avril 1789)," in *L'Affrique et le people affriquains*, D. Lamiral (Paris, 1789). On race and citizenship in eighteenth-century Saint-Louis, see Guillaume Aubert, "'Nègres ou mulâtres nous sommes tous français': race, genre et nation à Gorée et Saint-Louis du Sénégal, fin XVIIe–fin XVIIIe siècle," in *Être et se penser Français. Nation, sentiment national et identités dans le monde atlantique français du XVIIe au XIXe siècle*, ed. Cécile Vidal (forthcoming).

72. *Pétition nouvelle des Citoyens de couleur des isles françoises, à l'assemblée nationale, precede d'un avertissement sur les manoeuvres employees pour faire échouer cette petition, et suivie de pieces justificatives* (Paris, 18 March 1791), 8, 7. On Julien Raimond, see John D. *Garrigus*, "Opportunist or Patriot? *Julien Raimond* (1744–1801) and the Haitian Revolution," *Slavery & Abolition* 28 (2007): 1–21.

73. See, in particular, Laurent Dubois, *A Colony of Citizens: Revolution & Slave Emancipation in the French Caribbean, 1787–1804* (Chapel Hill, NC, 2004).

74. "Lettre originale des chefs des nègres révoltés, à l'assemblée générale, aux commissaires nationaux et aux citoyens de la partie française de Saint-Domingue du mois de juillet 1792," *Le Créole Patriote* 282 (9 February 1793), Bibliothèque Historique de la Ville de Paris; reproduced in Nathalie Piquionne, "Lettre de Jean-François, Biassou et Belair," *Annales Historiques de la Révolution Française* 311 (1998): 132–39, quotation on 133–34.

# Chapter 9

# Class Dimensions of Blood, Kinship, and Race in Brittany, 1780–1880

## Christopher H. Johnson

The problematic examined here concerns the shift in the discourse of *blood*—as a term connecting individuals—from kinship to race in eighteenth- and nineteenth-century France. I argue that a decline in the use of the word *blood* (*sang*) to define the relatives and antecedents of one's parents is perceptible among bourgeois and nobles alike in the later eighteenth century. This phenomenon corresponds with the horizontalization of kinship practices and the growth of consanguineal marriage, which blurs the distinction between consanguines and affines. Simultaneously, the language of kinship is appropriated by the discourse of nation and race, and blood becomes a universal metaphor signaling one's link with other members of the group. If the new kinship regime seems not to be class bound, the politics of the racial nation, in France, nevertheless has a significant class dimension.

This chapter grew out of the realization that the word *sang* was virtually absent from the vocabulary of kinship employed during the century between 1750 and 1850, in hundreds of personal letters exchanged by members of several closely related bourgeois families of Vannes, the chief city of the Morbihan region of Brittany.[1] At the same time, though more fully after 1800, "blood" became a crucial component in the language of an emergent Breton racial nationalism. But the bourgeois of Vannes and most other Breton cities, French speakers all, rarely participated in this discourse either. Its chief proponents were for the most part intellectuals of Breton aristocratic roots disgruntled by the consequences of the French Revolution, who saw in the Breton-speaking peasantry the authentic soul of their province. Two schools thus arose in the nineteenth century to debate Breton origins and historical development: one, arguing what might be called the "noble thesis," seeking to prove the province's "Celtic-Breton" origins and its separate historical path in order to justify claims to autonomy in a restored Bourbon monarchy; the other, putting forth the "bourgeois Francophone thesis," justifying a current politics of integration within the French nation, and arguing for the strength of Gallo-Roman roots and closer links historically with the developing French state. The stakes of this debate were high, and the outcome politically significant.

## The Changing Language of Blood as a Kin-Term

To provide a baseline for this study, I begin with a sampling of the discourse of blood as utilized in the later seventeenth century by Marie de Sévigné, a Breton by marriage, a noble of impeccable credentials, and arguably the century's most famous letter writer. A digital scan for the word *sang* in Mme de Sévigné's voluminous correspondence yields 193 instances.[2] Of these, 67, or approximately a third, relate directly to kinship: "princes du sang" or "princesses du sang," the formal titles for blood relatives of the king, occurring 25 times and references to her own kin or to relatives of her friends, 43 times. This number is all the more impressive when compared with *famille*, a much more inclusive term, which appears 69 times. The term *parent(s)*, for any relative, produced 72 entries. *Sang* appears in descriptions of specific individuals or of the quality of their lineage. It crops up in discussions of the role played by nobility in maintaining social harmony and morality, even in quotations of popular adages.[3] These usages cover the range of the place of blood in the seventeenth-century kin terminology among high aristocrats, but this language actually transcends class. It is common among all the propertied classes, for whom blood relationship through the agnatic lineage determined the transmission of property from generation to generation: blood, that is, defined as the substance passed on by males (with much confusion with semen in this age of the "fungibility of fluids").[4] Relatives of one's mother were also blood-kin, but identified by their fathers' lineages. Mme de Sévigné was unexceptional.[5]

But something happened to the notion of blood as a metaphor for kinship in the course of the eighteenth century. Using the same digital-scanning method, I have searched eighteenth-century memoirs and printed correspondence for instances of the word *blood* signifying consanguineal kin. There is nothing exhaustive about this research, but it does tend to confirm the decline of the blood language that was so common a century before. The best comparison with Mme de Sévigné can be found in a writer who mirrors his society and time just as she did hers: Restif de la Bretonne, whose memoir, *Monsieur Nicolas*, was published between 1794 and 1797.[6] Alongside the scores of *familles* and *parent(s)*, there are but eighteen sentences in which *sang* operates as a kinship term. Fifteen come from notes recorded in 1750s. Not only much fewer in number than with Sévigné, the references in this memoir are less varied, often appearing as afterthoughts.[7] Restif, who hailed from Burgundian landowning-peasant roots, became a master printer, which led him quickly into literary pursuits. His Parisian social milieu bridged the aristocracy and the *bonne bourgeoisie*. His status was quite similar to that of my Breton families, who were printer/publishers and notaries with relatives in the Parisian art world.[8]

I had originally assumed that while blood might have declined in bourgeois discourse, it would remain more deeply imbedded among nobles. As it turns out, this does not seem to have been the case. In scanning some thirty-five printed collections of personal correspondence from the later eighteenth and nineteenth centuries, I have found that the preferred word for describing biological kin, whether one was noble or bourgeois, was *famille*, with *parent(s)* and *parenté* a distant second, and *liens de sang* and other such blood concepts little in evidence. The demotion of *blood* actually began well before the unleashing of anti-noble sentiment in the 1789 Revolution; even among royalists of the emigration and counter-revolutions, blood terminology was rare.[9] Three examples will illustrate these points.

The first example is found in *L'école des moeurs*, a famous guide to "proper conduct in the world" for "young gentlemen" by Abbé Jean-Baptiste-Xavier Duchesne Blanchard (1731–97), which originally appeared in 1773.[10] Its three volumes are organized around "maxims" to prepare "un honnête homme."[11] Maxim VII deals with family, counseling the aspiring gentleman to be "a good father, good spouse, good master, without weakness" and enjoining him to "honor your kin [*parens*], especially in their old age." Throughout the book, the word *blood* appears forty-nine times, but of these instances, only six relate to kin. Three occur in the discussion of family obligations and honor: condemning "*parvenus*"; honoring relatives proportionate to their "*liens de sang*";

and sequencing *"reconnaissance"* (recognition, gratitude) in a hierarchy of moral obligation that begins with those "united with one by ties of blood."[12] The other three appear in Blanchard's pages on the concept of *"noblesse"* with their blistering remarks on any young man of noble birth whose actions shame his family. Such a wayward son not only "dishonors blood" but also "defames" his forebears (*aïeux*); he insults the "virtues" of his fathers (*pères*); and is a "rotten branch" from an "illustrious trunk."[13] *Blood* here is thus buried among several other terms for one's antecedents. The final passage, in which *blood* occurs twice, stresses the obligation to give assistance to a blood relative in distress, but not if he has dishonored the family.[14] Blood thus plays a minor role as a metaphor for kinship relations in this guide to noble comportment, always, when it is used at all, mixed up with an array of other terms and vastly outnumbered by them: *famille*, occurs seventy-two times and *parens/parent*, eighty-three. Like Restif, Blanchard is a transitional figure, but a noble writing for nobles who, by following his dictates, might retain their nobility in an age of challenges to their legitimacy. Blood alone could not prop them up.[15]

The second example is taken from the correspondence of a young noblewoman in exile, Théophile de Fernig, writing to her cousin, an army officer.[16] De Fernig gained fame as a *"femme militaire"* before her commander, General Dumouriez, went over to the enemy—a momentous turning point in the Revolution and in her life. In thirty-three letters written between 1797 and 1803, *blood* appears four times. Two instances concern her emotions and a third laments blood "spilled" in warfare. The single use of blood-kin terminology comes in a passage where she hopes that she can continue to serve as a go between with her cousin's "dear relatives, who are less close by ties of blood, but who could not be more so by those [ties] of the heart and of friendship."[17] This usage is far exceeded by the frequency of *family* and *relatives* (together appearing twenty times) and other collective terms, but above all by mention of specific kin both by name and relationship on nearly every page. This noble exile sounds, in fact, a great deal like my bourgeois in Vannes writing at about the same time.

The third example comes from Mme de Genlis's novels *Adèle et Théodore* (1782) and *Les veillées du chateau* (1784), which embrace both the social pedagogy of Blanchard and the exile experience of de Fernig. Mme de Genlis, countess, enormously popular novelist, children's writer, moralist, and *salonnière*, provided my initial evidence that later eighteenth-century aristocrats were shying away from the discourse of blood. In these, her two most widely read novels, as in her ten-volume personal memoirs (1825), *blood*, as a metaphor for kinship (always expressed as "ties of blood and friendship [*l'amitié*]"), appears exactly three times, totally eclipsed by *famille* and *parens*.[18]

*Blood* as a kin-term thus appears to be fading fast in the later eighteenth century. It would require more research to make such a case definitively, but clearly the discourse of blood was changing. Why did this happen? I would cite as significant two broad and rapid developments in the eighteenth century: the transformation of kinship structures and associated behaviors, and the formulation of racial definitions of the nation. In the first, bloodline and blood relatives became less important, while in the second, the notions of blood brotherhood and bloodlines stretching back to ancient and indeed mythic ancestors were transferred from kin groups to entire peoples united by language and culture but *defined* by one blood.

The first process has been investigated and demonstrated in recent work by students of European kinship and deftly summarized in the introduction by David Warren Sabean and Simon Teuscher to *Kinship in Europe: Approaches to Long-Term Development (1300–1900)*.[19] In a paradigm shift, inheritance, kin-reckoning, internal family authority, bonds of love, marriage practices, indeed the entire habitus of kin behavior, evolved during the period from the mid eighteenth to the mid nineteenth century, from vertical patterns of relationship to horizontal ones. This development saw the waning of primogeniture, the recognition of the status of younger brothers and of sisters, the decline of father-centered patriarchy with a marked shift of power to brothers and husbands, a discourse of romantic love punctuated by brother-sister incestuous desires, and a remarkable growth of consanguineal marriage. Cousin marriage among the propertied became almost routine, as families moved away from marriages arranged to enhance mutual advantage for often somewhat socially unequal partners to those between equals where "love" was prized—and what was deeper than love among those brought up "like brothers and sisters," as cousins often were.[20]

The practical consequence was the consolidation of property, status, and power, particularly among the bourgeoisie, but this consolidation depended on the family very broadly conceived so that distinctions such as "blood relatives" and "affines" or "in-laws" became blurred. Moreover, even in marriages with non-consanguineal kin, the affinal families, which were embraced immediately as "one's own" with appropriate intimate forms of address (the familiar *tu* was routinely extended to in-laws), quickly became sources for future marriage partners. The concept of the "bloodline" simply lost its salience.[21] On the broader scale, among the elites, generations of intermarriage produced a vast *cousinage* that achieved a remarkable social and political hegemony later in the century.[22] In place of *blood relations*, the simple word *famille* is everywhere. In short, as the distinction between "blood relatives" and relatives by marriage became more difficult to discern, the use of blood as a metaphor for kinship tended to disappear along with the passing of "father-right" patriarchy and the patriline.[23]

But another metaphorical usage of blood appeared in public discourse in Europe and America in the seventeenth century and exploded in the language of the age of revolution. This was the notion of the unity of blood among people of the same "race."[24] While Frenchmen abroad wrestled with the idea of race in their capacity as conquerors of indigenous peoples and as slave owners of non-Europeans, at home, in France itself, they turned to the race concept to support conflicting views on social divisions and the legitimate locus of sovereignty in the state. Henri, le comte de Boulainvilliers, who was aligned with aristocratic factions challenging royal absolutism, posited that the history of France had been wisely steered by the blond Frankish race (essentially a synonym for the nobility) until its role was vastly diminished by a crown bent on absolute power. Among the worst of royal policies was the practice of ennobling commoners, which effectively polluted the ancient lineage of the noble race. The original constitutional rights of this race had been established on the Champs de Mars when triumphant Frankish warriors elevated Clovis as king, thereby creating a *joint* stewardship with the monarch. The right to rule was both noble *and* racial. In 1734, Abbé Dubos countered, stressing the peaceful arrival of the Franks and their considerable intermarriage with the much larger Gallo-Roman population. The French "race" was thus predominately Gallo-Roman. Clovis's government, according to Dubos, was absolutist but had nevertheless guaranteed in law the rights and freedoms of citizens, like the current monarchy. Variations on these themes punctuated eighteenth-century politics, used by both the aristocratic defenders of the Frankish race in the parlements and provincial estates and by the proponents of the Gallo-Roman majority's right to sovereignty, the latter flowing directly into notions of popular sovereignty (into the racial undertones accompanying it, as well) of the French Revolution.[25]

The Revolution simultaneously witnessed the wholesale appropriation of still-powerful kinship terminology in the cause of the "nation," upending traditional authority relationships. The royal "father" and "mother" were forced to share power with their "children" under the Constitutional Monarchy of 1791, but their continued betrayal of the new contract led to their replacement by a disembodied parent—the father*land*—given life by "la famille nationale." "Allons enfants de la patrie," sang the *Marseillais*. The children soon declared their sovereignty as they took control of the parents' house, the Tuileries palace. "Sons of the nation" streamed into battle for the nation, promising "to irrigate its furrows with the blood of our enemies," while sons *and* daughters proposed law in their "maisons nationales," and the "filles de la Révolution" even created their own political organizations. But then the sons committed "parricide," and, as the trial of Marie Antoinette dragged on, the guilt-ridden "band of brothers" denied her motherhood entirely, transforming her into a harlot and lesbian, while simultaneously harassing and *dis*banding their "soeurs de la liberté," ultimately sending a number of them to the guillotine along with the queen. As the vast brotherhood of the nation mobilized during Year II, equality became the watchword—the French became "one blood," nation and race united against not only external enemies, but also against "aristocracy," anyone of Boulainvillier's "noblesse de race." Simultaneously, legislation on behalf of equality within the family reached a fevered pitch, to the point where inheritance rights were extended to illegitimate children. Divorce was legalized and equalized as well. And all *actual* children of the fatherland were to receive a free and equal education through primary school. Finally, there were to be only two families: the one of the private sphere, which would manage its own affairs with regard to marriage and child rearing, without strictures from the state (save in first-degree incest) but subject to complete equality under the law; and the other of the public sphere, the family of the nation, which would replace the royal family and be free of hierarchy—except, of course, when it denied political rights to the sisters. A third family of the old regime, the clerical "fathers, mothers superior, brothers, and sisters," so-named by the Church in its early struggle against Roman family authority, was effectively abolished by the Civil Constitution of the Clergy. All of this would be much modified by Napoleon and in later regimes, but the Revolution nevertheless infused the idea of the "nation" with the ideology of family and kinship and completed the transfer of "blood relations" from kindred to the metaphorically racialized nation.[26]

The French Revolution at once spawned the awakening of national sentiment everywhere in Europe, either in sympathy with or in opposition to its ideals and goals, and spread its familial-racial language. In general, aristocrats were wary of revolutionary nationalism because the accompanying egalitarian themes threatened their status. But the language of race and nation proved able also to serve the cause of resistance to the French armies, and provided ideas that would be mobilized to justify aristocratic leadership and traditional social structures. Nowhere was this truer than in the counter-revolutionary pockets of France itself where non-French languages, cultures, and—for now the term had arrived—"races" thrived. Brittany, with its complicated and murky cultural and political history, was the prime example.[27]

## Race and Class in Brittany: The Battleground of History

Any linguistic mapping of Brittany in the eighteenth century reveals that the pattern of language use has both geographic and socio-economic components. The division of Brittany into Upper Brittany (east of the dividing line created by the Vilaine and Rance rivers) and Lower Brittany (west of that line) also corresponds roughly to the division between French- and Breton-speaking populations. But this pattern holds true only for rural areas, and specifically for peasants. Bourgeois city dwellers everywhere in the province mostly spoke French, partook of French culture, and embraced an identity as citizens of the French nation. By and large, they knew little Breton and, at best, viewed the Breton-speaking peasantry paternalistically. The same could be said of most aristocrats, except that many of them, rooted also in rural Breton society and tradition, as bilingual lords enjoying seigneurial privileges and powers over peasants, were anything but enthusiastic in their loyalty to the French crown.

It would be anachronistic to argue that the counter-revolution in Brittany, known as the Chouannerie, pitted the Breton "nation" or "Celtic blood" against that of France, but the social and geographical alliances that characterized this conflict and the more-than-century-long history of alienation from the French state provided the groundwork upon which a Breton "race and blood" ideology arose. Counter-revolutionary mobilization was a rural phenomenon begun in 1792 as a guerilla movement among Breton-speaking peasants inspired by their non-juring priests, which evolved into an alliance with nobles who assumed officer roles as the war became more overt. City notables largely remained aloof from the conflict and accommodated or actively supported the political changes brought about by the Revolution in its moderate phase. But the nobility had always cherished its relative autonomy within the French state and successfully limited the centralizing thrust of Louis XIV, manifested especially in Colbert's "reformation" of 1668–72, a wholesale revocation of suspect titles of the nobility.[28] Jean Meyer shows that in Brittany, unlike in many other provinces and Paris, Colbert's policy greatly strengthened ancient and hugely wealthy Breton noble families and served as a "nearly sacred" symbol in the fight against any further encroachments by the central government. The subsequent arrival of the Intendancy, only in 1689, initiated an on-and-off struggle with the provincial Estates, supported by the Parlement.

Meyer argues that these circumstances created a "social rigidity" with profound implications for the future. At the same time, peasant unrest increasingly focused on royal fiscal exactions rather than on the still harsh seigneurial regime, which gave most nobles some direct contact with the peasant communities.[29] Seigneurial authority "resided less in the revenues that it procured than in the effective power that it conferred upon its holders."[30] Nobles dominated land ownership, especially in the Côtes-du-Nord and the Vannetais.[31] The most common form of tenure was the *domaine congéable*, in which everything but the land itself (*les fonds*) was owned by tenants on long-term leases providing *rentiers* with handsome incomes. This form of tenancy put a premium on stable relationships, not entrepreneurship. The Revolution broke seigneurial power but also threatened its bonds, and new authority invaded the autonomy of peasant communities, severing their warm relationship with their Breton-speaking and culturally tolerant priests and seeking to haul their young men off to a war they knew nothing about. Thus noble and peasant fought as officer and soldier until they finally joined with the invading noble exile army disembarked on the Quiberon peninsula in mid 1795. There they were crushed by the Republic's General Hoche, with most of the officers executed as traitors without the rights of prisoners of war.[32] The Quiberon took a place in the legends of Breton nationalism similar to other great defeats such as The Boyne and The Forty-Five for the Irish and the Scots. For many nobles, the blood that flowed became the symbol of revenge for an entire people, soon to be one "race."

Although the social and political foundations of a Breton racial nationalism were laid in the violence of the late eighteenth century, it would be given a historical justification only in the nineteenth-century by historians, philologists, and archeologists associated with provincial learned societies. The remarkable work by Jean-Yves Guiomar, *Le Bretonisme*, explores the historiography of the movement and provides a wonderful intellectual history of the flowering of scholarship among Breton *érudits* in the nineteenth century. He engages equally the formidable contingent of anti-Bretoniste writers. But while he appreciates the national-racial aspects of the conflict, he downplays its class dimensions. Working from my own study of the nationally prominent Société polymathique du Morbihan (SPM), based in Vannes, I argue here that anti-Bretoniste positions were largely taken by men from the milieu of the culturally French upper bourgeoisie of Vannes and elsewhere, who increasingly dominated the civic life of their cities in the nineteenth century, while Bretoniste positions were embraced in the milieu of an aristocracy claiming stewardship of a Breton peasantry depicted as the very heart and soul of the Breton race.[33] In this battle over the historical definition of Brittany and its destiny, the two sides thus replicated the urban-rural, bourgeois-noble, Francophone-Breton divide as evidenced in the Chouannerie. And, whereas the armory of the Bretonistes generously evoked the transformed kinship terminology of Celtic race and blood, such usages were largely absent from the language of their pro-French opponents.

In the search for racial origins and the continuity of blood, the dispute focused on the deepest and least accessible history of the Armorican peninsula. Unchallenged as the centerpiece of Breton pride were the "Celtic stones," the many monuments, megaliths, and tumuli concentrated in the Morbihan that everyone assumed had been constructed by the ancient Celtic conquerors of the peninsula. But were they in fact "Celtic" at all? The most incendiary questions, however, had to do with the nature of the interaction of peoples thereafter. To what extent was this western tip of continental Europe romanized? Can one speak of a "Gallo-Roman population" here—and how far west? How much of the original population survived the barbarian invasions? Thereafter, when the Anglo-Saxons drove Britons southward across the Channel, did these Celtic newcomers inhabit an empty land and mix with indigenous Celtic brethren, or were they themselves absorbed into a still strong Gallo-Roman population? How great was the Briton influence? How did Christianity come to Brittany? Already there or brought by "Breton saints" from the north? What remained of *Roman* Catholicism? And what happened with the arrival of the Franks, followed by the Normans? Who should be revered as the founding hero: Nominoë, who defeated Charles the Bald in 845–46, or Alain Barbetorte, who, in 939, removed Celtic Brittany's Norman yoke and established six hundred years of the Breton race's virtual independence as a duchy? And how "pure," with all these incursions, was that race?

The Bretoniste mainstream was led by accomplished scholars like ethnolinguist Baron Théodore Hersart de La Villemarqué (1815–95) and historian Arthur Lemoyne de La Borderie (1827–1901), both Breton aristocrats.[34] La Villemarqué unquestionably had the greatest impact, for his collection of songs and ballads of Brittany, *Barzaz Breiz* (1839), was received as an iconic symbol of the beauty and complexity of Breton popular culture and took a prominent place in the broad "Celtic renaissance" across the far western "captive" nations of Europe, from Spanish Galicia to the Hebrides. The literary revival celebrating the folk heritage was integral to the explosion of nationalist sentiment everywhere in Europe and mixed freely with the flowering of a discourse which regularly

confounded nation with race, based in the assumption that mental and
emotional qualities, the national characteristics of a people, were "in the
blood."[35] La Villemarqué would have a distinguished career, including
induction into the Académie française, marred late in life, however, as
new scholarship cast doubt on the validity of much of his masterwork.[36]
La Borderie was undoubtedly the leading Breton historian of his generation, a member of the Institut de France, and an ardent believer in docu-
ment-based history. Together with La Villemarqué, he became a leader
of the Association bretonne. The first province-wide learned society in
Brittany, the association would carry the torch of Breton racial nationalism until it was broken up by Napoleon III, who suspected its right-wing
political motives.

Founded in 1843, the Association bretonne was the child, not of the
right-wing Bretonistes who eventually dominated it, but of three pro-
gressives, Jules Rieffel, Geslin de Bourgogne, and Armand René Maufras du Chatellier, who were committed to the cause of agricultural
reform.[37] Strains of Saint-Simonianism and Fourierism ran through their
thought. It was assumed from the beginning that both the archeological
investigation and historical study of the monuments, megaliths, tumuli,
and medieval parish churches of the Breton countryside were integral
to such reform projects. Both, in their own ways, would bring public
attention and funds into a tradition-bound peasant society. Such a combination had been central to the work of the Société polymathique du
Morbihan since its founding in 1826, and the focus of its publication,
*L'Annuaire du Morbihan*. This society welcomed the new effort, sending
a contingent of its own membership to the first meeting, among them
lawyer and archeologist Alfred Lallemand, Mayor Armand Taslé, and
Prefect Édouard Lorois.[38] The SPM delegates assumed that the leadership of the new society would embrace the goal of joint archeological/
historical/agricultural reform. But in the organizing sessions of the 1843
congress, La Villemarqué and his allies pressed to separate the archeological and historical work from agricultural reform projects by creating
a parallel board of directors for the Classe archéologique. They were
opposed by the conveners, who feared that such a move would dilute
the association's dual purpose, and by Lallemand and other members of
the SPM.

It quickly became clear that what was at stake concerned the politics
of history. Both Lallemand, a conservative Catholic, and Louis Bizeul of
Nantes, a liberal and indefatigable researcher without strong religious
opinions, agreed on a view of Breton history that ran counter to the one
favored by the budding Bretoniste faction led by La Villemarqué. Labeled "Romanistes," Lallemand and Bizeul argued that Bretons were just

another variety of the Gallo-Romans, mixed in blood and culture, and sharing many traits and values with the rest of France, while also prizing their Breton distinctiveness. Lallemand's studies of the historical archeology of religious edifices were rooted in the belief that Brittany was one of the great bastions of *Roman* Catholicism; thus they downplayed Breton differences, writing them off as superstitions common to peasant cultures everywhere.[39] Bizeul, an expert on Roman roads in Brittany, argued that their network and excellence throughout the peninsula, along with much other evidence, showed that the province had been thoroughly romanized. Both men, and their local societies, cooperated fully with the Comité des travaux historiques in Paris, whose leader, the historian Augustin Thierry, had initiated a grand project to collect documents on the origins and development of the cities and towns in France. Thierry's interpretation of the history of the French nation reflected his belief in the overwhelming importance of the Gallo-Roman "race" on French soil. This race, he argued, led by the bourgeoisie, had overthrown the "Frankish" nobility in the Revolution and was steering the nation's current "bourgeois monarchy with republican institutions." Thierry's project inspired the creation of a nationwide system of departmental archives. In Vannes, the appointed archivists all stood firmly in the anti-Bretoniste camp.[40]

The Thierry campaign tended to further ideological biases against nobility, legitimism, and provincial nationalism. But his work also benefitted those camps, as its methodologies turned out to support a variety of historiographical interpretations and concomitant political ideologies. In Brittany, the salient example lies in the work of Aurélien de Courson, a close ally of La Villemarqué who was assigned to Rennes by Thierry in 1835.[41] While gathering documents in urban history, Courson also worked hard to bring cartularies and seigneurial archives into the public sphere, and in the process he developed a fascination with the nature of Breton feudalism. This he tied with emerging evidence of a large-scale Briton immigration in the fifth and sixth centuries to lay out the thesis that Breton feudalism was purely "Celtic" in origin, "having nothing to do with French feudalism": the latter, he argued, "was Germanic in origin, oppressive, and the source of inequalities; the former, all social harmony," was a system rooted in the insular Celtic institution of the clan, wherein hierarchy existed, but all members were of "one blood."[42] Courson supplemented this path-breaking publication with an overview, *L'histoire des peuples bretons* (Paris, 1846), which joined the early history of Bretons on both sides of the Channel into a single story. This was the first serious presentation of a "migration thesis." It posited a politically crucial belief: that Breton nobles and Breton peasants had always lived in happy, if differentiated, symbiosis, as racial father and child. In Courson's hands, paradoxically, the very methodologies that Thierry and his archivist allies had applied in support of the Gallo-Roman thesis became the instruments of a radically opposed historiography.

The Bretoniste camp of the Association bretonne lost the first round at Vannes in 1843, outvoted by the agriculturalists and the Romanists. But by 1845, it had generated sufficient membership to create a separate board for the Classe archéologique, which by then was bringing out many more studies than its agricultural counterpart. Indeed, the agricultural reformers in the organization had made so little headway with the large-landowning nobles they were attempting to recruit that progressive leaders like Rieffel turned their energies elsewhere, effectively leaving the association in the hands of the archeologists and historians.[43] Although the Classe archéologique still included many non-nobles and its annual *Bulletin* ran articles (especially by the workhorse Bizeul) contributing to the Romaniste perspective, its leadership, whether professional scholars like La Villemarqué, Courson, and La Borderie, or socially distinguished *amateurs* and civic activists like Aymar de Blois, the perennial president, was heavily aristocratic.[44]

That the dominant perspective within the archeology section had become Bretoniste was due in no small measure to the arrival of Arthur Lemoyne de la Borderie, who, in 1848, at the age of twenty-one, electrified his audience with his own migration thesis offering a complete vision of the deepest Breton historical past, essentially an anthropological "creation story" of the Breton nation.[45] It stressed the uniqueness of Brittany in France, linking it to the racial family to the north, in opposition to the Romaniste argument, which recognized the fact of the migrations but disputed claims about their scope and effects on the peninsula's population. From a "racial" point of view, the Romaniste line was simple. Evidence seemed overwhelming that romanization had effectively eliminated the "pure" Celtic Armoricans, whose roots went back to the original Celtic invaders, their Druids, and their stones. This romanized population of Armorica (like its champions, these mostly bourgeois Romaniste historians) had been part of the general entity Gaul (hence the term *Gallo-Roman*). The crucial historical problem then was what happened to these people as the Roman Empire fell apart: how was the population affected; how many inhabitants survived the brutal Alan and Saxon invaders? And were not the people of the far west, today's most Breton area, largely spared? The Romaniste thesis, of course, claimed that the Gallo-Romans weathered it all pretty well, mixing in later with the new Briton arrivals, though maintaining a greater Gallo-Roman presence in the south and east.

Now La Borderie conceded—and this was crucial—that Armorica was indeed quite romanized, even in the west. So, yes, *those* people were Gallo-Romans. But their numbers were disastrously reduced, impoverished by fiscal exactions associated with militarization, by an economy reduced to a subsistence form, and by depopulation due to low fertility and disease. When in the mid fifth century, Aëtius redirected the furies of the Alans on Brittany, the already stressed inhabitants fled to the forests. Their failed resistance "saved the honor of the race" in combat, but not their lands. Meanwhile, over many decades of the same century, the Saxons, that "race pillarde, voleuse et malfaisante," devastated huge swaths of the north and all of more prosperous eastern Armorica, evidenced by thousands of carbon remains.[46] What about the west? It had only small pockets of population anyway, he argued, and the center was virtually uninhabited. And so, when an entirely new population of Britons, driven by the Germanic invasion of their island, came across the sea, it took over the entire peninsula, including the Vannetais, establishing the four kingdoms of Lower Brittany.[47] Thus a largely peaceful migration to a new land by Grands Bretons created Petite Bretagne, giving the land the character and racial composition that still exists.

The migrants interbred with the surviving minority of Gallo-Romans, creating a "fusion of two races," but with clear Breton cultural and linguistic dominance. Racial bonds with the insular Celts were strong and enduring. Further migrations implanted the key civil institution of the *plou*, the colonial settlement that reassembled remnants of clans, which evolved into the foundation stone of Breton feudalism.[48] The seigneurial regime, which La Borderie made even more benign than Courson, was accompanied by systems of land tenure that prevented the establishment of serfdom and allowed lord and peasant to live co-operatively. The special case of the *domaine congéable*, which became widespread in the High Middle Ages, enhanced this relationship, and dated at least back to the eleventh century.[49] But the crucial institutional cement was the particular, ancient form of Christianity that, alive among the islanders in Britain, had blossomed after the migrations to a new "promised land," as scores of "Breton saints" crossed the peninsula performing good works and establishing colonial *lann*—later monasteries—everywhere. This was the intensely Catholic La Borderie's central contention, that contemporary Breton Christianity bore a Celtic Briton pedigree, that the earlier variant brought by Saint Martin had died out and with it, whatever Druidic influences it might have possessed.[50] His final argument for his thesis was linguistic and, he thought, definitive. Why, after all, was this peninsula thereafter called "Bretagne" and its language "Breton"?

The later history of the Breton people was riven with struggle against racial outsiders, first the Franks, then the Normans. The Merovingians, despite efforts, failed to control the Breton kingdoms, repelled by heroes mainly from the Vannetais. All of Brittany fell to Charlemagne, establishing a one hundred–year "Frankish yoke." Then came the epical moment when all the Breton chefs united under the great and wise Nominoë and crushed the forces of Charles the Bald in 845–49, thereafter creating the first "Kingdom of Brittany."

Let us listen to some of the language used by La Borderie in 1851 in a long serial article, "L'histoire de Nominoë," in the *Bulletin archéologique* of the Association bretonne. This great conflict would be engaged on the "battlefield of two races" between the Vilaine River and Vannes, the gateway to the entire peninsula. This was where "Breton blood germinated from the soil that it had watered with its torrents" since the time of Caesar: first the Gauls, then the Gallo-Romans, and now the predominant Briton colonists, all deriving from the ancient "Celtic race," whose triumphs and disasters La Borderie recounts in a paragraph. But on this field, "this debris of the great race refuses to die … ; the more fortune strikes [the Bretons], the more they persist in believing that they must live … and seize again that ancient power and glory whose memory their national traditions guard and from which Delphi and the Capitol had felt the blows." Now "two races of opposite instinct and character" who have confronted each other for centuries come to battle: one in control of a great empire, the other, "the Bretons, *une poignée d'hommes sur un sol étroit et maigre.*" But driven by "love of their native soil, hatred of the foreigner, and inextinguishable faith in the immortality of the fatherland and the race, this triple sentiment that no other nation perhaps has ever nurtured more," they will conquer.[51] And so they did at Ballon in 845 under Nominoë "The Liberator," who would be recognized as "king of Brittany" by Charles and the pope in 851, thereby initiating a quarter century of peace and glorious development, economically and institutionally.

Equally stirring was La Borderie's story of the repulsion of the Normans, the next great victory over an enemy race. Although Bretonistes were divided over who should be regarded as their nation's founding father, Nominoë or Alain Barbetorte, the final conqueror of the Normans and first duke of Brittany, Borderie anointed Nominoë. He was the culmination of the Breton creation story, the ancient voice of the Breton race.

His definition of that race resonated strongly with the pan-Celtic movement that animated the entire Celtic fringe of Europe. In 1867, the Société d'emulation des Côtes du Nord (Saint Brieuc) hosted the first Congrès celtique intérnationale, which drew participants from Britain but was dominated by the continental Celts. The official language, ironically, was French, since the Celtic dialects of the islands and Brittany were different enough to prevent easy communication. Moreover, while many of the participant scholars spoke and studied their own Celtic languages, they wrote mostly in French or English. The members of the organizing council were led by none other than La Villemarqué and La Borderie (then president of the archeological society at Rennes and a corresponding member of the Société polymathique du Morbihan), along with John Jenkins, the president of the Welsh archeological society, and Henri Martin, member of the Institut de France, arguably France's most famous historian. Martin had become an ardent researcher into the Breton past, offering opinions on everything from the megaliths to the origins of Breton "pardons," the colorful ritual processions of the faithful unique to Brittany, but he was above all a pan-Celticist. He was one of the few non-nobles in the leadership and honorary positions at the Congress. Geslin de Bourgogne, one of the agricultural reformers who had founded the Association bretonne, was now president of the Saint Brieuc society and an ardent Bretoniste. This congress was his crowning achievement—and the apogee of Breton pan-Celticism.

The language reflected the moment. The prefect, appropriately named De Manche, marveled at this "work of faith" that brought together "all the countries whose inhabitants are united by ties of blood and a common origin," noting that "the sons of the Celts have come ... to protest against the oblivion that threatens to overtake an entire past, an entire nationality, which the great crises of humanity may have held back without ever defeating." He then praised Bretons in particular for resisting all invaders with "tenacity and national spirit to preserve intact ... a race that time has done nothing to strip of its unique convictions and characteristics." But all Celts are "one race," as "modern science" has proved, bearing "distinct physiognomies, striking traits of resemblance."[52] De Manche remarked that the idea for this gathering was born in reflecting upon the "ancient Bards of our language" whose visions were so stirringly presented to the French-speaking world by our "national poet," Auguste Brizieux, in "Les Bretons."[53]

Geslin de Bourgogne welcomed participants and praised their unity, brought on by "a noble woman using the intelligent influence that her sex has never lost among the Celtic races." She is that "melodieuse enfant" of the first bard of Britain: "La harpe au triple rangs des cordes," the "divine voice who has brought men together since the beginning." The female as symbol—before an all-male audience—is again unveiled.[54] Geslin then introduced the keynote speaker, the venerable Henri Martin, who provided a grand overview of the history of the Celtic race from its "Aryan" roots onward. His remarks about the European Celtic populations provide a perfect summation of the largest theme of this chapter, the transfer of the blood-based language of the family from kinship to race and the passage of family values to racial values:

> The Bretons and the Kimris of Wales are brothers; the Gaels of Scotland and Ireland are their cousins german. There is for all a common base of primal language, origin, sentiments: the same consciousness of moral responsibility and human individuality; the same sense of duty—man to man, to the tribe, then to the fatherland; the same variability on the surface, the same persistence at the base, the same disposition to protect the weak from the strong. These cousins are indeed brothers.[55]

But, he continues, the "kinship goes beyond these who speak the same language," for most of the "masses of men" of western Europe and of France are Celtic in origin. And "many of those who no longer speak the language of our grandfathers, have conserved *le vieux coeur gaulois.* Your speaker is proud to be one of them."[56] Martin thus veered away from the emphasis on Brittany's separateness from France and French-speaking Gaulois or Gallo-Romans, showing that pan-Celticism bore within it the possibility of diluting notions of Brittany's divergent and racially unique history and its ideological potential to support autonomist politics. Inadvertently, he underlined the absurdity of the entire project.

La Villemarqué, in his presentation, "Les Bretons d'Angleterre et les Bretons de France," began by coupling family history and racial history in a manner also of great importance to the theme of this study. "Le sang parle!" he cries in stressing the bond of "father to son, brother to brother" in the traditions of the Breton countryside, where this usage remained.[57] But the link is simultaneously racial. For La Villemarqué, having invoked "our *vieille mère celtique,*" and the common memories of all in the room of our "young country comrades with whom we spoke *la langue naive* and shared our games," goes on to quote Brizieux that we are all Breton brothers in whom "one blood sparkles, all children of the same family." And "science unites us, proclaiming our ties of kinship." All the great students of linguistics and anthropology have "saved the genealogy of our race. Peoples, like individuals, love to have their genealogies traced." Thus La Villemarqué simply absorbs family history into racial history, the one duplicating the other.[58]

# The Critique

La Villemarqué, well aware that the Association bretonne had lost its authorization due to Napolean III's suspicions of separatism and legitimism, was also at pains to stress the non-political character of the search for Celtic and Breton origins.[59] In contrast, the Société polymathique du Morbihan, now Brittany's most active and respected learned society, had nothing to worry about and flourished during the Second Empire. Among the various departmental societies, it had benefited the most from the banning of the Association bretonne, when many of the members of the Classe archéologique, especially the Romanists, migrated to the SPM. In 1858, it began to publish its own journal. The SPM was now the center from which many of the verities of Breton nationalist history were questioned. Its work, however, was anything but a campaign of *parti-pris*, instead a process derived slowly from the fruits of its research.

The *érudits* of the SPM shared several important characteristics.[60] They were thoroughly intertwined by ties of kinship and friendship with the entire elite of Vannes, by this time largely bourgeois in origin. SPM members came from several generations of French-speaking stock, with largely Vannetais ancestors in small landholding, the liberal professions, lesser officialdom, the higher trades, the merchant communities, retail and especially wholesale, and the merchant marine. Some of their family names were Breton, but not many. The professions of SPM members mirror these patterns, but at a higher socio-economic level, with law, medicine, public employment, the military, academics, engineering, and architecture leading the way. Almost all were landed proprietors as well. Skilled professionals who came to Vannes from across the nation were quickly integrated into this society and the community. Many active members were also municipal and departmental officials and did volunteer work in other societies and agencies. The SPM combined community service and scholarly study, especially biology, geology, topography, agronomy, and meteorology, along with history and archeology. It made many contributions to civic improvement and mapped the region in all these fields. Its special province, however, was prehistorical and historical archeology, along with paleontology. One of the society's first campaigns was to save the vast alignments at nearby Carnac from the stonecutter's saw. In time, its membership included many of the leading investigators of these "Celtic monuments" and the hundreds of other menhirs, megaliths, and tumuli, which were denser here than anywhere else in the world.

Most of the SPM's papers reveal serious scholarship based on original research. Prudence was their watchword, their methodologies advancing incrementally. I am most familiar with the study habits of members of the Galles circle as evidenced in their works on paleontology, geology, archeology, and history. In an address of 1863, General René Galles, then the society's president and best-known archeologist, captured their spirit: "Modest pioneers in a science born yesterday, we shall never tire of research; let us multiply the facts, accumulate the discoveries. Let us with all our will shed light upon the grand questions that touch upon the origins and migration of the races; but we must beware, in our haste, of taking for rays of scientific truth those uncertain glimmers that seem to augur a hidden hypothesis."[61]

The SPM delivered some of the most damaging criticism of Bretoniste historiography, directly challenging its racist enthusiasm and its dreams of Breton autonomy. Contributors avoided the heroic language of Bretonisme, though like virtually everyone in later nineteenth-century Europe, they accepted the notion of "human races" as a biological fact and used the term *Celtic race*. They were proud Bretons and delighted in aspects of their regional culture. But they were "French" first, whether republican or royalist. From correspondence and other personal documents, one can discern that they had nothing against nobles, actively cooperating in scholarship and socializing with them, while rejecting their legitimist politics. They disdained the Breton language as a contemporary literary form, though they might thrill to La Villemarqué's translations of ancient bards or Brizieux's French poetry. They gave complete support to the *francisation* of public education. Though good Catholics for the most part, they found much in Breton Christianity superstitious and contrary to Roman Catholicism. They related to the peasantry largely as leaseholders, and while relations might be cordial enough, social intercourse was minimal. In general, these people lived in what might be called a "culture of moderation," where rationality should govern action, where dedication to civic life was an expectation, and where family and kinship ties extended across their entire social milieu, enforcing appropriate behavior.[62]

The major contribution of SPM research was to throw doubt on the first and unquestioned verity of Celtic pride: the Celtic origins of the great stoneworks stretching from Locmariaquer to Stonehenge commemorated in Brizieux's poem.[63] Henri Martin had just completed a general survey of them when he spoke at the 1867 Congrès celtique, adding his great weight to this assertion.[64] The Vannetais group did not use the term *Celtic* in its investigations until the 1840s, when outsiders adopted it. But overt skepticism began to appear in the pages of the *Bulletin* of the SPM in the 1860s, as their archeologists examined the grave sites "said to be Celtic" close to the visible alignments of Carnac. A paper by René Galles of 1863 was crucial. It reported the findings of his dig at the large tumulus called Manné-er-H'roëk (Mountain of the Fairy), where he had uncovered a dolmen (grave site) containing a *"pluralité"* of crypts. The first and most finished had mysterious symbolic markings, which he reproduced in drawings. Sifting the "debris" found at various levels yielded pieces of bronze, pottery, and polished stone seemingly in that order going downward, all suggesting "the image of one civilization succeeding another much more rudimentary." But which ones? His paper asks rhetorically, "Should we despair of finding the age of these monuments that we name *celtique, un peu à l'aventure* … ? Should we despair of knowing to what race we should attribute them? The stones speak, but we are ignorant of their language. … Who will teach it to us?"[65]

Although Doctor Gustave de Closmadeuc seemed certain already in 1866 that "these wondrous constructions" dated "from the stone age," over the following years, systematic exploration at one site after another uncovered such a variety of forms and materials that researchers remained unwilling to assign any designation to their original construction.[66] Louis Galles explored the question in depth and argued that evidence showed the presence in the tumuli of both Gaulois and pre-Celtic stone-age peoples, though the former seemed to predominate. His main point, however, was that dolmens of this sort were found everywhere in the world, that there was nothing uniquely Celtic about them.[67] An analysis by a prominent geologist argued that none of the stones used in the menhirs and megaliths were cut or shaped by hand, but rather were natural loose pieces, arranged in certain instances for some ritual purpose; also that the stones of the dolmens were found naturally as well.[68] René Galles was assigned as intendant militaire of Algeria in the late sixties and continued his archeological work there. His discovery of many menhirs and megaliths in Kabylia led him to research the phenomenon on a worldwide basis, from Mexico to Southeast Asia, and to conclude, simply, that they were ritual objects of many far-flung early civilizations.[69] Assessing the implications, he would write in 1882: does this reality not underline "the permanence of a confraternity of races resulting from a commonality of origin?"[70]

Space does not permit any detailed discussion of other aspects of SPM contributions to the anti-Bretoniste perspective. Suffice it to say that their papers built on Bizeul's Romaniste themes with further studies of Roman roads and fortifications, research into the persistence of the Gallo-Roman population and its early dedication to Christianity, and with studies of land tenure, particularly the *domaine congéable*, that linked the form, if not the name, to Roman law and Gallo-Roman practices; all of which were connected to the general point that the Morbihan and the southern coast was much less affected by the Briton migration from the north than other regions.[71] The implication was thus that "Brittany" owed as much to Gaul and the Roman occupation as it did to Celts from overseas. In general, if the SPM writers regarded the Celts as a race and explored its history, they eschewed the notion of a "Breton race" and rejected any claim of "blood" bonding a Breton nation.[72] The voluminous studies of ecclesiastical monuments and church history also stressed the integration of the Breton church into the French church and ties with Rome, though no one denied the early role of La Borderie's Breton saints in the conversion of the north and west. The society thus quietly did its work, living by the words of René Galles's last presidential address of 1883: "Facts, facts! cried Augustin Thierry, the only warp of the loom on which one can weave the stuff of history."[73]

## Conclusion

Overall, it made sense that the scholars within the Société polymathique du Morbihan, focusing as they did on the southeastern area of Lower Brittany, should lead the critique of Bretoniste history: they had by far the deepest knowledge of Brittany's prehistory, represented most significantly by the stones in their own back yard, and they inched their way toward the modern understanding of their pre-Celtic origins. Carbon dating now places the construction of these monuments from the fourth millenium to the early second, erected and often aligned with the sunrise and sunset at the solstices by (perhaps) sun-worshipers like the builders of Stonehenge. And again, modern understanding views the formation of the Breton people, their vital culture, and their historical institutions as a product of the mixing of Gallo-Roman and insular Briton influences (though the latter predominate), with regional differences southeast to west and north. It is a perspective from which race and blood are absent.[74]

But it is not the point of this analysis to say who was right or wrong. Rather it is to understand the stakes of a nineteenth-century race debate on this edge of Europe in which blood became a metaphor for entire populations putatively connected biologically. I have argued that Breton nationalist history incorporated the powerful impulse of race, as the concept was given "scientific" validity by biology and the new field of physical anthropology, and that it operated with a notion of purity of blood among most Breton-speaking people who descended from the ancestors of their cousin-brothers across the channel. This Celtic unity was as deep as their soul and somehow lodged in those mysterious stones. The Morbihan was included in this narrative on the belief that the migration had extended southward and absorbed most Gallo-Romans—and, of course, that was where the stones were! The other great force uniting the Breton people was its variant of Christianity, largely imported by saints from Britain. Although the banner of Bretonisme receded in the later nineteenth century due to work by scholars such as those in the SPM, its spirit lived on in right-wing and legitimist circles and gave historical grounding after 1873 to a revived Association bretonne, with a membership again drawn heavily from the nobility. The tepid atmosphere of this new organizaton, however, enraged younger members, and its secretary, Régis de l'Estourbeillon, eventually led them in 1898 to form Brittany's first nationalist-separatist political organization, the Union régionaliste bretonne. It should be underlined that La Borderie was still alive and brought out a fine new edition of his *Histoire de Bretagne* between 1905 and 1906. It and Villemarqué's *Barzaz Breiz* were the new party's historical bibles. Ultimately, noble-based Breton racial nationalism failed. Later nationalist movements in Brittany, which had only modest success in any case, drew from a base of the disaffected, both in the countryside and the towns with considerable social heterogeneity.[75]

The fact was that the majority of the population, retaining its culture and ways (though retaining the Breton language became more difficult with the Third Republic's campaign against all "patois") largely with support from the Breton Church (sermons and catechism lessons were in Breton), essentially rejected the stewardship of the nobility. Caroline Ford argues brilliantly that the guiding principles of social Catholicism, coupled with toleration and indeed encouragement of those "superstitious" practices scoffed at by bourgeois Catholics, gently awakened peasants to the practice of civic responsibility and brought them into the *French* nation via Christian Democracy.[76] This is, of course, the central political fact in modern Breton history.

What, then, of the bourgeois of Vannes and other Lower Breton cities? Their politics, whether republican or royalist, stressed moderation and the avoidance of extremes, and was French in orientation, though it certainly fought for local, regional, and provincial interests. It worked well to keep the elite in power (especially in the absence of much working-class resistance in weakly industrialized settings—Lorient and Brest excepted) and for civic improvement. It also succeeded in making Vannes, at least, the recipient of national administrative and especially military roles well beyond its obligations as departmental capital. René Galles and Jules Trochu, both Vannetais belonging to the military elite of the nation, were instrumental in the process. These bourgeois did little directly, however, to facilitate the crucial process of integrating Breton peasants into the French polity. But perhaps that's not quite true. After all, with the measured and careful scholarship of their learned

society, they helped disarm racial Breton nationalism, resolutely rejecting notions of the blood unity of a Breton people led by nobles and the
noble claims of social harmony in some idyllic pre-Revolutionary past,
thus contributing to the integration of Brittany into the French nation
in a context where the emotional power of race as a political force had
lost its salience. Breton peasants might still say "le sang parle," but they
would only be talking about their blood kin, not their race. Their bourgeois neighbors would not talk about either one.

# Notes

1. Archives départementales du Morbihan, fonds Galles, 2 J 71–84. This material provides the basis for several published articles and a book in progress.
2. *Lettres de Mme de Sévigné, de sa famille et de ses amis,* 8 vols. (Paris, 1863). All translations here and below are mine.
3. Mme de Sévigné's correspondence in this collection is largely with relatives, above
   all her cousin, the comte de Bussy Rabutin, and her daughter, Françoise-Marguérite
   de Grignan. A majority of blood references are phrases like "nous sommes proche,
   du même sang" (to her cousin) or "adieu, mon sang" (to her daughter) or "je recon-
   nois mon sang," about her daughter's nature (Sévigné, *Lettres,* 5:414, [1685]). In a
   lament about seeing her daughter so rarely after her marriage, she remarked, "Je le
   regrette tous les jours de ma vie, et j'en souhaiterois un pareil au prix de mon sang"
   (ibid., 1:352, [1671]). To her cousin, she wrote "Let us rejoice in the beautiful blood
   that flows so peacefully and agreeably in our veins" (ibid., 5:487, [1685]). Blood
   was more powerful than friendship. For example, her cousin writes: "Blood and the
   life that you have spent with Monsieur your uncle [who had died] rendered his loss
   much more painful than for me that of my dear friend Saint-Aignan" (ibid., 6:66,
   [1687]). More thoughtfully, Mme de Sévigné writes to de Bussy Rabutin in 1677,
   after some angry words, that it should not take long for them to rekindle their affection for "in any case there are vital spirits in our blood which will link us in spite
   of ourselves, if we only give in to it in good will" (ibid., 4:3–4). Hence their rapport
   is in the blood, instinctual. Such assumptions could also make her wonder how her
   cousin could occasionally write to her in a manner where "I don't recognize my
   blood ... or yours" (ibid., 1:144 [1669]). The count was less mystical. In an earlier
   letter to her, he expressed dismay that "the only person of my blood in the world
   that I love abandoned me in an affair of honor where she ran no risk"; that he had
   forgiven her entirely, having realized that he was mistaken (ibid., 1:117 [1668]).
   Many uses refer more generally to the noble blood of their line or that of others,
   including the famous phrase "good blood cannot lie" (in reference to another rec-
   onciliation with her cousin) or the "power of blood" will win out in a conflict. But
   "blood" relatives could also be condemned, as with a cousin who called in debts on
   a poverty-stricken aunt: the count was "disgusted that this evil beast [avarice] could
   be found in my blood" (ibid., 6:5 [1687]).
4. Thomas Laqueur, *Making Sex: Body and Gender from the Greeks to Freud* (Cambridge, MA, 1990), 103–8.
5. See the unpublished paper "Theological and Literary Discourses of Blood in Baroque Culture," by David Warren Sabean, of which chapter 7 in the current volume

is an abridged version. For an exhaustive analysis of the general notions of "noble blood" and "race" referring to the nobility as a breed (a term derived from animal husbandry), see André Devyver, *Le sang épuré. Les préjugés de race chez les gentilshommes français de l'Ancien Régime, 1560–1720* (Brussels, 1973).

6. *Monsieur Nicolas ou le coeur humain dévoilé, mémoires intimes de Restif de la Bretonne,* 14 vols. (Paris, 1794–97). It was based on notes he kept over sixty years and a "Calendre" "commemorating" some 366 women with whom he was intimate.

7. Examples: "Le sang parle," for an illegitimate child; "même sang," for sisters; no "sang pourri" (polluted blood) for the quality of his family; a grandmother from "beau sang"; and his own "sang roturier." My figures are compiled from a digital scan of the fourteen volumes of *Monsieur Nicolas.*

8. The Audran cousins were Gobelins tapestry artists, and the publishers had a branch in the capital. Interestingly, the only use of *sang* as a kin-term in my Breton bourgeois families' correspondence occurs in 1760, when a wife wondered whether her husband's bumbling brother was "of the same blood" or "exchanged by the wet nurse." See Jacquette Bertin Galles to Jean-Nicolas Galles, March 1760, in Bernard Frélaut, "Un Vannetais à la Bastille. Jean-Nicolas Galles en 1760 d'après sa correspondance inédite," *Mémoires de la Société polymathique du Morbihan* 116 (1990): 173–83, here 178.

9. The exceptions come from the royal family itself, from Marie-Antoinette to the comte de Chambord, the Bourbon pretender in the later nineteenth century. For a complete list of books digitally scanned, see the appendix.

10. It was reprinted many times thereafter. That it came out in a fine edition in 1812 indicates its appropriateness for the new nobility of the Empire. This is the version available for scanning and is unchanged, except for some additional historical exemplars: Blanchard, *L'école des moeurs,* 3 vols. (Paris, 1812).

11. It runs the gamut of advice, beginning and ending with seeking God's guidance, with a predictable list of virtues illustrated by the behavior of great men.

12. The sentence continues: "of marriage [*alliance*], of friendship, of country [*patrie*], of religion, for the law of charity, far from reversing that order, on the contrary establishes it, perfects it." There thus remains a distinction between relatives connected by fluid (this would include one's wife for this Churchman) and those not—the wife's direct relatives—a distinction, as we shall see, that becomes blurred in the nineteenth century. See Blanchard, *L'école,* 1:334–35 and 1:368–69.

13. Blanchard, *L'école,* 2:278–79 and ff.

14. Concerning the last point, Blanchard argues that if one is obliged to aid the poor in general "who are united with us by common ties of nature, how much stronger the reason to do so for those that [nature] has joined to us by ties more binding by those of the same blood." There lurk "enemies of our relatives [*parens*] in our hearts: hardness and pride." But there are at least three reasons for coming to their rescue: "*Homme droit*, oblige your parens out of justice and goodness of the heart: it is your *sang. Homme prudent*, aid them out of precaution: you could one day have need of them. *Homme dur*, assist them because it is *politique*, from fear that they will dishonor you by their conduct." Blanchard concludes, however, by saying there may be relatives undeserving of your largesse, whose "life is of such a nature as to dishonor your family." They should be refused, unless on the verge of death, and you should sever all ties with them. Blanchard, *L'école,* 2:371–74.

15. On the discourse of moral renewal, virtue, and the redefinition of "nobility" in the eighteenth century, see Jay Smith, *Nobility Re-imagined: The Patriotic Nation in Eighteenth-Century France* (Ithaca, NY, 2005). Smith does not cite Blanchard.

16. *Correspondance inédite de Mademoiselle Théophile de Fernig, aide de camp du général Dumouriez. Avec une introduction et notes par Honoré Bonnehomme* (Paris, 1873). See the "Introduction" for de Fernig's fascinating biography.

17. "Chers parents, qui me sont moins près par les liens du sang, mais qui ne peuvent l'être davantage pour ceux du coeur et de l'amitié"; *Correspondance inédite de Mademoiselle Théophile de Fernig,* 140 (letter sent from Harlem, dated 30 June 1801).

18. *Mémoires inédits de Madame la comtesse de Genlis, sur le dix-huitième siècle et la Révolution française, depuis 1756 à nos jours,* 10 vols. (Paris, 1825). The best biography is Gabriel de Broglie, *Madame de Genlis* (Paris, 2001).

19. *Kinship in Europe: Approaches to Long-Term Development (1300–1900),* ed. David Warren Sabean, Simon Teuscher, and Jon Mathieu (New York and Oxford, 2007), 16–24. See also the chapters by Gérard Delille, Christopher Johnson, and Sabean in this volume.

20. Christopher H. Johnson, "Das 'Geschwister Archipel': Bruder-Schwester Liebe und Klassenformation im Frankreich des 19. Jahrhunderts," *L'Homme. Zeitschrift für feministische Geschichtswissenschaft* 13, no. 1 (2002): 50–67. See now, above all, the volume edited by Christopher H. Johnson and David Warren Sabean, *Sibling Relations and the Transformations of European Kinship, 1300–1900* (New York and Oxford, 2011).

21. See Christopher H. Johnson, "Siblinghood and the Emotional Dimensions of the New Kinship System, 1800–1850: A French Example," in *Sibling Relations,* ed. Johnson and Sabean.

22. Christopher H. Johnson, "Kinship, Civil Society, and Power in Nineteenth-Century Vannes," in *Kinship in Europe,* ed. Sabean, Teuscher, and Mathieu: 258–83; Christophe Charle, *Les élites de la République, 1880–1900* (Paris, 1987); and Pierre Bourdieu, *La noblesse d'Etat* (Paris, 1989).

23. This does not mean, of course, that "dynasties" based on the transmission of a family name over several generations were not crucially important in nineteenth-century life, especially in private business organizations, where family partnerships predominated. David Sabean emphasizes the re-emergence of genealogy back to the founding father toward the end of the nineteenth century, in "German International Families in the Nineteenth Century: The Siemens Family as a Thought Experiment," in *Transregional and Transnational Families in Europe,* ed. Christopher H. Johnson et al. (New York and Oxford, 2011). Affines often contribute to the name itself and sons-in-law as well as distant relatives are often preferred to lead in the next generation because of their interest and ability. See, for example, Robert J. Smith, *The Bouchayers of Grenoble and French Industrial Enterprise, 1850–1970* (Baltimore, MD, and London, 2001).

24. The most thorough and up-to-date analysis, which also deals with the coupling of race and blood, is Ivan Hannaford, *Race: The History of an Idea in the West* (Washington, DC, and Baltimore, MD, 1996). See also Arlette Jouanna, *L'idée de race en France au XVIᵉ siècle et au début du XVIIᵉ siècle (1498–1614),* 2nd ed. (Montpellier, 1981), which explores the evolution of the concepts toward their modern meanings, and Arlette Jouanna, *Le devoir de révolte. La noblesse française et la gestation de l'Etat moderne* (Montpellier, 1989). I will not address here the complexities of the varying discourses of blood and race as they developed from the late Middle Ages onward, which are taken up in several chapters of this book, notably those of Teofilo F. Ruiz and Gérard Delille.

25. See above all, Jacques Barzun, *The French Race: Theories of Its Origins and their Social and Political Implications prior to the Revolution* (New York, 1932).

26. Among the many studies contributing to this analysis, see Suzanne Desan, *The Family on Trial in Revolutionary France* (Berkeley and Los Angeles, CA, 2004); Lynn Hunt, *The Family Romance of the French Revolution* (Berkeley, CA, 1992); *Women in Revolutionary Paris, 1789–1795*, ed. Darline Gay Levy, Harriet Branson Applewhite, and Mary Durham Johnson (Urbana, IL, 1980); Dominique Godineau, *Women in the French Revolution*, trans. Katherine Streip (Berkeley, CA, 1998); Joan Scott, *Only Paradoxes to Offer: French Feminists and the Rights of Man* (Cambridge, 1996); and Mona Ozouf, *La fête révolutionnaire* (Paris, 1976).

In emphasizing cultural, social, and political factors as the key forces undermining the place of blood in kinship discourse, I would not want to discount entirely the new medical knowledge that increasingly abandoned the notion that the fluids of sexual intercourse were reconstituted blood. Sperm and egg and their union in generation were well understood as was the anatomy of the sexual organs. But precisely what this had to do with heredity and the physical relatedness of the human beings produced by sex had not yet been explained and the science of genetics was a century away. Thus, biologically speaking, these relationships could still be discussed as those of people with the same, or at least similar, blood. New scientific knowledge had not really altered this possibility. But the use of the term for kinship declined rapidly. Hence the explanations offered above. It should also be noted that the original turn toward blood and bloodline in kinship terminology in the late Middle Ages, as analyzed in earlier chapters of this book—especially that of Anita Guerreau-Jalabert—could only be explained in cultural, social, and political terms, since this was a context in which medical knowledge about sex and generation changed not at all and did not enter the picture.

27. It was certainly not the only one to exploit this appeal for conservative ends, for regional autonomy (at least) was a theme of many right-wing movements. Best known, perhaps, is the "Félibrige" of Occitane France led by Frédéric Mistral and later recruited by Charles Maurras as a cultural adjunct of the Action Française.

28. But there was little sentiment for a return to the independent duchy that existed before 1532. Breton nobles benefited significantly from the union and, Jean Meyer argues, had been an agent for *francisation* until their liberties were challenged in the eighteenth century. Jean Meyer, *La noblesse de Bretagne au XVIIIᵉ siècle* (Paris, 1972), the abridged edition of his grand thèse, entirely recast to pursue the larger questions raised by the detailed research of the thèse.

29. See François Bluche, *Louis XIV* (New York, 1990), 203–04; Meyer, *La noblesse de Bretagne*, 47–59.

30. Meyer, *La noblesse de Bretagne*, 219. For an excellent analysis of Breton society and politics from union to the reign of Louis XIV, see James Collins, *Classes, Estates, and Orders in Early Modern Brittany* (Cambridge, 1980).

31. Meyer, *La noblesse de Bretagne*, 211–29; Timothy Le Goff shows that nobles owned as much as 70 percent of the land in parts of the Vannetais; see his *Vannes and its Region: A Study of Town and Country in the Eighteenth Century* (Oxford, 1981), chap. 5.

32. Donald Sutherland, *Les Chouans. Les origines sociales de la Contre-Révolution populaire en Bretagne, 1770–1796* (Rennes, 1990); Sutherland and Timothy Le Goff, "The Revolution and the Rural Community in Eighteenth-Century Brittany," *Past and Present* 62 (1974): 96–119; Patrick Huchet, *1795. Quiberon ou le destin de la France* (Rennes, 1995).

33. Johnson, "Kinship, Civil Society, and Power." See also Christopher H. Johnson, "'Into the World': Kinship and Nation Building in France, 1850–1885," in *Transregional and Transnational Families*, ed. Johnson et al.

34. There was a more radical minority, labeled "super-bretonistes" and led by Charles de Gaulle (the general's grandfather), who verged on separatism and clung to a legendary view (beginning with Conan Mériadec) of Breton power and independence.

35. There is of course a huge literature on the subject, which does not need to be cited here. Hannaford's discussion (*Race*, 180–324) covers these developments well.

36. Jean-Yves Guiomar, *Le bretonisme. Les historiens bretons au XIXe siècle*, pref. Michel Denis (Mayenne, 1987), 210–11. On Villemarqué, see Bernard Tanguy, *Aux origines du nationalisme Breton*, 2 vols. (Paris, 1977).

37. Jules Rieffel was an Alsatian who married into the upper bourgeoisie of Nantes; Geslin de Bourgogne, a journalist of Saint-Brieuc and a nobleman; and Armand-René Maufras du Chatellier, a minor noble, historian, and journalist of Quimper.

38. Taslé and Lorois, active SPM members, facilitated the association's first meeting. Lallemand's preservation work was being carried out in close cooperation with the national Comité des travaux historiques headed by Augustin Thierry.

39. For example, Alfred Lallemand, *Notice historique sur la très ancienne chapelle de sainte Anne et la statue miraculeuse qui en provenait* (Vannes, 1862).

40. In Vannes, Gustav Morand, a former négociant, led the study and became the Morbihan's first departmental archivist. He was succeeded in the 1850s by a professional historian trained at the Ecole des chartes, Louis Rozenzweig, who would be one of the most important figures in the anti-Bretoniste camp.

41. Guiomar, *Le bretonisme*, 99. De Courson came from an old Breton noble military family fallen on hard times. He married well and his wife's siblings connected with high aristocratic circles.

42. Guiomar, *Le bretonisme*, 110. The book in question was *Essai sur l'histoire, la langue et les institutions de la Bretagne armoricaine* (Paris, 1840), which Courson submitted for the Prix Gobert. In the running also was La Villemarqué, *Barzaz Breiz*. Neither entry won, but Courson's garnered Thierry's vote, an indication of the quality of the work and in a certain sense its agreement with the master's anti-Frankish perspective.

43. Guiomar recognizes that the conservative local seigneurs dotted across rural Brittany were largely unenthusiastic about fostering "progress." This is perhaps not surprising given their incomes (though certainly not all were rich) and their status in the villages. On the other hand (a point that Guiomar does not pursue), to have the opportunity to read in the emerging literature of Bretonisme about their ancestors and their primordial role in the making of the Breton nation, especially their stewardship of a peasantry with whom they were still intimately linked, could not help but make them proud and ponder, longingly, on how Breton autonomy had slipped away. In the context of the nationwide politics of the July Revolution, most were legitimists, feeling that another Bourbon Restoration might also restore that autonomy and their public role.

44. See the membership lists, 1849–56, in *Bulletin archéologique de l'Association bretonne*. Aymar's scholarship focused on the medieval Breton nobility; for example, "Étude historique sur les droits de sucession en Bretagne," *Bulletin archéologique* (1852) argued for the similarities between the Welsh and Breton systems.

45. Guiomar, *Le bretonisme*, 164–66. I will use Arthur Lemoyne de La Borderie, *Histoire de Bretagne*, vols. 1–4 (Rennes, 1904–6), the most complete edition with themes unchanged. On the notion of the creation story and its significance in the (gendered) culture of peoples, see Peggy Sanday, *Female Power and Male Dominance: On the Origins of Sexual Inequality* (Cambridge, 1981).

46. La Borderie, *Histoire*, 1:207–26; quotes, 1:217, 1:219.

47. La Borderie completely dispatched the original founding myth of Conan with excellent research that still stands.

48. La Borderie, *Histoire*, 1:227–392: on the non-romanization of the Britons, their maintenance of their language, and early Christianity, 1:267–79; on the invasion of Britain by the Anglo-Saxons, 1:229–46; on the "plou," 1:279–82. On further migrations and the establishment of the Breton kingdoms in the sixth and seventh centuries, 1:335–92.

49. La Borderie, *Histoire*, 2:142–275; 3:144–47.

50. La Borderie, *Histoire*, 2:335–92, 507–30. In a special index, La Borderie, lists 123 "Saints Bretons" mentioned in the volume.

51. *Bulletin archéologique* (1851): 36–48.

52. For these remarks by De Manche, see Congrès celtique internationale (Saint-Brieuc, 1868), Séance du mardi 15 octobre 1867, 2–3.

53. This book-length poem included twenty-four "songs" that attempt to encompass Breton culture, among them, "Pardon," "Carnac," "Le marché de Kemper," "Les fileuses," etc. Its twelfth song, "Encounter of Five Bretons," is a meeting of men from the four historic regions of Lower Brittany, Vannes, Tréguier, Cournouille, and Léon, with a Welsh bard, harp in hand. At the end, the four bid him well: Eh bien, à votre gré parcourez nos cantons, / Vous trouverez partout des frères Bretons. / Au fond de tous nos coeurs une même sang pétille, / Nous sommes tous les enfants d'une même famille. / (Well! Wander our cantons at your pleasure, / You will find brothers everywhere. / Deep in all our hearts a single blood sparkles, / For we are all the children of a single family). See Auguste Brizieux, *Les Bretons, poème couronné par L'Académie française* (Paris, 1848), 180. The link between the language of kinship and that of race could not be clearer.

54. Congrès celtique, Séance du mardi 15 octobre 1867, 9. It should be noted, however, that many male writers on the subject, while lauding the bravery and stolid persistence of the Celtic peoples, also emphasized the "feminine" quality of the Celtic soul, so such symbolism was appropriate. Ernest Renan was no doubt the most famous of them: *La poésie des races celtiques* (Paris, 1857).

55. Congrès celtique, Séance du mardi 15 octobre 1867, 15.

56. Congrès celtique, Séance du mardi 15 octobre 1867, 15–16.

57. The contrast with the bourgeois of Vannes, discussed earlier, is evident, but can no doubt be explained by the fact, as Martine Segalen has shown exhaustively, that consanguineal marriage, rampant among the French-speaking urban dwellers of the province in the nineteenth century, was extremely rare among Lower-Breton peasants because of the nature of property devolution among them. This conforms with one of my explanations for the decline of blood-kin language in close-marriage kinship regimes: *Fifteen Generations of Bretons: Kinship and Society in Lower Brittany, 1720–1980*, trans. J. S. Underwood (Cambridge, 1991).

58. Congrès celtique, Séance du 17 octobre 1867, 134–35.

59. Roger Price, *People and Politics in France, 1848–1870* (Cambridge, 2004), 83–95.

60. For details, see Christopher H. Johnson, "Kinship, Civil Society, and Power," in *Kinship in Europe*, ed. Sabean, Teuscher, and Mathieu, 269–75.

61. *Bulletin du Société polymathique du Morbihan* (1863): 101; hereafter BSPM.

62. These assessments are based on a perusal of the articles in BSPM, *l'Annuaire du Morbihan*, and certain contributions to the *Bulletin de l'Association bretonne*, as well as correspondence of the Galles circle (A. D. Morbihan 2 J 78–85). See also Johnson, "Kinship, Civil Society, and Power," in *Kinship in Europe*, ed. Sabean, Teuscher, and Mathieu, 269–72.

63. "Chant cinquième—Carnac," in Brizieux, *Les Bretons*, 67–77.

64. Martin, "De l'origine des monuments mégalithique," Congrès celtique, Séance du 16 octobre 1867, 37, and "Mémoire," 164–89. He also took into account the existence of megaliths in North Africa, but he attributed them to "blue-eyed, blond-haired Libyans" mentioned in ancient Egyptian inscriptions and argued they were Celts, too (188–89).

65. René Galles, "Manné-er-H'roëk: dolmen découvert sous un tumulus à Locmaria-quer," *BSPM* (1863): 18–40, quotation, 30–31. The previous year, Galles had opened investigation of the tumulus of Saint-Michel, which in the long run was more important in dating these sites.

66. "Allocution de M. de Closmadeuc en prenant le fauteuil de la présidence," *BSPM* (1867): 2.

67. L. Galles, "Comment les dolmens pourraient bien avait été construits par les Gaulois," *BSPM* (1873): 50–75.

68. M. A. Guyot-Jomard, "Sur la provenance des granits qui ont servi à élever les monuments dits celtiques," *BSPM* (1866): 101–6. This was only partially correct, but he was assuming that the builders were quite "primitive."

69. R[ené] Galles, "Un souvenir de Kabylie à propos des alignements de Carnac," *BSPM* (1881): 22–25.

70. "Allocution de M. Galles en prenant le fauteuil de la Présidance," *BSPM* (1882): 2.

71. See *BSPM*: on the Roman roads, Closmadeuc and others (1870s); on Breton ritual and relics, Lallemand and others (1870s); and on land tenure, Burgault, "Origine du domaine congéable" (1868 and 1869). The last was challenged by Courson, creating a heated controversy.

72. Emile Burgault was the future republican mayor of Vannes and situated at the very heart of its bourgeoisie. See his two long articles on Celtic origins and migrations in *BSPM* (1870 and 1871). In their rejection of a Breton race, SPM writers were joined by fellow urban Breton Ernst Renan, whose famous address, "Qu'est-ce qu' une nation," denouncing the equation of race and nation, was delivered at the Sorbonne in 1882.

73. "Allocution de M. Galles," *BSPM* (1885): 2.

74. Many of the debates are, appropriately, linguistic: see Leon Fleuriot, *Les origines de la Bretagne. L'émigration* (Paris, 1980). The most up-to-date general history is Joël Cornette, *Histoire de la Bretagne et des Bretons*, vol. 1, *Des âges obscurs à Louis XIV* (Paris, 2005). For southeastern Brittany, see Noël-Yves Tonnerre, *Naissance de la Bretagne. Géographie historique et structures sociales de la Bretagne méridionale (Nantais et Vannetais) de la fin du VIII<sup>e</sup> à la fin du XII<sup>e</sup> siècle* (Angers, 1994). For the view from Wales, which stressed the centrality of the migration, see Nora K. Chadwick, *Early Brittany* (Cardiff, 1969).

75. Jack E. Reece, *The Bretons Against France: Ethnic Minority Nationalism in Twentieth-Century Brittany* (Chapel Hill, NC, 1977).

76. Caroline Ford, *Creating the Nation in Provincial France: Religion and Political Identity in Brittany* (Princeton, NJ, 1993).

# Appendix

## Works entitled *Correspondance de* or *Lettres inédites de . . .*[a]

| AUTHOR(S) | LETTER DATES | WORDS USED FOR KIN | | | |
|---|---|---|---|---|---|
| | | *Sang* | *Sang* as *race* | *parent*, etc. | *famille*[b] |
| Voltaire | 1760–85 | 1 | 0 | 29 | 101 |
| Du Deffand | 1761–71 | 0 | 0 | 8 | 16 |
| De Sade | 1774–97 | 7 | 0 | 16 | 112 |
| Gilbert Romme | 1767–79 | 1 | 0 | 11 | 40 |
| Louis XVI | 1774–91 | 3 | 0 | 3 | 20[c] |
| Marie-Antoinette | 1770–92 | 9 | 0 | 5 | 46 |
| Père Lenfant[d] | 1790–93 | 1 | 0 | 3 | 20 |
| Charles Nodier | 1793–1809 | 1 | 0 | 0 | 40 |
| Théophile de Fernig | 1797–1805 | 1 | 0 | 6 | 14 |
| de Vaudreuil/d'Artois | 1798–1814 | 1 | 1 | 25 | 85 |
| Merlin de Thionville | 1798–1832 | 0 | 2 | 14 | 42 |
| Chateaubriand | 1800–1830 | 3 | 3 | 12 | 241 |
| de Staël/Meister | 1805–20 | 0 | 0 | 3 | 16 |
| Charles de Rémusat | 1814–23 | 1 | 0 | 6 | 9 |
| General Vandamme | 1810–40 | 0 | 0 | 0 | 25 |
| Hector Berlioz | 1819–69 | 0 | 0 | 4 | 25 |
| Lamennais/Vitrolles | 1810–53 | 0 | 0 | 0 | 18 |
| Auguste Comte | 1824–57 | 0 | 0 | 3 | 22 |
| P.-J. David d'Angers | 1825–56 | 0 | 0 | 0 | 41 |
| Béranger/Dupont | 1823–33 | 0 | 0 | 1 | 40 |
| Victor Jacquemont | 1824–32 | 0 | 3[e] | 4 | 21 |
| Lafayette | 1825–37 | 0 | 0 | 4 | 71 |
| Gustav d'Eichthal | 1828–71 | 0 | 0 | 0 | 17 |
| Victor Hugo | 1832–82 | 2 | 0 | 5 | 61 |
| Sainte-Beuve/Ollivier | 1837–69 | 0 | 0 | 3 | 28 |
| Allart/Sainte-Beuve | 1841–48 | 0 | 0 | 3 | 6 |
| Heinrich Heine | 1843–55 | 0 | 0 | 4 | 28 |
| L.-N. Rossel | 1844–71 | 0 | 0 | 2 | 29 |
| Pierre Lanfrey | 1850s | 1 | 1 | 1 | 9 |
| Famille Impériale | 1852–70 | 0 | 0 | 5 | 52 |
| Gustav Flaubert | 1845–80s | 0 | 6[f] | 4 | 40[g] |
| Le Cte de Chambord | 1841–71 | 5[h] | 0 | 0 | 44 |
| César Franck | 1870s–90s | 0 | 0 | 1 | 38 |
| Émile Zola | 1880s | 0 | 0 | 2 | 44 |

NOTES:

[a] Digital survey of kinship uses of sang, parent(s), parenté, and famille in full-text electronic reproductions of late eighteenth-century to nineteenth-century French books

(University of Michigan Library: Mirlyn). See the bibliography in this volume for complete citations.

[b] The use of *sang* as a kin-term is straightforward (*liens du sang, mon sang,* etc.) and can refer to immediate family or wider kin (see endnote 3). *Parent(s)* can mean one's own mother and/or father or more distant relatives. I have only sorted here for the latter, for much of the correspondence say, between siblings, will include multiple salutations to one's parents (in the English sense) and throw the count into confusion. In general, appearances of the term *parent(s)* for relatives decline significantly in the nineteenth century; *parenté* (kinship) comes into greater usage but remains unusual in everyday language. The distinction between wider kin and immediate family is easy to identify. This is not the case with *famille,* where lines are constantly blurred. I have therefore included all instances of the word's use in these texts. In general, reference to the wider family seems to be employed about half the time, though it depends a great deal on the nature of the correspondence. In any case, *famille* emerges in the nineteenth century as the normal reference to all relatives, whether close or distant.

[c] Including five instances of *la* (or *ma*) *grande famille des français.*

[d] Confesseur du Roi.

[e] Jacquemont uses *race* nineteen times to describe all sorts of peoples, from *race hollandaise* to *race noire.* He was an adventurer (son of a minister of public instruction) who traveled the world and died in Bombay in 1832. Prosper Merimée was a friend and arranged for the publication of his letters.

[f] Referring to Alfred de Musset, Flaubert also says, "sa vanité est de sang bourgeois"!

[g] Flaubert and several other letter writers refer to the "family of the French" or "of the nation" or indeed "of Europe."

[h] The Bourbon pretender also refers to his line as "la race" on three occasions.

SOURCE:
Compiled by Christopher H. Johnson with the aid of Mirlyn Classic, the University of Michigan Library Catalogue, at http://guides.lib.umich.edu/mirlynclassic.

# Chapter 10

# Nazi Anti-Semitism and the Question of "Jewish Blood"

## Cornelia Essner

## The NSDAP as a *Völkisch* Party

Anti-Semitism was the core of the *völkisch* movement that emerged with the foundation of the German Empire in 1871. A strange mixture of nationalistic and religious ideas, it was spread by various associations and federations that excluded members of "Jewish blood." All these relatively small organizations sought a new religion that would arise from the depths of the "German soul." This search for a German religion of the future implied the renunciation of traditional Christianity: the *Völkische* called either for purification from Jewish roots—and in consequence proposed an "Aryan Christ"—or for a total, neo-pagan renunciation of Christianity because of the ineradicable Jewish origin of Jesus.[1] *Völkisch* anti-Semitism focused on the notion of soul as much as on the notion of blood.

The *völkisch* Nationalsozialistische Arbeiterpartei only arose after the First World War. In 1920, the NSDAP stipulated in its program: "Only members of the nation may be citizens of the State. Only those of German blood, whatever their creed, may be members of the nation. Accordingly no Jew may be a member of the nation." It was no accident that they used the expression *German blood* but not the expression *Jewish blood*, because the *Jewish* was seen not only as a material-biological substance, but also as a spiritual substance. This underlined another point of the party program: the NSDAP postulated "a positive Christianity that is not linked to a special confession. It fights against the Jewish-materialistic spirit inside us and outside us."[2]

## Dinter's Sin Against the Blood

The omnipotent power attributed to "Jewish blood" is demonstrated in an anti-Semitic novel entitled *Die Sünde wider das Blut*. This book, which appeared in 1917, immediately became a bestseller and by 1921 had probably been read by more than one million people. The author of this bestseller was Artur Dinter (1876–1948), a scientist and *völkisch*-religious writer who after the First World War became a very close comrade of Adolf Hitler. But in 1928, Hitler parted company with him, albeit unwillingly, and Dinter was excluded from the NSDAP because of his intransigent fight for a new German Christian religion ("positive Christianity") based on the belief that Christ was of Aryan rather than Hebrew descent. This *völkisch* message no longer matched the vision of the party leaders, who after 1928 sought to win over larger segments of the voting public.

In *Die Sünde wider das Blut*, anti-Semitism in Germany gained a new "theoretical" foundation, which suggests the usefulness of a close reading of the novel. Its Aryan hero, Hermann Kämpfer (i.e., Hermann, the fighter), is a poor but gifted chemist who has to work for a rich Jewish entrepreneur. (All the Jews in the story have been baptized.) Hermann falls in love with Elisabeth, the daughter of the rich Jew and his Aryan wife. Before Hermann dares to ask this beautiful half-Jewish girl to marry him, he conjures up a spiritual kinship with her. By means of a very long monologue—forty pages in the book—Hermann wins Elisabeth and her mother over to German Christianity and a belief in the "Aryan Christ." "The unbridgeable difference between Jesus and the Jews," Dinter has his protagonist say, "could only be explained by the contrast between their races. Jesus was a Jew according to his education and to his religious creed, but never according to his race." At the end of his *völkisch* sermon Hermann cried out: "When will a new Luther appear to us German Christians, a Luther who will accomplish the first Luther's task and free our Christian religion from Judaism and free us from the Jew inside us and outside us; who will finally cut off the head of the Jewish Gorgon?"

At first Elisabeth's conversion to Aryan Christianity blotted out the stain of her Jewish extraction, allowing the marriage to Hermann to take place. But the couple's child turned out to be a "horrible monster" with all the signs of the "odious race" (he had "black curly hair" and was "monkey like"), a description fitting the stereotype of the Jew as well as that of the Negro. To explain the origin of the monster-child—who is only a "quarter-Jewish" arithmetically—Dinter used an old element of German superstition, *Versehen*, by which an unborn child is marked by a negative experience of the mother.[3] This popular idea, linked to earlier notions of human procreation, was well known to German intellectuals from Goethe's novel *Die Wahlverwandtschaften* (Elective Affinities) of 1809. In that story, two couples, imagining their counterparts at the moment of conception, beget children resembling the ones they were thinking about.[4]

During her pregnancy, Hermann's half-Jewish wife was unable to stop thinking of her former Jewish fiancé—and so she delivered herself to the "Jewish spirit." The belief in the force of female *Versehen* had been especially propagated in 1903 by Otto Weininger—admired by Hitler and Dinter—in his book *Geschlecht und Charakter.* "The urogenital tract is not the only, but the most efficient way," writes Weininger, "by which a woman could have sexual intercourse (*koitiert*)," adding that, "by a glance, by a word a woman could feel obsessed."[5] Still, Weininger, although himself Jewish and an anti-Semite, did not put *Versehen* to the service of anti-Semitism.

In *Die Sünde wider das Blut*, the half-Jewish wife died after giving birth to a second child, also monstrous. Thus *Versehen*—here turned into the dominance of the "Jewish spirit"—had spoiled her progeny forever. Kämpfer married a second time, this time to a pure Aryan woman. But this wife also gave birth to a monster-child. She was soon obliged to confess that she had had a stillborn child by a Jew. This second marriage between two Aryans articulates the model dear to the radical anti-Semites (whom I will call "contagionists"): sexual contact (followed by birth) with a Jewish man contaminates forever the capacity of an Aryan woman to bear Aryan children, even if her later children are engendered by an Aryan father. Dinter called this the "law of telegony" (or *Fernzeugung*, procreation at a distance).[6] He did not, however, indicate that telegony, conceived as a form of atavism, had been seriously discussed by animal breeders in the nineteenth century. The idea of telegony has a certain similarity with ideas about the transmission of syphilis: the Jewish man produces the "racial contamination," but the Aryan woman is like a prostitute who then transmits the venereal disease to Aryan men and to her children. It also is evident that the blood of a female, even an Aryan-German one, is considered the weaker blood.

The novel suggested that the contamination of "German blood" by the Jew was a well-organized operation. Motivated by the "devil's aim" of "racial contamination," Elisabeth's father, the rich businessman, had

provided support for more than a hundred poor Aryan girls. The stereotypes of Jewish economic power and "race defilement" (*Rassenschande*)
were here causally linked, in a bond that would be echoed in the Nuremberg laws when it was proclaimed that Jewish households were forbidden to keep female Aryan servants younger than forty-five years, that
is, in their childbearing years. Reinforcing the point about "race defilement," Dinter has his hero, Kämpfer, recall having once seduced and
impregnated a poor Aryan girl, who had died but had left him with a
splendid, if illegitimate, Aryan son. Kämpfer educated this son together
with his legitimate son—Jewish by the means of telegony. Each day their
tutor could see the inferiority of the latter. At the end of the novel, these
children die in accidents, and Kämpfer kills his second wife's Jewish se-
ducer. Brought to trial, he gives a long speech in which he calls for a law
prohibiting "mixed marriages" and "race defilement." Found not guilty
and celebrated by the public, the hero, now condemned to sterility because of the malediction of Jewish telegony, leaves for the war, thereby
sacrificing his life to his fatherland.

Besides the biological mechanism of "racial contamination" by sexual
intercourse in *Sünde wider das Blut*, there is also an immaterial mechanism: the *Versehen*. During her pregnancy the half-Jewish Elisabeth is obsessed by the memory of her former Jewish fiancé, an obsession caused,
not by her half-Jewish blood, but by her half-Jewish soul. The *Versehen*
appears like the reification of the elementary *völkisch* idea of the "Jew in
ourselves," which, according to Weininger, is "Judaism as a platonic idea,"
a "psychic constitution that forms a possibility for all human beings" that
must be fought against, just as Jesus overcame the Judaism in himself.[7]
Weininger, who in a footnote mentioned his Jewish origins, finished off
his "interior Jew" in his own way: very soon after the publication of his
book, he killed himself. The suicidal, inherently self-destructive aspect
of the idea of the "interior Jew" was felt by the adherents of the *völkisch*
movement. "What would we gain," a *völkisch* leader asked in 1924, of
those who called for a pogrom against the Jews, "if we killed all the Jews
around us, but left the Jew in ourselves still alive?"[8] The only efficient
protection against the omnipresence of the "Jewish," suggested Dinter, is
the belief in the "Aryan Christ."

Dinter's biological theory of telegony, developed in 1917, was totally
incompatible with the contemporary paradigm of the biology of heredity and eugenics in Germany based on Mendel's rediscovered laws of
heredity and recent knowledge of human generation, which postulated
an equal mixture of the male and the female germ cells and which was
linked to the discoveries of Oskar Hertwig in 1875 and popularized in
the writings of August Weismann.[9] It must have been clear to every edu-

cated reader that telegony was totally at odds with the modern biology of heredity.

## Julius Streicher, Dinter's Continuator

Dinter's most influential successor in contagionist anti-Semitism was Julius Streicher, who became the Nazi Gauleiter of Franconia. He abandoned the Christian-Aryan elements of Dinter's message and reduced the ideas of *Die Sünde wider das Blut* to pornographic anti-Semitism, published in series in *Der Stürmer.* Here stories about the dangerous Jewish *Rassenschänder* (defiler of the race) were indefatigably reported. In 1935, Streicher started a periodical with more scientific ambitions, called *Deutsche Volksgesundheit aus Blut und Boden,* which survived only one year. The co-publisher was Gerhard Wagner—head of the party office for national health—who was to play a central role in the elaboration of the Nuremberg laws. In the first pages of the periodical appeared Streicher's scandalous speech of 1 December 1934, delivered at Fürth in southern Germany: "The sperm of a man of a foreign race is a dissimilar [*artfremd*] albumen, which is absorbed with the copulation by the female mother soil [*Mutterboden*] and so goes into the blood," explained Streicher.

Contrary to Dinter, who considered that "racial contamination" started only with childbirth, Streicher now said: "A single copulation of a Jew with an Aryan woman is sufficient to poison her blood forever. With sperm foreign to the German species [*artfremd*], she takes over the foreign soul. Never again will this Aryan woman be able to have purely Aryan children, even by marrying an Aryan man. She will have only bastards ... [whose] children too will be bastards, *Mischlinge,* ugly, sickly human beings with bad characters. This process is called *Imprägnation.*"[10] With Streicher, the Jewish sperm also transmits the Jewish soul, and Dinter's complicated and quasi-mystical idea of *Versehen* has vanished. The Latin derivative *Imprägnation* sounded familiar to German listeners, being related to the German word *Prägung* (character, impression). *Imprägnation* conjures up old ideas of pregnancy (German: *Schwangerschaft*) visible in the English word.

## The Rise of the Nuremberg Laws

Although contagionist thinking was very strong in the party, it was officially condemned in October 1935. The NSDAP Office for Racial Policy distributed a flyer that read: "The belief in a so-called *Imprägnation* is not only without scientific basis, but also presents a great political danger and has caused great unrest because it defames numerous members of the nation of good German origin. This corresponds neither to the will of the Führer nor to the will of the party. Therefore he wishes to end the spread of this heresy."[11] Appealing to common sense, the flyer went on to argue that if the assertion that an Aryan woman becomes biologically Jewish by means of sexual intercourse with a Jewish man were true, then "inversely any Jewish woman must become Aryan by means of sexual intercourse with an Aryan man. Then the Jewish question could indeed find a very simple solution, but unfortunately this is not the case." The conclusion made the point very clear: "The racial idea of National Socialism is based on the acknowledgment of the fact that a person's racial characteristics are determined by heredity."[12]

The inconsistency between contagionist anti-Semitism and the modern biology of heredity had become a growing problem for the National Socialist state after Hitler had revealed in July 1933, by the proclamation of the Law for Prevention of Hereditary Illness (*Gesetz zur Verhütung erbkranken Nachwuchses*), that he wanted to base Nazi ideology on eugenics and the biology of heredity. With such an orientation, the Nazi state could be considered modern and should find international approval, since eugenic movements existed in different European countries and in America. It was no accident that the official condemnation of the *Imprägnation* theory happened just in October 1935. At this time a vehement tug-of-war about the future definition of a Jew was taking place behind the scenes. On 15 September 1935, at the end of the annual party rally at Nuremberg, the Nuremberg laws had been promulgated. Their central features were the Citizenship Law of the Reich (*Reichsbürgergesetz*) and the Law for the Protection of German Blood and German Honor (*Gesetz zum Schutz des deutschen Blutes und der deutschen Ehre*) or *Blutschutzgesetz*, prohibiting marriage and sexual intercourse between persons of "Jewish blood" and of "German blood." But the new Nuremberg laws did not as yet offer a solution for the "Jewish question": Who in Germany henceforth had to be treated as a Jew? Any person with one Jewish grandparent? From April 1933 on, the Law for the Purification of the National Civil Service (*Gesetz zur Wiederherstellung des Berufsbeamtentums*) used the construction of the "quarter-Jew." But should this widespread notion of a Jew—corresponding to the wishes of contagionists—be imposed on German society as a whole? The controversy about the genealogical reach of Jewish blood became inflamed at the party rally in Nuremberg.[13]

"The racial law arose in the night from Saturday to Sunday" (from 14 to 15 September 1935), wrote a racial expert of the Saxon Gauleitung, "and this the Führer wished, because the conflict between Streicher and Schacht [Minister of the Economy] was becoming alarming." The following phrase reveals what the conflict mainly was about: "The so-called theory of *Imprägnation*, notably defended by Dinter and Streicher, is completely without reason. Therefore an Aryan girl will not be defiled for life by contact with a Jew."[14] Hjalmar Schacht was a chief opponent of contagionist anti-Semitism. Together with bureaucrats from the Foreign Ministry and the Interior Ministry, he wanted a general law that would have combined racially organized nationality and the prohibition of undesirable marriages with anti-Semitic economic laws.[15] However, this larger project—the anti-Semitic orientation of which was less obvious because it was concerned with everything "racially foreign"—was blocked by Hitler at the party rally when he suddenly ordered the development of a purely anti-Semitic law of *Blutschutz*.

The 15 September 1935 laws thus formalized Hitler's orders: marriages between "Jews" and the "German blooded" were prohibited, any sexual intercourse between these two groups was punishable, and Jewish households were forbidden to keep female German-blooded servants under the age of forty-five. The *Reichsbürgergesetz* introduced two new legal categories—"citizen of German or related blood" (*Staatsangehöriger deutschen oder artverwandten Blutes*) and "citizen of the Reich" (*Reichsbürger*)—which were intended to create a racial and political elite. Jews were forbidden to become *Reichsbürger* or to exercise any official function. But the new national categories were never implemented, and all Germans who were classified as "Jews" kept their German citizenship until deportation.[16]

## The Conflict About the Reach of "Jewish Blood"

In these laws of 15 September 1935, the definition of a Jew had still not been settled and the question of which persons were prohibited from marrying remained unsolved. How deep should *Blutschutz* be? What degree of "Jewish blood" should be kept away from kinship with "German blood"? What would happen to the estimated 200,000 "half-Jews" or *Mischlinge*? Could they be absorbed by "German blood"; could they marry people of "German blood"? Or on the contrary should they be counted as "Jewish blood" and therefore not be allowed to marry people of "German blood"? The debate between the more rational bureaucracy of the state and the leaders of the party persisted for two months. Roughly thirty drafts of the future application decrees to the Nuremberg laws were created, discussed, and dropped, one after the other.

Finally, at the end of October, Gerhard Wagner—the friend of Streicher—presented a draft law obviously transmitting the idea of telegony or *Imprägnation*. Wagner, already of great influence on Hitler during the party rally, was said to be speaking the will of the Führer. The draft law stipulated that all "half-Jews" should be treated in general as "Jews." This equalization was to be retroactive to the generation of their parents: "The non-Jewish spouse of a Jew is also ranked as a Jew." But a possibility remained for the non-Jewish Jew to escape from the legally ordered change of race: "If a childless mixed marriage ceases other than by death, the consequences of this clause are invalidated with the end of the marriage."[17] This stipulation indirectly required that the Aryan partner of a mixed marriage either stay voluntarily childless or divorce. An Aryan spouse who had become contaminated by transmitting "Jewish blood" to offspring became a Jew forever. It is evident that Wagner's draft law mainly considered the case of mixed marriages where the man was Jewish and the woman Aryan. The possibility for the Aryan part to return to Germanity, if childless, demonstrates that Streicher's theory of *Imprägnation* had reverted to Dinter's original idea: it was the birth of a child, not the mere fact of sexual intercourse, that activated eternal contamination.

In Wagner's draft law, "half-Jews," therefore, became "Jews," with two exceptions: First someone could become "Aryan" by order of the Führer. Second, a half-Jew could retain mixed status by marrying an Aryan but would lose that status and become a Jew in the event of a divorce. This change back to the lower category applied only to a man: if a half-Jewish woman divorced, she remained half-Jewish. Once more it was apparent that the "danger" transmitted by "Jewish blood" was linked to the male. If Wagner's draft law had been realized, most of the estimated 200,000 half-Jews would have been reclassified as Jews, and the question of how to deal with *Mischlinge* would have been limited mainly to the roughly 40,000 "quarter-Jews."

The bureaucrats at the Ministry of the Interior's Department of Nationality Affairs, who had been in charge of the "Jewish question" since 15 September 1935, vehemently opposed Wagner's draft law. Change of race from Aryan to Jew, they argued, is not compatible with the science of hereditary biology, which teaches the constancy of race. Besides, since 1913, the racial biology of Eugen Fischer had been teaching that the *Mischling* should be considered as a special human being who was not similar, as earlier dogma had claimed, to the "inferior parent-race."[18] The state bureaucrats, pressing for the application of racial biology, practiced an anti-Semitism that I would like to call "rationalizing." As lawyers, they argued on behalf of the administration's need for rational, logical consistency. They thought it imperative to settle immediately upon a durable and unambiguous—in their mind, equitable—definition of the Jew. Wagner's draft law would have created a group whose definition as Jew or as Aryan depended on childlessness or divorce. The experts of the Ministry of Interior (Bernhard Lösener, Hans Globke) emphasized that a fluctuating notion of the Jew contradicted the administration's need for unchangeable personal identity.[19] They also argued that the disappearance of half-Jews among Jews would be dangerous in light of the biology of heredity, because the gift of 50 percent "precious German genetic material" to Jews would enrich them with strong and politically dangerous personas.

A draft law expressing the ideas of Eugen Fischer existed as well, having been circulated immediately after the party rally, but it had completely disappeared from discussion by the end of October. In this draft, the physician Artur Gütt, a leading eugenicist in the Ministry of the Interior until 1939, and a rival to the contagionist physician Wagner, had proposed to classify every *Mischling* at the moment of his marriage as either "Jewish" or "Aryan." But this project also had been overthrown by the lawyers, who told Hitler that it did not cover the danger produced by uncontrolled premarital sexuality of not-yet-classified "half-Jews."

At the end of October 1935, six weeks after the party rally at Nuremberg, the front line between contagionist and rationalizing anti-Semites appeared as hardened as it had been during the party rally. It was not Hitler who finally made a decision and ended the fight for a definition of the Jew, but Wilhelm Stuckart, state secretary at the Ministry of the Interior and head of the Department of Nationality Affairs. Stuckart, an early party member, succeeded in negotiating a compromise between Wagner's draft law and the one of his own department.

## The Codified Degrees of "Jewish Blood" in November 1935

Finally, on 14 November 1935, the first two application decrees to the 15 September Nuremberg laws appeared in the *Reichsgesetzblatt*. These decrees did not codify the new term "*German blood*" that the category "citizen of German or related blood" (*Staatsangehöriger deutschen und artverwandten Blutes*) had added to the legal definition of citizenship, but they did codify three degrees of "Jewish blood" and of separation in

German-Jewish kinship: "A Jew is one who is descended from at least three racially fully-Jewish grandparents." "A Jewish *Mischling* is one who is descended from one or two racially fully-Jewish grandparents." The proof of being "racially fully Jewish" was furnished by the Jewish religion of the grandparents—regardless of whether the grandchild was Jewish, Christian, or without confession. A "German-blooded" grandmother counted as Jewish if she had converted to Judaism.[20] People who had two fully Jewish grandparents were classified as *Mischlinge 1. Grades* unless they belonged to the Jewish religion or were married to a Jew. In that case, these "Mischlinge" were considered to be Jewish just like children from "race defilement" (*Geltungsjuden*).

The first application decree to the *Blutschutzgesetz* contained in particular the matrimonial impediments and prescriptions for *Mischlinge 1. Grades* (Half-Breeds of the First Degree), that is, half-Jews, and *Mischlinge 2. Grades* (Half-Breeds of the Second Degree), that is, quarter-Jews, or people with one Jewish grandparent. Half-Jews had better marry each other, suggested the decree indirectly, as this would guarantee reproduction of the first-degree classification in their children. The marriage of a half-Jew with a German-blooded person was not officially prohibited, but it required the approbation of the Ministry of Interior, which regularly refused the requests and then forwarded the records to the Gestapo. The key figure in this system of classification was the "quarter-Jew," who represented the "moment" wherein "Jewish blood" could change into "German blood": henceforth a quarter-Jew marrying a full-blooded Aryan would create an eighth-Jew whose "Jewishness" would "disappear" because he would be legally defined as an Aryan. But the party organizations and Himmler's SS went on applying the far-reaching and, in principle, endless (contagionist) definition of the Jew that the arrangement of 14 November 1935 had intended to eradicate from public memory, that is, that "Jewish blood" would persist in the "eighth-Jews" of the future.

The logic of the bureaucratic arithmetic of blood yielded, on the one hand, the imperative for a person categorized as *Mischling 2. Grades* to marry a person of "German blood" and, on the other hand, the prohibition of that individual's marriage to a "Jew" or to someone of the same category. The marriage between two "quarter-Jews" was forbidden because it would have generated children classified as "German blood" whose strong "Jewish blood-inheritance" (two-eighths Jewish, or Jewishness from two different family lines) would have been lost to the German memory of kinship.[21]

With the Nuremberg legislation of gradated categories of "Jewish blood," the modern German state "succeeded" in realizing the old racist utopian ideal of finding a way to draw a legal boundary between people of "positive" and "negative" groups. It is very likely that the bureaucracy's lawyers had learned from the example of the German colonial past.[22] In the last years of the German colonial empire before the outbreak of the First World War, the administration was working to develop racial legislation, with the prohibition of mixed marriages at its core. Especially in the colony of Southwest Africa (present-day Namibia), which had a long history of white settlement, the administration tried to find a racial definition of a "native." In 1908, the Windhoek High Court stipulated that anybody whose genealogy, either on the paternal or the maternal side, went back to a native was to be considered a native. This unlimited definition of the native created some unrest in the "German Southwest" because white inhabitants suddenly saw themselves changed into natives if, for instance, a native great-grandmother emerged from their genealogy. The question of whether we can speak of a causal continuity between Windhoek and Nuremberg is a very interesting matter that I have studied in another article.[23]

## Two Proceedings for the Separation of Jewish-German Kinship

It is not the aim of this chapter to describe the exclusion and persecution of those Germans to whom the notion of Jew, according to the decrees of 14 November 1935, was applied. It should only be emphasized that the administration was very aware of the *Mischling 1. Grades* because members of this category made numerous demands for exemption from the discriminatory acts that now regulated their lives. The more the state administration had to deal with the *Mischlinge*, the less interested society became in the destiny of the "full-Jews," whose persecution was increasingly practiced by the new institutions of the police like the Geheime Staatspolizei (Gestapo) and the SS-Sicherheitspolizei. In the autumn of 1941, the deportation and finally the murder of men, women, and children covered by the legal definition of *Jew* began.

We should perhaps briefly mention two proceedings for the separation of Jewish-German kinship that had their origin in the Nuremberg laws. The first were the court cases concerning "race defilement" (*Rassenschande*), which continually demonstrated to German society the importance of "blood protection" (*Blutschutz*). Every trial about "race defilement" began with an assessment of the Jewish "quality" of the perpetrator or the victim. If a Jewish "race defiler" or his victim could prove that he was only a *Mischling 1. Grades*, a trial would not take place. The trials were full of pornography. In 1937 the Court of Justice of the Reich ruled that "perverse" sexuality would be considered a form of race defilement, and, therefore, that physical contacts between Jews and the "German-blooded" for sexual satisfaction were punishable.[24] The Jew who visited a "German-blooded" prostitute was punishable, and likewise the SS-man who had a mistress in an extermination camp. However, as the contagionist anti-Semites, and especially Hitler, considered women to be generally passive and victims of sexuality, the female partner in "race defilement"—Jewish or Aryan—was not to be punished.[25] This was stipulated in the *Blutschutzgesetz* in 1935. The second proceeding was a new type of trial established in 1938, allowing the status as "Jew" or *Mischling 1. Grades* to be contested. The *Abstammungsklage* (Petition about Descent) was utilized mainly by *Mischling 1. Grades*. If it could be proved that the legal, Jewish father was not the biological father of the *Mischling*, that the *Mischling* was in fact the child of maternal adultery with an Aryan, then the *Mischling* would be declared Aryan, but of illegitimate birth. The trials of *Rassenschande* were rooted in contagionist thinking, but the *Abstammungsklage* had its origin in the thinking of rational anti-Semites: each successful petition saved a part of the "precious German genetic material" from vanishing among the Jews.

## The "Wannsee-Conference" and After: The Persistent Conflict About the Reach of "Jewish Blood"

The endeavor of contagionist anti-Semites to make the "half-Jews" into "full Jews" never stopped and actually intensified in the summer of 1941, when the war against the Soviet Union—with its large Jewish population—finally started. The party leadership and the SS-Office for the Security of the Reich (RSHA, SS-Reichssicherheitshauptamt), founded in 1939, worked together on this. The phrase "final solution of the Jewish question" was at this time not yet a camouflage for the murder of the Jews, but referred instead to a project—described here in the words of Eichmann, the instructor for Jewish affairs in the RSHA—to "determine definitively the group of people of Jewish blood who should be extracted from the European people" and transported outside Europe.[26]

On 20 January 1942, a meeting of nine state secretaries and five high-ranking SS officers took place in Berlin-Wannsee. Reinhard Heydrich, head of the RSHA, which had been organizing the deportation of the German Jews since the autumn of 1941, had initiated the "Wannsee-Conference." The protocol for the meeting was found in March 1947—when the Americans were preparing the Nuremberg trials against the

Nazi bureaucracy—in a special record of the Nazi Foreign Office labeled "Endlösung der Judenfrage." The American prosecuting body was happy to take the document as proof that there had been a well-organized plan for the murder of the European Jews. This view, however, is no longer shared by all Holocaust researchers, and I would argue that the meeting dealt primarily with the genealogical "final solution of the Jewish question," as shown by the long-neglected second part of the protocol.[27]

Heydrich presented the state bureaucracy with his project "to equate the *Mischlinge 1. Grades* with the Jews as regards the final solution of the Jewish question."[28] That meant applying the notion of the Jew according to the Nuremberg laws to this group, thus making them "capable of deportation." (At this time deportations did not end in extermination camps like Auschwitz but in the newly established ghettos of the occupied Baltic countries.) The legal notion of the Jew had become the basis both of all the exclusion measures and of the deportation lists. Heydrich proposed exempting from deportation only a few first-degree *Mischlinge* who would then have had to accept sterilization. After that procedure, they would no longer have been officially distinguished from the people of "German blood." The *Mischlinge 2. Grades* would on the contrary generally be categorized among the German-blooded and only as an exception considered as Jews. Heydrich's project became most detailed when it listed the criteria that would allow the deportation of the partners of *Bastard-Ehen* (marriages between *Mischlinge* of different degrees). The ideological goal behind the long and seemingly complicated new scheme of classification was simple: to define once and for all the people of "Jewish blood" in Europe and then to remove them from Europe. Thus the old *völkisch* "Jewish question" would finally be resolved.

The Ministry of the Interior protested against Heydrich's project. State Secretary Stuckart offered a different plan: the forcible sterilization of all "half-Jews" of fertile age, who were then to be kept in the Reich, still marked by the constraints of their special juridical status. Stuckart further demanded the forcible divorce of all "mixed marriages" (after which the deportation of the Jewish partner would have been possible). His main objection to Heydrich's project was that it called for "endless administrative work." This choice of argument was of great importance because Hitler had said in June 1941 that for the duration of the war the "Jewish question" had to be treated, if at all, with a minimum of administrative work—and this was his last formal order about the "Jewish question."[29]

A second meeting, to discuss a "final solution of the question of mixed breed" (*Mischlingsfrage*), took place on 6 March 1942. Here the participants mainly discussed the pros and cons of the racial-biological theory that Stuckart had explained in detail and that his department at the Ministry of the Interior had defended in the autumn of 1935: principally, the concern that the equalization of "half-Jews" with Jews runs the risk of these people with their "precious German genetic material" becoming leaders of Slav resistance if deported to the East. The protocol of this meeting shows clearly that only the Führer was considered empowered to make a decision in favor of one of the rival plans for the "final solution of the question of mixed breed." But it was well known that the Führer was against any change to the Nuremberg laws.

In June 1942, Heydrich was assassinated. Himmler, the head of the German police, took over the direction of the RSHA for one year. By now, deportation meant murder, and Auschwitz had been equipped as the largest extermination camp. In this context, what happened to the conflict over the enlargement of the notion of the Jew? The discussion was frozen. Then, against the background of the murderous policy toward the Jews, although this was kept as secret as possible, the project to equate "half-Jews" with "Jews" became enormously incendiary. The extension of the definition of the Jew would create a constant potential for unrest among the population, wrote Stuckart and Lösener of the Ministry of the Interior to Himmler in September 1942: once racial policy "involved the field of the mixed breed, then there would no longer be a perceptible limit to considering ever more distant degrees of mixed breed. That is why this limit should be defined soon in the clearest and most definitive way."[30] The ultimately self-destructive and identity-destroying structure of contagionist anti-Semitism is here clearly named by its rivals, the rationalizing anti-Semites: What German could be certain of his non-Jewish origin, if ever more distant degrees of "Jewish blood" were taken into consideration?

Now, seven years after the promulgation of the Nuremberg laws, the German population was so accustomed to the idea that "full-Jews" were no longer a part of the German nation that they watched the deportation of the now alien "full-Jewish" families without compassion or concern. But what would happen if *Mischlinge*, with their widely ramified "German-blooded" kinship, were to be deported? The protest by Germans, mostly women, in the Rosenstraße of Berlin gave a foretaste of the possibilities. At the end of February 1943, the male Jewish partners of "mixed marriages" had been abruptly arrested, and the concerned spouses and children had gathered defiantly in front of the Rosenstraße prison. The formal operation was ultimately reversed—instead, later, the Jewish partners of "mixed marriages" were deported individually, so that their disappearances would not attract public attention.[31] They were mostly deported to Theresienstadt, the only camp where an exchange of letters was possible.

Any communication about the delicate genealogical "Jewish question" signified for Himmler a threat to his policy of systematic murder of the "full-Jews." At the end of October 1942, the official discussion about the "final solution of the question of mixed breed" was formally stopped. On the third meeting about this question, thanks "to new insights into the field of sterilization" (the new idea of forced sterilization by X-ray), it was decided "to sterilize all *Mischlinge 1. Grades.*" But the resolution taken at the meeting was never put into practice.

## The *Völkisch* "Jewish Question" Outlived Even the Genocide

The discussion about the "final solution of the question of mixed breed" did not stop. While the murder of the "full-Jews" from the whole of Europe was reaching a peak in the summer of 1943, the tug-of-war about the genealogical Jewish question shifted back to its old core in the party and the SS. Starting in December 1943, a vehement controversy broke out within the SS about the extent of "Jewish blood," when two SS officers who happened to be related asked for permission to marry. Their genealogies revealed that back at the end of the seventeenth century they had a common Jewish ancestor. An expert racial biologist demonstrated by means of acrobatic calculations that "Jewish chromosomes"—this "modern" notion now replacing the old notion of "Jewish blood"—would normally have disappeared after three generations, provided that new "Jewish chromosomes" were not added again by marriage. Himmler was not convinced. He argued: "It could equally be claimed that the non-Jewish chromosomes would vanish after the third generation. Therefore I have to ask: Where does the human being get his genetic material from?"[32] In the following months, Himmler's incurable contagionist conviction of the prior-potency (*Präpotenz*) of "Jewish blood"—the idea that in a mixed-blooded individual, the Jewish blood would take priority over the German blood in determining the identity of offspring—produced a hallucinatory dispute, expressed in memoranda, about the question of whether "Jewish blood" could, with confidence, be limited. Some racial experts who had already expressed their opinions during the debate about the notion of the Jew in autumn 1935 also took part in this dispute. So the *völkisch* "Jewish question" outlived even the genocide.

# Notes

1. For *völkisch* Christianity and its splitting, see Edouard Conte and Cornelia Essner, *La Quête de la race. Une anthropologie du nazisme* (Paris, 1995), 13–63; and Cornelia Essner, *Die "Nürnberger Gesetze" oder die Verwaltung des Rassenwahns 1933–1945* (Paderborn, 2002), 21–31.
2. The NSDAP program can be found in Wolfgang Treue, ed., *Deutsche Parteiprogramme seit 1861*, 4th ed. (Göttingen, 1968).
3. It derives from the German word *sehen* (to see); the prefix *ver* means "intensifying."
4. See Cornelia Essner, "Das Geheimnis der menschlichen Reproduktion. Zeugungstheorien in Deutschland zwischen 1750 und 1900," *Historische Mitteilungen* 22 (2009): 257–70.
5. Otto Weininger, *Geschlecht und Charakter*, 22nd ed. (Vienna and Leipzig, 1921), 551.
6. "Telegonie" is the name of an epic (*Epos*) in the sixth century before Christ that continues Homer's *Odyssey*. The hero is Telegonos—who is procreated at a distance—son of Odysseus and Circe. Like Oedipus, Telegonos kills his father without knowing it. At the end, Telegonos marries Penelope and Circe marries Telemachos, the son of Odysseus and Penelope. Cf. Homère, *Odysse* (Paris, 1969), 504.
7. Weininger, *Geschlecht*, 404.
8. Cited in *Die Sonne. Volksdeutsche Wochenschrift* 1 (1924): 394.
9. See further Essner, "Das Geheimnis."
10. Cited in Léon Poliakov and Josef Wulf, *Das Dritte Reich und seine Denker. Dokumente* (Munich, 1978), 424.
11. This office was founded in 1934, with the aim of controlling and diminishing the strong disagreements about racial theories.
12. Cited in *Die Sonne* 11 (1935): 514.
13. For the debates on the Nuremberg laws, which I sketch in the next paragraphs, see Essner, *Die "Nürnberger Gesetze,"* 134–73.
14. Report of Vellguth to Gestapo, Sonderarchiv Moskau, Bestand Reichssicherheitshauptamt, 500-1-343.
15. See Essner, *Die "Nürnberger Gesetze,"* 155–56.
16. See Essner, "Kommentar zu den 'Nürnberger Gesetzen'," in *100(0) Schlüsseldokumente zur deutschen Geschichte im 20.Jahrhundert*, at www.1000dokumente.de/index .html.
17. Wagner, "Entwurf zu den ersten Ausführungsverordnungen zum *Blutschutzgesetz* und zum *Reichsbürgergesetz*," Bundesarchiv Berlin-Lichterfelde, R 18/5513, fol. 176 and R 18/5514, fol. 9.
18. Eugen Fischer, *Die Rehobother Bastards und das Bastardisierungsproblem beim Menschen* (Munich, 1913).
19. Hans Globke was from 1953 to 1963 the secretary of the state under Adenauer. Most influential for the development of the bureaucratic arguments was Bernhard Lösener, whose memorandum—which misled a whole generation of researchers—was published in 1961: "Als Rassereferent im Reichsinnenministerium," *Vierteljahrshefte für Zeitgeschichte* 9 (1961): 263–313. For a general critique of the Lösener source, see Essner, *Die "Nürnberger Gesetze,"* 113–33.
20. For instance in Prussia before 1875, when obligatory civil marriage was introduced, conversion offered the only way for partners of different religions to obtain a valid marriage, because the churches stipulated the religious unity of the partners.

21. The new system of 14 November 1935, which turned away from the idea of the "fraction-Jew" in the first anti-Semitic law of 7 April 1933, counted only the "full-Jewish" grandparents and so led to an Aryanizing effect.

22. The second paragraph of the *Blutschutzgesetz* indicates knowledge of the prohibition of mixed marriages in the German colonies before 1914: if the marriage prohibition of 15 September 1935 is avoided by means of a marriage ceremony in a foreign country, the marriage will be declared invalid. The Imperial Colonial Office spent a lot of effort trying to solve the international problem resulting from the prohibition of mixed marriages; the prohibition could be avoided if the couple married abroad and returned afterward to the German colony.

23. See Cornelia Essner, "'Border-line' im Menschenblut und Struktur rassistischer Rechtsspaltung: Koloniales Kaiserreich und Drittes Reich," in *Gesetzliches Unrecht. Rassistisches Recht im 20. Jahrhundert*, ed. Monica Brumlik, Susanne Meinl, and Werner Renz, Jahrbuch 2005 zur Geschichte und Wirkung des Holocaust (Frankfurt, 2005), 27–64.

24. See Essner, *Die "Nürnberger Gesetze,"* 219–32.

25. But nevertheless persecuted by the Gestapo.

26. Feldscher, Note of 13 August 1941, Munich, Institut für Zeitgeschichte, F 71/3.

27. See Essner, *Die "Nürnberger Gesetz,"* 384–441.

28. NG–2586 [Beweisdokument der Anklage im 11. Nürnberger Folgeprozess], Besprechungsprotokoll vom 20 January 1942.

29. NG–1123 [Beweisdokument der Anklage im 11. Nürnberger Folgeprozess], Letter from Lammers to Bormann, 7 June 1941.

30. NG–2982 [Beweisdokument der Anklage im 11. Nürnberger Folgeprozess], Letter from Stuckart and Lösener to Himmler, 16 September 1942.

31. See Wolf Gruner, *Widerstand in der Rosenstraße. Die Fabrik-Aktion und die Verfolgung der "Mischehen" 1943* (Frankfurt, 2005).

32. Letter of Himmler to Hildebrandt, 17 December 1942, Bundesarchiv Berlin-Lichterfelde, NS/1047.

# Chapter 11

# Biosecuritization
## *The Quest for Synthetic Blood and the Taming of Kinship*

## Kath Weston

The dream of synthesizing blood is an old one.[1] Since at least the seventeenth century, physicians, naturalists, merchants, military planners, and more recently biotechnology firms have searched for an industrially manufactured, easily replicable, non-toxic replacement for human blood, variously figured as "synthetic blood," "artificial blood," or a "blood substitute."[2] They have experimented with polymerized hemoglobin and perfluorocarbons, platelets, and plasma, looking for ways to address issues of compatibility, infection, religious restrictions, storage, and scarcity that attend the redistribution of blood from body to body.

By the early twenty-first century, blood that was both manufactured and marketable remained a dream, perpetually on the edge of discovery. Technically speaking, researchers no longer aspired to create a blood substitute as such, but rather a red cell substitute that would carry oxygen and carbon dioxide to and from the body's tissues without performing other key tasks such as coagulation.[3] However diminished, the dream continued to be pursued, with synthetic blood configured from the start as a blood *product*, alienated from the body, with all the implications of estrangement, abstraction, and alienated labor that production under capitalism entails.[4] Some of the latest experiments seek to customize the properties of red blood cells (e.g., viscosity) for niche marketing to patients with specific ailments.[5] Synthetic blood has always represented a resolutely commodified prospect, unlike the act of "giving blood," which has oscillated between the ethical poles of sale and gift in Europe and North America.

It might be tempting to conclude that the quest for synthetic blood has confined itself to scientists and investors hoping to accumulate a stake in what would now be termed *biocapital*, but that is far from the case. In societies that symbolically privilege *sang* as a source of consanguinity, kinship relations have long generated arrangements for blood synthesis of a more metaphorical but no less ambitious sort. Adoption is the obvious example, if only the most famous. Aspiring parents use adoption to assuage desires for childbearing that fertility treatments cannot accommodate. Childless entrepreneurs seek "outside" sons to take over the family business. Long-haul truckers rescue small bundles from the side of the road and raise them as their own. From the families of friends assembled by lesbians and gay men in the San Francisco of the 1980s, to the affirmations of blood brotherhood incorporated into gangs and secret societies, people have busily synthesized kinship in ways presumed to be unalienated.

Even the most naturalized of kinship ties—the ones described as blood relations in Europe and North America—must be synthesized in some sense, insofar as they are meaningfully constituted through culturally and historically located practices.[6] Drawing up a genealogy, deciding whom to invite to a family vacation, lending a poor cousin a few Euros, debating how to apply the injunction never to talk politics with family: these are the sorts of practices that mark kinship and call it into being as such. In speaking of the synthesis of kinship, then, it is not a matter of mimicry grounded in some untenable split between "real" and "fictive" relations. The process of synthesis is not so much one of social construction as it is a compounding of various elements and practices that can yield new and quite specific forms of relatedness.[7]

The essay that follows brings together the social synthesis of blood in these contrasting yet intertwined senses. In the first sense, synthetic blood replaces red blood cells produced by the body with a material substance that lends itself to metaphor even as it shrouds the social relations involved in its production. In the second, the blood synthesis involved in the manufacture of kinship ties metaphorically invokes blood in ways that are equally dependent on a material scaffolding—the bodies of parents, siblings, adoptees, and other already synthesized relations. I argue that the appeal of one can lie in an attempt to evade or renegotiate the imperatives of the other. Although backers of blood substitutes have often framed their development as a quest for a safer, more serviceable, and incidentally(!) more profitable way of supplying blood on demand, they have also responded to a culturally inflected desire to control the volatility and "messiness" historically associated with maintaining a steady stream of donors.

Since blood kin are often in a position to deny or permit reassignment of corporeal substances from one body to another and since blood kin continue to represent the donors of choice for certain maladies, the invention of synthetic blood appears to offer a way to defuse the often fraught parleys with relatives that clear the way for transfers of bone marrow, organs, and blood cells. Taming kinship relations through the commodification of blood may not have universal appeal, especially for groups whose ethnicity and/or nationality is bound up with the valorization of family, but as we shall see, it is a vision that has become integral to capital's search for ever-expanding markets.

The implementation of this liberation story has, in turn, been shaped by the political economy through which it has emerged. While the financialization of blood transfusion has been around for some time—witness the introduction of blood "banking"—there is something novel about the revival of the search for synthetic blood in the twenty-first century. Biotech companies obtained funding for research on synthetic blood by tapping into the kind of high finance that gave us hedge funds, derivatives, venture capitalists, and structured credit products. Promoters enlisted the same type of securitization schemes that, during the Great Financial Crisis of 2007–2008, would bankrupt governments and bring commercial lending to its knees.[8] Gillian Tett dates the practice of securitization to the 1960s–70s, when bankers experimented with dividing loans and bonds into financial "instruments" that would, at least in principle, be easily transferable.[9] By the 1990s these innovations had proliferated into vehicles such as "synthetic collateralized debt obligations" (note the language of synthesis), which could mean investment in derivatives of derivatives.[10] As these products, along with slivers (tranches) of collections of asset-backed securities such as mortgages, were sold to investors farther down the chain of debt, relations of ownership and obligation became increasingly obscured.[11] The difficulties faced by investors who tried to authenticate their claims to these products in the face of their impending dissolution during the credit crisis testifies to the alienated character of securitization per se, which can place so many mediated transactions between the parties involved that no one can tell who the parties are.

Efforts to synthesize blood during the same period have featured a kind of *biosecuritization*. Biosecuritization echoes the operations of other derivatives markets in its attempt to introduce new forms of social investment that veil aspects of the production, circulation, and labor embedded in commodities. In its current form, the push to biosecuritize bodies integrates two neoliberal preoccupations: (1) the development of biosecurity regimes ostensibly designed to protect against threats of disease or terrorism, and (2) the securitization of nature, in which investment in derivatives such as reprocessed hemoglobin transforms biological substances into de-natured products whose social debts can only with difficulty be traced. In that, the quest for synthetic blood participates in a broader capitalization of nature that promises to domesticate kinship, at least in the form of ties that *bind*, even as it participates in its reconstitution.

## Liquid Suture: *Amar Akbar Anthony,* Transfusion, and the Blood Tie

Transfers of blood and other bodily substances can serve as either suture or solvent, drawing people together into new forms of belonging or dissolving the claims of ostensibly indissoluble ties. Much depends on how it's done. With its focus on freezers and cell lines, the biosecuritization of blood through its synthesis presumes, as it calls into being, a body divided into ever more alienated, expendable pieces. So many exchanges have mediated this long awaited substitute for a key bodily fluid that the "natural" organisms joined and the "natural" substances replaced can scarcely be discerned. Bovine plasma is purchased, factories established, products licensed, stem cell technology advanced, nervous investors reassured that the moment for recouping their assets lies just down the road. Biosecuritization also presumes, even as it constitutes, a body synthesized in parts that appear to be independent and self-contained: product $x$, substitute for $y$. There is not much room for relatedness here, much less for kinship relations, and that, as we shall see, is perhaps the point. The entire process is a far cry from the days of direct vein-to-vein transfusion, when a length of tubing that stretched from arm to arm transformed two human bodies into a single circulating system and made the connection visible.

The quest to biosecuritize living organisms takes place in counterpoint to a long history in which material transfers of blood have signified and secured belonging, rather than perpetuating exchanges of substances already alienated from the body. Elsewhere I have written about the race/class controversies that attended blood transfusion in the United States in the days when white and black bodies were not supposed to share a water fountain, much less a bloodstream.[12] Before the abolition of Jim Crow laws, people who crossed racial lines to exchange blood, often under circumstances of great exigency, had to confront segregated hospitals and doctors who refused to treat them. Medical facilities prohibited interracial transfusions. Anonymous foes issued death threats.

At issue was the kind of relatedness that blood transfers appeared to establish. Direct transfusions, which sent corpuscles on their way between bodies located in the same room, broke through the illusion of separateness by piercing the barriers that skin appeared to maintain. At that time, in that place, direct transfusions lent visceral support to the politicized contention that regardless of the hue of a person's skin, "everybody bleeds red." Images of the transfusion process often depicted the tubing that linked the bodies as transparent, the better to see through to color.

In the 1954 novel by John Oliver Killens, *Youngblood*, characters protest when the protagonist decides to give blood to his injured white coworker, the closest thing he has to a friend at the turpentine plant where the two work together. Why would you help this man who belongs to a people who have done nothing but persecute your own? No need, the other characters insist, and the terms of their objections are telling: "Y'all ain't no kin." This transfer of blood ends up generating a kind of race/class solidarity, figured in kinship terms, that no amount of talk or union organizing had managed to produce.

And what kind of solidarity is that? A solidarity that refigures divisions and alliances by casting them as kinship. A solidarity that exceeds friendship or kinship in its attempt to take on the politics of the day. And, in the case of *Youngblood*, a solidarity that insists upon equality.

The capacity of direct, me-to-you transfusion to generate such solidarities was not limited to North America. A non-commodified form of blood transfusion also figures prominently in the 1977 classic of Bollywood cinema, *Amar Akbar Anthony*, directed by Manmohan Desai, in ways that bear intimately on kinship. In the film, three brothers become separated after their father leaves them in a park at the foot of a statue of Mahatma Gandhi while he tries to elude the mob. The vehicle he is driving, stolen from his employer, crashes. By the time he regains consciousness and goes back to the park to retrieve his sons, they have disappeared. Their mother, believing her sons to have perished in the crash, goes blind. The boys' names in the title hint at their impending adoption into different communities: Hindu, Muslim, and Christian. Amar is taken home by a Hindu police inspector and retains his original name. Raju is adopted by a Muslim tailor, who decides to call him Akbar. Chhotey is reincarnated as Anthony after finding refuge with a Christian priest. Will their paths cross again? Yes, the inveterate watcher of Hindi movies suspects, but how?

The reunion takes place in a hospital, where the three brothers, now grown, have each arrived separately to donate blood to a woman gravely injured in an accident. This is not yet a recognition scene, for the brothers are unknown to one another as such and the identity of the injured woman has not yet been established as that of their mother. In the film, it is the transfusion that brings them into a proximity in which recognition becomes possible. What's more, because the transfusion requires compatibility of a blood type that all of them happen to share, the transfusion provides supporting evidence for a kinship connection that the mother's faltering vision cannot supply. This being Bollywood, in the end the mother regains not only her sons but also her sight.

Of course, any appeal to blood to establish relatedness must be culturally and historically situated, not universally inferred. The debates over blood quantum in indigenous communities illustrate just how high the stakes can be when people use blood to calculate affiliation, not to mention how persistent colonial classifications for bodies have become. Who is Hawaiian? Who is Hopi? J. Kēhaulani Kauanui opens her book *Hawaiian Blood* with the story of her cousin's son's grandfather, who accosts her at a family party and will not rest until she transforms her claim on Hawaiian identity into fractions.[13] Eva Marie Garroutte describes the complexities that emerged as Native Americans grappled with colonial legacies of racialized belonging. The title for the second chapter of her book *Real Indians*, "If He Gets a Nosebleed, He'll Turn into a White Man," pokes fun at the reliance on "degrees of blood" to determine who is and who isn't Indian, as opposed to relying, say, on living culturally, linguistic ability, adoption, a history of fighting the federal government together during the colonial period, or other non-biological bases for affiliation.[14] In the strange calculus of the State, 50 percent plus 50 percent can add up to 50 percent: a person with papers that describe him as half Lakota and half Cheyenne might not count as "full blood" in the eyes of a tribal government because those ties span different groups.[15] Federal and local agencies have demanded documentation of blood quanta that they themselves refused to issue, denying land claims and treaty rights to groups whose identity was otherwise never questioned. For a procedure such as direct transfusion to produce the solidarities and conflicts that it does, blood has to signify belonging, at least for some, and signify it in ways that may be open to painful reinterpretation.

More is at stake in blood synthesis than recognition scenes and tropes of discovery, modes of reckoning relationships that inscribe divisions and solidarities that reach across them. Even in the lost-and-found formula applied to kinship in movies, what is found can never be the original form of whatever was lost. Time passes. The sons are grown, the years they might have spent with their first set of parents cannot be recovered, and the memory of inhabiting a body that grieved or worshipped in a certain way persists. After the transfusion, when a woman and three donors meet as mother and sons, they must synthesize a new sort of relation.

Nikolas Rose has written eloquently about the "biological games of truth and identity" that medical technologies such as genetic screening and organ transplants can inspire.[16] While he might not have had blood transfusion in mind, his work on economies of vitality draws attention to the significance of the distinctions between various technologies for building, repairing, or supplementing a body. In the case of direct blood transfusion, the proximate, non-commodified, body-to-body relationships called into being promote the kind of social relations that can draw upon kinship yet are not easily reducible to it.

Synthetic blood, in contrast, offers a very different technology of life, even through its perpetually deferred invention. So-called blood substitutes cull cells from widely dispersed bodies and incorporate nonhuman life forms into the process. When doctors administer synthetic blood, if only in the imagination, transfusions of life-giving fluids that once served to suture people together into creative relations of belonging diffuse any sense of interdependency and speed them on their separate ways.

## From Suture to Solvent: The Rise of Blood Banking and Other Alienated Forms of Sharing Substance

By the 1930s and 1940s in Europe and North America, the mode of acquiring blood in cases of illness or injury began to shift away from direct transfusion. New arrangements borrowed heavily from the rhetoric of finance and mass production. Hospitals and nonprofit organizations established blood "banks," where workers parceled blood into "units" and "warehoused" those units for later "withdrawal," at which point they would be "administered" to recipients. While most facilities kept records that allowed blood to be traced back to the bodies that had donated or sold it, the stored packets bore labels that indicated qualities ascribed to the blood itself (e.g., blood type) with few references to personhood. "One unit of O negative" is a very different thing indeed from "some more of Mrs. Johnson's blood," even though these phrases might describe the same material substance.

Blood banking introduced standardization as well as abstraction. In most countries, an order for a unit of blood dispensed 450 milliliters.

Schemes for describing the factors and types that governed compatibility between donor and recipient crossed national borders. Organizations such as the Red Cross temporally reorganized donation into drives that encouraged employees to give blood together at the workplace on particular days.

Most significantly, the banking model fostered increasingly alienated forms of corporeal substance. Banks transformed blood into a series of components: packed red blood cells (RBCs), fresh frozen plasma (FFP), cryoprecipitate (a concentrated FFP derivative), immune globulins, and the like. Even folk categories such as white blood cells shape-shifted into acronyms (WBCs). In the guise of products, blood could be packaged, dated, and retailed like any other industrially produced commodity.[17]

The abstraction entailed in alienated forms of production is a double-edged sword. On the one hand, it may slice through ignorance and provide a measure of protection against discrimination. Given a racist refusal to transfer blood between bodies that fall into different color categories, not knowing a donor's race can help secure access. Perhaps it is no coincidence that an African American, Dr. Charles Drew, invented the blood bank. At the same time, alienation can be devastating, creating what Marx called a "realm of estrangement" that separates people from their life activity as well as one another. The alienated person herself becomes an abstraction, mistaking disconnection for independence, her laboring body mortified and her apprehension of the world shattered into bits.[18]

Like any corporation, blood banks developed bureaucratic rules for donation that drew on old prejudices and new cultural vocabularies. They began to assess potential donors based on non-kinship criteria such as "risk," prohibiting donations from members of so-called high-risk groups. In 1983, the US Food and Drug Administration issued guidelines that barred men who had had sex with another man since 1977 from giving blood. At the time, popular media held gay men, rather than unsafe sex, responsible for the spread of HIV. By 2009, researchers and community groups were still protesting the ban, still arguing that unsafe sex should be the issue, not personhood or the gender of partners. An HIV-infected man who engaged in unprotected anal intercourse with a woman could certainly transmit the infection to her, yet blood donation centers seldom asked screening questions directed at the implications of this encounter for blood safety.[19] Meanwhile "emerging agents" of infection such as West Nile virus took time to appear on questionnaires, when they appeared at all.

The estranged character of transfusion in an era of blood banking can also be seen in the periodic calls to "replenish the blood supply" that go out whenever the stock at blood banks falls perilously low. In any embodied sense, of course, blood supply is never lacking. The supply of blood rises and falls, not in warehouses, but in blood vessels; not with fluctuating demands due to accident or disaster, but with demographics. To claim that "more than two-thirds of the developing world's nations do not have enough blood" as a reason to manufacture alternatives is, on the face of it, nonsensical.[20] Only in the sense of a substance already alienated from bodies can the blood supply be said to diminish. Only in the sense of a substance already alienated from persons can the blood supply be proclaimed safe on behalf of a nation.[21]

All this does not mean that face-to-face relations disappeared from the *discourse* that became integral to securing blood once blood banks started mediating transfusion. Blood drives might have borrowed the language of supply and demand from neoclassical economics, but they also traded upon the impression that donations go directly to the assistance of "real people" who have been injured in earthquakes or lie stricken in a hospital ward waiting for a donor. In North India, for example, Jacob Copeman describes how donation campaigns melded the categories of finance, Hinduism, and reproductive kinship when they portrayed blood donation as an accumulation of spiritual "credit" for "the future generativity of those that are 'saved.'"[22]

The idea of person-to-person transfer still motivates, but there's a catch: The *New England Journal of Medicine* reported that of the estimated 475,000 units of blood collected in the United States following the attacks of September 11, 2001, the number of units used by survivors of the attack numbered just 258.[23] Donors may imagine their blood flowing into the bodies of the victims, but in most cases their blood will find other uses, in whole or in part. It is a measure of the degree of alienation inherent in the blood banking system that the number of units actually transferred to 9/11 victims could only be ascertained with a study.

Any pitch that alludes to person-to-person transfer in an effort to get people to donate to a banking system is complicated by the fact that donors no longer share a room with recipients. In 2007, the American Red Cross circulated an advertisement that featured a toll-free phone number, 1-800-GIVE-LIFE, below an image of an Asian/Asian American man in a café gazing directly at the camera. "You wouldn't recognize me in an elevator," the bold copy in the ad reads, "but if you ever needed it, I would give you my blood."[24] Here is the eye-to-eye connection, the face behind the donation, coupled with the tacit reassurance for a multiracial audience that interracial transfusion has become acceptable.

When you read the fine print you will find yourself the target of a classic advertising maneuver: the bait and switch. "And with someone in

America needing blood every two seconds, there's someone who needs you to roll up your sleeve today." First you are hailed as the recipient in need; by the time you finish reading the ad, you discover that you have become the prospective donor. This interchangeability of parts, transmuted through empathy—I could have been the one in need!—brings the personal encounter from the days of direct transfusion forward into a time when bodily substances retail *en masse.*[25]

The creative paradox of alienated production is that it can still yield an almost haptic sense of unalienated connection. People may be hailed by ideologies of supersession—from direct exchange to abstract exchange, the forward march of progress—while simultaneously experiencing a visceral bond with someone imagined though not always imaginary. This allows the institutional apparatus associated with blood banking and blood synthesis to be cynically manipulated for nationalist or corporate ends, but also to be placed in the service of generosity, compassion, and other culturally construed ways of reaching for something that exceeds capitalist production.

And who is this "someone" in the ad who requires your blood? At first it seems to be the person who lies at the end of a commodity chain of advertisements, centrifuges, bloodmobiles, freezers, plastic IV bags, and tubing. Readers can conjure a vision of an embodied recipient out there somewhere, however difficult that person might be to discern. But wait—that someone had better not be an embodied person, for s/he would be in bad shape indeed, requiring blood "every two seconds"! This second meaning of *someone* turns out to be a statistical average, derived from who knows where and dropped into the text of the ad. With its unimaginable face and divided character, the second someone offers the reader just the sort of derivative that lends itself to biosecuritization.

In many ways the quest for synthetic blood extends the process of the alienation of bodily substances that blood banking began. Claims that artificial blood will enhance "shelf life"—that is, allow a longer period of storage before the blood "goes bad"—elaborate the corporate metaphors in which blood products are already packaged.[26] Claims that the invention of blood substitutes will provide "unlimited supplies" of blood evoke the free market utopia of a world without scarcity where entrepreneurs can still manage to turn a profit.[27] Lest blood banks become redundant, they may have to provide "a new service, namely the collection of red cells for further manufacture."[28] Because the social relations, including labor, involved in production of synthetic blood are nowhere evident in the disembodied product, blood substitutes promise to serve more as solvent than suture for kinship ties. There will be no movies about estranged relatives reunited at the hospital as a liter of synthesized blood courses from vein to vein, not even an appeal to donate to the imagined stranger a substance that becomes readily replicable.

To tame the "problems" of safety and supply constraints is also to tame the "problems" posed by kin who might otherwise refuse to give, or who give only grudgingly. For all the romanticism infused into vignettes of face-to-face encounters between long-lost brothers, the transfer of body parts and bodily fluids between relatives does not always proceed amicably. The very alienation implicit in blood synthesis promises to domesticate kinship, or at least some of the obligations, demands, hopes, and requests that kinship ties can generate.

## Unrequited Love: *Un Conte de Noël* and the Kinship Politics of Donation

While the semiotic movement of blood from suture to solvent presents a resolutely linear story of scientific modernization, commodification, and increasing abstraction, many types of bodily transfer still preserve the intimacies of person-to-person transmission. Storing blood for one's own elective surgeries represents the ultimate instance, insofar as it collapses the identities of donor and recipient by making them self-same. Organ transplants sometimes involve knowledge of the donor's identity or, lacking that, a yearning to know.[29] But because organ and bone marrow transplants require compatibilities that are difficult to obtain, the search for a suitable donor often begins with consanguineal relatives.

Prospective donors who sign up for the National Marrow Donor Program Registry in the United States are welcomed into a "global movement of more than 11 million donors who stand ready to give someone a future."[30] Lest that "someone" in need of a bone marrow transplant prove too anonymous to motivate readers to part with a yet-to-be-shared bodily substance, the NMDP features "Mary's story" on its homepage. Mary was "a typical teenager, busy with cheerleading, dance, theater and gymnastics—until she was diagnosed with aplastic anemia when she was only 18." By age twenty, post-transplant, she is "healthy and hopeful," returning to gender-prescribed dreams of becoming "an actress, a model, or a nurse."

Dig a little further into the NMDP website, however, and you will come across another passage that testifies to the continuing salience of blood ties in bone marrow transfers: "If you need an allogeneic transplant (which uses donated cells from a family member, unrelated donor or cord blood unit), *and do not have a suitable donor in your family*, your transplant center can search the National Marrow Donor Program

(NMDP) Registry for an unrelated donor or cord blood unit for you [my emphasis]." Unrelated donors, then, continue to represent a fallback option, the sort of alternative that presents itself when familial alternatives have been exhausted.

The process of bone marrow transplantation seems simple enough. Following radiation and/or chemotherapy, "the bone marrow is infused into the patient intravenously in much the same way that any blood product is given."[31] Yet the reassuring information available on websites stops short at giving advice about how to coax one's reluctant brother to donate or how to say "no" when your sense of being, say, Chicano tells you a relative shouldn't even have to ask. How much more complicated does this simple process become when it has to traverse the often roiled waters of kinship?

Such negotiations bear some of the hallmarks of arranging a marriage between people whose emphatically non-conjugal, non-sexual connection has, by birth, already been arranged. Are we compatible? Will our bodies work together? Should I offer? Should I beg? If I say no, how will it affect the webs of kinship relations in which we are already enmeshed? In contrast to the organ recipients studied by Lesley Sharp, who traced out new forms of belonging and sometimes claimed kinship with donors, these negotiators already acknowledge an embodied connection.[32] Like blood transfers back in the days of direct transfusion, bone marrow transplants between relatives offer people a chance to rematerialize their relationships, but also to refuse to share.

In the feel bad / feel good movie *Un Conte de Noël*, directed by Arnaud Desplechin and released to coincide with the 2008 Christmas season, the need for a bone marrow transplant continuously reorganizes family dynamics.[33] As the Vuillard family gathers to celebrate the holidays, something appears to be bothering Junon, played by Catherine Deneuve. Years ago her first son, Joseph, had been diagnosed with Burkitt lymphoma, a fast-growing malignancy. Doctors considered a bone marrow transplant his only hope, but neither the parents nor Joseph's sister, Elizabeth, proved suitable donors. In desperation, the parents conceived a third child, Henri, hoping for compatibility. Much to the parents' dismay, Henri's marrow did not match either, and at the age of six, Joseph died. Now Junon has contracted an equally rare cancer, but her case is somewhat different: Henri is the only adult in the family whose bone marrow can extend her hold on life.

Of course, there is a catch. Henri's sister, Elizabeth, has fallen out with Henri. In exchange for freeing him from debt, she banishes him—*Bannis!*—from contact with the Vuillards whenever she is around, and not just temporarily, but *jamais à tout*. "Wherever I go," she declares,

"Henri won't be there. Wherever I am, he won't be part of the family."
What's more, Junon and Henri, though mother and son, have never particularly cared for one another and affirm as much in the course of the
reunion that eventually transpires. Theirs is an unrequited love of the
sort occasionally explored in Bollywood romances but rarely acknowledged for consanguineal relations.

Haunted by the death of her eldest child and by the face of the middle son who could not save him, the character of Junon incarnates the
question that the search for synthetic blood seems to beg. It is clear from
the historical transformation of body parts into products, the shift from
direct transfusion to commodified forms of blood banking, that transfers
of bodily substances can be alienated. But blood ties, too, can partake of
estrangement. Is it possible to repair alienated blood ties through non-
alienated transfers of shared substance, through a body-to-body transplant of marrow unmediated by the apparatus of a registry? In the end,
it is not transfer but the prospect of transfer that brings Henri back to
the family. It is the hope and fantasy of shareable substance that recon-
ceives the blood tie, rather than vice versa.

Under such difficult circumstances, it is not surprising that synthetic
blood exerts an appeal, at least to those with an investment in hegemonic forms of European and American kinship. Why go to relatives if
you can buy your way out of manipulative, confused, ethically compromised, and otherwise vexed family histories? (Presuming, of course, you
have the money: in that, the synthesis of blood products represents a
bourgeois dream.) Why hold your life hostage to kinship?

Of course, not everyone shares the perception of kinship as the kind
of tie that may need to be given the slip. For people of color in the
United States, the value placed on family often serves as a marker of
what sets a group apart from the rest of society. When that's the case,
as Teo Ruiz adroitly puts it, "if you have to ask, you are lost."[34] But that
will not stop capital from trying to expand its markets by enhancing
the appeal of evasion. In "Risky Business," Geeta Patel explores how the
explosion of financial services enterprises on the Indian subcontinent
has created "new forms of personhood, disciplining, and sociality" by en-
ticing people to switch from relatives to banks when they need money.
"The person taking the loan," she continues, "no longer needs to depend
on (read: be financially connected to) his family and friends."[35]

Attempts to market the taming of kinship in the form of synthetic
blood (or bank loans, or what have you) promise an end to the search
for a donor, an end to the imperative to resolve all that ails a body in any
familial sense. Whether or not the backers of red blood cell technologies

ever make good on their investments, the appeal itself exerts an influence. It remains to be seen what kind of body, politic or impolitic, will be created along the way.

## Putting Paid to Kinship:
## From Biocapital to Biosecuritization

*Kinship*, then, has become a shadow term in the quest for synthetic blood. Much of the discussion of tissue economies focuses on commodification, exploitation, and safety/risk, rather than kinship per se.[36] Yet it is the progressive alienation of social ties, first through the shift from direct transfusion to blood banking, then through the biosecuritization associated with synthetic blood, that has promised to put paid to kinship in all such transactions. "Put paid" in the sense of commodification, of course: manufacturers aspire to realize a profit. "Put paid," too, in the sense of obviating any back-and-forth with relatives when vital bodily substances require a supplement.

What does it mean to biosecuritize the human body and how does the process of biosecuritization involved in blood synthesis differ from treating bodies as just another source of biocapital? A clue resides in the form taken by the yearning for the very product that has eluded researchers for so many years, despite massive infusions of investment. "If only," writes Linda Wang, "there were substitutes that could fill some of blood's roles in the body, artificial substances that would be free of the supply constraints and contamination vulnerabilities of the real stuff."[37] If only.

The form that yearning takes here, as in much of the literature on blood substitutes, is one of freedom *from*—freedom from "the real," freedom from limitations and restraints, be they economic or social. The fantasy is not one of a world without blood ties or kinship, but rather of a world without conflicts or breaks. But under conditions of alienation, the process that you expect to free you binds you ever more tightly into unequal relations—the exploitation of labor hidden in new technologies, the debt incurred to purchase medical treatments at market rates—even as it isolates you from life-giving dependencies you may already have.

As mentioned earlier, biosecuritization has two sides: (1) a preoccupation with biosecurity of the sort instituted by national security states when they discipline bodies in the name of protecting them, and (2) the slicing, dicing, and transmogrification of bodies that are then inserted into commodity chains in pieces in such a way that social investments become ever more difficult to trace. Let us examine each in turn in relation to the quest to synthesize blood during the era of securitization in global finance.

Biosecurity discourse tethers "personal" safety to the defense of the nation-state. Thus it is Thailand's or Portugal's blood supply that is said to require protection, rather than "the world's," "the Loire valley's," or the two units that will course through your veins during your next operation. Protection in this context seldom takes the form of nourishment or environmental justice. Instead, the State cultivates preparedness by instituting surveillance and traceback mechanisms to handle "threats," or, in the case of blood substitutes, sponsors new products directed at improving upon the human body, here figured as a source of infection.[38]

There are, to be sure, many compelling safety concerns associated with transfusion. Researchers are not wrong when they claim that an affordable blood substitute with universal compatibility would alleviate the potentially fatal clerical errors that have resulted in administering blood of the wrong type. Be that as it may, to date synthetic blood has proved much *more* hazardous than "the real stuff." Clinical trials of various products have shown side effects that include fever, gastrointestinal problems, thrombocytopenia, kidney toxicity, flu-like syndromes, a rise in arterial blood pressure, and interference of hemoglobin with nitric oxide metabolism.[39] Proper metabolism of nitric oxide, to take just one, is essential for protecting the liver from ischemic damage and for preventing the kind of vascular collapse associated with septic shock. Because hemoglobin-based synthetics can still carry diseases, the dream of biosecuring the human body is likely to remain just that: a dream.

The process of securitizing biology, in contrast, is already well underway. Under this model, debt was not only distributed but also fractionated and reified into products at a great remove from *matériel*. The tide may or may not have turned against financial securitization, as governments and investors have come to appreciate its destabilizing effects on capitalist institutions.[40] But no shift in political economy has yet put paid to the era that, in Ian Hacking's view, has divided our neo-Cartesian bodies into parts, an era with a habit of parsing all things corporeal into organs, cells, molecules, even nanoparticles for the purposes of transplant, recombination, and synthesis.[41] Indeed, the very conceptualization of a body as an organism composed of replaceable parts and metabolic economies of scale makes it susceptible to the slicing and dicing already so familiar from the operations of capital markets, where synthesized derivatives are pooled, assigned a risk/safety rating, and sold to buyers all over the world.

Yet biosecuritization involves much more than some highly capitalized synecdoche that sets up new relationships between part and whole. Securitization reduces bodies to so much extractable hemoglobin, so many titers of white blood cells, in a way that elides kinship. Like freeze-dried coffee or canned chickpeas, the ideal blood substitute will be retailed in a form "capable of prolonged storage under adverse conditions."[42] Its alienated production will obscure the exploitation involved in production of the so-called raw materials (perfluorocarbons, hemoglobin) for synthesis, the body-to-body contact submerged in commodity chains, and the contretemps that helps make kinship what it is if not always what we will it to be.

Biosecuritization enlists the same kinds of technologies that transform breathing, squirming, worshipping, cycling, and sleeping bodies into profitable bits of biocapital, but it does not stop there.[43] There is something discernible in today's quest for synthetic blood besides the modern mantra of better living through (bio)chemistry. What Neal Smith considers the subsumption or vertical integration of nature into capital, via its replication in laboratories and factories, "involves not just the production of nature 'all the way down,' but its simultaneous financialization 'all the way up.'"[44] Replication has its price. The investor's hope is that one day the invention of a marketable blood substitute will generate a lucrative business. With securitization, it gets harder and harder for blood donation to signify altruism, much less belonging, as it has done in many European and North American settings.[45]

## All My Bloody Relations

Once it has been biosecuritized, blood no longer synthesizes kinship. Bodies fall to pieces. Those pieces can be sutured only through purchase, rather than through transfers of bodily substance with the power to make social debts visible, or through face-to-face negotiations with the power to call solidarities into being. What's missing from the packaging of blood substitutes are not reified ties but social relations, the vis-à-vis that makes life what it is.

By focusing on biocapital alone, or the mining of bodies for parts, social theorists risk subsuming nature with a replication attempt of their own: the replication of market ideology. Karen Ho has argued that a similar process occurred for analysts of globalization, whose breathless critiques of the global have reproduced an element of market hype and disguised the unevenness of developments.[46] The quest for blood substitutes is, after all, still a quest. Health crises that require marrow and organ transplants still draw relatives into deliberations. If and when blood substitutes are licensed, their initial applications will be limited. Indeed, the very first products brought to market have been restricted to veterinary use.

To grasp the social implications of biotechnology requires a certain critical perspective on the political economy of the historical moment that so resolutely slices and dices bodies into parts in the first place. There is more going on in the quest to synthesize blood than a bid for profits or a technology-incited shift in scale in our perceptions of bodies from visible to microscopic to nano, of the sort that Ian Hacking and Paul Gilroy have observed.[47] The triumph of financial capital, with its concomitant financialization of everyday life, has infiltrated organisms and insinuated itself into the corpse.[48] Like a securitized loan or a bond whose worth can scarcely be assessed, the biosecuritized body divides into ever-more-alienated pieces, with transfers of tissues and bodily fluids mediated by so many exchanges that the elements of sociality they bring into play become scarcely perceptible.

"As organisms, we live together," Ed Cohen reminds his readers in *A Body Worth Defending*.[49] We live together not as cell cultures, not as fermented batches of hemoglobin, not as self-contained fortresses guarded by an immune system, but as organisms who will die without what Cohen calls a "modulated openness" to oxygen, bacteria, and other people. And why do we need reminding? In part because the alienated means by which finance capital securitizes bodies encourage us to cordon off "my body" from "yours," to misconceive the operations of power, to forget.

Having placed even the gift in the service of capital, biosecuritization goes on to distance. Producers, buyers, and recipients become insulated from what happens in the other room, inside their skin, or half a world away, wherever the synthesis of blood and kinship takes place. What biosecurity promises, the securitization of the body forestalls. The marketable dream is that with synthetic blood, you'll be safe because you'll know just what you're getting. Except, of course, as with any commodified product that is industrially sourced, widely distributed, and synthesized from fragments, you'll know less and less about the conditions of its production. You'll know less and less about all that has been given and all that has been taken away. The memory of a sister's generosity that convinces a brother to sign the donation forms, the liters sold to pay for a meal? A family fortune made in perfluorocarbon manufacturing? The blood seeping into the grass after they have hauled off the body, those red marks spattered on the wall? The most you can do is wonder about the price while you watch things congeal.

# Notes

1.  Heartfelt thanks to participants in the "Kinship and Blood" conference held in Frankfurt in 2009 for their provocative comments on an earlier version of this chapter, and to Roberto Armengol, Cassandra Fraser, Susan McKinnon, and Geeta Patel for alternative readings, suggestions, encouragement, and citations that helped shape the version you have before you.
2.  The term *synthetic blood* is sometimes restricted to the class of blood substitutes derived from perfluorocarbons, which are chemically synthesized molecules, as opposed to hemoglobin-based blood substitutes that are typically derived from animals. In this essay, I use *synthetic blood* to embrace any type of industrially manufactured blood product, regardless of the materials sourced in its production. The term *artificial blood* is less satisfactory, in light of the dichotomy between "real" and "artificial" it encodes, especially considering that many attempts to produce synthetic blood begin by fermenting "real" hemoglobin extracted from "real" bodies.
3.  On efforts in Europe and the Americas to develop synthetic blood in previous centuries, following the "discovery" of the circulatory system, see Suman Sarkar, "Artificial Blood," *Indian Journal of Critical Care Medicine* 12 (2008): 140–44; Douglas Starr, *Blood: An Epic History of Medicine and Commerce* (New York, 1998); and Robert M. Winslow, Kim D. Vandegriff, and Marcos Intaglietta, eds., *Advances in Blood Substitutes: Industrial Opportunities and Medical Challenges* (Boston, MA, 1997). For updates on research and investment strategies that target synthetic blood, see Maria Burke, "Is Artificial Blood the Way of the Future?" *The Times*, 6 January 2006; Evan Hessel, "Dracula: Steven Gould Has Sucked Up Millions of Investors' Dollars to Develop a Blood Substitute. Why Hasn't It Been Approved?" *Forbes*, 6 June 2005, 80–82; H. G. Klein, "Blood Substitutes: How Close to a Solution?" in *Advances in Transfusion Safety*, ed. G. N. Vyas and A. E. Williams (Basel, 2005), 45–52; Wil McCarthy, "Strange Blood: Cataclysmic Shortages. Tainted Supplies. There is a Solution: Artificial Blood," *Wired*, August 2002, 108–13; Alan S. Rudolph, Reuven Rabinovici, and Giora Z. Feuerstein, eds., *Red Blood Cell Substitutes: Basic Principles and Clinical Applications* (New York, 1997); Toshiaki Sato, "Japan Looks for New Blood," *World Press Review*, July 2001, 45; Zbigniew M. Szczepiorkowski and Christopher P. Stowell, "Red Blood Cell Substitutes," in *Blood Safety and Surveillance*, ed. Jeanne V. Linden and Celso Bianco (New York, 2001), 543–67; Eishun Tsuchida, ed., *Blood Substitutes: Present and Future Perspectives* (Burlington, MA, 1998); Linda Wang, "Blood Relatives: First-Generation Artificial Blood is about to Hit the Market," *Science News* 159 (2001): 206–7; Robert M. Winslow, "How Do Scientists Make Artificial Blood? How Effective Is It Compared With the Real Thing?" *Scientific American* (21 October 1999); Robert M. Winslow, "Blood Substitutes: Refocusing an Elusive Goal," *British Journal of Haematology* 111 (2000): 387–96; and Robert M. Winslow, "Current Status of Blood Substitute Research: Towards a New Paradigm," *Journal of Internal Medicine* 253 (2003): 508–17.
4.  Here and throughout, when I refer to *alienation*, I do so in the multivalent sense in which Marx used the term in the *1844 Manuscripts;* see Karl Marx, *Economic and Philosophical Manuscripts of 1844* (New York, 1964). Alienation, then, condenses aspects of estrangement, abstraction, illusion, isolation, misrecognition, unrealized potential, and loss, in ways realized for both workers and capitalists, albeit differently. Recent scholarship on biocapital and the environment extends Marxist concepts

such as alienation and surplus beyond the human and beyond a holistic conception of the organism. See, for example, Teresa Brennan, *Globalization and Its Terrors*
(New York, 2003); Melinda Cooper, *Life as Surplus: Biotechnology and Capitalism
in the Neoliberal Era* (Seattle, WA, 2008); and John Bellamy Foster, *Marx's Ecology:
Materialism and Nature* (New York, 2000).

5. Klein, "Blood Substitutes"; Szczepiorkowski and Stowell, "Red Blood Cell Substitutes."
6. Kath Weston, *Families We Choose: Lesbians, Gays, Kinship*, 2nd ed. (New York,
   1997).
7. For a creative exploration of changes in the meaning and lived experience of relatedness in the wake of new technologies that enlist bodily substances, see Janet Carsten,
   *After Kinship* (Cambridge, 2003).
8. The term *Great Financial Crisis* comes from Foster and Magdoff, who employ it
   with an emphasis on the increasing dominance of finance capital in the era of ma-
   ture or late capitalism, when speculation offers an outlet, however inadequate, for
   ever-greater surpluses in search of places to invest; see John Bellamy Foster and Fred
   Magdoff, *The Great Financial Crisis: Causes and Consequences* (New York, 2009).
9. Gillian Tett, *Fool's Gold: How the Bold Dream of a Small Tribe at J. P. Morgan Was
   Corrupted by Wall Street Greed and Unleashed a Catastrophe* (New York, 2009).
10. For example, a securitized bond backed by a pool of credit default swaps that them-
    selves represented a financial instrument of insurance against corporate default.
11. Gretchen Morganson, "Foreclosures Hit a Snag for Lenders," *New York Times*, 15
    November 2007.
12. Kath Weston, "Kinship, Controversy, and the Sharing of Substance: The Race/Class
    Politics of Blood Transfusion," in Sarah Franklin and Susan McKinnon, eds., *Relative
    Values: Reconfiguring Kinship Studies* (Durham, NC, 2001), 147–74.
13. J. Kēhaulani Kauanui, *Hawaiian Blood: Colonialism and the Politics of Sovereignty and
    Indigeneity* (Durham, NC, 2008).
14. Eva Marie Garroutte, *Real Indians: Identity and the Survival of Native America*
    (Berkeley, CA, 2003). See also Garroutte's essay, "The Racial Formation of American
    Indians: Negotiating Legitimate Identities within Federal and Tribal Law," *American
    Indian Quarterly* 25 (2001): 224–39.
15. Andrea Appleton, "Blood Quantum: A Complicated System that Determines Tribal
    Membership Threatens the Future of American Indians," *High Country News* 41
    (2009): 14–18.
16. Nikolas Rose, *The Politics of Life Itself: Biomedicine, Power, and Subjectivity in the
    Twenty-First Century* (Princeton, NJ, 2007), 229.
17. Witness the emergence of the notion of "outdated blood" (i.e., blood stored outside
    the body too long to function reliably after transfusion). Outdated blood became
    a key source material in the experimental production of hemoglobin-based blood
    substitutes.
18. See Marx, *Economic and Philosophical Manuscripts of 1844*, and Bertell Ollman, *Alien-
    ation: Marx's Conception of Man in Capitalist Society*, 2nd ed. (Cambridge, 1976).
19. On the politics of questionnaires and risk assessments associated with blood dona-
    tion, see Anne Eder and Celso Bianco, eds., *Screening Blood Donors: Science, Reason,
    and the Donor History Questionnaire* (Bethesda, MD, 2007), and Eric A. Feldman
    and Ronald Bayer, eds., *Blood Feuds: AIDS, Blood, and the Politics of Medical Disaster*
    (New York, 1999).
20. In Klein, "Blood Substitutes," 50.

21. See also Cooper, who observes in passing that "the public, nation-based blood bank is the biological equivalent of the national reserve bank," in the sense that it established a reservoir of biological wealth that "became integral to Keynesian growth strategies" in the post–World War II era of welfare nationalism (*Life as Surplus,* 178).

22. Jacob Copeman, "Blood, Blessings, and Technology in India," *Cambridge Anthropology* 25 (2005–6): 39–51, here 41. For ethnographic treatments of blood donation in various cultural and economic circumstances, see Jacob Copeman, ed., "Blood Donation, Bioeconomy, Culture," *Body & Society* 15 (2009), a special issue of this journal.

23. Paul M. Schmidt, "Blood and Disaster—Supply and Demand," *New England Journal of Medicine* 346 (2002): 617.

24. American Red Cross, "You Wouldn't Recognize Me ..." (advertisement), *Wired,* May 2007, 32.

25. Alternatively and perhaps complementarily, Susan McKinnon has suggested that one could read the ad as an invitation to delayed reciprocity that takes the form of generalized exchange, in the context of an economy where the standardized extraction of blood, repackaged into units, creates "a sense of national unity between abstractly equal citizens" (personal communication).

26. See Wang, "Blood Relatives." Significantly, synthetic blood privileges life on the shelf—the life of merchandise—over life in the body, since none of the red blood cell substitutes developed to date lasts nearly as long in the human body as a transfusion of non-synthetic blood (typically a matter of hours in the case of RBCs, versus a month or more for whole blood).

27. See Roger Highfield, "Stem Cell Technology May Make Blood Donations Thing of the Past," *Telegraph,* 20 August 2008.

28. Christopher P. Stowell and Peter Tomasulo, "The Impact of Blood Substitutes on Blood Banking Worldwide," in *Red Blood Cell Substitutes: Basic Principles and Clinical Applications,* ed. Alan S. Rudolph, Reuven Rabinovici, and Giora Z. Feuerstein (New York, 1998), 1–16, here 12.

29. Catherine Waldby and Robert Mitchell, *Tissue Economies: Blood, Organs, and Cell Lines in Late Capitalism* (Durham, NC, 2006).

30. Quotations that refer to the National Marrow Donor Program come from the NMDP website, http://www.marrow.org, consulted 3 March 2009.

31. Columbia Presbyterian Medical Center, "The Nuts and Bolts of Bone Marrow Transplants," http://cpmcnet.columbia.edu/dept/medicine/bonemarrow/bmtinfo.html, consulted 3 March 2009.

32. Lesley A. Sharp, *Strange Harvest: Organ Transplants, Denatured Bodies, and the Transformed Self* (Berkeley, CA, 2006).

33. *Un Conte de Noël* paved the way for other cinematic releases that focus on ethical dilemmas associated with the transfer of corporeal substance between kin, including the 2009 film *My Sister's Keeper,* which introduced the concept of medical emancipation to the screen. Medical emancipation statutes allow legal minors to determine their own course of medical treatment and to give or withhold consent to medical procedures, regardless of the wishes of their parents.

34. A comment made in the course of discussions at the "Kinship and Blood" conference. I am grateful to Teo Ruiz for pushing me to think through this part of the analysis.

35. Geeta Patel, "Risky Subjects: Insurance, Sexuality, and Capital," *Social Text* 24 (2006): 25–65, here 42.

36. The phrase comes from Waldby and Mitchell, *Tissue Economies*. An argument has been made for treating blood transfusion as a kind of tissue transplantation, based on evidence that transfused lymphocytes can establish themselves in the bodies of transfusion recipients; see Winslow, "Blood Substitutes," 388.
37. Wang, "Blood Relatives," 206.
38. On biosecurity and preparedness, see Andrew Lakoff, "The Generic Biothreat, or, How We Became Unprepared," *Cultural Anthropology* 23 (2008): 399–428, and Andrew Lakoff and Stephen J. Collier, eds., *Biosecurity Interventions: Global Health and Security in Question* (New York, 2008). On state-sponsored traceback initiatives, see Kath Weston, "Lost Intimacies: Surveillance and Face-to-Face Relations in the Food Chain," manuscript in progress. National security regimes have supplied a hefty portion of the capital that has kept the quest for synthetic blood going. The US Army, for example, has funded research into "resuscitation solutions" that include blood substitutes for use on the battlefield; see Institute of Medicine, *Fluid Resuscitation: State of the Science for Treating Combat Casualties and Civilian Injuries* (Washington, DC, 1999).
39. Abdu I. Alayash, "Hemoglobin-based Blood Substitutes and the Hazards of Blood Radicals," *Free Radical Research* 33 (2000): 341–48; Klein, "Blood Substitutes"; and Winslow, "Blood Substitutes."
40. At the onset of the crisis, many commentators singled out securitization as the culprit and predicted its demise; see Tony Jackson, "Has the Supercharged Banking Model Run Out of Road?" *Financial Times*, 21 January 2008, 19. By late 2009, however, the *Financial Times* described financial institutions as "desperate to salvage the basic elements of securitisation"; Jennifer Hughes, "Bankers Seek to Detoxify the Alphabet Soup," *Financial Times*, 13 October 2009, 232. The idea was to rehabilitate discredited financial instruments in the guise of "smart securitization" that renounces the "excesses" of the past; Patrick Jenkins, "Banks Reinvent Securitisation to Cut Capital Costs," *Financial Times*, 6 July 2009, 1; and Gillian Tett and Aline van Duyn, "Under Restraint: Credit," *Financial Times*, 7 July 2009, 7. This move came as no surprise to John Bellamy Foster and Robert McChesney, who followed Paul Sweezy in regarding the contemporary period of rampant financial innovation as integral to monopoly-finance capital's attempts to ward off stagnation; John Bellamy Foster and Robert W. McChesney, "Monopoly-Finance Capital and the Paradox of Accumulation," *Monthly Review* 61 (2009): 1–20; Paul M. Sweezy, "The Triumph of Financial Capital," *Monthly Review* 46 (1994): 1–11. For a critical perspective on discourse about derivatives (and, by implication, securitization), see Bill Maurer's "Repressed Futures: Financial Derivatives' Theological Unconscious," where he argues that the discursive power accorded to derivatives in accounts both pro and con, popular and scholarly, relies upon bracketing the mathematical techniques on which derivatives depend. By sidelining the so-called black box where the algorithms reside, analysts evoke the historical split between religion and statistics, between epistemological and stochastic thought, which effectively renders the black box "a moral argument"; Maurer, "Repressed Futures: Financial Derivatives' Theological Unconscious," *Economy and Society* 31 (2002): 15–36.
41. Ian Hacking, "Our Neo-Cartesian Bodies in Parts," *Critical Inquiry* 34 (2007): 78–105.
42. Winslow, "Blood Substitutes," 387.
43. For three excellent takes on how to theorize the life forms emerging from the latest investments in technology, see Kaushik Sunder Rajan's discussion of "lively capital"

in *Biocapital: The Constitution of Postgenomic Life* (Durham, NC, 2006); Adriana Petryna's study of biological citizenship in the wake of the Chernobyl nuclear disaster, *Life Exposed: Biological Citizens after Chernobyl* (Princeton, NJ, 2002); and Nikolas Rose's pursuit of biopolitics over the rough terrain of medicine and subjectivity in *The Politics of Life Itself.*

44. Neal Smith, "Nature as Accumulation Strategy," in *Coming to Terms with Nature,* ed. Leo Panitch and Colin Leys (New York, 2006), 16–36.

45. For the classic discussion of the relationship between blood donation and altruism, see Richard M. Titmuss, *The Gift Relationship: From Human Blood to Social Policy* (New York, 1997). On cultural twists associated with voluntarism, see Jacob Copeman's work on the participation of devotional movements in India in blood campaigns, *Veins of Devotion: Blood Donation and Religious Experience in North India* (New Brunswick, NJ, 2009). Note that when it comes to transfers of corporeal substances, the rhetoric of donation increasingly extends to bodies that can by no stretch of the imagination be described as voluntary participants, altruistically inclined or otherwise. A recent article in *Science News* described a thoroughbred mare named Twilight as donating DNA to the Horse Genome Project, while a Duroc pig named T. J. Tabasco "donated DNA" to researchers engaged in decoding the pig genome. Unnamed cassava and cucumber plants in the same article, less subject to anthropomorphism, merely "served up leads" and "revealed information" about their chromosomes; Tina Hesman Saey, "Whoa, Nellie! Horse Genome Is Revealed," *Science News* (5 December 2009): 5–6.

46. Karen Ho, *Liquidated: An Ethnography of Wall Street* (Durham, NC, 2009); and Karen Ho, "Situating Global Capitalisms: A View from Wall Street Investment Banks," *Cultural Anthropology* 20 (2005): 68–96.

47. Hacking, "Our Neo-Cartesian Bodies in Parts"; Paul Gilroy, *The Status of Difference: From Epidermalisation to Nano-Politics,* Critical Urban Studies Occasional Paper Pamphlet (London, 1995).

48. Here I am indebted to Randy Martin and Geeta Patel for their deft expositions of how the fiduciary operations of credit, debt, and insurance become lived instruments that reconstitute subjectivity; Randy Martin, *Financialization of Daily Life* (Philadelphia, PA, 2002); Geeta Patel, "Risky Subjects"; and Geeta Patel, "Imagining Risk, Care, and Security," *Anthropological Theory* 7 (2007): 99–118.

49. Ed Cohen, *A Body Worth Defending: Immunity, Biopolitics, and the Apotheosis of the Modern Body* (Durham, NC, 2009), 280.

*Chapter 12*

# Articulating Blood and Kinship in Biomedical Contexts in Contemporary Britain and Malaysia

## Janet Carsten

My contribution to this volume on kinship and blood arises from research that aims to investigate blood as an object rather than as a particular domain of practices.[1] The research highlights the pathways along which blood travels, crucially, between areas of knowledge and practice that we think of as "scientific" or "biomedical," and those that are apparently more "social"—such as kinship, ethnicity, or religion. As the chapters in this volume demonstrate, blood is in many cultures and at different historical junctures a core symbol of kinship, ethnicity, and religion. It is also a scientific or medical object of investigation, and a valued source of medical treatment. If the separation of scientific knowledge from other, more "social," orders of knowledge, such as kinship, seems paradigmatic of modernity, then this suggests that the boundaries separating these categories are worthy of scrutiny. What kinds of work go into creating such boundaries? How strictly are these separations maintained? Are there areas in which we can detect seepage between one kind of knowledge and another?

The research, which is still continuing, investigates the intersection between popular and biomedical understandings of blood through comparative fieldwork in Malaysia and the UK. It builds on my previous work on kinship in both states but extends the quest into the fields of medical anthropology and science studies.[2] In 2008, I undertook seven months of fieldwork in the blood banks and clinical pathology labs of two urban private hospitals in Penang, to which I returned for a brief visit in February and March 2009. A further phase of research is planned to take place in Edinburgh in 2010. This chapter thus reflects the fact that I have barely begun the European work. In keeping with long-standing anthropological practice, however, I use ethnography from Penang to bring into focus a more general discussion about the complex articulations between blood, biomedicine, and kinship.

The first part of this chapter is a description of the project and the questions that underlie it. What follows is a rather eclectic juxtaposition of material drawn from my recent fieldwork in Penang, including public discourses about blood and organ donation in Malaysia, vignettes of blood donation, and a depiction of kinship connections in the clinical pathology labs. After some brief reflections on participating in a major health research project in the UK, the conclusion draws out the more general implications of the connections between these different contexts. It makes some suggestions about the exceptional status of blood resting on its overdetermined participation in different realms of practice and its function as a vector between domains that are generally kept separate.

# From Kinship to Biomedicine

The participation of blood in many different fields, its social and historical construction, and its range of symbolic and metaphorical connotations—what Sarah Franklin in this volume refers to as the "plasticity" of blood as an idiom—are central to this study. As well as being the focus of notions of kinship and ethnicity, blood is also a major object of biomedical procedures, including donation, testing, analysis, and transfusion. How do professionals with medical, scientific, and technical expertise move between different understandings and practices when carrying out laboratory or clinical procedures? In what ways do they compartmentalize their knowledge? In what ways do understandings deriving from cultural or moral domains inflect biomedical practices or knowledge? For such questions, the extensive social science and historical literature on idioms of blood in religious, political, and familial life provide a rich source of background material.[3]

In both Malaysia and Britain, blood is a dominant idiom for kinship relations, but its significance is different in the two cases. In my fieldwork of the 1980s, I explored how blood, in Malay kinship, is understood as something both "given" at birth and acquired through consuming food that has been cooked in the household hearth (as opposed to the hearth in some other house). Maternal milk and rice meals are regarded in Malay ideas as of prime importance in the formation of blood. Because maternal milk is conceived both as a form of blood—produced primarily through the consumption of rice meals—and as a prime contributor, through maternal feeding, to the blood of infants, it is accorded a special value in these ideas as a vector of bodily substance linking mothers and their children and thus as a source of similarity between siblings. The centrality of bonds of siblingship in Malay kinship means that, rather than the inheritance or sharing of bodily substance between parents and children, it is the identity of the blood of siblings that is often singled out for comment and elaborated symbolically.[4] In the UK, the symbolic significance of blood in terms of kinship is primarily as an inherited substance and as an idiom of continuity and connection. In this sense, what is inherited "in the blood" is often contrasted to what is acquired from the environment (whereas in Malay articulations environment and inheritance tend not to be seen in opposition to each other and may indeed be merged).[5] The titles of several recent British literary memoirs, such as Andrew Motion's *In the Blood* (2006) or Lorna Sage's *Bad Blood* (2000), underline the resonance of blood in terms of inheritance. This has different implications from the Malay articulations that I encountered in the 1980s, in which the emphasis on rice meals as a source of blood and on the latter as a source of breast milk implied that, as a bodily substance, blood could be viewed as falling as much within the field of what in European ideas would count as "nurture" as within a symbolically opposed domain of "nature."[6]

Extending the scope of my previous work on the distinctions made in everyday life between "biological" and "social" kinship, I have set out to examine the links between cultures of kinship and medical knowledge in Britain and Malaysia.[7] This involves being attentive to all the registers in which people talk about blood—drawing on religious, ethnic, and kinship idioms.[8] For example, on an investigative visit to Penang in 2005, I was told by hospital physicians that local ideas about ethnic difference affected the availability of blood for transfusion and the willingness of patients to accept donated blood. Rather than assuming the cultural uniformity of such ideas in Malaysia or the UK, I aim to explore how blood encodes ethnic difference and how medical and scientific practices are affected by and articulate notions of cultural difference.

By focusing on blood as a bodily substance central to kinship and notions of identity, on the one hand, and as the subject of biomedical procedures, on the other, I examine the interconnections between these domains of knowledge. And I look at ways in which these interconnections inform how the boundary between the social and biological is perceived. I thus hope to illuminate how professionals with medical, scientific, and technical expertise move between different understandings and practices when carrying out research or clinical procedures. In what follows I draw on recent work in medical anthropology, science studies, and the anthropology of kinship, to highlight some of the general questions raised by the status of blood as a biomedical object and by its participation in different fields of knowledge.

## Blood as a Biomedical Object

What kind of medical object is blood when it becomes the object of scientific or clinical investigation? How is it treated? What professional and ethical protocols apply to it? Both the classic study of blood donation and social policy in Britain by Richard Titmuss and the one of French DNA by Paul Rabinow demonstrate how narratives about blood are politically and historically contingent and show the myriad ways in which donated blood is imbued with moral qualities.[9] The "gift relationship" that Titmuss argued was central to the efficient organization of blood donation in the UK and the benevolent voluntary sacrifice of members of the French resistance discussed by Rabinow can be contrasted to the inefficiencies of the US market in blood, or to the moral corruption of Vichy-regime collaborators, who were paid to donate blood in wartime France. Both authors demonstrate how these historically situated moral qualities of blood crucially affect the availability of blood products and their freedom from contamination.

In the extraction of blood, its many separations into samples and blood products, and their storage and analysis, how is blood transformed from bodily substance into information? What kinds of information are involved and how are they embodied?[10] Tracing the complex "social life" of blood and its separations in medical, research, and clinical settings, I do not assume either that blood is a commodity or that it has inherent moral qualities.[11] Rather, drawing on the work of Bruno Latour and on studies that focus on specific scientific or medical *practices*, I explore some of the specific networks in which blood participates for diagnostic and clinical purposes and the particular contexts and registers in which blood can be differently constructed as an object.[12]

# Articulations Between Domains of Knowledge

In what ways do clinical and research professionals maintain boundaries between different domains of knowledge and practice? How do they traverse these domains? Rayna Rapp's discussion of the social impact of amniocentesis in the US suggests that, "at stake in the analysis of the traffic between biomedical and familial discourses is an understanding of the inherently uneven seepage of science and its multiple uses and transformations into contemporary social life."[13] I find the notion of "uneven seepage" helpful, both for examining how the domains of social life and biomedicine may impinge on each other and for undermining any simple assumption of the hegemonic force of the categories of biomedicine. In fact, it is quite possible that the influence might go in the other direction. Thus I ask: In what ways do the categories of kinship or religion or politics inflect the practices of scientists or health professionals? In what ways are their experiences of kinship, their family histories of illness, or their attention to public debates or ethical issues reflected in scientific practice or the categories of biomedicine? Recent studies suggest that kinship has been transformed by biomedical advances.[14] But clinicians, researchers, technicians, and students are also part of kinship networks and participate in public debates about what is ethical. This would suggest not only that the boundaries between these domains may be blurred but also that "reverse traffic" between familial and biomedical discourses can take place.

Studies demonstrating the formative influence of kinship ideas on the reception of biomedical concepts have recently begun to add weight to Jonathan Marks's contention that the powerful metaphorical connections between blood and heredity make scientific investigations of blood both an appropriate locus for investigating the modeling of disease causation and an excellent site for observing the traffic between familial, moral, and biomedical discourses.[15] For example, Sarah Franklin, pursuing the question of how far recent advances in genetic medicine have transformed understandings of kinship, suggests in this volume that contrary to what some anthropologists have expected, ideas about genes have in fact been reshaped by those about blood.[16] Blood, as she remarks, is "thicker than genes." In a similar vein, and using the example of genetic markers for late-onset Alzheimer's disease, Margaret Lock has recently demonstrated that when educated middle-class Canadians are given information about their own genetic susceptibility that has uncertain consequences, far from adopting the idiom of genetic predispositions, they translate this back into more familiar idioms of kinship.[17] Here I seek to extend Lock's insights by investigating the interface between practices

based on scientific knowledge and those based on everyday understandings of kinship and ethnicity among professionals working in biomedical
fields.

## Locations

During the first phase of my ethnographic research in Penang in 2008,
I focused on medical lab technologists working with blood in two pri-
vate-sector, hospital-based, clinical pathology labs and in blood banks.
Since I am interested in the links and articulations between different
domains of knowledge and practice, I have not, however, treated these
personnel only in terms of their professional identities. Their insertion
into networks of kinship and participation in everyday experiences of
family life, health, and illness, as well as in public debates about moral issues, have been central to this study. Contexts for investigation included
blood donation drives (in various locations, such as factories, temples,
community halls), blood banks, dialysis units, and clinical pathology
laboratories charged with routine blood-screening as well as diagnostic
testing of blood samples. I have had conversations with doctors, nurses,
lab technicians, receptionists, nursing students, and blood donors, and
have observed the settings in which they operate.

## Public Discourses of Donation: Malaysia

During an exploratory visit to Penang in 2005, I was quite surprised to
find the medical practitioners to whom I talked immediately engaged by
this project. In their view, the local shortage of donated blood is a result
of "cultural factors" inhibiting the willingness to donate blood or to receive it from particular sources. It is generally accepted that most blood
in Malaysia is donated by Malays. Blood donation campaigns have high
media exposure, and this is particularly the case just before and during
Ramadan, when a fall in donations from Malays results in severe shortages. Visiting Malaysia again, shortly before Ramadan in 2007, I could
hardly fail to be struck by the almost daily reports on blood drives in the
newspapers and the accompanying exhortations to donate.

That ethnicity is at issue in bodily exchanges is also suggested by
local media coverage of a heart transplant operation that took place in
Kuala Lumpur in October 2007. Newspaper reports highlighted the fact
that one of the two donors was Malay, while the teenage girl who was
the recipient was Malaysian Chinese. The political mileage to be gained

from this incident was recognized by leaders who praised it as testimony to harmonious inter-ethnic relations. Thus one newspaper, in an article headed "Transplant touches Hearts," reported:

> Umno Youth chief Datuk Seri Hishammuddin Tun Hussein said the noble deed of a Malay boy's family donating his heart to Hui Yi transcended race and religion. "It is so special and touching. In a time when there are issues relating to racial and religious divisions. The act has given us hope. This is exactly what the Barisan Nasional [National Front] tries to do. We need to highlight more such stories," said Hishammuddin at the opening of the Gerakan Youth and Wanita delegates' conference at Menara PGRM yesterday.[18]

The same article began:

> The double transplant case of 14-year old Tee Hui Yi had the Gerakan Youth delegates and VIPs engrossed yesterday. Tan Sri Dr Koh Tsu Koon said a heart transplant was more dramatic than blood donation, which was now a normal procedure. "When blood is transfused into one's body, no one would ask whether this is blood from a Chinese or Malay. To all of us, it is just human blood," he said, adding that Malaysians should be grateful for the advances. "There are many things we have taken for granted. Mutual help and inter-marriages, it is happening in this country," he said.[19]

In these politically inflected commentaries, the connections between organ transfers, blood donation, and harmonious ethnic relations encompassing cooperation and intermarriage, are laid out in a logically implied sequence that is also a highly charged moral discourse. Such dense interconnections between the realms of kinship, ethnicity, behavior deemed ethical, and resultant political harmony are so common as to go almost unremarked in the Malaysian public sphere. The ease with which it is possible to extend this range of associations to also include biomedical practices is indicative of how deeply ingrained these interconnections are and how "natural" and unquestionable they seem. Moral idioms of donation as well as the particular ethical value attached to gifts of blood or human organs apparently enhance the capacity of such extensions to appear self-evident. And, as I discuss in the conclusion to this chapter, it is not just in the Malaysian context that this observation is pertinent.

## Blood Donation: Penang

We tend to take for granted that the act of donating blood is an ethical act that draws on the kind of moral discourse alluded to above, but the case in Penang proved not to fit this assumption so neatly. When I asked donors why they had come to donate blood, the replies would often come in the form of the stock phrases employed in public education campaigns and hospital posters, such as "to save a life" or "to help people." Such posters were prominently displayed in blood banks and at shopping malls, temples, community halls, and factories selected as sites for mass donation campaigns. Additional questioning sometimes elicited more complex motivations tied to the life stories and kinship relations of donors. For example, one donor told me that she had been giving blood for the previous twelve years. When I asked her what had first motivated her to donate, she told me that her father had regularly given blood, and that after his death, she had decided to begin donating blood herself, as a way of perpetuating his memory. Other stories revealed further interconnections of kinship and memory. Often, donors told me that they had been giving blood for many years and had first started to donate with members of their family. And this association of blood donation with ties of kinship was visibly demonstrated at many blood donation campaigns I observed, where donors were accompanied by their spouses and children. Large-scale blood drives were generally held on a Sunday and had the air of a festive family excursion. In fact, the organizers of such events enthusiastically drew my attention to the "family spirit" of these occasions and explained how they aimed to encourage it by various organizational features, such as holding the campaigns on a non-working day, cooking food, and encouraging donors to bring their families—especially their children.

I was intrigued by the way that the booklet carried by blood donors, which records dates and locations of each donation, could become a material record of a life. I was shown many such booklets in which a long list of donations taking place over many years, in fact, traced not just the events of donation but the history of a life: where a donor had lived and worked, and the reasons that had dictated donating in a particular hospital, town, or city. Often donors took some time to explain the background story of family or employment history, alluded to in the list of donations recorded in their donor booklets but left in the shadows.

In one somewhat eccentric case, a man in his mid fifties came to one of the hospital blood banks that I was observing, to give blood, as he explained proudly, for the 104th time in his life. The donor booklets he carried, which were attached to each other, attested to a long history of such donations, stretching back thirty-two years and encompassing not just several hospitals in Penang but also others in different states of peninsular Malaysia. Along with his donor booklets, this man carried other mementoes of his previous donations: certificates from hospitals, bus tickets to neighboring states, photographs of one of the hospitals that he favored, an envelope that had held a supermarket voucher given as a token of appreciation by one of the blood banks, a special cup that was a souvenir for regular donors from another hospital. In response to my interest, he carefully unwrapped these various artifacts from document cases and boxes and displayed them, while at the same time lamenting the loss of an inscribed donor's T-shirt, a reward from one blood bank, which, he said, had been stolen by a drug addict. I was struck, not just by the expansive detail with which this man told me about his history of blood donation (all the more notable because it seemed that he was carrying his personal archive by chance or habit and not because he had been aware beforehand that a researcher might have a particular interest in it), but also by how truncated his answers became when I asked about his family. His wife had died some years before, he told me, and his only daughter did not live with him. For many donors it seemed easy to locate their acts of donation in stories of kinship and family lives, which were part of their personal significance, but for this man it seemed as though blood donation had itself expanded to become the guiding principle giving meaning to his life.

Private hospitals not only took blood from voluntary donors but also encouraged replacement donations from the families of patients who needed blood transfusions.[20] Many donors were probably encouraged to donate by staff keen to maintain the supply of blood available in the hospital blood bank. Still others might have been offered remuneration by families unable or unwilling to meet hospital requests themselves. Thus, at the same time that the enthusiastic voluntary donor whom I described above was enlarging on his life history of donation, another person, lying on the next bed, was also giving blood. In marked contrast to the first donor, this young man spoke very little and was clearly feeling quite unwell after donating. Several times, he tried to get up from the bed where he was resting but was seemingly overcome by nausea and giddiness. His mother explained that her son was there as a replacement donor for his grandmother, a patient at the hospital, and that he had a phobia about giving blood. His older, more voluble and more experienced neighbor on the next bed told him that if he gave blood more often he would soon become accustomed to it and it would get easier.

These two cases highlight some of the differences between donors and point to the issue of pressure from family or friends. But as commentators pointed out to me, the contrast could also be misleading, since voluntary donors are subject to constraints or persuasions of various kinds. Notoriously, soldiers and police in Malaysia are sometimes more or less ordered to volunteer. And one university lecturer recalled that when she had been up for promotion and had nothing much to write under the heading "community service," the easiest remedy would have been to donate blood at the university clinic. So, between "saving a life," "doing good," "helping others," and other statements of virtuous altruism, and acting as a replacement donor or donating more or less to order, a range of motivating factors come into play. These include the material signs of recognition with which blood banks sometimes reward donors, such as certificates, special T-shirts, and the like, as well as more overtly material recompense, including supermarket vouchers, and even, in some cases, transactions that would not be visible to hospital staff, such as cash offered by the families of patients. While for many donors, less tangible emotions of pride or satisfaction are the central consequences of donating, other factors clearly also play their part. And it is possible to see how these complex motivations are also woven into career paths and family histories.

## Laboratory Connections: Penang

It was during lunch with small groups of associates from the labs that I learned many of the most interesting things about the lives of staff in the clinical pathology labs and blood banks in Penang. On one occasion, over a Kentucky Fried Chicken lunch, it occurred to me to ask one young couple, a medical lab technologist and a hospital administrator, how they had originally gotten together. With some laughter and embarrassment, Stephen, the young man from the human resources department, first told me to ask Mr. Khoo, the lab manager. But he then related that Mr. Khoo had invited him to come on a mobile blood drive, along with other staff four years earlier, where he had met his future wife-to-be, and that about a month later, he had asked her out on a date. Blood donation campaigns are, of course, serious work events, but they sometimes have the air of an office outing, especially on occasions during which ten or more staff travel together to temples, factories, Chinese association halls, or shopping malls as much as several hours away, taking most of the day and stopping for lunch along the way. Given the potential air of festivity, it is perhaps unsurprising that a match such as the one between Stephen and his fiancée might occasionally be a result. Stephen told me that Mr. Khoo now claims he arranged their match. I asked him whether he knew he was being set up before he went on the blood drive, and he told me he did. Meanwhile, his partner (whom I knew somewhat better) was looking more and more surprised as she listened to this exchange. She told me that until I asked about it she hadn't heard that her fiancé had known about the matchmaking intentions of her boss, although she had known that her boss was somehow involved. This young couple was planning their wedding a few months hence, and it was expected that, as custom would have it, they would invite all their colleagues.

Over the months I was in Penang, I learned of several marriages between lab staff and members of other departments, and of other matchmaking attempts involving lab staff. Quite a few people had relatives working elsewhere in the same hospital. In one of the hospitals this was so much the case that I was advised never to say anything about staff working elsewhere in the same hospital just in case it turned out to concern a relative of the person to whom I was talking. One quite senior medical lab technologist was married to a colleague in the same lab; another's husband had previously worked in the same lab before leaving for further studies. Although it took me some time to learn about these connections, they were not particularly hard to find once I started looking.

Children and babies were another source of connection between staff. They were often the subject of conversations between colleagues who would relate problems they were having to each other, issues about feeding and diet, funny stories, or achievements of their children. During lulls in working hours, they also often showed each other recent pictures of their children, which they carried on their mobile phones. Babies were regularly brought into the hospital for the health checks and blood tests available to staff at reduced rates, and so they might be brought to greet colleagues in the lab. Similarly, parents of staff were eligible for treatment at reduced rates. Indeed, staff were usually familiar with the grandparents, parents, spouses, and children of their colleagues.

There were many different ways then for kinship to be the basis of connections between staff who worked in the blood bank and clinical pathology labs. These connections could be quite loose—perhaps the shared concerns of women who have young children of the same age. Or they could be the kind of connection that builds up gradually between colleagues who have worked together over several decades, developing mutual interests, like the construction and daily maintenance of a set of decorative fish ponds in the area just outside the labs, or the visiting of each other's homes. In one case of colleagues who had worked together over a very long period, one of them had lodged for some time in the other's parental home. Sometimes the connections were direct and intimate—two marriages among lab colleagues and an engagement between a staff member and a former trainee.

It is difficult to say how these different kinds of connection affected work. In both sets of labs and blood banks, it seemed to me that relations were in many ways warm and mostly harmonious—although in one lab there were more obvious signs of friction than in the other. In the latter, colleagues routinely helped each other out during times of high pressure, while in the former, staff tended to ask the manager to send them someone to help, with consequent delays and periods of stress. In general, there was a higher "density" of social relations than might be expected in similar settings in the UK, resulting partly from the considerable length of time colleagues had been working together and also from locally accepted cultural practices and norms. In any case, I was struck by the regularity with which I observed lab staff, their spouses, and their connections elsewhere in the hospital coming to donate blood and by the number of staff who told me that they or their spouses had donated blood in the past.

One other way in which close relations among colleagues or between staff and their families impinged directly on the working life of the lab was through blood tests themselves. Because staff and their families qualified for medical treatments at reduced rates, medical lab technologists often carried out blood tests on their own or close relatives' blood, or on the blood of colleagues or their family members. They could very easily track results as they were being processed by the lab, and they frequently did so. Thus when my own daughter was unwell, the staff in the lab helpfully went into the data system to let me know that nothing serious had shown up on her results. It goes without saying that not all information was so benign in its potential consequences.

Childbirth intersected with the professional knowledge of lab staff in less predictable ways. The majority of the medical lab technologists were married women with young children. When I asked them individually about their experiences of childbirth, I was quite surprised to learn that almost all of them had gone through a lengthy period of special post-natal practices and taboos involving special diet, restrictions on bathing, and the application of heat to their stomach. These are very widespread in Malaysia, and I had already encountered them in the 1980s when carrying out fieldwork in a Malay fishing village.[21] In urban contexts in contemporary Malaysia, it is common to hear middle-class people talk of a period of "confinement" (they used the English term) after childbirth, and in Penang there are a number of private "confinement homes" where women can spend this period if it is more convenient than being looked after at home. The women I interviewed in the labs, however, spoke about being under the care of a mother-in-law or their own mother during confinement and often attributed the fact that they followed these restrictions to the strictness and insistence of their senior kin. They also talked about blood in terms I had not expected to hear: The central idea of these post-natal rituals is that giving birth involves the loss of blood, which is a "cooling" process. This means that after giving birth, in order to restore the body to its normal state, women should stay in the house and avoid various kinds of food classified as "cooling" (especially raw fruit and vegetables and iced drinks). They should also avoid bathing in cold water, and they may have heat applied in various ways to their body, especially to the stomach. The period of confinement, which lasts for forty-four days for Malays and one month for Chinese and involves subjecting the body to heat, is arduous in a tropical climate. Such practices strongly indicate that for these medical lab technologists, biomedical or scientific knowledge about blood does not necessarily dominate their thinking or actions.

While I did not carry out direct research with patients needing transfusions or their families, blood bank and laboratory staff did sometimes speak about the preferences of patients for using blood from particular sources. Thus I was told that occasionally patients would try to ensure that the transfused blood they received came from members of their own families through the replacement donor system. Blood bank staff, however, emphasized to me that receiving blood from family members did not automatically ensure its safety. The replacement system of donation normally operated indirectly because the blood from replacement donors was not to be used for direct transfer to specific patients but was intended to maintain the overall supply of blood in the blood bank. Sometimes a conversation with medical lab technologists about a particular patient's preference for blood from a family member would progress to a discussion about the preferences of certain patients for blood from Malay Muslim donors. Here the almost imperceptible transition from kinship to ethnicity and religion recalls the newspaper reports cited earlier. In Malaysia both ethnicity and religion (categories that in popular discourse often signify each other) are highly sensitive, and it is indicative that medical lab technologists always spoke in hushed tones when referring to issues of either category. My impression was that, at least in the hospitals where I carried out research, questions about the ethnic or religious source of blood did not arise frequently, and most transfused patients received blood from sources that were not known to them. This mirrored the preferences of the voluntary donors to whom I spoke, who expressed their disapproval of any exclusionary practices that might limit the availability of the blood they had donated.

# UK Biobank

My last and rather different ethnographic vignette comes from another site—this time in Edinburgh. In the autumn of 2007, by chance, I received an invitation to join a national medical research project. The UK Biobank, as I was informed in the invitation letter, would "involve around 500,000 people aged 40–69 from all around the UK" and was being set up by the UK Department of Health, the Medical Research Council, the Scottish Executive, and the Wellcome Trust medical charity. Designed to study "the prevention and treatment of cancer, heart attacks, strokes, diabetes, dementia, joint problems, and many other serious diseases," this research in progress requires participants to answer an extensive touchscreen questionnaire on lifestyle, medical history, diet, sexual history, familial relations, and other matters; to agree to have some physical measurements and tests; and to donate blood and urine samples for analysis.[22] Participants are asked to "allow UK Biobank to access [their] medical and other health-related records," to consent to the "long-term storage and use of blood and urine samples for health-related research purposes (even after incapacity or death)," and to "relinquish all rights to these donated samples."[23] The language of the gift figures prominently in the information provided to potential participants. Thus the information leaflet accompanying the letter of invitation states: "Like giving blood for transfusions, UK Biobank is not intended to help directly those who take part—but it should give future generations a much better chance of living their lives free of diseases that disable and kill."[24]

Unable to resist such a timely opportunity, I duly found myself taking up this invitation and providing answers to wide-ranging questions about what kind of accommodation I live in, whether I have a gas fire, how often I exceed speed limits on motorways, what breakfast cereal I eat (the categorization sometimes baffling, as in the separation of "muesli" from "oat based cereals"), how many portions of various kinds of vegetables and meat I habitually consume, whether anyone has ever complained that I snore, how many brothers or sisters I have (not including step- or half-siblings); along with others about the medical histories of parents, the number and gender of my sexual partners, my own previous medical procedures, drug regimes, illnesses and disabilities, smoking history, alcohol consumption, and weight at birth; and concluding with questions testing my short-term memory and reaction times. The list, as I have indicated, was long, and my summary is not exhaustive. The final memory tasks seemed designed to highlight the fallibility of memory or knowledge on which the answers one had just supplied rested—but exactly how they connected to the other information provided was unclear. By contrast, the physical measures taken were few and seemed disconcertingly precise: height, weight, grip strength, pulmonary function, and bone density were all measured and noted before the taking of blood and urine samples (perhaps significantly left to the last). A printout of the physical measures as well as the signed consent form (but not the questionnaire or the answers provided to it) was given to participants before they left.

The UK Biobank study is a quintessential piece of state-supported modern scientific investigation—indeed, as I was told by one of the nurses, it is the biggest medical study currently being undertaken in the UK. Despite—or perhaps because of—this grand scale, the perceived contrast among the kinds of information being collected makes me pause. Most notably, there seems an obvious disjunction between the apparently unambiguous physical samples and measures, and the presumably hazy or approximate recollections of participants about various obscure aspects of their lifestyles, past circumstances, and family histories. And I would guess that many participants subsequently worry about the accuracy of their answers. Of course, it more or less goes without saying that one could point to innumerable ways in which assumptions about kinship and relatedness (not to mention other kinds of assumptions) are implicitly incorporated into the framing of the questionnaire. And this makes one wonder what will result when all of the information on the 500,000 participants is collated—particularly as the accumulation of a mass database is the point of the study.

The UK Biobank aims to provide new treatments for diseases and new insights for their prevention by joining a vast amount of information on "lifestyle" with physical measures and medical histories. But it also provides social scientists with insights about what kinds of information medical practitioners, epidemiologists, and geneticists think could be relevant to such aims and about how different kinds information can be collected, put together, and quantified. The collation of all this information appears already to presuppose a radical separation between the "social"—coded as "lifestyle"—and the "scientific"—encompassed in bodily measurements and the analysis of samples. And this separation is constantly reenacted in the way the study is conducted. One might juxtapose these processes with the accounts of bodily transfers in the Malaysian press that I quoted earlier. In the Malaysian accounts, what seemed to be at issue was the explicit separation or removal of "cultural factors" from physiological processes of donating, transfusing, and transferring blood or organs, whereas the UK Biobank project aims to put together what is assumed to be radically separated. But one effect of the intense effort required to keep these domains separate is that their overt reintegration in the UK Biobank study is not easy to achieve. Indeed, it seems to require active and rather cumbersome performance—a more or less visible demonstration of the difficulties of making the incommensurable commensurable.

# Conclusion

I have sketched some apparently quite discontinuous contexts in which blood makes an appearance. From Malaysia, newspaper stories about donation; vignettes of blood donors; a description of kinship connections in the lives of those who work in clinical pathology labs and blood banks, whose work comprises the routine collecting, screening, and diagnostic testing of blood; from the UK, a state-sponsored research project that rests on the collection of blood samples and physiological measures, together with information about "lifestyle" from many thousands of participants.

The work I have described here is designed to illuminate the connections and separations between kinship and scientific or biomedical knowledge and practices. It is also a particular kind of urban ethnography of the two very different places in which it is conducted—Edinburgh and Penang. It is far too soon to pronounce on the comparative scope of this work, which might eventually be expected to illuminate important cultural and historical differences between these sites, the one British and a key locus of the institutionalization of enlightenment knowledge practices, the other Southeast Asian with a long colonial past and a complex migration history. In spite of their wide cultural and historical divergences, however, I would hesitate to suggest that separations between domains of knowledge would be clearer or more securely anchored in one place than another. While the particular resonances and meanings that attach to blood or to kinship or ethnicity may differ, global continuities of laboratory practices, medical training, and career pathways, as well as other continuities in scientific knowledge suggest that there may be more connections between these apparently very different locations than might initially be predicted. For the moment, therefore, my conclusions are general ones.

My starting point has been that blood, as a bodily substance of everyday significance, has a peculiarly extensive symbolic repertoire. This has led me to consider ways in which blood travels between domains that in other contexts are actively kept separate. While Richard Titmuss highlighted the importance of "the gift" of blood, I argue that the social significance of blood is not limited to donation. On the contrary, the meanings of blood are created partly through its seemingly overdetermined participation in many different spheres. In this respect, Titmuss's discussion of the "gift relationship," whereby, in the British NHS, free donation is the guarantor of the safety of blood from contamination, could be viewed as part of the ethnography one might wish to examine. Titmuss's argument hinged precisely on the importance of strictly separating blood from commerce. I suggest that this process of distinction is fraught with difficulties precisely because of the way blood flows between domains. The openness of medical lab technologists to non-biomedical ideas about blood and the importance of histories of kinship to acts of blood donation and to relations between staff in the clinical pathology labs provide some indications of the many pathways along which blood may travel and the permeability of boundaries between kinship and biomedicine.

The exceptionality of blood partly rests on the fact that the associations between the symbolic resonance of blood in terms of family connection, the moral discourses surrounding blood donation, and the biomedical properties and functions of blood are not just contingent but rely on and imply each other, in a series of interconnections difficult to sever because they are endlessly self-reinforcing. This is demonstrated through the discourses, practices, and sites that I have examined here. Intricate chains of association link the rhetoric surrounding blood donation, the way donors themselves perceive their acts of donation and situate them in their own histories of kinship, and the working practices of staff in blood banks and clinical pathology labs. These associations both ensure the adequate supply of blood for medical purposes and place in question the degree to which it is possible to seal off a separate domain of scientific or biomedical practices involving blood from other socio-cultural practices and discourses. In this respect, blood could be viewed as an object that is in fact always incompletely objectified. Its subjective qualities, deriving from multiple symbolic, relational, moral, and practical spheres, are not only impossible to shed but have important implications for different forms of relationality—including those of scientific and medical practice.

# Notes

1. The research on which this chapter is based was funded by a Leverhulme Major Research Fellowship with further funds for fieldwork in Malaysia provided by a British Academy Small Research Grant. I am grateful to the Leverhulme Trust and the British Academy for making this work possible, to the staff of the hospitals where I carried out fieldwork, and to the editors of this volume for their helpful comments on an earlier draft.
2. Janet Carsten, "The Substance of Kinship and the Heat of the Hearth: Feeding, Personhood and Relatedness among Malays of Pulau Langkawi," *American Ethnologist* 22 (1995): 223–41; Janet Carsten, *The Heat of the Hearth: The Process of Kinship in a Malay Fishing Community* (Oxford, 1997); Janet Carsten, ed., *Cultures of Relatedness: New Approaches to the Study of Kinship* (Cambridge, 2000); Janet Carsten, *After Kinship* (Cambridge, 2004).

3.  See, for example, Caroline Walker Bynum, *Wonderful Blood: Theology and Practice in Late Medieval Germany and Beyond* (Philadelphia, PA, 2007); Jacob Copeman, *Veins of Devotion: Blood Donation and Religious Experience in North India* (New Brunswick, NJ, and London, 2009); Gillian Feeley-Harnik, *The Lord's Table: Eucharist and Passover in Early Christianity* (Philadelphia, PA, 1981); Steve Jones, *In the Blood* (London, 1996); Anastasia Karakasidou, *Fields of Wheat, Hills of Blood: Passages to Nationhood in Greek Macedonia* (Chicago, IL, 1997); Christopher Knight, *Blood Relations: Menstruation and the Origin of Culture* (New Haven, CT, 1991); David M. Schneider, *American Kinship: A Cultural Account*, 2nd ed. (Chicago, IL, 1980); Douglas Starr, *Blood: An Epic History of Medicine and Commerce* (New York, 1998); Richard Titmuss, *The Gift Relationship: From Human Blood to Social Policy*, orig. ed., with new chaps., ed. Ann Oakley and John Ashton (New York, 1997).

4.  See Carsten, *Heat of the Hearth*; Roziah Omar, *The Malay Woman in the Body: Between Biology and Culture* (Kuala Lumpur, 1994). These ideas are specifically Malay. Malaysia is, however, a multiethnic society, and my earlier work did not explore Chinese Malaysian or Indian Malaysian kinship.

5.  See Jeanette Edwards, *Born and Bred: Idioms of Kinship and New Reproductive Technologies in England* (Oxford, 2000); Schneider, *American Kinship*.

6.  See Carsten, "The Substance of Kinship."

7.  See Carsten, *After Kinship*, chap. 6.

8.  Richard Tutton, "Gift Relationships in Genetics Research," *Science as Culture* 11, no.4 (2002): 523–42.

9.  Titmuss, *The Gift Relationship*; Paul Rabinow, *French DNA: Trouble in Purgatory* (Chicago, IL, 1999).

10. Tutton, "Gift Relationships."

11. Arjun Appadurai, "Introduction: Commodities and The Politics of Value," in *The Social Life of Things: Commodities in Cultural Perspective*, ed. Arjun Appadurai, (Cambridge, 1986), 3–63; Margaret Lock, *Twice Dead: Organ Transplants and the Reinvention of Death* (Berkeley, CA, 2002); Rabinow, *French DNA*; Titmuss, *The Gift Relationship*; Tutton, "Gift Relationships."

12. Bruno Latour, *The Pasteurization of France* (Cambridge, MA, 1988); Bruno Latour, *We Have Never Been Modern* (New York, 1993); Marc Berg and Annemarie Mol, eds., *Differences in Medicine: Unraveling Practices, Techniques, and Bodies* (Durham, NC, 1998); Annemarie Mol, *The Body Multiple: Ontology in Medical Practice* (Durham, NC, 2002); Annemarie Mol and Marc Berg, "Differences in Medicine: An Introduction," in *Differences in Medicine*, ed. Berg and Mol (Durham, NC, 1998); Annemarie Mol and J. Law, "Regions, Networks, and Fluids: Anaemia and Social Topology," *Social Studies of Science* 24 (1994): 641–71.

13. Rayna Rapp, *Testing Women, Testing the Fetus: The Social Impact of Amniocentesis in America* (New York and London, 1999), 303. Here Rapp makes use of Paul Rabinow's notion of "biosociality" as a process of identity formation governed by categories of biomedicine. See Paul Rabinow, "Artificiality and Enlightenment: From Sociobiology to Biosociality," in *Incorporations*, ed. John Crary and Sanford Kwinter (New York, 1992); Paul Rabinow, *Making PCR: A Story of Biotechnology* (Chicago, IL, 1996).

14. Kaja Finkler, *Experiencing the New Genetics: Family and Kinship on the Medical Frontier* (Philadelphia, PA, 2000).

15. Jonathan Marks, "98 percent Chimpanzee and 35 percent Daffodil: The Human Genome in Evolutionary and Cultural Context," in *Genetic Nature/Culture: Anthropology and Science Beyond the Two-Culture Divide*, ed. Alan H. Goodman, Deborah Heath, and M. Susan Lindee (Berkeley, CA, 2003).

16. See also Sarah Franklin, "Biologization Revisited: Kinship Theory in the Context of the New Biologies," in *Relative Values: Reconfiguring Kinship Studies*, ed. Sarah Franklin and Susan McKinnon (Durham, NC, and London, 2001).

17. Margaret Lock, "Eclipse of the Gene and the Return of Divination," *Current Anthropology* 46, Supplement (December 2005): 47–70.

18. Star Online at http://thestar.com.my/news/story.asp?file=/2007/10/6/nation/1909 7515; accessed 31 October 2007.

19. Star Online at http://thestar.com.my/news/story.asp?file=/2007/10/6/nation/1909 7515; accessed 31 October 2007.

20. This is not the case for public hospitals in Malaysia, which only operate a system of voluntary blood donation in line with WHO protocols.

21. Carsten, "The Substance of Kinship"; Carsten, *Heat of the Hearth*.

22. Quotations taken from introductory letter sent to potential participants, "Invitation to join a national medical research project," UK Biobank, 19 October 2007. The letter was sent out under the signatures of Rory Collins, UK Biobank Principal Investigator and Professor of Medicine and Epidemiology, University of Oxford, and Dr. Harry Burns, Chief Medical Officer.

23. Quotations taken from Consent Form Version: 20061124 Amendment One Final Version, dated 24 November 2006, UK Biobank; signed 8 November 2007. The consent form includes seven clauses, to which participants are separately asked to agree, including, "I understand that my participation is voluntary and that I am free to withdraw at any time without giving any reason."

24. Biobankuk Information Leaflet 2007:2.

# Chapter 13

# From Blood to Genes?

## *Rethinking Consanguinity in the Context of Geneticization*

### Sarah Franklin

Kinship has returned to the pages of anthropology journals with a vengeance, but also with a twist. With the revitalization of one of its hallmark concepts, anthropology is once again plunged into controversy about blood, genes, inheritance, descent, and reproductive biology—just as in its founding throes a century ago, although today with a greater focus on industrialized societies, and on the role of biomedicine and the new genetics.[1] Central to this reconfiguration of kinship studies is a resurgence of interest in European societies within social anthropology, as well as a re-examination of the concepts of the biological and the technological. This chapter explores the new connections between blood and genes in anthropology—particularly in the context of biomedicine—in three parts. The first section provides a brief and very basic overview of the historical importance of kinship studies to anthropology. This sets the context for examining the new focus within anthropology on geneticization and new genetic technologies in the second and third sections.[2]

# The Importance of the Kinship Concept to Anthropology

In modern European society, knowledge about reproductive substance and the hereditary transmission of characteristics is largely taken to be knowledge about the natural facts of life (biology), so that kin relations are seen to have a basis in natural facts—themselves often depicted as the material substances of kinship, such as blood, genes, or DNA. These models of substantial connection, organized as a bilateral, brachiating structure, are also crucial to the emergence of modern biological science. Darwin famously borrowed the analogy of blood relations to describe life's genealogical interconnectedness in the late nineteenth century, and from this, Foucault has argued, modern biology and its foundational concept of "life itself" were derived.[3] In return, as Marilyn Strathern has argued, the blood-based analogy of biological relations "travelled back" to naturalize human kin connections: a family's genealogical unity recapitulated the genealogical unity of all mankind and, indeed, the natural system (evolution) connecting all living things.[4] We can thus refer both ordinarily and literally today to a biological, or even a genetic, relative.

How people in different societies interpret the significance of connections established through "biological" ties in terms of kin obligations, family formation, marriage proscriptions, and so forth, has long been held to be a matter of social, cultural, and historical diversity, and within Anglo-American kinship theory, this topic was classically investigated in relation to a presumed opposition between "natural and social facts."[5] However, since the 1980s, with the rise of feminist anthropology as well as scholarly attention to the social construction of gender more widely, the natural and social/cultural dichotomy as a cultural and historical artifact has been subjected to a serious and productive critique.[6] From this perspective, kinship is no longer interpreted as deriving from a set of immutable biogenetic facts but must be read as a system of cultural knowledge through which biological and social practices are constantly remixed and remade in what is described as a hybrid, or plural, fashion. The question of kinship within social anthropology therefore turns not so much on the question of how ideas of relatedness are "culturally constructed" on a naturalized or "real biological" base, but on the wider question of how kinship models enact or perform culturally specific ways of knowing about the world at large.

Descent and parenthood are not the only sources of kinship models in social anthropology. In European societies, the relations that are considered kinship are also considered to be those derived through, or modeled on, marriage, residence, filiation, and locality. The study of marriage systems, including both fields of relations established through the prohibition of ties based on consanguinity (incest) and affinal relations of marriage (alliance), comprises a major strand of theoretical interest within social anthropology and also a source of divergence between its different articulations. The focus on marriage and exchange patterns has been most notably a result of the influential work of Lévi-Strauss, who sought to establish a universal basis for the analysis of human cultural systems (structuralism), and to verify a single hypothesis connecting the origins of marriage to the incest taboo.[7] In contrast to the emphasis on biology and descent in British and US anthropology, the Francophile tradition, focused on alliance and filiation, has tended to be less biologically orientated in favor of an emphasis on complex marriage patterns, following the precepts of structuralism.[8]

Considerable debate in the past has occasioned the question of the extent to which kinship systems derive their sociological importance from their role in structuring inheritance patterns, and it is an interest in African unilineal descent groups that shapes much of the work on jural and political relations associated with the British structural functionalism of Radcliffe-Brown, Meyer Fortes, and Evans-Pritchard.[9] This focus is also associated with a strand of social historical literature examining structural inheritance patterns. In the European context, a significant conjuncture between anthropology and social history has resulted in a large body of research investigating changing family formations over time, often through the use of genealogical records and other documents.[10] These studies, partially based on the analysis of rural peasant societies and often tied to the analysis of gender and household structure, comprise a large area of research in which kinship has a particular descriptive meaning and empirical importance that overlaps substantially with usages of these terms in social anthropology.[11]

In addition to ties through procreation, marriage, filiation, descent, and inheritance, the study of kinship within anthropology includes a wide range of so-called fictive, ritual, or spiritual kinship practices. On the one hand, there are types of honorary or ceremonial kinship, such as the institution of *compadrazgo*, which is a form of baptism, godparenthood, or "second birth" found widely in Europe, the Middle East, and Latin America.[12] Similarly, there are numerous practices of fostering and adoption, sometimes related to substances, as in "milk kinship" practices that are found worldwide.[13] On the other hand, there are numerous practices related to friendship and support networks, in which the establishment of reciprocal ties and obligations creates a kinship network of sorts.[14] These ties may replace, parallel, or complement consanguineal or conjugal relationships. The use of the term *fictive*, like the adjective *pseudo*, is consequently used less often, as it reflects the essentialist presumption of a biological "base" to the kinship superstructure.

Finally, relations built on kinship may be seen as those involving residence and household composition, reciprocal ties of mutual support and obligation concerned with nurture, child rearing, and other, often domestically related activities through which recognized definitions of closeness and distance are established practices—what could also be called kinship "processes."[15] An important component of such studies is the emphasis upon the range of kinship practices that may affect an individual over the life course, the wide range of persons who may play kinship roles, and the broad range of how such roles can be defined (for example, through the adoption of sibling terminologies of *brotherhood* and *sisterhood*).

In sum, kinship studies comprise both a major area of study within anthropology and a significant point of conjuncture between anthropology and other disciplines, in the European context most notably with sociologists, historians, and demographers. Quite a wide range of behavior may be classed as kinship or kinship-related activity, and several schools of thought have historically cohered around specific questions concerning kinship as a cultural idiom and as a mode of social organization.

Although the study of kinship is central to the discipline of social anthropology, neither the study of European societies in general, nor of European kinship systems in particular, has figured prominently within the discipline's foundational literature—which is instead largely focused on non-Western societies. It is only in the latter half of the twentieth century that ethnographic studies of the social relations of kinship and the cultural values ascribed to them in modern European societies have begun to play a more prominent role, and only in the past two decades that such studies have begun to gather momentum in the kinship literature. Several factors account for this pattern, which deserve brief mention. In part, this tendency is the result of the general orientation of anthropologists toward non-Western and pre-industrial societies throughout much of their discipline's development. The importance of kinship within anthropology, for example, can be seen to be in approximate proportion to its significance within the societies studied by anthropologists. In the late nineteenth century, when anthropology began to emerge as a discipline, much attention was focused on social formations in which kinship was seen as a primary institution providing the organizational structures of social and political life. This pattern continued as anthropology expanded, with the consequence that the study of kinship remained central to those theoretical concerns focused on social organization, most notably in the British functionalist and structural-functionalist traditions.[16]

An increase in attention to the cultures of modern industrialized nations accompanied the growing European interest in American cultural
anthropology in the 1970s. Consequently, theoretical interest in kinship
in terms of social structure began to diminish somewhat, although the
influence of structuralism remained strong, and continues to hold great
sway in the French traditions. Several developments in the 1980s and
1990s signaled a renewed interest in kinship in Europe. One was the
recognition that although as social institutions kinship systems may not
have had the same prominence in Europe as they do in societies organized into corporate descent groups, they are nonetheless integral to
cultural identities. Indeed, as many kinship theorists in the 1990s began
to argue, their importance had probably been underestimated.[17]

Alongside this renewed interest in kinship was also evident a surge in
anthropological activity within Europe. This was most readily evident in
the formation of the European Association of Social Anthropologists in
1990 (now with more than a thousand members), which in turn functioned as a major impetus for a resurgence of interest in kinship studies,
in general, within the discipline of social anthropology. This trend has
been reinforced by an increasing emphasis on kinship in the context of
new reproductive and genetic technologies—a literature that includes
a large number of influential studies based in the industrialized West.
In sum, kinship was most theoretically important to social anthropology when the societies of Europe were most neglected. Notwithstanding numerous significant exceptions, the broad pattern characterizing
mid-twentieth-century anthropology was a non-European focus and a
predominant concern with Third World societies. As the study of contemporary European culture began to emerge as a field in its own right
toward the end of the twentieth century, the theoretical importance of
kinship studies within anthropology had waned significantly, and even
come in some quarters to be considered indexical of an old-fashioned,
colonial anthropology that had rightly been left behind.

Although for all of the reasons outlined above, European kinship has
not been as widely studied as its counterparts in many other parts of
the world, it should also be stated that a substantial body of literature
addressing a wide range of kinship phenomena across Europe was nonetheless published during the mid to late twentieth century.[18] Indeed,
a 1991 survey, "Kinship Studies in Europe," revealed an unexpectedly
large and coherent body of scholarship on this topic, confirming that the
alleged decline of kinship studies was partly misperceived.[19] Were one to
speculate that loss of its former theoretical prominence (the importance
of kinship to anthropology has been compared to that of the nude to
art) perhaps partially eclipsed the actuality of its continuing empirical

importance, the complexity of the situation would no doubt be better captured.

Two final points need to be made concerning the origins of a return of anthropological attention to kinship, and these are of particular importance as they bring us into conversation with the question of kinship in the context of new reproductive and genetic technologies—which began to acquire increasing prominence from the 1980s onward. To begin with, an important source of the impetus to re-examine kinship derived not only from its long-standing theorization as a social practice that, though incontrovertibly rooted in the actual biological facts of sexual reproduction, nevertheless varied cross-culturally, but also from the entire nineteenth- and twentieth-century model of biology as a set of "true facts" on which society is "based." As noted earlier, the critique of the taken-for-granted equation of biological facts with incontrovertible and pre-determined social truths—such as the idea that the association of women with the domestic sphere derives from their biological role as mothers—had taken considerable impetus from feminist anthropology. Famously, in her 1985 paper at the American Anthropological Association meetings in Washington, DC, at a panel honoring the American anthropologist and kinship theorist David Schneider, feminist anthropologist Sylvia Yanagisako argued that Schneider's entire theory was flawed in that he had overlooked the most important implications of his own argument, which concerned the gender differences necessary for biological reproduction.[20] Schneider's presentation, "Doctrine of the Genealogical Unity of Mankind," was intended as a mocking jibe toward the Anglo-American over-reliance on a presumed genealogical (biological) "base" to kinship superstructures everywhere. He claimed this "doctrine" was ethnocentric: biology, in his view, was doing "symbolic" work not only within kinship systems but also in the anthropological study of kinship. In essence, he argued that anthropologists were projecting their own kinship values onto the people they studied and masking this ethnocentrism as scientific objectivity.[21] Yanagisako argued that "the model of natural difference" implied in the "biological facts of sexual reproduction" organized far more than kinship: it organized gender too and by implication also reproductive labor, family structure, and so forth (this argument was to reach a much fuller form shortly afterward in Judith Butler's *Gender Trouble*, probably the single most influential work of feminist theory since *The Second Sex*).[22]

A second major influence contributing to the resurgence of kinship studies was the re-evaluation of scientific knowledge coming from the broad area now known as science studies. Work by feminist theorists such as Donna Haraway from the 1970s onward, and also from scholars such as Bruno Latour, who took a quasi-anthropological approach to the laboratory in his famous study, *Science in Action*, began to introduce new models of "fact-making" in science that began to unsettle the categories of the "natural" and the "biological."[23] Since the 1980s, a steady stream of such studies by a growing number of scholars, including anthropologists, has contributed to the emergence of the study of science as culture as a subdiscipline in its own right.[24] This has been further aided by an increase in the number of ethnographic studies dedicated to bioscience and biomedicine.[25] The "biological facts of sexual reproduction" took a further stride into uncertainty with the onset of "the age of assisted conception," followed quickly by the scientific excitement and popular debate over cloning and stem cells. Today, of course, we live in a context in which, as Ian Wilmut has said, "nothing is biologically impossible anymore."[26]

While self-evident, the value of studying such changes anthropologically has been offset by the considerable debate about how best to do so. Moreover, while disappointing, it would be fair to say the question of kinship and the new biologies remains somewhat marginal to mainstream anthropology in Britain, Europe, and the United States. That said, there is nonetheless a significant core of studies of kinship in the context of new genetic technologies—and in particular genetic screening—to which this chapter will now turn.

## Kinship and the New Genetics: From Blood to Genes

Despite the diversity represented within existing studies of kinship in Europe, and at the risk of oversimplifying, two broad patterns can be generalized across the European frame that are of particular relevance to anthropological investigation of kinship in the context of new reproductive and genetic technologies: that European kin-reckoning is primarily bilateral and that blood predominates as the main idiom of shared bodily substance. Bilateral or cognatic kinship systems are defined by a dual tracing of descent through both the mother's and the father's "sides," and this is, of course, the system of kin-reckoning familiar to most Europeans. The system with which it is usually contrasted is unilateralism, as exemplified by patrilineal or matrilineal descent systems creating agnatic or uterine kin groups (unilineal descent groups) as a consequence. It is the absence of unilineal descent systems, and of corporate kin groups of the kind described in the literature for Africa and Oceania, that is one of the most notable characteristics of the European kinship pattern. Equally notable is the evidence, as demonstrated in the very impressive set of chapters prepared for this publication, that blood is a ubiquitous and overdetermined cultural idiom in Europe, which has taken a wide variety of often conflicting forms. Despite, or more likely because of, this often paradoxical and ambivalent capacity to signify, blood remains a paradigmatic substance of kin connection in Europe. In addition to being a very ancient component of privileged social ties denoted by concepts of spiritual and corporeal personhood, blood and blood connection are widely embedded idioms, central to the scriptures of the early church, to Roman and Teutonic law, and to a range of other foundational and historic traditions grounding contemporary European societies. Through blood is expressed a complex cultural knowledge of origins, descent, inheritance, and degrees of relatedness, in which the content of the blood connection is inseparable from its form (as in coats of arms, which both symbolically and literally, that is, materially, recapitulate and represent the bilateral nature of specific genealogies). Such knowledge is not only essential to individual identity and fundamental to understandings of inheritance and descent, but also the basis for a range of social institutions and practices, now and in the past. A typical example of the characteristic significance of blood in relation to kinship is provided by Elliot Leyton in his study of an Irish village: "A man's 'blood,' the physical and moral qualities of his ancestors, gives him the prestige he will bear as a child. ... The significance of the one blood is a consequence of the villager's beliefs that biological reproduction transmits not only physical characteristics, but also personality and worth. It follows from this that a man is his ancestors."[27]

The combination of a blood idiom that connects descent to procreation and a bilateral reckoning system which traces kinship equally from both parents is of particular significance in relation to the questions raised by the human genome project and new genetic technologies. What is striking, of course, is the close resemblance between the model of inheritance described by blood-based bilateralism and that described by biogenetics.[28] The cognatic model of shared bodily substance emphasizing equal and impartible links through procreation to both parental lines provides the basis on which knowledge about genes represented by scientific discourse can appear to be about "kinship," while kinship reckoning can similarly be understood to be "about genes." Significantly, there is simultaneously great "plasticity" to the blood, so that while a general pattern of bilateral descent based on an idiom of blood ties is evident across Europe, this pattern is enormously diverse in its expression and cross-cut, mediated, and filtered by numerous other kinship practices.[29] Very importantly, kinship practices are also "strategic": they may be regarded as part of the natural order of events (especially practices based on ideas about growth, nurture, parental care), or be considered of a different order altogether, such as in definitions of relatedness based on law or divine sanction.[30] This "switching-back-and forth" capacity, both of the blood idiom and the semi-naturalized connections it is often seen to represent, is very important in terms of what we later learn about genes. As it turns out, this lesson is not exactly what we might have expected.

To understand not only how the rising importance of genes, DNA, and the genetic sciences have reshaped understandings of blood connection, but also the reverse, how blood connection has reshaped ideas of genes, DNA, and the genetic sciences, we need to keep in mind two important facts about bilateralism. Unlike those unilateral descent systems that produce group boundaries by a rule of outmarriage (exogamy), bilateral kinship systems open up an infinite universe of potential kinship, in which "everyone" is eventually "related" by consanguinity. (It is possible that even the complexity of canonical restrictions governing acceptable degrees of relatedness for marriage to occur may derive in part from this "rimless wheel" effect of bilateralism.) It is for this reason that anthropologists studying the blood-based bilateral kinship systems of Europe continuously have pointed out that these systems not only create connections but, due to the unbounded scope of potential interconnectedness, also require means of producing disconnections. There are numerous ways in which this dual process of connection and disconnection can be seen to occur. The means through which individuals discriminate among consanguines, for example, is the focus of a considerable literature, particularly in the British Isles.[31] The importance of distinctions between "close" and "distant" kin, or "effective" and "ineffective" relatives, and the role of individuals in negotiating these degrees of distance and proximity have been stressed. Strathern expresses this as a fundamental opposition within the cultural values ascribed to English kinship: on the one hand there is a set of a priori ascriptions, on the other, a degree of individual choice.[32]

The embeddedness of blood-based kinship ties within other mechanisms for defining relatedness, the necessity for systems of disconnection to curtail the unlimited kin universe produced by bilateralism, and the active selection and negotiation of kin definition and degrees of acknowledged proximity by individual social agents or groups are but three of the well-documented mechanisms through which a potentially endless number of bilateral and cognatic "relations" are delimited in social practice. The mechanisms by which the kinship universes of individuals are extended, altered, restricted, and otherwise manipulated are crucial and exist both in tension and in necessary complementarity with blood as an idiom for "diffuse, enduring solidarity."[33] It should be emphasized that the perspective offered from social anthropology affirms repeatedly and across a wide range of contexts that the definition and recognition of kin is selective. Far from formulaic (despite the existence of complex, formal systems of rules and prohibitions), kinship is the focus of concerted activity at the levels of both content and form.

If new genetic technologies may be thought of, then, as new means of representing kinship, their significance thus also lies in both their content and their form: they offer new information about relatedness and a new language for it, as well as new signifiers that belong not to the traditional "soil-based" arboreal idioms used to express "sides," "lines," or "relations," but to the recent history of molecular biology in the scientific laboratory. This overlap between the biogenetic and European blood-based bilateral models of inheritance, descent, and relatedness creates a new means of switching back and forth between knowledge systems. In both cases, "ties" based on shared bodily substance can be "traced" through procreation, the same two "sides" are recognized, and descent is imagined as a line of connection based on shared bodily substance, etc. This similarity has consequences for understanding, but these consequences have proven somewhat different from initial expectations, not only because the systems are partially isomorphic but also because significant gaps divide them.

The early predictions, for example by British and European governments, about genetic literalization—that it would exercise a colonizing effect on the older and more colloquial idiom of blood-based consanguinity—foresaw the "language of the blood" becoming, in effect, a subordinated meaning system. Much of the fear of geneticization stemmed from this almost knee-jerk response to the increasing power of the genetic sciences and their object—the gene—a fear that rightly cannot be separated from the use of genetic science to legitimate the German racial hygiene program during World War II. One unwelcome possibility was that far from strengthening existing kinship ties, new forms of "genetic information" might cause conflict among kin. For example, in its Report to the British Government, published in January 1992, the Committee on the Ethics of Gene Therapy expressed the concern this way:

> The special qualities of genes and genetic events [may] give rise to different, and possibly conflicting, interests of kindred, including those yet unborn, who share, or might share, the same genes. For example, an individual might be the source of genetic information which is important to relatives. It might be important to their health care, decisions on parenthood, or life

plans which might be influenced by known health risks. Conversely, information which is important to a particular individual might only be obtainable from relatives.[34]

The difference between blood and genes as idioms of relatedness may be phrased as a contrast between forms of cultural knowledge. Within scientific discourse, genes (despite uncertainty regarding their precise nature) are seen to belong to an empirical order of truth as precise but abstract and disembodied "genetic information." In contrast, the truth of a blood tie is generally recognized to denote a wide range of diffuse, embodied, and physically shared cultural meanings. This "loose" quality of the blood tie is what enables its continual negotiation, or social "adjustment"—indeed this is what might be imagined to facilitate the use of blood to "make and unmake kin" because, like a bicycle, the blood idiom is ready to hand, and can be made to go "off road" quite easily. Hence, although "blood," as a symbol of the biological mechanism for the transmission of traits by procreation, may stand for genes, the reverse is not as readily envisaged because genes do not represent all of the meanings of blood—they are, in a sense, "narrower."

The reason for this can be stated simply. A significant distinction between the concept of blood as an idiom of kin ties and the science of biogenetics as a model of inheritance and relatedness lies in the location of these two knowledge systems. Blood could be described as "thicker than genes" in its longstanding cultural entrenchment in European history, whereas genes are deliberately symbolically impoverished within the system they "belong" to—namely, the authoritative, expert, exclusive, and elite knowledge system of science. Whereas the idea of blood may be encountered in a variety of contexts, among them traditional institutions of European society, such as the church or heraldry, the idea of genes is more likely to be encountered in the context of institutionalized medicine (e.g., prenatal or other genetic screening programs), in media discussions of scientific innovation, or in legal contexts, such as in criminal or family law.

Initially, then, while it seemed that genes, in becoming part of nonexpert discourse, might "map onto blood," it was also feared they might "geneticize" consanguinity—in effect replacing blood with genes. But as the gene has entered increasingly into ordinary speech, in car advertisements showcasing "BMW's DNA," or in references to someone as "not my genetic father," the question of the relationship of geneticization to consanguinity has had to be posed anew. As we shall see, the first crop of anthropological studies over the past decade has shown this relationship is far from straightforward or predictable.

# The Blooding of the Gene

Since the 1990s, a small specialist literature has arisen in anthropology concerning kinship and the new genetics, much of which has been focused on Britain, Europe, and the United States. Taken together, these studies can be characterized as largely addressing the most "obvious" context of the geneticization of consanguinity—that of people (mostly women) in medical settings having to make decisions about either reproductive outcomes (prenatal screening, amniocentesis, pre-implantation genetic diagnosis) or pathology (breast cancer screening). Some other studies have examined adoption. For the purposes of attempting to identify certain of the key dynamics in this literature, instead of providing a comprehensive summary, it is worth looking at two influential recent monographs—by American anthropologists Kaja Finkler and Rayna Rapp—that examine the new social powers of DNA by using the methods and perspectives of ethnography.[35]

In contrast to the claims of many commentators, such as Paul Rabinow, who have famously argued that new genetic technologies will break down older socialities based on the idea of natural facts and instead will create new "biosocialities" based on cultural values, a minority of scholars, including medical anthropologist Kaja Finkler, have argued that the new genetics have not precipitated the decline of the natural facts / social facts dichotomy, but have instead strengthened this distinction.[36] Controversially, Finkler argues that "biomedical explanations reinforce our notions that family and kinship are anchored in genetic ties, flowing from past to future, possessing a permanence that transcends time."[37] She calls this process the "medicalization of kinship," claiming that "our kinship relations have been given a new dimension that stresses faulty genes."[38] Like the British Ethics Committee report mentioned above, albeit for rather different reasons, Finkler's main thesis is that "the medicalization of kinship subverts the ideology of choice regarding the people one selects as one's kin."[39]

Using case studies of adoptees in search of their biological parents and women at risk of inherited breast cancer, Finkler provides examples of the ways in which individuals become reconnected to wider kin networks through "inherently impersonal" DNA molecules.[40] By means of family medical history, Finkler argues, peoples' day-to-day realities are changed by reconnecting to their genetic heritage, acquiring "a new sense of continuity with the past" through ties of suffering.[41] These ties, though urgently prominent, are, in Finkler's view, fundamentally ambivalent, as she illustrates with examples such as the following case of Karen. At the suggestion of her genetic counselor, Karen, a 39-year-old woman at risk of breast cancer, initiated a reunion with her 77-year-old maternal aunt, Alice, in order to learn more about her medical background. Finkler describes Karen's feelings of guilt about having lost contact with her mother's sister and re-establishing the connection only to acquire a blood sample. Moreover, Finkler depicts Karen's "contradictory feelings" about the positive outcome of the genetic tests—the option of a prophylactic mastectomy—"which will touch her at the core of her being as a traditional mother and wife and may physically convert her to the protected child she feels she is."[42] Alice, Karen's aunt, is willing to contribute a blood sample out of a sense of family obligation, even though she herself does not believe the disease is inherited and complains that "Karen just called me because I knew a lot, but they never come to see me."[43] Alice, then, may well be what Finkler describes as a paradigmatic "example of someone reunited with a family member only because of genetic ideologies of inheritance," but it is less clear that the example is as "remarkable" as Finkler claims.[44] The experiences of Alice and Karen may be "especially instructive in how the ideology of genetic inheritance defines for them a relationship with family and kin," but they are less so about what kind of relationship this is: Karen's case is cited as one in which "the belief in the genetic inheritance of disease has unwittingly brought [her] closer to [her] family," yet it is not clear what the "closeness" consists of. It could be said to reinforce their continuing distance in spite of genetic proximity.[45]

Leaving aside the important question of the extent to which such studies might be seen as tautological—by assuming a medical connection is one of "kinship"—the question remains as to whether "the medicalization of kinship" and "the hegemony of the gene" actually have the effect of reinforcing consanguineal ties, de-emphasizing conjugal and affinal ties, and deepening the significance of biological ties to distant kin, as Finkler claims.[46] In Finkler's view, the language of genetic inheritance "distanc[es] the person from his or her being," opening up a gap between experience and genetic identity.[47] She describes this situation as a phenomenological paradox in the form of a collision between everything known and familiar in a person's biography and experience and abstract medical knowledge about a genetic disorder. Hence, as Finkler notes, "the compartmentalized postmodern fragmented individual has become joined to his or her ancestors by DNA and to living relatives by the ideology of genetic inheritance."[48]

Rayna Rapp uses the somewhat different analogy of "moral pioneers" in her study of prenatal genetic testing in New York City, which introduces yet another set of "partial connections" at the level of both individual experience and institutional structures.[49] Rather than alien-

ated postmodern subjects reunited by the truth of their DNA, Rapp
finds resourceful immigrants on a new frontier, foregrounding what we
might call "discursive resourcefulness," or what was referred to above,
more simply, as switching back and forth. In attempting to provide a
"topography" of amniocentesis through a multi-sited ethnographic account of personal and professional encounters with prenatal chromosomal analysis, Rapp describes at length the "inadvertent imbrications"
that "frame the social conditions under which prenatal diagnosis became
conceivable."[50]

These "inadvertent imbrications" produce in Rapp's study, not a genetic gap so much as a genetic knowledge gap, that is a gap between
genetic information, which is often highly technical but incomplete, and
meaningful knowledge, which, by definition, is socially, not medically,
defined, evaluated, and acted upon. This gap is compounded both by the
time lag built into the technique of amniocentesis (between extraction
of amniotic fluid and analysis of its chromosomal content) and by the
social stratifications that mark encounters with the forms of reproductive choice and control the technique is designed to facilitate. Although
medical information is understood as "objective," and genetic counseling
is dedicated to the principles of non-interference and neutrality, no one
comes to amniocentesis with an objective or neutral social positioning,
individual identity, or cultural background. To the contrary, the difficult
choices involved in amniocentesis are highly stratified and differentiated
by personal circumstances, including gender, racial, ethnic, and class-
based forms of privilege, exclusion, and subordination.

These factors produce the "multiple intersections" that require "complex choreography" for both patients and professionals in the world
of prenatal genetic diagnosis and decision making.[51] Rapp shows how
"alternative and sometimes competing rationales" must be weighed up
and evaluated, often in complicated marital or family settings that can
generate what she describes as "kinship friction."[52] Initially based on
her own experience of amniocentesis, involving a positive diagnosis for
Down's syndrome and the subsequently painful decision to terminate
her pregnancy, Rapp's own retrospection about her encounter with
prenatal genetic diagnosis frames her investigation of the experiences
of others. She is attentive both to the burdens of decision making for
those in a position of disenfranchisement and social deprivation, and
to the very different burdens of privileged middle-class women, who
frequently become highly self-critical despite doing everything in their
power to act responsibly toward others. Both the burdens of lack—of
literacy, language, entitlement, financial resources, adequate healthcare,
and basic social support—and the costs of middle-class privilege, with all

of its overvaluation of control, rationality, and medical technology, are exhaustively chronicled in Rapp's nuanced and compassionate study of what has come to be called the geneticization of reproductive choice.

The concept "inadvertent imbrications" is thus another way to describe the complex linking up of the ordinary and the quotidian into odd, sometimes bizarre, combinations in the context of the new genetics.[53] This phrase could describe the circumstances of the well-educated woman who changed her mind about having an amniocentesis because, by coincidence, she met three women who had lost pregnancies after the test shortly before she was scheduled to have it herself—a situation Rapp attributes to "the gap between statistical risk figures and phenomenological experience."[54] It could also describe the "ordinary laboratory occurrence" of reading a cell with a chromosome count of 47, identifying the extra chromosome as number 21, counting thirty more cells to be sure, and logging a diagnosis of Down's syndrome, destined "to set off an extraordinary reaction in the hearts and minds of pregnant women and their supporters to whom it is shortly reported."[55] The macrosociological histories of birth control, access to abortion, attitudes toward disability, and the development of DNA amplification technology are also part of the "potent and heterogeneous social mix" Rapp refers to in her linkage analysis of what is "testing" about genetic tests.

The following case from Rapp's account provides what might be described as an ethnographic fragment, of conjoined and simultaneous dialogue, which is tellingly incoherent, and in which two different logics of genetic interpretation are seamlessly interwoven to produce what Rapp describes as a diagnostic "stand-off."[56] The background to the case is the discovery of "something ambiguous on the #9 chromosome of the sample" and a provisional diagnosis of "#9+." The closest condition to which this could be assimilated is "some clinical reports on trisomy 9," resulting in physical anomalies and mental retardation. After counseling, the mother decides to keep the pregnancy and gives birth in early June. A month later the genetics laboratory requests a consultation via the mother's obstetrician, and she agrees to attend with her baby son.

> He was a six-week-old Haitian boy named Etienne St-Croix. His mother, Veronique, spoke reasonably good English and good French. His grandmother, Marie-Lucie, who carried the child, spoke Creole and some French. The two geneticists spoke English, Polish, Hebrew, and Chinese between them. I translated into French, ostensibly for the grandmother and mother. ... The geneticist was gracious with Veronique but after a moment's chit-chat asked to examine the baby. She never spoke again to the mother during the examination. Instead, she and a second geneticist, both trained in pediatrics, handled the newborn with confidence and interest. The counselor took notes

as the geneticists measured and discussed the baby. "Note the oblique palpebral fissure and micrognathia," one called out. "Yes," answered Veronique in perfect time to the conversation, "he has the nose of my uncle Herve and the ears of Aunt Mathilde." As the geneticists pathologized, the mother genealogized, the genetic counselor remained silent, furiously taking notes, and the anthropologist tried to keep score.[57]

This episode, from Rapp's chapter "Refusing," is presented as an example of the problem of diagnostic ambiguity, and also as "a dramatic instance of interpretive standoff between biomedical discourse and family life."[58] The geneticists are working from known precedents to increase their scientific understanding by comparing a new case with previous cases through physical examination of the newborn "trisomy 9." Rapp observes that

> while the geneticists are confident that this child will share the developmental pattern reported in the literature for other children with very similar chromosomal patterns, the mother was quite aware of the idiosyncratic nature of the case, its lack of a clear-cut label and known syndrome. She therefore decided that the contest for interpretation was still an open one.[59]

Here, then, is the opposite finding from Finkler, in which a medicalized version of a genetic tie is resisted in favor of a more colloquial and adamantly familial one. The rejection of the medicalized version of genealogical connection is, furthermore, underscored by the decision to have the child—more or less against the medical advice. Asked about her decision after the examination is over, on the way to the subway, Veronique explains,

> If it had been Down's, maybe, just maybe I would have had an abortion. Once I had an abortion, but now I am a Seventh Day Adventist, and I don't believe in abortion anymore. Maybe for Down's, just maybe. But when they told me this, who knows? I was so scared, but the more they talked, the less they said. They do not know what this is. And I do not know either. So now, it's my baby. We'll just have to wait and see what happens. And so will they.[60]

In one sense, a perfectly comprehensible exchange has taken place between two sets of interested parties who have both different relationships to Etienne's birth and different knowledge priorities about the future. The shared context of diagnostic ambiguity is not a source of conflict: all of the parties involved, including the genetic counselor and the anthropologist, leave the conversation with their pre-existing assumptions unaffected, despite their lack of a shared interpretation or standpoint having been reinforced and the seriousness of the occasion in terms of what is at stake in the form of suspected genetic impairment.

For Rapp, what is important about this scene is not only that it is paradoxical, contradictory, and made up of "alternative and competing rationales," but also that it involves a direct rejection of biomedical expertise.[61] Using Rabinow's concept of biosociality discussed above, Rapp argues that "biomedicine provides discourses with hegemonic claims ... encouraging enrolment in the categories of biosociality. Yet these claims do not go uncontested, nor are these new categories of identity used untransformed. Religious orientations and practices, informal folk beliefs, class-based and ethnic traditions as well as scientifically-inflected counter discourses also lay claim to the interpretation of extra chromosom[al material]."[62]

What is clear from both Finkler's and Rapp's ethnographic accounts of the new genetics is the resilience of strategic agency in the face of conflicting versions of normality and abnormality. There is a lot of picking and choosing at the level of determining which information is accepted as useful knowledge, what kinds of authority are relied upon, and how individual decisions are reached amidst often conflicting individual, marital, and familial priorities. The central paradox of prenatal testing is that it is primarily sought as a form of reassurance that everything is "normal," when it is designed to detect exactly the reverse. Moreover, it is only in the event a test returns a "positive" finding that there are difficult decisions to be made. The most difficult decisions of all occur when normality is no longer a predicted outcome, which is, ironically, after the test has been "successful" in detecting genetic disease.

However, two different models of geneticization also emerge from these ethnographies. In Finkler's terms, geneticization is the cause of genealogical reconnection—it re-establishes kinship. For Rapp, existing social definitions of kinship can supersede geneticization, displacing it in favor of stronger, pre-existing kinship ties.

As Rapp notes, "in some sense, all positive diagnoses appear ambiguous to pregnant women" because genetic information is always partial.[63] Even when a chromosomal analysis is known with all possible certainty, it will not reveal how serious the disease will be, when its onset will occur, or how it may affect a child's lifespan. Even in the very rare cases of single gene disorders such as Tay-Sachs disease, spinal muscular atrophy, or Duchenne's muscular dystrophy, where the outcome can be predicted with tragically accurate clinical precision, the potential offspring is never fully reducible to a potential syndrome, even if the condition is terminal. Hence, the assumption that genes make us who we are is both too true to ignore and too partial to be enough truth by itself.

# Conclusion

Jeanette Edwards and Marilyn Strathern describe the "recombinant" quality of European kinship as one of its defining features: "at the core of English kinship thinking for much of the twentieth century has been the combination and division of phenomena for which at the end of the century we are just beginning to find metaphors."[64] While it would not be appropriate to generalize from this English example to the rest of Europe—where Anglophone accounts of kinship have already held too much sway—the framing of the question in this way is suggestive. What is noticeable is that this "recombinant" quality, the ability to shift explanatory registers and thus to "negotiate" the genetic "gap" that often arrives in lieu of genetic knowledge or understanding appears all the more prevalent in the context of the new genetics. While increasingly more precise authoritative scientific information about genes might be imagined to confirm beyond any doubt that kinship is indeed a social system "based on" the biological facts of genetic connection, the question of what this information means to people and the overwhelming ethnographic evidence that it is far from straightforward—no matter how "scientifically literate," well-educated, middle-class, or even medically trained its interpreters are—suggests a new paradox to kinship thinking: that greater scientific precision about shared genetic substance exists in inverse relation to the plasticity of kinship thinking. In other words, far from the impartiality of scientific discourse narrowing the meanings of genes, their revealed partiality actually increases their plasticity in social contexts.

In the context of this volume, we might ask further if this paradox presents another occasion to examine "what the blood is all about" as well. Certainly one of the most predominant findings in recent studies of the new genetics—so much so that it is increasingly hard to find any exceptions—is that the somewhat worrying, and flattening, effect of a geneticization of consanguinity, which it was imagined might possibly confirm the colonizing power of expert scientific discourse on DNA, is less in evidence than something that looks like the reverse. We would better describe the empirical findings from at least a dozen major studies were we to claim that expert discourse on DNA has in fact been "blooded" by being remodeled on the template of the traditional plasticity of the blood idiom. This suggests the "traffic in analogies" between blood and genes may be more defined by the lengthy history of the blood idiom than it is by the much shorter history of DNA. This ambiguity of genes is confirmed by the fact that the imagined causal power of the gene is in some disarray scientifically at present.[65] We can safely conclude that we may be just beginning to appreciate how much more the kinship significance of blood has to teach us about understandings of genetic relations, rather than the other way around.

# Notes

1. Several recent monographs and anthologies address the "new kinship studies," including Sarah Franklin and Susan McKinnon, eds., *Relative Values: Reconfiguring Kinship Study* (Durham, NC, 2001); Janet Carsten, ed., *Cultures of Relatedness: New Approaches to the Study of Kinship* (Cambridge, 2002); Janet Carsten, *After Kinship* (Cambridge, 2004); Marilyn Strathern, *Kinship, Law and the Unexpected: Relatives are Always a Surprise* (Cambridge, 2005); Ladislav Holy, *Anthropological Perspectives on Kinship* (London, 1996); Linda Stone, ed., *New Directions in Anthropological Kinship* (Lanham, MD, 2000).
2. This chapter draws on two previous publications. I am grateful to Marilyn Strathern for permission to reproduce sections of a co-authored 1991 Report for the European Commission Human Genome Division, Ethical, Legal and Social Implications Programme; Sarah Franklin and Marilyn Strathern, *Kinship and the New Genetic Technologies: An Assessment of Existing Anthropological Research* (Department of Social Anthropology, University of Manchester and EC, Brussels, DG VII). I am also grateful to the editors of *Anthropological Theory* for permission to reprint sections from "Re-thinking Nature-Culture: Anthropology and the New Genetics," *Anthropological Theory* 3, no. 1 (2003).
3. Charles Darwin *On the Origin of Species by Means of Natural Selection* (New York, 1864); Michel Foucault, *The Order of Things: An Archaeology of the Human Sciences* (New York, 1970).
4. Marilyn Strathern, *Reproducing the Future: Anthropology, Kinship and the New Reproductive Technologies* (Manchester, 1992); Marilyn Strathern, *After Nature: English Kinship in the Late Twentieth Century* (Cambridge, 1992)
5. J. A. Barnes, "Physical and Social Kinship," *Philosophy of Science* 28 (1961): 296–99; J. A. Barnes "Physical and Social Facts in Anthropology," *Philosophy of Science* 1 (1964): 294–97.
6. See in particular Carol MacCormack and Marilyn Strathern, eds., *Nature, Culture and Gender* (Cambridge, 1980); and Jane Collier and Sylvia Yanagisako, eds., *Gender and Kinship: Essays Toward a Unified Analysis* (Palo Alto, CA, 1987).
7. See Claude Lévi-Strauss, *Structural Anthropology* (London, 1963); and Claude Lévi-Strauss, *The Elementary Structures of Kinship* (London, 1969). For the expansion of these themes in contemporary French anthropology, see Françoise Héritier, *L'exercice de parenté* (Paris, 1981); and Marc Augé, ed., *Les domaines de la parenté* (Paris, 1975). For a review of the history of French kinship theory, see Martine Segalen, "The Shift in Kinship Studies in France: The Case of Grandparenting," in *Relative Values*, ed. Franklin and McKinnon, 246–73.
8. See Segalen, "The Shift in Kinship Studies in France."
9. Meyer Fortes, *Kinship and the Social Order* (Chicago, IL, 1969); E. E. Evans-Pritchard, *The Nuer: A Description of the Modes of Livelihood and Political Institutions of a Nilotic People* (Oxford, 1940); A. R. Radcliffe-Brown, *Structure and Function in Primitive Society* (Glencoe, IL, 1952).

10. Peter Laslett and R. Wall, eds., *Household and Family in Past Time* (Cambridge, 1972); J. L. Flandrin, *Families in Former Times: Kinship, Household and Sexuality* (Cambridge, 1979); Philippe Ariès, *Centuries of Childhood: A Social History of Family Life* (New York, 1965); Leonore Davidoff and Catherine Hall, *Family Fortunes: Men and Women of the English Middle Class, 1780–1950* (London, 1987); Elizabeth Bott, *Family and Social Networks*, 2nd ed. (London, 1971).

11. See in particular Martine Segalen, *Historical Anthropology of the Family* (Cambridge, 1986); Jack Goody, Joan Thirsk and E. P. Thompson, eds., *Family and Inheritance* (Cambridge, 1976); Jack Goody, *The Development of the Family and Marriage in Europe* (Cambridge, 1983).

12. Maurice Bloch and Stephen Guggenheim, "Compadrazgo, Baptism and the Symbolism of a Second Birth," *Man* 16, no. 3 (1981): 376–86.

13. Peter Parkes, "Milk Kinship in Southeast Europe: Alternative Social Structures and Foster Relations in the Caucasus and the Balkans," *Social Anthropology* 12, no. 3 (2004): 341–58; Morgan Clarke, "The Modernity of Milk Kinship," *Social Anthropology* 15, no. 3 (2007): 287–304; Peter Parkes, "Milk Kinship in Islam: Substance, Structure, History," *Social Anthropology* 13, no. 3 (2005): 307–29; Corinne Fortier, "Blood, Sperm and the Embryo in Sunni Islam and in Mauritania: Milk Kinship, Descent and Medically Assisted Procreation," *Body Society* 13 (2007): 15–36.

14. Sandra Bell and Simon Colemen, eds., *The Anthropology of Friendship* (Oxford, 1999).

15. See Janet Carsten, *The Heat of the Hearth: The Process of Kinship in a Malay Fishing Community* (Oxford, 1997), for a useful discussion of kinship systems based on feeding and dwelling rather than descent or filiation—an approach that has come to be associated with kinship as a processual, cumulative activity (an approach I refer to as the feeding rather than seeding approach).

16. For example, see Jack Goody, ed., *The Character of Kinship* (Cambridge, 1975).

17. This interest lay less in the power of kinship as a form of social organization than as a mode of perception, or cultural knowledge. See, for example, Mary Bouquet, *Reclaiming English Kinship: Portuguese Refractions of British Kinship Theory* (Manchester, 1993); Joan Bestard-Camps, *What's In a Relative: Household and Family in Formentara* (London, 1991); Strathern, *After Nature;* and Strathern, *Reproducing the Future.*

18. Anthony Cohen's anthology *Belonging: Identity and Social Organisation in British Rural Cultures* (Manchester, 1982) offers an excellent example of the strong tradition of kinship studies that continued in the context of the study of regional and rural identities. Urban identities were also linked to kinship, as in Raymond Firth, Jane Hupert, and Anthony Forge's famous 1969 publication, *Families and Their Relatives: Kinship in a Middle-Class Sector of London* (London, 1969); see also C. C. Harris, ed., *Readings in Kinship in Urban Society* (Oxford, 1970).

19. David Schneider *American Kinship: A Cultural Analysis* (Englewood Cliffs, NJ, 1968).

20. Sylvia Yanagisako, "The Elementary Structure of Reproduction in Kinship and Gender Studies," paper presented to the American Anthropological Association, Washington, DC (1985); and see Sylvia Yanagisako and Jane Collier, eds., *Gender and Kinship.*

21. David Schneider, *A Critique of the Study of Kinship* (Ann Arbor, MI, 1984).

22. For a fuller discussion of Schneider's work and Yanagisako's critique, see Sarah Franklin, *Embodied Progress: A Cultural Account of Assisted Conception* (London, 1997), esp. 17–72; Carsten, *After Kinship;* and Strathern, *After Nature.* In the same

way Yanagisako re-read Schneider as identifying a problem he did not fully diagnose, Butler reads De Beauvoir, but more radically: one does indeed become a woman— but through the repetitive, "stylising" effects of gender, rather than by the pre-given biological fact of sex; see Judith Butler, *Gender Trouble: Feminism and the Subversion of Identity* (New York, 1990).
23. Donna Haraway, *Simians, Cyborgs and Women: The Reinvention of Nature* (London, 1991); Bruno Latour, *Science in Action: How to Follow Scientists and Engineers Through Society* (Cambridge, MA, 1987); Bruno Latour and Steve Woolgar, *Laboratory Life: the Social Construction of Scientific Facts* (Beverley Hills, CA, 1979).
24. Sarah Franklin, "Science as Culture, Cultures of Science," *Annual Review of Anthropology* 24 (1995): 163–84.
25. See, for example, Paul Rabinow, *Making PCR: The Story of a Biotechnology* (Chicago, IL, 1996); Paul Rabinow, *Essays on the Anthropology of Reason* (Princeton, NJ, 1996); Paul Rabinow, *French DNA: Trouble in Purgatory* (Princeton, NJ, 2002); Sarah Franklin and Margaret Lock, eds., *Remaking Life and Death: Towards an Anthropology of the Biosciences* (Santa Fe, NM, 2003).
26. Ian Wilmut, Keith Campbell, and Colin Tudge, *The Second Creation: The Age of Biological Control by the Scientists Who Cloned Dolly* (London, 2000).
27. Elliot Leyton, "The One Blood: Kinship and Class in an Irish Village," Newfoundland Social and Economic Studies No. 15, Institute of Social and Economic Research (Saint Johns, 1975), 20.
28. See for example Carina Dennis, Richard Gallagher, and Philip Campbell, "Everyone's Genome," *Nature* 409 (2001): 815.
29. For a comprehensive account of this plasticity, see Jeanette Edwards and Carles Salazar, eds., *European Kinship in the Age of Biotechnology* (Oxford, 2009).
30. Charis Thompson devised the phrase "strategic naturalisation" to refer to the disembedding, re-embedding, and selective emphasis that enables couples using nonstandard means of conception, involving genetic contributions from third parties, to re-normalize their family structures through a highly intentional and selective use of some biological facts to the exclusion of others. See Charis Thompson, *Making Parents: the Ontological Choreography of New Reproductive Technology* (Cambridge, MA, 2005).
31. See, for example, Marilyn Strathern, *Kinship at the Core: An Anthropology of Elmdon, a Village in North-West Essex, in the 1960s*, foreword by Audrey Richards (Oxford, 1981).
32. See Strathern, *After Nature;* and also Jeanette Edwards, *Born and Bred: Idioms of Kinship and New Reproductive Technologies* (Oxford, 2000).
33. The expression "diffuse, enduring solidarity" comes from David Schneider, who used it to describe the character of the "American" kinship tie; see Schneider, *American Kinship*, 65.
34. *Report of the Committee on the Ethics of Gene Therapy*, col. 1788 (London: Her Majesty's Stationery Office, 1992), 16.
35. Kaja Finkler, *Experiencing the New Genetics: Family and Kinship on the Medical Frontier* (Philadelphia, PA, 2000); Rayna Rapp, *Testing Women, Testing the Fetus: the Social Impact of Amniocentesis in America* (New York, 1999).
36. For one example of this position, see Paul Rabinow, *Essays on the Anthropology of Reason* (Princeton, NJ, 1996).
37. Finkler, *Experiencing the New Genetics*, 43.
38. Finkler, *Experiencing the New Genetics*, 181.
39. Finkler, *Experiencing the New Genetics*, 185.

40. Finkler, *Experiencing the New Genetics*, 187.
41. Finkler, *Experiencing the New Genetics*, 186.
42. Finkler, *Experiencing the New Genetics*, 69.
43. Finkler, *Experiencing the New Genetics*, 73.
44. Finkler, *Experiencing the New Genetics*, 74.
45. Finkler, *Experiencing the New Genetics*, 74.
46. Finkler, *Experiencing the New Genetics*, 208.
47. Finkler, *Experiencing the New Genetics*, 209.
48. Finkler, *Experiencing the New Genetics*, 209.
49. Rapp, *Testing Women*, 306.
50. Rapp, *Testing Women*, 34.
51. Rapp, *Testing Women*, 24, 100.
52. Rapp, *Testing Women*, 10, 153.
53. Rapp, *Testing Women*, 34.
54. Rapp, *Testing Women*, 175.
55. Rapp, *Testing Women*, 219.
56. Rapp, *Testing Women*, 188.
57. Rapp, *Testing Women*, 187.
58. Rapp, *Testing Women*, 188.
59. Rapp, *Testing Women*, 188.
60. Rapp, *Testing Women*, 188.
61. Rapp, *Testing Women*, 10.
62. Rapp, *Testing Women*, 302, emphasis added.
63. Rapp, *Testing Women*, 188.
64. Jeanette Edwards and Marilyn Strathern, "Including Our Own," in *Cultures of Relatedness*, ed. Carsten, 163.
65. See Wilmut, Campbell, and Tudge, *Second Creation;* and Evelyn Fox Keller, *The Mirage of a Space Between Nature and Nurture* (Durham, NC, 2010).

# Bibliography

The following bibliography lists only printed primary and secondary sources, apart from classical Latin and medieval Latin texts. These last, according to US bibliographic custom, have been omitted except where they have been cited in translation, or in specified editions, by page numbers. Information on all omitted sources has been preserved, of course, in the individual chapter endnotes.

Alain of Lille [Alanus de Insulis]. *Distinctiones dictionis theologicum. Patrologia Latina* 201.

Alayash, Abdu I. "Hemoglobin-based Blood Substitutes and the Hazards of Blood Radicals." *Free Radical Research* 33 (2000): 341–48.

Albanese, Bernardo. *Le persone nel diritto privato romano.* n.p. [Palermo?], 1979.

Albornoz, Claudio Sánchez. *Estudios sobre las instituciones medievales españolas.* México, 1965.

Alighieri, Dante. *Convivio.* Edited by Giorgio Inglese. Milan, 1997.

Alonso, Hilario Casado. "Una familia de mercaderes castellanos extendida por toda Europa: Los Bernuy." Chapter in *El triunfo de Mercurio. La presencia castellana en Europa (siglos XV y XVI)*, 136–62. Burgos, 2003.

American Red Cross. "You Wouldn't Recognize Me …" (advertisement). *Wired,* May 2007, 32.

Amyraut, Moyse. *La morale chrestienne.* 4 pts. in 6 vols. Saumur, 1652–60.

Andreae, Ioannes [Johannes Andreae]. *Arbor consanguinitatis, mit Kommentar von Heinrich Greve.* Leipzig, not before 1492.

———. "Consanguinitas per tres regulas declaratur." In *Decretum Magistri Gratiani*, vol. 1 of *Corpus iuris canonici*, edited by Emil Friedberg, col. 1427–36. Leipzig, 1879.

———. *Super arboribus consanguinitatis, affinitatis et cognationis spiritualis* [German]. Strasbourg, before 1482.

———. "Commentarium in quartum decretalium librum Novella. De cons. et affinitate cap. VIII." In *In quinque decretalium libros novella commentaria*. Venice, 1581. Repr. Turin, 1963.

Antón, José Monsalvo. *Teoría y evolución de un conflicto social. El antisemitismo en la corona de Castilla en la baja Edad Media*. Madrid, 1985.

Appadurai, Arjun. "Introduction: Commodities and The Politics of Value." In *The Social Life of Things: Commodities in Cultural Perspective*, edited by Arjun Appadurai, 3–63. Cambridge, 1986.

Appleton, Andrea. "Blood Quantum: A Complicated System that Determines Tribal Membership Threatens the Future of American Indians." *High Country News* 41 (2009): 14–18.

Aquinas, Thomas. *Aquinas: Summa theologiae, Questions on God*. Edited by Brian Davies and Brian Leftow. Cambridge Texts in the History of Philosophy. Cambridge, 2006.

———. "Quaestio LIV, 'De impedimento consanguinitatis.'" In vol. 7 of *"Summa theologica" diligenter emendata Nicolai et al., notis ornata*. 8 vols. Luxemburg, 1870.

Ariès, Philippe. *Centuries of Childhood: A Social History of Family Life*. 1st Vintage ed. New York, 1965.

Aristotle. *Generation of Animals*. Translated by A. L. Peck. Loeb Classical Library 366. Cambridge, MA, 1942.

Arnauld, Antoine. *Lettres de Monsieur Antoine Arnauld*. 9 vols. Nancy, 1727.

Arrêt du Conseil d'État du Roi du 5 avril 1778. In *Race et esclavage*, by Pierre Boulle, 258. Paris, 2007.

Arteta, Antonio Ubieto, ed. *Crónica de Alfonso III*. Valencia, 1971.

Aubert, Guillaume. "'Nègres ou mulâtres nous sommes tous français.' Race, genre et nation à Gorée et Saint-Louis du Sénégal, fin XVIIᵉ–fin XVIIIᵉ siècle." In *Être et se penser Français. Nation, sentiment national et identités dans le monde atlantique français du XVIIᵉ au XIXᵉ siècle*, edited by Cécile Vidal (forthcoming).

———. "'The Blood of France.' Race and Purity of Blood in the French Atlantic World." *William and Mary Quarterly*, 3rd ser., 61 (July 2004): 439–78.

———. "'To Establish One Law and Definite Rules': Race, Religion, and the Transatlantic Origins of the Louisiana Code Noir." In *Louisiana and the Atlantic World*, edited by Cécile Vidal (forthcoming).

Aubigné, Théodore Agrippa d'. *Les tragiques*. Edited by A. Garnier and J. Plattard. Paris, 1932.

Augé, Marc, ed. *Les domaines de la parenté*. Paris, 1975.

Aurell, Martin. "La parenté en l'an mil." *Cahiers de civilisation médiévale* 43 (2000): 125–42.

Autrand, Françoise. *Naissance d'un grand corps de l'Etat. Les gens du Parlement de Paris, 1345–1454*. Paris, 1981.

———. "Tous parens, amis et affins: Le groupe familial dans le milieu de robe parisien au XVᵉ siècle." In *Commerce, finances et société*, edited by Philippe Contamine, Thierry Dutour, and Bertrand Schnerb, 347–57. Paris, 1993.

Aymar [Aymar de Blois]. "Étude historique sur les droits de sucession en Bretagne." *Bulletin archéologique* (1852).

Baer, Yitzhah. *A History of the Jews in Christian Spain*. 2 vols. Philadelphia, PA, 1966.

Bailey, David R. Shackleton. *Two Studies in Roman Nomenclature*, 2nd ed. New York, 1991.

Barnes, J. A. "Physical and Social Facts in Anthropology." *Philosophy of Science* 1 (1964): 294–97.

———. "Physical and Social Kinship." *Philosophy of Science* 28 (1961): 296–99.

Barry, Laurent. *La Parenté*. Paris, 2008.

Bartlett, Robert. "Medieval and Modern Concepts of Race and Identity." In "Race and Ethnicity in the Middle Ages," edited by Thomas G. Hahn. Special issue, *Journal of Medieval and Early Modern Studies* 31 (2001): 39–56.

Barton, Simon. *The Aristocracy in Twelfth-Century León and Castile*. Cambridge, 1997.

Barzun, Jacques. *The French Race: Theories of Its Origins and Their Social and Political Implications prior to the Revolution*. New York, 1932.

Baudy, Dorothea. "Matralia," *Der Neue Pauly* 7 (1999): 1027–28.

———. "Parentalia," *Der Neue Pauly* 9 (2000): 330–31.

Bechstedt, Johann [Johannes Bechstadius]. *Collatio jurium connubalium, tam universorum et communium, quam municipalium quorundam, inter congnatos et affines.* ... Coburg, 1626.

Bell, David. *The Cult of the Nation: Inventing Nationalism, 1680–1800*. Cambridge, MA, 2001.

*Bell, Sandra, and Simon Coleman, eds. The Anthropology of Friendship. Oxford, 1999.*

Bellavitis, Anna, Laurence Croq, and Monica Martinat, eds. *Mobilité et transmission dans les sociétés de l'Europe moderne*. Rennes, 2009.

Belleforest, François de. *Les grandes annales et histoire générale de France.* ... Paris, 1579.

Berceo, Gonzalo de. *Milagros de Nuestra Señora*. Madrid, 1982.

Berg, Marc, and Annemarie Mol, eds. *Differences in Medicine: Unraveling Practices, Techniques, and Bodies*. Durham, NC, 1998.

Bernáldez, Andrés. *Historia de los Reyes Católicos*. In vol. 70 of *Biblioteca de autores españoles*, 599–699. Madrid, 1953.

Berriot-Salvadore, Évelyne. "Le discours de la médecine et de la science." Chap. 11 in *XVIe–XVIIIe siècle*. Sous la direction de Natalie Zemon Davis and Arlette Farge. Vol. 3 of *Histoire des femmes en Occident*. Edited by Georges Duby, Michelle Perrot, et al. Paris, 2002.

Bertaut, J. *Les oeuvres poetiques*. Paris, 1611.

Bérulle, Pierre de. "Discours de l'estat et des grandeurs de Jesus." In vol. 1 of *Oeuvres complètes de Cardinal Bérulle*. 2 vols. Paris, 1644. Repr. Montsoult, 1960.

———. *Oeuvres complètes*. Texte établi et annoté by Michel Dupuy. Paris, 1995–.

Beseler, Gerhardt. "*Aequitas*." *Zeitschrift der Savigny-Stiftung für Rechtsgeschichte* 45 (1925): 454.

Bestard-Camps, Joan. *What's In a Relative: Household and Family in Formentara*. London, 1991.

Bettini, Maurizio. *Familie und Verwandtschaft im antiken Rom*. Frankfurt am Main and New York, 1992.

Biale, David. *Blood and Belief: The Circulation of a Symbol between Jews and Christians*. Berkeley, CA, 2007.

Biet, Christian. *Œdipe en monarchie: Tragédie et théorie juridique à l'âge classique*. Paris, 1994.

Bildhauer, Bettina. *Medieval Blood*. Cardiff, 2006.

Billacois, François. *Le duel dans la société française des XVIe–XVIIe siècles. Essai de psychologie historique*. Paris, 1986.

Biondi, Biondo. *La giustizia. Le persone*. Vol. 2 of *Il diritto romano cristiano*. Milan, 1952.

Blaise, Albert. *Dictionnaire latin-français des auteurs chrétiens*. Strasbourg, 1954. http://www.brepolis.net.

Blanchard, Abbé Jean-Baptiste-Xavier Duchesne. *L'école des moeurs*. 3 vols. Paris, 1812.

Bloch, Maurice, and Stephen Guggenheim. "Compadrazgo, Baptism and the Symbolism of a Second Birth." *Man*, n.s. 16, no. 3 (1981): 376–86.

Bluche, François. *Louis XIV.* Translated by Mark Greengrass. New York, 1990.
Bondio, Mariacarla Gadebusch, ed. *Blood in History and Blood Histories.* Florence, 2005.
Bonfante, Pietro. *Diritto di famiglia.* Vol. 1 of *Corso di diritto romano.* Rome, 1925.
Bonnassie, Pierre. "Consommation d'aliments immondes et cannibalisme de survie dans l'Occident du Haut Moyen Age." Chap. 5 of *Les sociétés de l'an mil. Un monde entre deux âges.* Brussels, 2001.
Bononiensis, Tancredus [Tancredus of Bologna]. *Tancredi summa de matrimonio.* Edited by Agathon Wunderlich. Göttingen, 1841.
Borchardt, Karl. "Tancred v. Bologna." In vol. 8 of *Lexikon des Mittelalters.* Edited by Robert-Henri Bautier et al. Munich, 1997.
Bossuet, Jacques-Bénigne. *De la connaissance de Dieu et de soi-même.* In vol. 23 of *Oeuvres complètes,* edited by F. Lachat. Paris, 1864.
————. *Élévations sur les mystères.* Edited by Maturin Dréano. Paris, 1962.
————. *Méditations sur l'évangile.* Critical edition by M. Dréano. Études de théologie et d'histoire de la spiritualité. Paris, 1966.
————. *Oeuvres complètes de Bossuet.* 12 vols. Paris, 1845–46.
————. *Oeuvres complètes de Bossuet.* ... Edited by F. Lachat. 31 vols. Paris, 1862–75. Gallica.bnf.fr.
————. *Oraison funèbre de très haute et très puissante princesse Anne de Gonzague de Clèves.* In vol. 6 of *Oeuvres oratoires,* edited by J. Lebarq, revised and expanded by Ch. Urbain and E. Levesque. Paris, 1922–27.
————. "Précis d'un sermon pour la fête de la nativité de la Sainte Vierge." In vol. 11 of *Oeuvres complètes de Bossuet,* edited by F. Lachat, 121–29. Paris 1863.
————. "Premier sermon pour la fête de la conception de la Sainte Vierge." In vol. 11 of *Oeuvres complètes de Bossuet,* edited by F. Lachat, 1–20. Paris, 1863.
————. "Second sermon pour la fête de la conception de la Sainte Vierge." In vol. 11 of *Oeuvres complètes de Bossuet,* edited by F. Lachat, 20–42. Paris, 1863.
————. "Sermon sur le mystère de la très-Sainte Trinité." In *Sermons.* Vol. 4 of *Oeuvres complètes de Bossuet,* 1–8. Paris, 1846.
————. "Troisiéme sermon pour la fête de l'annonciation." In vol. 11 of *Oeuvres complètes,* edited by F. Lachat, 164–176. Paris, 1863.
————. "Troisième sermon pour la fête de la nativité de la Sainte Vierge." In *Sermons.* Vol. 4 of *Oeuvres complètes de Bossuet,* 152–58. Paris, 1846.
————. "Troisième sermon pour la fête de la nativité de la Sainte Vierge." In vol. 11 of *Oeuvres complètes,* edited by F. Lachat, 100–21. Paris, 1863.
Bott, Elizabeth. *Family and Social Network.* 2nd ed. London, 1971.
Boulle, Pierre. *Race et esclavage dans la France de l'Ancien Régime.* Paris, 2007.
Bouquet, Mary. *Reclaiming English Kinship: Portuguese Refractions of British Kinship Theory.* Manchester, 1993.
Bourdaloue, Louis. "Second sermon sur l'annonciation de la Vierge." In vol. 5 of *Oeuvres complètes de Bourdaloue de la compagnie de Jésus.* New ed., 6 vols. Paris, 1905.
Bourdieu, Pierre. *La noblesse d'État. Grandes écoles et esprit de corps.* Paris, 1989.
Boureau, Alain. "Hérédité, erreurs et vérité de la nature humaine (XIIᵉ–XIIIᵉ siècles). In Van der Lugt and Miramon, *L'hérédité entre Moyen Âge et Époque moderne,* 67–82.
Braun, Christina von, and Christoph Wulf, eds. *Mythen des Blutes.* Frankfurt am Main and New York, 2007.
Brennan, Teresa. *Globalization and Its Terrors.* New York, 2003.
Brizieux, Auguste. *Les Bretons, poème couronné par L'Académie française.* Paris, 1848.
Broglie, Gabriel de. *Madame de Genlis.* Paris, 2001.

Brückner, Hieronymus. *Hieronymi Bruckneri I.U.D., Consil. Saxo-Gothani aulici et consistorialis decisiones iuris matrimonialis controversi.* Frankfurt and Leipzig, 1692.

Brunelle, Gayle K. "Dangerous Liaisons: Mésalliances and Early Modern French Noble Women." *French Historical Studies* 19 (1995).

Burgault, Emile. "Origine du domaine congéable." *Bulletin du Société polymathique du Morbihan* (1868; 1869).

Burguière, André. "Un nom pour soi. Le choix du nom de baptême en France sous l'Ancien Régime (XVIe–XVIIIe siècles)." *L'Homme* 20, no.4 (1980): 25–42.

Burke, Maria. "Is Artificial Blood the Way of the Future?" *The Times*, 6 January 2006.

Burke, Peter. *Languages and Communities in Early Modern Europe.* Cambridge, 2004.

Burkert, Walter. "'Blutsverwandtschaft': Mythos, Natur und Jurisprudenz." In Braun and Wulf, *Mythen des Blutes*, 245–56.

Butler, Judith. *Antigone's Claim: Kinship between Life and Death.* New York, 2000. Repr. New York, 2002.

———. *Gender Trouble: Feminism and the Subversion of Identity.* New York, 1990.

Bynum, Caroline Walker. *Holy Feast and Holy Fast: The Religious Significance of Food to Medieval Women.* Berkeley, CA, 1987.

———. *The Resurrection of the Body in Western Christianity: 200–1336.* New York, 1995.

———. "Der weibliche Körper und religiöse Praxis im Spätmittelalter." In *Fragmentierung und Erlösung. Geschlecht und Körper im Glauben des Mittelalters*, edited by Caroline Walker Bynum, 148–225. Frankfurt am Main, 1996.

———. *Wonderful Blood: Theology and Practice in Late Medieval Northern Germany and Beyond.* Philadelphia, PA, 2007.

Camus, Jean-Pierre. *Homélies des États Généraux (1614–1615).* Edited by Jean Descrains. Geneva, 1970.

Carlo De Lellis. *Discorsi delle famiglie nobili del Regno di Napoli.* 3 vols. Ed. anast., Bologna, 1968.

Carsten, Janet. *After Kinship.* Cambridge, 2003; Cambridge and New York, 2004.

———. *The Heat of the Hearth: The Process of Kinship in a Malay Fishing Community.* Oxford, 1997.

———. "The Substance of Kinship and the Heat of the Hearth: Feeding, Personhood and Relatedness among Malays of Pulau Langkawi." *American Ethnologist* 22 (1995): 223–41.

———. "Substantivism, Antisubstantivism, and Anti-Antisubstantivism." In Franklin and McKinnon, *Relative Values: Reconfiguring Kinship Studies*, 29–53.

Carsten, Janet, ed. *Cultures of Relatedness: New Approaches to the Study of Kinship.* Cambridge, 2000.

Cartagena, Alonso de. *Defensorium Unitatis Christiana: tratado en favor de los judios conversos.* Edited by Manuel Alonso. Madrid, 1943.

Castelnuovo, Guido. "Revisiter un classique. Noblesse, hérédité et vertu d'Aristote à Dante et à Bartole (Italie communale, début XIIIe–milieu XIVe siècle)." In Van der Lugt and Miramon, *L'hérédité entre Moyen Âge et Époque moderne*, 105–55.

Castiglione, Baldassar. *Il libro del cortegiano.* Edited by Amedeo Quondam and Nicola Longo. Milan, 2009.

Cerda, Juan de la. *Weiblicher Lustgarten.* Teil 1. Translated by Aegidius Albertinus. Munich, 1605.

Cervantes, Miguel de. *Don Quijote de la Mancha.* Edited by Martín de Riquer. 2 vols. 12th ed. Barcelona, 1995.

Chadwick, Nora K. *Early Brittany.* Cardiff, 1969.

Champeaux, Ernest. "*Jus sanguinis*, trois façons de calculer la parenté au Moyen Age." *Revue historique de droit français et étranger* 4, no. 12 (1933): 241–90.

Charle, Christophe. *Les élites de la République, 1880–1900*. Paris, 1987.

Chenu, Marie-Dominique. "Sang du Christ." In vol. 4 of *Dictionnaire de théologie catholique*, cols. 1094–97.

Clarke, Morgan. "The Modernity of Milk Kinship." *Social Anthropology* 15, no. 3 (2007): 287–304.

Clichtove, Josse. *Le livre et traicté de toute vraye noblesse (par J. Clichtove), nouvellement translaté de latin en françoys.* Lyon, 1533.

Closmadeuc, M. de. "Allocution de M. de Closmadeuc en prenant le fauteuil de la présidence." *Bulletin du Société polymathique du Morbihan* (1867): 2.

Cloud, Duncan. "*Parricidium:* From the *lex Numae* to the *lex Pompeia de parricidiis.*" *Zeitschrift der Savigny-Stiftung für Rechtsgeschichte* 88 (1971): 1–66.

Cohen, Anthony. *Belonging: Identity and Social Organisation in British Rural Cultures.* Manchester, 1982.

Cohen, Ed. *A Body Worth Defending: Immunity, Biopolitics, and the Apotheosis of the Modern Body.* Durham, NC, 2009.

Collett, Pierre. *Traité des dispenses en général et en particulier, dans lequel on résout les principales difficultés, qui regardent cette matière.* 3 vols. 3rd ed. Paris, 1752–53.

Collier, Jane, and Sylvia Yanagisako, eds. *Gender and Kinship: Essays Toward a Unified Analysis.* Palo Alto, CA, 1987.

Collins, James. *Classes, Estates, and Order in Early Modern Brittany.* Cambridge, 1994.

Columbia Presbyterian Medical Center. "The Nuts and Bolts of Bone Marrow Transplants." http://cpmcnet.columbia.edu/dept/medicine/bonemarrow/bmtinfo.html.

Comitibus, Prosdocimus de. "Tractatus de arbore consanguinitatis et affinitatis." In vol. 9 of *Tractatus universi iuris, duce, et auspice Gregorio XIII in unum congesti*, fols. 141r–144v. Venice, 1584–86.

Condorcet, Jean-Antoine-Nicolas de Caritat, Marquis de. *Réflexions sur l'esclavage des Nègres.* Neufchastel, 1781.

*Congrès celtique internationale tenu à Saint-Brieuc (Cotes-du-Nord), Bretagne, en octobre 1867: séances, mémoires.* Saint-Brieuc, 1868.

Conte, Edouard, and Cornelia Essner. *La Quête de la race. Une anthropologie du nazisme.* Paris, 1995.

Cooper, Frederick, and Ann Laura Stoler, eds. *Tensions of Empire: Colonial Cultures in a Bourgeois World.* Berkeley and Los Angeles, CA, 1997.

Cooper, Melinda. *Life as Surplus: Biotechnology and Capitalism in the Neoliberal Era.* Seattle, WA, 2008.

Copeman, Jacob. "Blood, Blessings, and Technology in India." *Cambridge Anthropology* 25 (2005–6): 39–51.

———. *Veins of Devotion: Blood Donation and Religious Experience in North India.* New Brunswick, NJ, and London, 2009.

Copeman, Jacob, ed. "Blood Donation, Bioeconomy, Culture." Special issue, *Body & Society* 15 (2009).

Corneille, Pierre. *Théatre complet de Corneille.* Edited by Maurice Rat. 3 vols. Paris, n.d. [1942]. See especially *Agésilas, Andromède, Héraclius, Horace, Le Cid, Médée, Nicomède, Polyeucte, Pompée, Rodogune, Sertorius, Théodore,* and *Toison d'or.*

Cornette, Joël. *Des âges obscurs à Louis XIV.* Vol. 1 of *Histoire de la Bretagne et des Bretons.* Paris, 2005.

Corominas, Joan. *Diccionario crítico etimológico de la lengua castellana.* 4 vols. Madrid, 1954–57.

*Corpus de la littérature médiévale.* http://www.championelectronique.net.

*Corpus iuris canonici.* Edited by Emil Friedberg. 2 vols. Leipzig, 1879. Microform repr. Graz, 1959.

*Correspondance inédite de Mademoiselle Théophile de Fernig, aide de camp du général Dumouriez … Avec une introduction et notes par Honoré Bonnehomme.* Paris, 1873.

Corro, Juan Escobar del. *Tractatus bipartitus de puritate et nobilitate probanda … Philippo IV latae, Matriti, 10. februarii … 1623.* Lyon, 1637.

Cosandey, Fanny. "La maîtresse de nos biens. Pouvoir féminin et puissance dynastique dans la monarchie française d'Ancien Régime." *Historical Reflections/Réflexions historiques* 32, no. 2 (2006): 381–401.

*The Council of Trent: The Canons and Decrees of the Sacred and Oecumenical Council of Trent.* Edited and translated by J. Waterworth. London, 1848. http://history.hanover.edu/texts/trent.html.

Courson, Aurélien-Marie, Comte de. *Essai sur l'histoire, la langue et les institutions de la Bretagne armoricaine.* Paris, 1840.

*Coûtumes générales du Duché d'Aoste, proposées et rédigées par écrit en l'Assemblée des trois États: gens d'église, nobles, patriciens et coûtumiers […] confirmé et approuvé par Son Altesse.* Aoste, 1684.

Cox, Cheryl A. *Household Interests: Property, Marriage Strategies, and Family Dynamics in Ancient Athens.* Princeton, NJ, 1998.

Crawford, Michael H., ed. *Roman Statutes.* 2 vols. London, 1996.

Crébillon, P. J., père [Prosper Jolyot Crébillon]. *Idoménée.* In vol. 1 of *Oeuvres.* Paris, 1831.

*Crónica de Alfonso III.* Edited by Antonio Ubieto Arteta. Valencia, 1971.

Curty, Olivier. *Les parentés légendaires entres cités grecques.* Geneva, 1995.

Cyntholtz, Ioannes [Lintholtz]. "Tractatus seu commentaria in arborem consanguinitatis, affinitatis, cognationis spiritualis atque legalis." In vol. 9 of *Tractatus universi iuris,* fols. 145r–58r. Venice, 1584–86.

Darmon, Pierre. *Le mythe de la procréation à l'âge baroque.* Paris, 1977.

Darwin, Charles. *On the Origin of Species by Means of Natural Selection.* New York, 1864.

Davies, Brian, and Brian Leftow, eds. *Aquinas: Summa theologiae, Questions on God.* Cambridge Texts in the History of Philosophy. Cambridge, 2006.

*Déclaration du Roi du 8 février 1726.* In vol. 3 of *Loix et constitutions des colonies françaises de l'Amérique sous le vent,* edited by Médéric-Louis-Elie *Moreau de Saint-Méry.* 6 vols. Paris and Cap Français, Saint-Domingue, 1784–90.

*Le Defensoire de la conception de la glorieuse Vierge Marie, en forme de dialogue a Rouen chez Maistre Martin Morin, l'An de grace 1515.* In *Monumenta Italo-Gallica ex tribus auctoribus maternâ linguâ scribentibus pro Immaculata Virginis Mariae Conceptione. Scilicèt, P. Domenico de Carpane, Nicolao Grenier, et anonymo colloquio inter sodalem et amicum. Pars secunda.* Edited by Pedro de Alva y Astorga. 3 vols. in 2. Louvain, 1666. Repr. Bruxelles, 1967.

Deissmann, Marie-Luise. "Inzest." In *Antike Medizin. Ein Lexikon,* edited by K.-H. Leven, 462–63. Munich, 2005.

Delille, Gérard. "Kinship, Marriage, and Politics." In Sabean, Teuscher, and Mathieu, *Kinship in Europe: Approaches to Long-Term Development (1300–1900),* 163–83.

———. *Le maire et le prieur. Pouvoir central et pouvoir local en Méditerranée occidentale (XVᵉ–XVIIIᵉ siècle).* Rome, 2003.

———. "Parenté et alliance en Europe occidentale. Un essai d'interprétation générale." *L'Homme,* no. 193 (2010): 75–136.

Dennis, Carina, Richard Gallagher, and Philip Campbell. "Everyone's Genome." *Nature* 409 (2001): 815.

Derouet, Bernard. "Le partage des frères. Héritage masculin et reproduction sociale en Franche-Comté aux XVIII<sup>e</sup> et XIX<sup>e</sup> siècles." *Annales. Économies, Sociétés, Civilisations* [*Annales ESC*] (1993): 453–74.

———. "Pratiques de l'alliance en milieu de communauté familiales (Bourbonnais, 1600–1750)." In *Le choix du conjoint,* edited by G. Brunet, A. Fauve-Chamoux, M. Oris, 227–51. Lyon, 1998.

———. "Territoire et parenté. Pour une mise en perspective de la communauté rurale et des formes de reproduction familiale." *Annales. Histoire, Sciences Sociales* [*Annales HSS*] (1995): 645–86.

Desan, Suzanne. *The Family on Trial in Revolutionary France.* Berkeley and Los Angeles, CA, 2004.

Descimon, Robert. "Chercher de nouvelles voies pour interpréter les phénomènes nobiliaires dans la France moderne. La noblesse, 'essence' ou rapport social?" *Revue d'histoire moderne et contemporaine* 46, no. 1 (1999): 5–21.

Descimon, Robert, and Elie Haddad, eds. *Les preuves de noblesse.* Paris, 2010.

Devyver, André. *Le sang épuré. Les préjugés de race chez les gentilshommes français de l'Ancien Régime (1560–1720).* Editions de l'Université de Bruxelles. Brussels, 1973.

Dewald, Jonathan. *Aristocratic Experience and the Origins of Modern Culture: France, 1570–1715.* Berkeley, CA, 1993.

*Diccionario de la lengua castellana en que se explica el verdadero sentido de las voces.* ... 6 vols. Madrid, 1737. Facsimile ed. Madrid, 1979.

*Dictionnaire de L'Académie françoise dédié au Roy.* 1st ed. Paris, 1694.

*Dictionnaire de L'Académie françoise.* 4th ed. Paris, 1762.

*Dictionnaire du Moyen Français.* Edited by Robert Martin. http://www.atilf.fr/dmf.

*Digesta Iustiniani Augusti recognouit adsumpto in operis societatem Paulo Kruegero, Th. Mommsen.* Berolini [Berlin], 1868–70.

*Discours sur le congé impétré par Monsieur le Cardinal de Lorraine.* ... s.l., 1565.

Dominici, Domenico. *De sanguine Christi tractatus reueren. D.d. Dominici de Dominicis veneti, episcopi Torcellani & Brixiensis theologi praestantissimi. Accessit Tractatus eiusdem de filiazione Ioannis Evangelistae ad b. Virginem pulcherrimus. Indicem quaesitorum quarta pagina explicabit.* Venice, 1557.

Donati, Claudio. *L'idea di nobiltà in Italia. Secoli XIV–XVIII.* Rome and Bari, 1988.

Doubleday, Simon R. *The Lara Family: Crown and Nobility in Medieval Spain.* Cambridge, MA, 2001.

Doumerc, Bernard. "'De lignée antique et consanguine.' L'idéologie nobiliaire à Venise (fin XV<sup>e</sup>–début XVI<sup>e</sup> siècle)." In *Le sang au Moyen Age. Actes du quatrième colloque international de Montpellier, Université Paul-Valéry, 27–29 novembre 1997,* 87–108. Montpellier, 1999.

Du Laurens, André. *Toutes les oeuvres, trad du Latin par Gelée.* Paris, 1621.

Dubois, Laurent. *A Colony of Citizens: Revolution and Slave Emancipation in the French Caribbean, 1787–1804.* Chapel Hill, NC, 2004.

Duby, Georges. "Lignage, noblesse et chevallerie au XII<sup>e</sup> siècle dans la région maconnaise. Une révision." *Annales. Économies, Sociétés, Civilisations* [*Annales ESC*] 27 (1972): 803–23.

———. *Hommes et structures du Moyen Age.* Paris and The Hague, 1973.

———. "La noblesse dans la France médiévale. Une enquête à poursuivre." *Revue historique* 226 (1961): 1–22.

Duden, Barbara. *The Woman Beneath the Skin*. Translated by Thomas Dunlap. Cambridge, MA, 1991.

Duhamelle, Christophe. *L'héritage collectif. La noblesse d'Eglise rhénane, 17ᵉ et 18ᵉ siècles*. Paris, 1998.

Dupont, Clémence. *Les constitutions de Constantin et le droit privé au début du IVᵉ siècle. Les personnes*. Lille, 1937.

Dupont, Florence. "Le lait du père romain." In *Corps romains*, edited by Philippe Moreau, 115–37. Grenoble, 2002.

Dupont-Sommer, André, and Marc Philonenko, eds. *La Bible. Ecrits intertestamentaires*. Paris, 1987.

Dussaussoy, Maille. *Le citoyen désintéressé, ou diverses idées patriotiques*. Paris, 1767.

Eder, Anne, and Celso Bianco, eds. *Screening Blood Donors: Science, Reason, and the Donor History Questionnaire*. Bethesda, MD, 2007.

Edwards, Jeanette. *Born and Bred: Idioms of Kinship and New Reproductive Technologies*. Oxford, 2000.

Edwards, Jeanette, and Marilyn Strathern. "Including Our Own." In *Cultures of Relatedness: New Approaches to the Study of Kinship*, edited by Janet Carsten. Cambridge, 2000.

Edwards, Jeanette, and Carles Salazar, eds. *European Kinship in the Age of Biotechnology*. Oxford, 2009.

Egitanensis, Ioannes [Ioannes Hispanus Egitanensis]. *Lectura arborum consanguinitatis et affinitatis magistri Ioannis Egitaniensis*. Edited by Isaías da Rosa Pereira. *Studia Gratiana* 14 (1967): 155–82.

Elisabeth, Léo. *La société martiniquaise au XVIIᵉ et XVIIIᵉ siècles, 1664–1789*. Paris, 2003.

Essegern, Ute. "Kursächsische Eheverträge in der ersten Hälfte des 17. Jahrhunderts." In *Witwenschaft in der frühen Neuzeit: Fürstliche und adlige Witwen zwischen Fremd- und Selbstbestimmung*, edited by Martina Schattkowsky, 116–34. Leipzig, 2003.

Essner, Cornelia. "'Border-line' im Menschenblut und Struktur rassistischer Rechtsspaltung: Koloniales Kaiserreich und Drittes Reich." In *Gesetzliches Unrecht. Rassistisches Recht im 20. Jahrhundert*, edited by Monica Brumlik, Susanne Meinl, and Werner Renz, 27–64. Jahrbuch 2005 zur Geschichte und Wirkung des Holocaust. Frankfurt am Main, 2005.

———. "Das Geheimnis der menschlichen Reproduktion. Zeugungstheorien in Deutschland zwischen 1750 und 1900." *Historische Mitteilungen* 22 (2009): 257–70.

———. "Kommentar zu den 'Nürnberger Gesetzen.'" In *100(0) Schlüsseldokumente zur deutschen Geschichte im 20.Jahrhundert*. www.1000dokumente.de/index.html.

———. *Die "Nürnberger Gesetze" oder die Verwaltung des Rassenwahns 1933–1945*. Paderborn, 2002.

Evans-Pritchard, E. E. *The Nuer: A Description of the Modes of Livelihood and Political Institutions of a Nilotic People*. Oxford, 1940.

F. Vattioni, ed. *Sangue e antropologia biblica*. Rome, 1981.

———. *Sangue e antropologia biblica nella patristica*. Rome, 1982.

———. *Sangue e antropologia nella letteratura cristiana*. Rome, 1983.

Fair Bestor, Jane. "Ideas about Procreation and Their Influence on Ancient and Medieval Views of Kinship." In *The Family in Italy from Antiquity to the Present*, edited by D. I. Kertzer and R. P. Saller, 150–67. New Haven, CT, and London, 1991.

Fanizza, Lucia. "Il parricidio nel sistema della *lex Pompeia*." *Labeo* 25 (1979): 266–89.

Fayard, Janine, and Marie Claude Gerbet. "Fermeture de la noblesse et pureté de sang en Castille à travers les procès de *hidalguía* au XVIe siècle." *Histoire, économie et société* 1, no. 1 (1982): 51–75.

Fayer, Carla, ed. *Aspetti giuridici ed antiquari, sponsalia, matrimonio, dote.* Vol. 2 of *La familia Romana.* Rome, 2005.

Feeley-Harnik, Gillian. *The Lord's Table: Eucharist and Passover in Early Christianity.* Philadelphia, PA, 1981.

Feldman, Eric A., and Ronald Bayer, eds. *Blood Feuds: AIDS, Blood, and the Politics of Medical Disaster.* New York, 1999.

Festus, Sextus Pompeius. *Sextii Pompei Festi De verborum significatu quae supersunt cum Pauli epitome. Thewrewkianis copiis usus edidit Wallace M. Lindsay.* Reprographischer Nachdruck der Ausg. Leipzig, 1913. Hildesheim, 1965.

*Financial Times* (UK).

Finkler, Kaja. *Experiencing the New Genetics: Family and Kinship on the Medical Frontier.* Philadelphia, PA, 2000.

Firth, Raymond, Jane Hubert, and Anthony Forge. *Families and Their Relatives: Kinship in a Middle-Class Sector of London.* London, 1969.

Fischer, Eugen. *Die Rehobother Bastards und das Bastardisierungsproblem beim Menschen.* Munich, 1913.

Flandrin, J. L. *Families in Former Times: Kinship, Household and Sexuality.* Cambridge, 1979.

Fleuriot, Léon. *Les origines de la Bretagne. L'émigration.* Paris, 1980.

Ford, Caroline. *Creating the Nation in Provincial France: Religion and Political Identity in Brittany.* Princeton, NJ, 1993.

Fortes, Meyer. *Kinship and the Social Order.* Chicago, IL, 1969.

Fortier, Corinne. "Blood, Sperm and the Embryo in Sunni Islam and in Mauritania: Milk Kinship, Descent and Medically Assisted Procreation." *Body Society* 13 (2007): 15–36.

Foster, John Bellamy. *Marx's Ecology: Materialism and Nature.* New York, 2000.

Foster, John Bellamy, and Fred Magdoff. *The Great Financial Crisis: Causes and Consequences.* New York, 2009.

Foster, John Bellamy, and Robert W. McChesney. "Monopoly-Finance Capital and the Paradox of Accumulation." *Monthly Review* 61 (2009): 1–20.

Foucault, Michel. *An Introduction.* In vol. 1 of *The History of Sexuality.* New York, 1978.

———. *The Order of Things: An Archaeology of the Human Sciences.* New York, 1970.

———. *Les mots et les choses. Une archéologie des sciences humaines.* Paris, 1966.

Fourth Lateran Council (1215). Constitutions. http://www.ewtn.com/library/councils/lateran4.htm

Franklin, Sarah. "Biologization Revisited: Kinship Theory in the Context of the New Biologies." In Franklin and McKinnon, *Relative Values: Reconfiguring Kinship Studies.*

———. *Dolly Mixtures: The Remaking of Genealogy.* Durham, NC, and London, 2007.

———. *Embodied Progress: A Cultural Account of Assisted Conception.* London, 1997.

———. "Re-thinking Nature-Culture: Anthropology and the New Genetics." *Anthropological Theory* 3, no. 1 (2003).

———. "Science as Culture, Cultures of Science." *Annual Review of Anthropology* 24 (1995): 163–84.

Franklin, Sarah, and Margaret Lock, eds. *Remaking Life and Death: Towards an Anthropology of the Biosciences.* Santa Fe, NM, 2003.

Franklin, Sarah, and Susan McKinnon, eds. *Relative Values: Reconfiguring Kinship Studies.* Durham, NC, and London, 2001.

Fumagalli, M. Balestri. "L'incapacità successorale delle *adgnatae* non consanguinee et la *lex Voconia.*" Chap. 2 in *Riflessioni sulla* lex Voconia. Milan, 2008.

Galles, Louis. "Comment les dolmens pourraient bien avait été construits par les Gaulois." *Bulletin du Société polymathique du Morbihan* (1873): 50–75.

Galles, René. "Allocution de M. Galles." *Bulletin du Société polymathique du Morbihan* (1885): 2.

———. "Allocution de M. Galles en prenant le fauteuil de la Présidance." *Bulletin du Société polymathique du Morbihan* (1882): 2.

———. "Manné-er-H'roëk. Dolmen découvert sous un tumulus à Locmariaquer." *Bulletin du Société polymathique du Morbihan* (1863): 18–40.

———. "Un souvenir de Kabylie à propos des alignements de Carnac." *Bulletin du Société polymathique du Morbihan* (1881): 22–25.

García y García, Antonius. *Constitutiones concilii quarti Lateranensis una cum commentariis glossatorum*. Vatican City, 1981.

Gardner, Jane. *Family and Familia in Roman Law and Life*. Oxford, 1998.

———. *Women in Roman Law and Society*. London and Sydney, 1995.

Garrigus, John D. *Before Haiti: Race and Citizenship in French Saint-Domingue*. New York, 2006.

———. "Opportunist or Patriot? *Julien Raimond* (1744–1801) and the Haitian Revolution." *Slavery & Abolition* 28 (2007): 1–21.

Garroutte, Eva Marie. "The Racial Formation of American Indians: Negotiating Legitimate Identities within Federal and Tribal Law." *American Indian Quarterly* 25 (2001): 224–39.

———. *Real Indians: Identity and the Survival of Native America*. Berkeley, CA, 2003.

Gauvard, Claude. *"De grace especial." Crime, État et société en France à la fin du Moyen Age*. Paris, 1991.

"Généalogies de la Maison de Toulouse." In vol. 3, pt. 4 of *Europäische Stammtafeln*, n.s., Tables 763–772. Marburg, 1989.

Genlis, [Stéphanie Félicité Ducrest de Saint-Aubin], La comtesse de. *Mémoires inédits de Madame la comtesse de Genlis, sur le dix-huitième siècle et la Révolution française, depuis 1756 à nos jours*. 10 vols. Paris, 1825.

Gerbet, Marie-Claude. *Les noblesses espagnoles au Moyen Age. XIᵉ–XVᵉ siècles*. Paris, 1994.

Gerson, Jean. "Sermon de la conception nostre dame." *Six sermons français inédits*. Edited by Louis Mourin. Études de théologie et d'histoire de la spiritualité 8. Paris, 1946.

"Gesetz zum Schutze des deutschen Blutes und der deutschen Ehre" [*Blutschutzgesetz*]. http://www.documentarchiv.de/ns/nbgesetze01.html.

Gilbert, Maurice. "Une seule chair." *Nouvelle révue théologique* 100 (1979): 66–89.

Gilroy, Paul. *The Status of Difference: From Epidermalisation to Nano-Politics*. Critical Urban Studies Occasional Paper Pamphlet. London, 1995.

Ginzburg, Carlo. *Ecstasies: Deciphering the Witches' Sabbath*. Translated by Raymond Rosenthal. Chicago, IL, 2004.

Godefroy, Frédéric. *Dictionnaire de l'ancienne langue française, IXᵉ–XVᵉ siècles*. Paris, 1881–1902.

Godineau, Dominique. *The Women of Paris and Their French Revolution*. Translated by Katherine Streip. Berkeley, CA, 1998.

González, Fernán. *Poema de Fernán González*. Edited by John Lihani. East Lansing, MI, 1991.

González, María Asenjo. *Espacio y sociedad en la Soria medieval. Siglos XIII–XV.* Soria, 1999.

———. *Segovia. La ciudad y su tierra a fines del medievo*. Segovia, 1986.

Goody, Jack. *The Development of the Family and Marriage in Europe*. Cambridge, 1983.

———, ed. *The Character of Kinship*. Cambridge, 1975.

Goody, Jack, Joan Thirsk, and E. P. Thompson, eds. *Family and Inheritance: Rural Society in Western Europe, 1200–1800*. Cambridge, 1976.

Gourevitch, Danielle. "Le sang dans la médecine antique." *La Recherche* 254 (1993): 510–17.

*Gratiani decretum: La traduction en ancien français du Décret de Gratien.* Edited by Leena Löfstedt. 5 Vols. Commentationes humanarum litterarum 95, 99, 105, 110, 117. Helsinki, 1992–2001.

Greer, Margaret R., Walter D. Mignolo, and Maureen Quilligan, eds. *Rereading the Black Legend: The Discourses of Religious and Racial Difference in the Renaissance Empires.* Chicago, IL, 2007.

*The Greek Anthology: Volume 5, Books 13–16.* Translated by W. R. Paton. Loeb Classical Library 86. London and Cambridge, MA, 1918.

Grenier, Nicole. *Tome second du Bouclier de la foy contenant l'antidote contre les adversaires de la pure conception de la mere de Dieu.* Vol. 2 of *Monumenta Italo-Gallica ex tribus auctoribus materna lingua scribentibus,* edited by Pedro de Alva y Astorga. 3 vols. in 2. Brussels, 1967.

Gruner, Wolf. *Widerstand in der Rosenstraße. Die Fabrik-Aktion und die Verfolgung der "Mischehen" 1943.* Frankfurt am Main, 2005.

Guastella, Gianni. "La rete del sangue. Simbologia delle relazioni e modelli dell'identità nella cultura romana." *Materiali e discussioni per l'analisi dei testi classici* 15 (1985): 49–123.

Guazzo, Stefano. *La civil conversatione del sig. Stefano Guazzo gentiluomo di Casale di Monferrato. Divisa in quattro libri ... i modi, che s'hanno a serbare nella domestica conue.* Brescia, 1574.

Guenée, Bernard. "Le roi, ses parents et son royaume en France au XIVᵉ siècle." In *Un roi et son historien: Vingt études sur le règne de Charles VI et la "Chronique du Religieux de Sain- Denis,"* 301–24. Paris, 1999.

Guerreau-Jalabert, Anita. "Aimer de fin cuer. Le coeur dans la thématique courtoise." In "Il Cuore/The Heart." Special issue, *Micrologus. Natura, Scienze e Società Medievali* XI (2003): 343–71.

———. "La désignation des relations et des groupes de parenté en latin médiéval." *Archivum Latinitatis Medii Aevi* 46–47 (1988): 65–108.

———. "Le graal, le Christ et la chevalerie." In *Pratiques de l'eucharistie dans les Eglises d'Orient et d'Occident (Antiquité et Moyen Age),* edited by Nicole Bériou, Béatrice Caseau, and Dominique Rigaux, 1057–72. Paris, 2009.

———. "*Spiritus et caritas.* Le baptême dans la société médiévale." In *La parenté spirituelle,* edited by Françoise Héritier and Elisabeth Copet-Rougier, 133–203. Paris, 1995.

———. "Sur les structures de parenté dans l'Europe médiévale (Note critique)." *Annales. Économies, Sociétés, Civilisations [Annales ESC]* (1981): 1028–49.

Guerreau-Jalabert, Anita, Michel Sot, and Jean-Patrice Boudet. *Le Moyen Age.* Vol. 1 of *Histoire culturelle de la France.* Paris, 1997.

Guerreau-Jalabert, Anita, Régine Le Jan, and Joseph Morsel. "Familles et parentes. De l'histoire de la famille à l'anthropologie de la parenté." In *Les tendances actuelles de l'histoire du Moyen Âge en France et en Allemagne,* edited by Jean-Claude Schmitt and Otto Gerhard Oexle, 433–46. Paris, 2002.

Guiance, Ariel. "To Die for Country, Land, or Faith in Castilian Medieval Thought." *Journal of Medieval History* 24 (1998): 313–32.

Guillaumin, Colette. "Usages théoriques et usages banals du terme race." *Mots* no. 33 (1992): 59–65.

Guiomar, Jean-Yves. *Le bretonisme. Les historiens bretons au XIXᵉ siècle.* Preface by Michel Denis. Mayenne, 1987.

Guyot-Jomard, M. A. "Sur la provenance des granits qui ont servi à élever les monuments dits celtiques." *Bulletin du Société polymathique du Morbihan* (1866): 101–6.

Hacking, Ian. "Our Neo-Cartesian Bodies in Part." *Critical Inquiry* 34 (2007): 78–105.

Haddad, Elie. *Fondation et ruine d'une "maison." Histoire sociale des comtes de Belin (1582–1706)*. Limoges, 2009.

Hahn, Thomas G., ed. "Race and Ethnicity in the Middle Ages." Special issue, *Journal of Medieval and Early Modern Studies* 31 (2001).

Hall, Catherine. *Family Fortunes: Men and Women of the English Middle Class, 1780–1950.* London, 1987.

Hanard, Gilbert. "Observation sur l'*adgnatio*." *Revue internationale des droits de l'Antiquité* 27 (1980): 169–204.

Hanley, Sarah. "Engendering the State: Family Formation and State Building in Early Modern France." *French Historical Studies* 16, no. 1 (1989): 4–27.

———. "The Monarchic State in Early Modern France: Marital Regime Government and Male Right." In *Politics, Ideology and the Law in Early Modern Europe*, edited by Adrianna E. Bakos, 107–26. Rochester, NY, 1994.

Hannaford, Ivan. *Race: The History of an Idea in the West.* Washington, DC, and Baltimore, MD, 1996.

*Harangve faicte par la Noblesse de Champagne & de Brie.* s.l., 1615. http://gallica.bnf.fr/ark:/12148/bpt6k999621.

Haraway, Donna. *Simians, Cyborgs and Women: The Reinvention of Nature.* London, 1991.

Harders, Ann-Cathrin. *Suavissima Soror. Untersuchungen zu den Bruder-Schwester-Beziehungen in der römischen Republik.* Munich, 2008.

Harris, C. C., ed. *Readings in Kinship in Urban Society.* Oxford, 1970.

Hartmann, Elke. *Heirat, Hetärentum und Konkubinat im klassischen Athen.* Frankfurt am Main and New York, 2002.

Harvey, William. *Anatomical Exercitations Concerning the Generation of Living Creatures: To which are added Particular Discourses of Births, and of Conceptions, &c.* London, 1653.

Hauser-Schäublin, Brigitta. "Blutsverwandtschaft." In Braun and Wulf, *Mythen des Blutes*, 171–83.

———. "Politik des Blutes. Zur Verkörperung sozialer Ungleichheit als naturgegebene Verschiedenheit am Schnittpunkt zwischen Geschlecht, Klasse und Rasse." *Zeitschrift für Ethnologie* 120 (1995): 31–49.

Heers, Jacques. *Le clan familial au Moyen Age. Étude sur les structures politiques et sociales des milieux urbains.* Paris, 1974.

Henricus de Segusio [Hostiensis]. *Summa. Una cum summariis et adnotationibus Nicolai Superantii.* Lyon, 1537. Repr. Aalen, 1962.

Héritier, Françoise. *Les deux soeurs et leur mère.* Paris, 1994.

———. *L'exercice de la parenté.* Paris, 1981.

———. *Masculin/féminin. La pensée de la différence.* Paris, 1996.

Héritier-Augé, Françoise. "Semen and Blood: Some Ancient Theories Concerning Their Genesis and Relationship." In vol. 3 of *Fragments for a History of the Human Body.* Edited by Michel Feher, Ramona Nadaff, and Nadia Tazi. New York, 1989.

Hessel, Evan. "Dracula: Steven Gould Has Sucked Up Millions of Investors' Dollars to Develop a Blood Substitute. Why Hasn't It Been Approved?" *Forbes,* 6 June 2005, 80–82.

Highfield, Roger. "Stem Cell Technology May Make Blood Donations Thing of the Past." *Telegraph,* 20 August 2008.

Hincmar de Reims. "Epistulae 22." *Patrologia Latina* 126, col. 136A.

Ho, Karen. "Situating Global Capitalisms: A View from Wall Street Investment Banks." *Cultural Anthropology* 20 (2005): 68–96.

———. *Liquidated: An Ethnography of Wall Street*. Durham, NC, 2009.

*Hochangelegene/ und bißhero vielfältig bestrittenen Gewissens-Frage/ Nemlich: Ob Jemand seines verstorbenen Weibes Schwester/ sonder Ubertrettung Göttlicher und Natürlicher Gesetze/ in wiederholter Ehe zu heuraten berechtiget? Durch auff dem in der Fürstliche Residentz zu Oettingen den 10. Octobr. Anno 1681 gehaltenen COLLOQUIO Ergangene Wechsel-Schriften/* Responsa_und hochvernünfftige Judicia; *Nach höchtes Fleisses überlegten beyderseitigen* Rationibus, *und hierüber gefaßten Grund-Schlüssen Erörtert: Und als ein Curiöses und ungemeines Zweiffel-Werck/ Zu eines jeden genugsamen Unterricht in offentlichem Truck ausfertiget*. Frankfurt and Leipzig, 1682.

Holy, Ladislav. *Anthropological Perspectives on Kinship*. London, 1996.

Homère [Homer], *Odysse*. Paris, 1969.

Honorius Augustodunens. "Eucharistion." *Patrologia Latina*, 172.

Hostiensis. *See* Henricus de Segusio.

Huchet, Patrick. *1795. Quiberon, ou, le destin de la France*. Rennes, 1995.

Hughes, Jennifer. "Bankers Seek to Detoxify the Alphabet Soup." *Financial Times*, 13 October 2009, 232.

Hunt, Lynn. *The Family Romance of the French Revolution*. Berkeley, CA, 1992.

Institute of Medicine. *Fluid Resuscitation: State of the Science for Treating Combat Casualties and Civilian Injuries*. Washington, DC, 1999.

Jackson, Tony. "Has the Supercharged Banking Model Run Out of Road?" *Financial Times*, 21 January 2008, 19.

Jacques, François. "*Obnoxius curiae*. Origines et formes de l'astreinte à la cité au IVᵉ s. de notre ère." *Revue historique de droit français et étranger* 63 (1985): 303–85.

Jaenen, Cornelius. *Friend and Foe: Aspects of French-Amerindian Cultural Contact in the Sixteenth and Seventeenth Centuries*. New York, 1976.

Jaher, Frederic Cople. "Nineteenth-Century Elites in Boston and New York." *Journal of Social History* 6 (1972): 32–77.

Jenkins, Patrick. "Banks Reinvent Securitisation to Cut Capital Costs." *Financial Times*, 6 July 2009.

*The Jesuit Relations and Allied Documents: Travels and Explorations of the Jesuit Missionaries in New France, 1610–1791*. Edited by R. G. Thwaites. 73 vols. Cleveland, 1896–1901.

Johnson, Christopher H. "Das 'Geschwister Archipel': Bruder-Schwester-Liebe und Klassenformation im Frankreich des 19. Jahrhunderts." *L'Homme. Zeitschrift für feministische Geschichtswissenschaft* 13, no. 1 (2002): 50–67.

———. "'Into the World': Breton Bourgeois Families Make Their Way in the Nation, 1750–1890." In Johnson et al., *Transregional and Transnational Families in Europe and Beyond: Experiences Since the Middle Ages*. New York and Oxford, 2011.

———. "Kinship, Civil Society, and Power in Nineteenth-Century Vannes." In Sabean, Teuscher, and Mathieu, *Kinship in Europe: Approaches to Long-Term Development (1300–1900)*, 258–83.

———. "Siblinghood and the Emotional Dimensions of the New Kinship System, 1800–1850: A French Example." In Johnson and Sabean, *Sibling Relations and the Transformations of European Kinship, 1300–1900*. New York and Oxford, 2011.

Johnson, Christopher H., and David Warren Sabean, eds. *Sibling Relations and the Transformations of European Kinship, 1300–1900*. New York and Oxford, 2011.

Johnson, Christopher H., David Warren Sabean, Simon Teuscher, and Francesca Trivellato, eds. *Transregional and Transnational Families in Europe and Beyond: Experiences Since the Middle Ages*. New York and London, 2011.

Jones, Christopher P. *Kinship Diplomacy in the Ancient World*. Cambridge, MA, and London, 1999.

Jones, Steve. *In the Blood*. London, 1996.

Jones, William Jervis. *German Kinship Terms (750–1500)*. Berlin and New York, 1990.

Jonin, Michel. "De la pureté de la foi vers la pureté de sang. Les ambiguïtés bien orthodoxes d'un discours chrétien de défense des *conversos*." In Van der Lugt and Miramon, *L'hérédité entre Moyen Âge et Époque moderne*, 83–104.

Jori, Alberto. "Blut und Leben bei Aristoteles." In *Blood in History and Blood Histories*, edited by Mariacarla Gadebusch Bondio, 19–38. Florence, 2005.

Jouanna, Arlette. *Le devoir de révolte. La noblesse française et la gestation de l'État moderne*. Paris, 1989.

———. *L'idée de race en France au XVIᵉ siècle et au début du XVIIᵉ*. Lille, 1976. Rev. ed. Montpellier, 1981.

Karakasidou, Anastasia. *Fields of Wheat, Hills of Blood: Passages to Nationhood in Greek Macedonia*. Chicago, IL, 1997.

Kaser, Max. *Das römische Privatrecht. Erster Abschnitt: Das altrömische, das vorklassische und klassische Recht*. 2nd ed. Munich, 1971.

Kaster, Robert A. *Cicero, Speech on Behalf of Publius Sestius*. Oxford, 2006.

Kauanui, J. Kēhaulani. *Hawaiian Blood: Colonialism and the Politics of Sovereignty and Indigeneity*. Durham, NC, 2008.

Keller, Evelyn Fox. *The Mirage of a Space Between Nature and Nurture*. Durham, NC, 2010.

Klapisch-Zuber, Christiane. "La genèse de l'arbre généalogique." In *L'arbre. Histoire naturelle et symbolique de l'arbre, du bois et du fruit au Moyen Âge*, edited by Michel Pastoureau, 41–81. Paris, 1993.

———. *L'ombre des ancêtres. Essai sur l'imaginaire médiéval de la parenté*. Paris, 2000.

———. "Le nom refait." *L'Homme* 20, no. 4 (1980): 77–104.

———. *Retour à la cité. Les magnats de Florence, 1340–1440*. Paris, 2006.

Klein, H. G. "Blood Substitutes: How Close to a Solution?" In *Advances in Transfusion Safety*, edited by G. N. Vyas and A. E. Williams, 45–52. Basel, 2005.

Knight, Christopher. *Blood Relations: Menstruation and the Origin of Culture*. New Haven, CT, 1991.

La Boétie, Étienne de. *Discours de la servitude volontaire*. In *Oeuvres complètes d'Estienne de la Boétie*. Edited by Paul Bonnefon. Paris, 1892.

La Borderie, Arthur Le Moyne de. *Histoire de Bretagne*. Vols. 1–4. Rennes, no later than 1904–6.

La Primaudaye, Pierre de. *Academie Francoise en laquelle il est traicté de l'institution des moeurs*. Paris, 1581.

La Roque, Gilles-André de [La Roque de La Lontière]. *Traité de la noblesse*. Paris, 1678.

La Villemarqué, Théodore Hersart, Vicomte de. *Barzaz Breiz. Chants populaires de la Brétagne. …* Paris, 1840.

Lakoff, Andrew. "The Generic Biothreat, or, How We Became Unprepared." *Cultural Anthropology* 23 (2008): 399–428.

Lakoff, Andrew, and Stephen J. Collier, eds. *Biosecurity Interventions: Global Health and Security in Question*. New York, 2008.

Lallemand, Alfred. *Notice historique sur la très ancienne chapelle de sainte Anne et la statue miraculeuse qui en provenait*. Vannes, 1862.

Lamaison, Pierre, and Elisabeth Claverie. *L'impossible mariage. Violence et parenté en Gévaudan, XVII^e, XVIII^e, et XIX^e siècles.* Paris, 1982.

Lamy, Marielle. *L'immaculée conception. Étapes et enjeux d'une controverse au Moyen-Age (XIIe–XVe siècles).* Collection de Études Augustiniennes. Série Moyen-Age et temps modernes 35. Paris, 2000.

Laqueur, Thomas. *Making Sex: Body and Gender from the Greeks to Freud.* Cambridge, MA, 1990.

Laslett, Peter, and R. Wall, eds. *Household and Family in Past Time.* Cambridge, 1972.

Latour, Bruno. *The Pasteurization of France.* Cambridge, MA, 1988.

———. *Science in Action: How to Follow Scientists and Engineers Through Society.* Cambridge, MA, 1987.

———. *We Have Never Been Modern.* New York, 1993.

Latour, Bruno, and Steve Woolgar. *Laboratory Life: The Social Construction of Scientific Facts.* Beverley Hills, CA, 1979.

Le Goff, Timothy. *Vannes and Its Region: A Study of Town and Country in Eighteenth-Century France.* Oxford, 1981.

*Le sang au Moyen Age. Actes du quatrième colloque international de Montpellier, Université Paul-Valéry, 27–29 novembre 1997.* Montpellier, 1999.

Letter of Jacquette Bertin Galles to Jean-Nicolas Galles, March 1760. In "Un Vannetais à la Bastille. Jean-Nicolas Galles en 1760 d'après sa correspondance inédite," by Bernard Frélaut. *Mémoires de la Société polymathique du Morbihan* 116 (1990): 173–83.

Lettre de Colbert à Talon, 5 avril 1667. In *Rapport de l'archiviste de la Province de Québec pour 1930–1931.* Québec, 1931.

Lettre du Gouverneur general de Fayet au Gouverneur du Cap, 7 décembre 1733. In vol. 3 of *Loix et constitutions des colonies françaises de l'Amérique sous le vent,* edited by Médéric-Louis-Elie *Moreau de Saint-Méry.* 6 vols. Paris and Cap Français, Saint-Domingue, 1784–90.

Lettre du Ministre aux Administrateurs contenant une décision aux trois points relatifs aux Races Noires et Indiennes, 7 janvier 1767. In vol. 5 of *Loix et constitutions des colonies françaises de l'Amérique sous le vent,* edited by Médéric-Louis-Elie *Moreau de Saint-Méry.* 6 vols. Paris and Cap Français, Saint-Domingue, 1784–90.

Lettre du Ministre aux Administrateurs, qui défend d'accorder aucun passage pour la France aux esclaves et aux nègres libres, 30 juin 1763. In vol. 4 of *Loix et constitutions des colonies françaises de l'Amérique sous le vent,* edited by Médéric-Louis-Elie *Moreau de Saint-Méry.* 6 vols. Paris and Cap Français, Saint-Domingue, 1784–90.

"Lettre originale des chefs des nègres révoltés, à l'assemblée générale, aux commissaires nationaux et aux citoyens de la partie française de Saint-Domingue du mois de juillet 1792." *Le Créole Patriote* 282 (9 février 1793). Bibliothèque Historique de la Ville de Paris. Reproduced in Nathalie Piquionne. "Lettre de Jean-François, Biassou et Belair." *Annales Historiques de la Révolution Française* 311 (1998): 132–39.

Lévi-Strauss, Claude. *The Elementary Structures of Kinship.* London, 1969.

———. *Structural Anthropology.* London, 1963.

Levy, Darline Gay, Harriet Branson Applewhite, and Mary Durham Johnson, eds. *Women in Revolutionary Paris, 1789–1795.* Urbana, IL, 1980.

Leyton, Elliot. "The One Blood: Kinship and Class in an Irish Village." *Newfoundland Social and Economic Studies* No. 15, Institute of Social and Economic Research. Saint Johns, Newfoundland, 1975.

*Library of Latin Texts.* http://www.brepolis.net.

Liébault, Jean. *Trois livres des maladies et infirmitez des femmes.* Rouen, 1649.

Lignac, Louis Luc de. *De l'homme et de la femme.* 2 vols. 1st ed. Lille, 1772.

Lintholtz, Ioannes. *See* Cyntholtz, Ioannes.

Livy. *Summaries. Fragments. Julius Obsequens. General Index.* Translated by A. C. Schlesinger. Vol. 14 of Livy, *History of Rome.* London and Cambridge, MA, 1959.

Lochak, Danièle. "La race: une catégorie juridique?" *Mots* no. 33 (1992): 291–303.

Lock, Margaret. "Eclipse of the Gene and the Return of Divination." *Current Anthropology* 46, Supplement (December 2005): 47–70.

———. *Twice Dead: Organ Transplants and the Reinvention of Death.* Berkeley, CA, 2002.

Löfstedt, Leena, ed. *Gratiani decretum: La traduction en ancien français du Décret de Gratien.* 5 vols. Commentationes humanarum litterarum 95, 99, 105, 110, 117. Helsinki, 1992–2001.

*Loix et constitutions des colonies françaises de l'Amérique sous le vent.* Edited by Médéric-Louis-Elie *Moreau de Saint-Méry.* 6 vols. Paris and Cap Français, Saint-Domingue, 1784–90.

Lomellini, Leonardo. *Risposta a Marco Antonio Sauli.* In "La pubblicistica politica genovese durante le guerre civili del 1575," by Rodolfo Savelli. *Atti della società ligure di storia patria,* n.s. 20 (1979): 82–105.

Lösener, Bernhard. "Als Rassereferent im Reichsinnenministerium." *Vierteljahrshefte für Zeitgeschichte* 9 (1961): 263–313.

Lubich, Gerhard. *Verwandtsein: Lesarten einer politisch-sozialen Beziehung im Frühmittelalter (6–11. Jahrhundert).* Cologne, 2008.

MacCormack, Carol, and Marilyn Strathern, eds. *Nature, Culture and Gender.* Cambridge, 1980.

Malouet, Pierre-Victor. *Mémoire sur l'esclavage des nègres.* Neufchâtel, 1788.

Manrique, Jorge. *Coplas por la muerte de su padre.* In *Ten Centuries of Spanish Poetry.* Edited by Eleanor L. Turnbull. Baltimore, MD, 1955.

Marks, Jonathan. "98% Chimpanzee and 35% Daffodil: The Human Genome in Evolutionary and Cultural Context." In *Genetic Nature/Culture: Anthropology and Science Beyond the Two-Culture Divide,* edited by Alan H. Goodman, Deborah Heath, and M. Susan Lindee. Berkeley, CA, 2003.

Martin, Henri. "De l'origine des monuments mégalithique." In "Séance du 16 octobre 1867" of *Congrès celtique internationale ... octobre 1867.*

———. "Mémoire." In *Congrès celtique internationale ... octobre 1867.*

Martin, Jochen. "Formen sozialer Kontrolle im republikanischen Rom." In *Demokratie, Recht und soziale Kontrolle im Klassischen Athen,* edited by D. Cohen, 155–72. Munich, 2002.

———. "Das Vaterland der Väter. Familia, Politik und cognatische Verwandtschaft in Rom." In *Bedingungen menschlichen Handelns in der Antike. Gesammelte Beiträge zur Historischen Anthropologie,* by Jochen Martin, 311–27. Stuttgart, 2009.

———. "Zur Anthropologie von Heiratsregeln und Besitzübertragung. 10 Jahre nach den Goody-Thesen." *Historische Anthropologie* 1 (1993): 149–62.

———. "Zwei Alte Geschichten. Vergleichende historisch-anthropologische Betrachtungen zu Griechenland und Rom." *Saeculum* 48 (1997): 1–20.

Martin, Randy. *Financialization of Daily Life.* Philadelphia, PA, 2002.

Martin, Robert, ed. *Dictionnaire du Moyen Français.* http://www.atilf.fr/dmf.

Marx, Karl. *Economic and Philosophical Manuscripts of 1844.* New York, 1964.

Maurer, Bill. "Repressed Futures: Financial Derivatives' Theological Unconscious." *Economy and Society* 31 (2002): 15–36.

Mayerne-Turquet, Louis de. *Histoire générale d'Espagne.* Lyon, 1587.

McCarthy, Wil. "Strange Blood: Cataclysmic Shortages. Tainted Supplies. There is a Solution: Artificial Blood." *Wired*, August 2002, 108–13

Mencacci, Francesca. *"Sanguis/Cruor.* Designazioni linguistiche e classificazione antropologica del sangue nella cultura romana." *Materiali e discussioni per l'analisi dei testi classici* 17 (1986): 25–91.

Mertens, Dieter, and Thomas Zotz. "Einleitung der Herausgeber." In *Karl Schmid. Geblüt, Herrschaft, Geschlechterbewusstsein: Grundfragen zum Verständnis des Adels im Mittelalter. Aus dem Nachlass herausgegeben,* edited by Dieter Mertens and Thomas Zotz, ix–xxxiii. Sigmaringen, 1998.

Meyer, Jean. *La noblesse bretonne au XVIII<sup>e</sup> siècle.* Paris, 1972.

Meyerson, Mark D. *A Jewish Renaissance in Fifteenth-Century Spain.* Princeton, NJ, 2005.

———. *Jews in an Iberian Frontier Kingdom: Society, Economy and Politics in Morvedre, 1248–1391.* Leiden, 2004.

Miramon, Charles de. "Aux origines de la noblesse et des princes du sang. France et Angleterre au XIVe siècle." In Van der Lugt and Miramon, *L'hérédité entre Moyen Âge et Époque moderne,* 157–210.

*Mittellateinisches Wörterbuch.* Munich, 1959–.

Mitterauer, Michael. *Warum Europa? Mittelalterliche Grundlagen eines Sonderwegs.* Munich, 2003.

Mol, Annemarie. *The Body Multiple: Ontology in Medical Practice.* Durham, NC, 2002.

Mol, Annemarie, and J. Law. "Regions, Networks, and Fluids: Anaemia and Social Topology." *Social Studies of Science* 24 (1994): 641–71.

Mol, Annemarie, and Marc Berg, "Differences in Medicine: An Introduction." In *Differences in Medicine,* edited by Marc Berg and Annemarie Mol. Durham, NC, 1998.

Molière [Jean-Baptiste Poquelin]. *Oeuvres complètes.* Edited by E. Despois. Paris, 1873. See especially *Le malade imaginaire, L'étourdi,* and *Le médicin volant.*

Mommsen, Theodor, and Paul Krueger, eds. *Digesta Iustiniani Augusti.* … Berolini [Berlin], 1868–70.

Mont'Albano, Marco de la Frata et [Marco Montalbani]. *Il nobile. Ragionamenti di nobiltà partiti in cinque libri.* Florence, 1548.

Montaigne, Michel de. "Of the Resemblance of Children to Fathers." In *The Complete Essays of Montaigne.* Translated by Donald M. Frame. Stanford, CA, 1958.

Montemagno, Buonaccorso da. "De nobilitate tractatus." In *Prose e rime de' due Buonaccorsi da Montemagno,* 2–97. Florence, 1718.

*Monumenta Germaniae Historica.* http://www.brepolis.net.

Moore, Robert I. *The Formation of a Persecuting Society: Authority and Deviance in Western Europe, 950–1250.* 2nd ed. Malden, MA, 2007.

Moreau, Philippe. "La *domus Augusta* et les formations de parenté à Rome." *Cahiers Glotz* 16 (2005): 17–20.

———. "Domus Augusta: L'autre maison d'Auguste." In *L'expression du pouvoir au début de l'Empire. Autour de la Maison Carrée à Nîmes,* edited by M. Christol and D. Darde, 28–38. Paris, 2009.

———. *Incestus et prohibitae nuptiae. L'inceste à Rome.* Paris, 2002.

———. "Sangs romains. Taxinomie du sang dans la Rome ancienne." In *Penser et représenter le corps dans l'Antiquité. Actes du colloque international de Rennes, 1–4 septembre 2004,* edited by F. Prost and J. Wilgaux, 319–32. Rennes, 2006.

Morganson, Gretchen. "Foreclosures Hit a Snag for Lenders." *New York Times,* 15 November 2007.

Morsel, Joseph. "Geschlecht als Repräsentation. Beobachtungen zur Verwandtschaftskonstruktion im fränkischen Adel des späten Mittelalters." In *Die Repräsentation der*

*Gruppen. Texte—Bilder—Objekte*, edited by Otto Gerhard Oexle and Andrea von Hülsen-Esch, 259–325. Göttingen, 1998.

————. "Le médiéviste, le lignage et l'effet de réel. La construction du *Geschlecht* par l'archive en Haute Allemagne à partir de la fin du Moyen Age." *Revue de Synthèse* 125 (2004): 83–110.

Moxó, Salvador de. "De la nobleza vieja a la nobleza nueva. La transformación nobiliaria castellana en la baja edad media." *Cuadernos de historia: Anexos de Hispania* 3 (1969): 1–210.

Münzer, Friedrich. *Römische Adelsparteien und Adelsfamilien*. Stuttgart, 1920.

Murray, Oswyn. *Early Greece*. London, 1993.

*My Sister's Keeper*. Film in English. Directed by Nick Cassavetes. 2009.

Naevius, Johann Karl [Johann Karl Naeve]. *Jus conjugum, Oder das Ehe-Recht*. Chemnitz, 1709.

National Marrow Donor Program [NMDP]. http://www.marrow.org.

Nebrija, Antonio de. *Gramática de la lengua castellana*. Salamanca, 1492. http://elies .rediris.es/elies16/Niederehe1.html.

Nelson, Janet. "Family, Gender and Sexuality in the Middle Ages." In *Companion to Historiography*, edited by Michael Bentley, 153–76. London and New York, 1997.

Nenna, Giovanni Battista [Jean-Baptiste]. *Il Nennio. Nel quale si ragiona di nobilta*. Venice, 1542.

————. *Traicté de la noblesse*. Paris, 1583.

Nicot, Jean. *Le Thresor de la langue françoyse tant ancienne que moderne*. Paris, 1606.

Nirenberg, David. *Communities of Violence: Persecution of Minorities in the Middle Ages*. Princeton, NJ, 1996.

————. "Race and the Middle Ages: The Case of Spain and Its Jews." In *Rereading the Black Legend. The Discourses of Religious and Racial Difference in the Renaissance Empires*, edited by Margaret R. Greer, Walter D. Mignolo, and Maureen Quilligan, 71–87. Chicago, IL, 2007.

O'Callaghan, Joseph F. *A History of Medieval Spain*. Ithaca, NY, 1975.

Ollman, Bertell. *Alienation: Marx's Conception of Man in Capitalist Society*. 2nd ed. Cambridge, 1976.

Omar, Roziah. *The Malay Woman in the Body: Between Biology and Culture*. Kuala Lumpur, 1994.

Otalora, Juan Arce de. *Summa nobilitatis hispanicae et immunitatis Regiorum … recognita*. Salamanca, 1559.

Ozouf, Mona. *La fête révolutionnaire, 1789–1799*. Paris, 1976.

Paré, Ambroise. "De la Generation." In bk. 24 of *Les oeuvres d'Ambroise Paré*. 4th ed. Paris, 1585.

Parkes, Peter. "Milk Kinship in Islam: Substance, Structure, History." *Social Anthropology* 13, no. 3 (2005): 307–29.

————. "Milk Kinship in Southeast Europe: Alternative Social Structures and Foster Relations in the Caucasus and the Balkans." *Social Anthropology* 12, no. 3 (2004): 341–58.

Paruta, Paolo. "Della perfezione della vita politica libri tre." In *Opere politiche*, edited by C. Monzani, 35–413. Florence, 1852.

Patel, Geeta. "Imagining Risk, Care, and Security." *Anthropological Theory* 7 (2007): 99–118.

————. "Risky Subjects: Insurance, Sexuality, and Capital." *Social Text* 24 (2006): 25–65.

*Patrologia Latina: The Full Text Database*. CD-ROM with web support. http://pld .chadwyck.co.uk/.

Peabody, Sue. *There Are No Slaves in France: The Political Culture of Race and Slavery in the Ancien Régime*. Oxford, 1996.

Pech, Sarah. "L'influence des nourrices sur la formation physique et morale des enfants qu'elles allaitent selon les médecins et moralistes espagnols des XVI^ème et XVII^ème siècles." *Paedagogica Historica* 43, no. 4 (2007): 493–507.

Pennaforte, Raymundus de [Raymond of Peñafort]. *Summa Sancti Raymundi de Peniafort Barcinonensis de poenitentia et matrimonio cum glossis Ioannis de Friburgo*. Rome, 1603.

Pereira, Isaías da Rosa, ed. *Lectura arborum consanguinitatis et affinitatis magistri Ioannis Egitaniensis*. *Studia Gratiana* 14 (1967): 155–82.

*Pétition nouvelle des Citoyens de couleur des isles françoises, à l'Assemblée nationale, précédée d'un avertissement sur les manoeuvres employées pour faire échouer cette petition, et suivie de pièces justificatives*. Paris, 1791.

Petryna, Adriana. *Life Exposed: Biological Citizens after Chernobyl*. Princeton, NJ, 2002.

Piquionne, Nathalie. "Lettre de Jean-François, Biassou et Belair." *Annales Historiques de la Révolution Française* 311 (1998): 132–39.

*Poem of the Cid*. Bilingual edition. English translation by W. S. Merwin. New York, 1959.

Poliakov, Léon, and Josef Wulf. *Das Dritte Reich und seine Denker. Dokumente*. Berlin, 1959. Repr. Munich, 1978.

Pomata, Gianna. "Blood Ties and Semen Ties: Consanguinity and Agnation in Roman Law." In *Gender, Kinship and Power: A Comparative and Interdisciplinary History*, edited by Mary Jo Maynes et al., 43–64. New York and London, 1996.

———. "Legami di sangue, legami di seme: Consanguineità e agnazione nel diritto romano." *Quaderni Storici* 86 (1994): 299–334.

Pontas, Jean (Dr. en droit-canon, Fac. de Paris). "Empêchement de l'affinité." In *Dictionnaire de cas de conscience: ou decisions des plus considerables difficultez touchant la morale et la discipline ecclesiastique, tirées de l'ecriture, des conciles, des decretales des papes, des peres, et des plus célebres théologiens et canonistes*. 2 vols. with supp. Paris, 1715; with supp., 1718.

Price, Roger. *People and Politics in France, 1848–1870*. Cambridge, 2004.

*Primera crónica general. Estoria de España que mando componer Alfonso el Sabio y se continuaba*. … 2 vols. 3rd reprint. Madrid, 1977.

Puliatti, Salvatore. *Incesti crimina. Regime giuridico da Augusto a Giustiniano*. Milan, 2001.

Moreau, Philippe. "Incestus et prohibitae nuptiae." *Conception romaine de l'inceste et histoire des prohibitions matrimoniales pour cause de parenté dans la Rome antique*. Paris, 2002.

Quevedo y Villegas, Francisco de. *Letrilla*. In *Ten Centuries of Spanish Poetry*. Edited by Eleanor L. Turnbull. Baltimore, MD, 1955.

Quinlan, Sean M. *The Great Nation in Decline: Sex, Modernity and Health Crises in Revolutionary France c. 1750–1850*. Ashgate, 2007.

Rabinow, Paul. "Artificiality and Enlightenment: From Sociobiology to Biosociality." In *Incorporations*, edited by John Crary and Sanford Kwinter. New York, 1992.

———. *Essays on the Anthropology of Reason*. Princeton, NJ, 1996.

———. *French DNA: Trouble in Purgatory*. Chicago, IL, 1999.

———. *Making PCR: A Story of Biotechnology*. Chicago, IL, 1996.

Rabutin-Chantal, Marie de, Marquise de Sévigné. *Correspondence*. Texte établi, présenté et annoté par Roger Duchêne. 3 vols. Paris, 1972–78.

———. *Lettres de Mme de Sévigné, de sa famille et de ses amis*. 8 vols. Paris, 1862–63.

Racan, Honorat de Bueil, Seigneur de. *Les Psaumes*. Vol. 2 of *Oeuvres complètes*. New edition, revised and annotated by Tenant de Latour. Paris, 1857.

Radcliffe-Brown, A. R. *Structure and Function in Primitive Society.* Glencoe, IL, 1952.

Ragueau, François. *Indice des droits royaux et seigneuriaux des plus notables dictions, termes et phrases de l'estat et de la justice et practique de France.* Paris, 1583.

Rajan, Kaushik Sunder. *Biocapital: The Constitution of Postgenomic Life.* Durham, NC, 2006.

Rapallo, Umberto. "Linguistica e antropologia del sangue: convergenze macroreali." In *Sangue e antropologia nel Medioevo: atti della VII settimana, Roma, 25–30 novembre 1990.* Centro Studi Sanguis Christi. Rome, 1993.

Rapp, Rayna. *Testing Women, Testing the Fetus: The Social Impact of Amniocentesis in America.* New York and London, 1999.

Ray, Jonathan. *The Sephardic Frontier: The Reconquista and the Jewish Community in Medieval Iberia.* Ithaca, NY, 2005.

Raynal, Guillaume-Thomas. *Histoire philosophique et politique, des établissemens & du commerce des Européens dans les deux Indes.* Geneva, 1780.

———. *Histoire philosophique et politique, des établissemens & du commerce des Européens dans les deux Indes, Tome quatrieme.* Amsterdam, 1770 and La Haye, 1774.

Reece, Jack E. *The Bretons Against France: Ethnic Minority Nationalism in Twentieth-Century Brittany.* Chapel Hill, NC, 1977.

Régent, Frédéric. *Esclavage, métissage, liberté. La révolution française en Guadeloupe 1789–1802.* Paris, 2004.

Reif, Heinz. *Westfälischer Adel 1770–1860. Vom Herrschaftsstand zur regionalen Elite.* Göttingen, 1979.

Renan, Ernest. *La poésie des races celtiques.* Paris, 1854.

———. "Qu'est-ce qu'une nation." Paris, 1882.

*Report of the Committee on the Ethics of Gene Therapy*, col. 1788. London: Her Majesty's Stationery Office, 1992.

Restif de la Bretonne, Nicolas-Edme [Rétif de la Bretonne]. *Monsieur Nicolas ou le coeur humain dévoilé, mémoires intimes de Restif de la Bretonne*, 14 vols. Paris, 1794–97.

Rigaux, Dominique. "Autour de la dispute De Sanguine Christi. Une relecture de quelques peintures italiennes de la seconde moitié du XVe siècle." In *Le sang au Moyen Age. Actes du quatrième colloque international de Montpellier, Université Paul-Valéry, 27–29 novembre 1997*, 393–403. Montpellier, 1999.

Rogers, Dominique. "On the Road to Citizenship: The Complex Paths of the Integration of Free People of Colour in the Two Capitals of Saint-Domingue." In *The World of the Haitian Revolution*, edited by David Geggus and Norman Fiering, 65–78. Bloomington, IN, 2009.

Rose, Nikolas. *The Politics of Life Itself: Biomedicine, Power, and Subjectivity in the Twenty-First Century.* Princeton, NJ, 2007.

Rosenwein, Barbara H. *To Be the Neighbor of Saint Peter: The Social Meaning of Cluny's Property.* Ithaca, NY, 1989.

Roumy, Franck. "La naissance de la notion canonique de *consanguinitas* et sa réception dans le droit civil." In Van der Lugt and Miramon, *L'hérédité entre Moyen Âge et Époque moderne*, 41–66.

Rousseau, Vanessa. *Le goût du sang. Croyances et polémiques dans la chrétienté occidentale.* Paris, 2005.

Routrou, Jean [Jean de Routrou]. *Le véritable Saint Genest. Tragédie.* Edited by E. T. Dubois. Geneva, 1972.

Rouvroy, Louis de, Duc de Saint-Simon. *Mémoires.* 20 vols. Paris, 1691–1723. Paginated by ARTFL: www.lib.uchicago.edu/efts/ARTFL/databases/TLF/.

Rucquoi, Adeline. *Valladolid en la Edad Media.* 2 vols. Valladolid, 1987.

Rudolph, Alan S., Reuven Rabinovici, and Giora Z. Feuerstein, eds. *Red Blood Cell Substitutes: Basic Principles and Clinical Applications.* New York, 1997.
Ruiz, Teofilo F. *Crisis and Continuity: Land and Town in Late Medieval Castile.* Philadelphia, PA, 1994.
———. *From Heaven to Earth: The Reordering of Castilian Society, 1150–1350.* Princeton, NJ, 2004.
———. "Jews, Muslims, and Christians." In *Medieval Christianity,* edited by Daniel E. Bornstein, 265–99. Vol. 4 of *A People's History of Christianity,* edited by Denis R. Janz. Minneapolis, MN, 2009.
———. *Spanish Society, 1400–1600.* Harlow, 2001.
———. *Spain's Centuries of Crisis: 1300–1474.* Oxford, 2007.
———. "The Transformation of the Castilian Municipalities: The Case of Burgos." *Past & Present* 77 (1977): 3–33.
———. "Two Patrician Families in Late Medieval Burgos: The Sarracín and the Bonifaz." Chap. 6 in *The City and the Realm: Burgos and Castile 1080–1492.* Aldershot, Hampshire, Great Britain, 1992.
Rüpke, Jörg. *Die Religion der Römer. Eine Einführung,* 2nd ed. Munich, 2006.
———. *Religion of the Romans.* Translated by Richard Gordon. Cambridge, UK, and Malden, MA, 2007.
Sabean, David Warren. "Constructing Lineages in Imperial Germany: Eingetragene Familienvereine." In *Alltag als Politik, Politik im Alltag. Dimensionen des Politischen in Vergangenheit und Gegenwart,* edited by Michaela Fenske, 143–57. Berlin and Münster, 2010.
———. "From Clan to Kindred: Thoughts on Kinship and the Circulation of Property in Premodern and Modern Europe." In *Heredity Produced. At the Crossroad of Biology, Politics and Culture, 1500–1870,* edited by Staffan Müller-Wille and Hans-Jörg Rheinberger, 37–60. Cambridge, MA, 2006.
———. "German International Families in the Nineteenth Century: The Siemens Family as a Thought Experiment." In Johnson et al., *Transregional and Transnational Families in Europe and Beyond: Experiences Since the Middle Ages.* New York and Oxford, 2011.
———. *Kinship in Neckarhausen, 1700–1870.* Cambridge, 1998.
———. *Landbesitz und Gesellschaft am Vorabend des Bauernkriegs.* Stuttgart, 1972.
Sabean, David Warren, and Simon Teuscher. "Kinship in Europe: A New Apporach to Long-Term Development." In Sabean, Teuscher, and Mathieu, *Kinship in Europe: Approaches to Long-Term Development (1300–1900),* 1–32.
Sabean, David Warren, Simon Teuscher, and Jon Mathieu, eds. *Kinship in Europe: Approaches to Long-Term Development (1300–1900).* Oxford and New York, 2007.
Sachers, Erich. "Das Recht auf Unterhalt in der römischen Familie der klassischen Zeit." In vol. 1 of *Festschrift F. Schulz,* 310–63. Weimar, 1951.
Saey, Tina Hesman. "Whoa, Nellie! Horse Genome Is Revealed." *Science News* (5 December 2009): 5–6.
Sahlins, Peter. *Unnaturally French: Foreign Citizens in the Old Regime and After.* Ithaca, NY, 2004.
Saint Julien, Pierre de [Saint-Julien de Balleure]. *Meslanges historiques.* Lyon, 1588.
Saint-Aubin. *See under* Genlis, [Stéphanie Félicité Ducrest de Saint-Aubin], La comtesse de.
Saint-Simon. *See under* Rouvroy, Louis de, Duc de Saint-Simon.
Sales, Saint François de. "Sermon LXVII, 'Sermon pour la fête de l'immaculée conception de la sainte vierge'." In vol. 10 of *Oeuvres de Saint François de Sales: évêque de Genève*

*et docteur de l'Eglise: édition complète, d'après les autographes et les éditions originales.* ... 27 vols. (Annecy, 1892–1964).

Salutati, Colucci. *De nobilitate legum et medicinae. De verecundia.* Edited by E. Garin. Vol. 8 of Edizione nazionale dei classici del pensiero italiano. Florence, 1947.

"Sanc." In *Dictionnaire du Moyen Français.* Edited by Robert Martin. http://www.atilf .fr/dmf.

Sanday, Peggy. *Female Power and Male Dominance: On the Origins of Sexual Inequality.* Cambridge, 1981.

"Sangre." In *Diccionario de la lengua castellana en que se explica el verdadero sentido de las voces.* ... 6 vols. Madrid, 1737. Facsimile ed. Madrid, 1979.

Sardi, Alessandro. *Discorsi del S. Alessandro Sard. Della bellezza. Della nobilità.* ... *Di novo posti in luce.* Venice, 1586.

Sarkar, Suman. "Artificial Blood." *Indian Journal of Critical Care Medicine* 12 (2008): 140–44.

Sassoferrato, Bartolo da. "Tractatus de dignitatibus." In *In secundam Codicis partem ... Novissime accesserunt Additiones Iacobi Menochii.* Venice, 1585.

Sato, Toshiaki. "Japan Looks for New Blood." *World Press Review,* July 2001, 45.

Schadt, Hermann. *Die Darstellungen der Arbores Consanguinitatis und der Arbores Affinitatis. Bildschemata in juristischen Handschriften.* Tübingen, 1982.

Schalk, Ellery. *L'épée et le sang. Une histoire du concept de noblesse (vers 1500–vers 1650).* Paris, 1996.

———. *From Valor to Pedigree: Ideas of Nobility in France in the Sixteenth and Seventeenth Centuries.* Princeton, NJ, 1986.

Schmid, Karl. *Gebetsgedenken und adliges Selbstverständnis im Mittelalter.* Sigmaringen, 1983.

———. "Zur Problematik von Familie, Sippe und Geschlecht, Haus und Dynastie beim mittelalterlichen Adel. Vorfragen zum Thema 'Adel und Herrschaft im Mittelalter'." *Zeitschrift für Geschichte des Oberrheins* 105 (1957): 1–62.

Schmidt, Paul M. "Blood and Disaster—Supply and Demand." *New England Journal of Medicine* 346 (2002): 617.

Schneider, David Murray. *American Kinship: A Cultural Account.* 1st ed. Englewood Cliffs, NJ, 1968; 2nd ed. Chicago, IL, 1980.

———. *A Critique of the Study of Kinship.* Ann Arbor, MI, 1984.

Schudt, Johann Jacob. *Jüdische Merckwürdigkeiten vorstellende Was sich Curieuses und denckwürdiges in den neuern Zeiten bey einigen Jahr-hunderten mit denen in all IV.Theile der Welt/ sonderlich durch Teutschland/ zerstreuten Juden zugetragen.* Frankfurt am Main and Leipzig, 1714.

Schultz, Celia E. *Women's Religious Activity in the Roman Republic.* Chapel Hill, NC, 2006.

Schwartz, M. *See* Condorcet, Jean-Antoine-Nicolas de Caritat, Marquis de.

Scott, Joan. *Only Paradoxes to Offer: French Feminists and the Rights of Man.* Cambridge, MA, 1996.

Scullard, Howard H. *Festivals and Ceremonies of the Roman Republic.* London, 1981.

Segalen, Martine. *Fifteen Generations of Bretons: Kinship and Society in Lower Brittany, 1720–1980.* Translated by J. S. Underwood. Cambridge, 1991.

———. *Historical Anthropology of the Family.* Cambridge, 1986.

———. "The Shift in Kinship Studies in France: The Case of Grandparenting." In Franklin and McKinnon, *Relative Values: Reconfiguring Kinship Studies,* 246–73.

Sévigné, Marquise de. *See under* Rabutin-Chantal, Marie de, Marquise de Sévigné.

Sevilla, Margarita Torres. *Linajes nobiliarios de León y Castilla, siglos IX–XIII.* Salamanca, 1999.

Sharp, Lesley A. *Strange Harvest: Organ Transplants, Denatured Bodies, and the Trans-formed Self.* Berkeley, 2006.

Sicroff, Albert A. *Les controverses des statuts de "pureté de sang" en Espagne du XV<sup>e</sup> au XVII<sup>e</sup> siècle.* Paris, 1960.

Sissa, Giulia. "Subtle Bodies." In vol. 3 of *Fragments for a History of the Human Body,* edited by M. Feher, 133–41. New York, 1989.

Smith, Jay. *Nobility Re-imagined: The Patriotic Nation in Eighteenth-Century France.* Ithaca, NY, 2005.

Smith, Neal. "Nature as Accumulation Strategy." In *Coming to Terms with Nature,* edited by Leo Panitch and Colin Leys, 16–36. New York, 2006.

Smith, Robert J. *The Bouchayers of Grenoble and French Industrial Enterprise, 1850–1970.* Baltimore, MD, and London, 2001.

*Die Sonne. Volksdeutsche Wochenschrift.*

Souvigny, Comte de. *Mémoires.* Edited by Ludovic de Contenson. 3 vols. Paris, 1906–9.

Spiess, Karl-Heinz. *Familie und Verwandtschaft in deutschen Hochadel des Spätmittelalters.* Stuttgart, 1993.

Spring, Eileen. *Law, Land, and Family: Aristocratic Inheritance in England, 1300–1800.* Chapel Hill, NC, and London, 1993.

Sreenivasan, Govind P. *The Peasants of Ottobeuren, 1487–1726: A Rural Society in Early Modern Europe.* Cambridge, 2004.

*The Star Online.* Property of Star Publications (Malaysia) Berhad. http://thestar.com.my.

Starr, Douglas. *Blood: An Epic History of Medicine and Commerce.* New York, 1998.

Stoler, Ann Laura. *Carnal Knowledge and Imperial Power: Race and the Intimate in Colonial Rule.* Berkeley and Los Angeles, CA, 2002.

———. *Race and the Education of Desire: Foucault's History of Sexuality and the Colonial Order of Things.* Durham, NC, 1995.

Stone, Linda, ed. *New Directions in Anthropological Kinship.* Lanham, MD, 2000.

Stowell, Christopher P., and Peter Tomasulo. "The Impact of Blood Substitutes on Blood Banking Worldwide." In *Red Blood Cell Substitutes: Basic Principles and Clinical Applications,* edited by Alan S. Rudolph, Reuven Rabinovici, and Giora Z. Feuerstein, 1–16. New York, 1998.

Strathern, Marilyn. *After Nature: English Kinship in the Late Twentieth Century.* Cambridge, 1992.

———. *Kinship at the Core: An Anthropology of Elmdon, a Village in North-West Essex, in the Nineteen-Sixties.* Foreword by Audrey Richards. Oxford, 1981.

———. *Kinship, Law and the Unexpected: Relatives are Always a Surprise.* Cambridge, 2005.

———. *Reproducing the Future: Anthropology, Kinship and the New Reproductive Technologies.* Manchester, 1992.

Strathern, Marilyn, and Sarah Franklin. *Kinship and the New Genetic Technologies: An Assessment of Existing Anthropological Research.* Department of Social Anthropology, University of Manchester and EC, Brussels, DG VII.

Strohmaier, Gotthard. "Blut und Blutbewegung im arabischen Galenismus." In *Blood in History and Blood Histories,* edited by Mariacarla Gadebusch Bondio, 39–47. Florence, 2005.

Sutherland, Donald. *Les Chouans. Les origines sociales de la Contre-Révolution populaire en Bretagne, 1770–1796.* Rennes, 1990.

Sutherland, Donald, and Timothy Le Goff. "The Revolution and the Rural Community in Eighteenth-Century Brittany." *Past & Present* 62 (1974): 96–119.

Sweezy, Paul M. "The Triumph of Financial Capital." *Monthly Review* 46 (1994): 1–11.

Szczepiorkowski, Zbigniew M., and Christopher P. Stowell, "Red Blood Cell Substitutes." In *Blood Safety and Surveillance*, edited by Jeanne V. Linden and Celso Bianco, 543–67. New York, 2001.

Tancredus Bononiensis [Tancredus de Bologna]. *Tancredi summa de matrimonio*. Edited by Agathon Wunderlich. Göttingen, 1841.

Tanguy, Bernard. *Aux origines du nationalisme Breton*. 2 vols. Paris, 1977.

Tellenbach, Gerd. "Vom karolingischen Reichsadel zum deutschen Reichsfürstenstand." In *Herrschaft und Staat im Mittelalter*, edited by Hellmut Kämpf, 190–242. Darmstadt, 1956.

Tett, Gillian. *Fool's Gold: How the Bold Dream of a Small Tribe at J. P. Morgan Was Corrupted by Wall Street Greed and Unleashed a Catastrophe*. New York, 2009.

Tett, Gillian, and Aline van Duyn. "Under Restraint: Credit." *Financial Times*, 7 July 2009.

Teuscher, Simon. *Bekannte–Klienten–Verwandte. Soziabilität und Politik in der Stadt Bern um 1500*. Cologne, Weimar, and Vienna. 1998.

*The Theodosian Code and Novels, and the Sirmondian Constitutions*. Translated by Clyde Pharr. Princeton, NJ, 1952.

*Thesaurus linguae latinae*. Leipzig, 1990–.

Thietmar of Merseburg. "Chronicon." *Patrologia Latina* 139, col. 1409D.

Thomas, Yan. "The Division of Sexes in Roman Law." In *From Ancient Goddesses to Christian Saints*, edited by P. Schmitt Pantel, 83–138. Vol. 1 of *A History of Women in the West*. Edited by Georges Duby and Michelle Perrot. Cambridge, MA, 1992–94.

———. "*Parricidium* I. Le père, la famille et la cité." *Mélanges de l'École française de Rome. Antiquité* 83 (1981): 643–713.

———. "*Vitae necisque potestas*. Le père, la cité, la mort." In *Du châtiment dans la Cité. Supplices corporels et peine de mort dans le monde antique. Table ronde organisée par l'École française de Rome avec le concours du Centre National de la Recherche Scientifique (Rome 9.–11. novembre 1982)*, 499–548. Rome, 1984.

Thompson, Charis. *Making Parents: The Ontological Choreography of New Reproductive Technology*. Cambridge, MA, 2005.

Thompson, Wesley E. "The Marriage of First Cousins in Athenian Society." *Phoenix* 21 (1967): 273–82.

Thwaites, R. G., ed. *The Jesuit Relations and Allied Documents: Travels and Explorations of the Jesuit Missionaries in New France, 1610–1791*. 73 vols. Cleveland, OH, 1896–1901.

*The Times* [London].

Titmuss, Richard M. *The Gift Relationship: From Human Blood to Social Policy*. Orig. ed. with new chaps. Edited by Ann Oakley and John Ashton. New York, 1997.

Tobler, Alfred, and Ernst Lommatzsch. *Altfranzösisches Wörterbuch*. Wiesbaden, 1925–2002.

Tonnerre, Noël-Yves. *Naissance de la Bretagne. Géographie historique et structures sociales de la Bretagne méridionale (Nantais et Vannetais) de la fin du VIIIe à la fin du XIIe siècle*. Angers, 1994.

*Tractatus universi iuris, duce, et auspice Gregorio XIII in unum congesti*. Venice, 1584–86.

Tranensis, Goffredus [Gottofredo da Trani]. *Summa super titulis decretalium. Novissime cum repertorio et numeris principalium et emergentium questionum impressa*. Lyon, 1519. 2nd reprint, Aalen, 1992.

Treggiari, Susan. *Roman Marriage: Iusti Coniuges from the Time of Cicero to the Time of Ulpian*. Oxford, 1991.

Trenard, Louis. "Les fondements de l'idée de race au XVIIIe siècles." *L'Information Historique* 43 (1981): 166.

"Très-humbles doléances et remontrances des Habitans du Sénégal, aux Citoyens Français tenant les Etats-Généraux (15 avril 1789)." In *L'Affrique et le peuple affriquains considérés sous tous leurs rapports avec notre commerce et nos colonies* ... , by Dominique Harcourt Lamiral. Paris, 1789.

Treue, Wolfgang, ed. *Deutsche Parteiprogramme seit 1861.* 4th ed. Quellensammlung zur Kulturgeschichte, Bd. 3, Ed. 4. Göttingen, 1968.

Tsuchida, Eishun, ed. *Blood Substitutes: Present and Future Perspectives.* Amsterdam and New York, 1998.

Turlan, Juliette M. "Amis et amis charnels d'après les actes du Parlement au XIV$^e$ siècle." *Revue historique de droit français et étranger* 47 (1969) 645–98.

——. "Amis et amis charnels. D'après les actes du parlement au XIV$^e$ siècle." *Revue historique du droit français et étranger* 47 (1969): 645–98.

Turnbull, Eleanor L., ed. *Ten Centuries of Spanish Poetry.* Baltimore, MD, 1955.

Tutton, Richard. "Gift Relationships in Genetics Research." *Science as Culture* 11, no. 4 (2002): 523–42.

*Un Conte de Noël.* Film in French. Directed by Arnaud Despleschin. 2008.

Valdeavellano, Luis García de. *Historia de España antigua y medieval.* 2 vols. Madrid, 1988.

Valin, René-Josué. *Nouveau commentaire sur l'Ordonnance de la Marine, du mois Août, 1681.* 2 vols. La Rochelle, 1776.

Van der Lugt, Maaike, and Charles de Miramon. "Penser l'hérédité au Moyen Âge: une introduction." In Van der Lugt and Miramon, *L'hérédité entre Moyen Âge et Époque moderne,* 3–40.

Van der Lugt, Maaike, and Charles de Miramon, eds. *L'hérédité entre Moyen Âge et Époque moderne. Perspectives historiques.* Florence, 2008.

Vandermonde, Charles-Augustin. *Essai sur la manière de perfectionner l'espèce humaine.* 2 vols. Paris, 1756.

Venette, Nicolas. *De la generation de l'homme, ou, Tableau de l'amour conjugal.* Paris, 1696.

——. *Tableau de l'amour considéré dans l'estat du mariage.* Amsterdam, 1687.

Venturino, Diego. "Race et histoire. Le paradigme nobiliaire de la distinction sociale au début du XVIIIe siècle." In *L'idée de "race" dans les sciences humaines et la littérature (XVIII$^e$-XIX$^e$ siècles), Proceedings from the International Conference held in Lyon (November 16–18, 2000),* edited by Sarga Moussa, 19–39. Paris, 2003.

Vila, Anne C. *Sensibility in the Literature and Medicine of Eighteenth-Century France.* Baltimore, MD, 1998.

Villegas, Francisco de Quevedo y. *See* Quevedo y Villegas, Francisco de.

Visceglia, Maria Antonietta. "Gli 'humori' delle nazioni. La rappresentazione della Spagna nella Francia del primo Seicento (1590–1635)." *Dimensioni e problemi della ricerca storica* 2 (1995): 39–68.

Voci, Pasquale. *Parte speciale. Successione ab intestato. Successione testamentaria.* Vol. 2 of *Diritto ereditario romano.* Milan, 1963.

Voisinet, Jacques. "Le tabou du sang dans les pénitentiels du Haut Moyen Age." In *Le sang au Moyen Age. Actes du quatrième colloque international de Montpellier, Université Paul-Valéry, 27–29 novembre 1997,* 111–25. Montpellier, 1999.

Wagner, Herbert. *Studien zur allgemeinen Rechtslehre des Gaius (ius gentium und ius naturale in ihrem Verhältnis zum ius civile).* Zutphen, 1978.

Waldby, Catherine, and Robert Mitchell. *Tissue Economies: Blood, Organs, and Cell Lines in Late Capitalism.* Durham, NC, 2006.

Waltzing, Jean-Pierre. *Les collèges professionnels considérés comme institutions officielles.* Vol. 2 of *Etude historique sur les corporations professionnelles chez les Romains: depuis les origines jusqu'à la chute de l'Empire d'occident.* Louvain, 1896.

Wang, Linda. "Blood Relatives: First-Generation Artificial Blood is about to Hit the Market." *Science News* 159 (2001): 206–7.

Watson, Alan. *The Law of Succession in the Late Roman Republic.* Oxford, 1971.

Weininger, Otto. *Geschlecht und Charakter.* 22nd ed. Vienna and Leipzig, 1921.

Wesel, Uwe. *Rhetorische Statuslehre und Gesetzesauslegung der römischen Juristen.* Cologne, 1967.

Weston, Kath. *Families We Choose: Lesbians, Gays, Kinship.* 2nd ed. New York, 1997.

———. "Kinship, Controversy, and the Sharing of Substance: The Race/Class Politics of Blood Transfusion." In Franklin and McKinnon, *Relative Values: Reconfiguring Kinship Studies,* 147–74.

Wharton, Edith. *A Backward Glance.* Teddington, 2008.

Williams, Elizabeth. *The Physical and the Moral: Anthropology, Physiology, and Philosophical Medicine in France, 1750–1850.* Cambridge, 1994.

Wilmut, Ian, Keith Campbell, and Colin Tudge. *The Second Creation: The Age of Biological Control by the Scientists Who Cloned Dolly.* London, 2000.

Wilson, Kathleen. *The Island Race: Englishness, Empire and Gender in the Eighteenth Century.* London, 2003.

Wincler, Benedict. *Principiorum iuris.* Leipzig, 1615.

Winslow, Robert M. "Blood Substitutes: Refocusing an Elusive Goal." *British Journal of Haematology* 111 (2000): 387–96.

———. "Current Status of Blood Substitute Research: Towards a New Paradigm." *Journal of Internal Medicine* 253 (2003): 508–17.

———. "How Do Scientists Make Artificial Blood? How Effective Is It Compared With the Real Thing?" *Scientific American* (21 October 1999).

Winslow, Robert M., Kim D. Vandegriff, and Marcos Intaglietta, eds. *Advances in Blood Substitutes: Industrial Opportunities and Medical Challenges.* Boston, 1997.

Winston, Michael. "Medicine, Marriage, and Human Degeneration in the French Enlightenment." *Eighteenth-Century Studies* 38 (2005): 263–81.

Winterling, Aloys. *Politics and Society in Imperial Rome.* London, 2009.

Wunderlich, Agathon, ed. *Tancredi summa de matrimonio.* Göttingen, 1841.

Zoz, Maria Gabriella. "In tema di obbligazioni alimentari." *Bollettino dell'Istituto di diritto romano* 73 (1970): 323–55.

# Contributors

**Guillaume Aubert** is visiting assistant professor at the College of William & Mary. He has also been a visiting professor at McGill University and is a member of the French Atlantic History Group based in Montreal, Quebec. He is finishing a book on constructions of race and nation in the French Atlantic and has started a new project on the transatlantic histories of Gorée and Saint-Louis du Sénégal from the seventeenth to the early nineteenth century.

**Janet Carsten** is professor of social and cultural anthropology at the University of Edinburgh. She is the author of *The Heat of the Hearth: The Process of Kinship in a Malay Fishing Community* (1997) and *After Kinship* (2004). Her edited books include *Cultures of Relatedness: New Approaches to the Study of Kinship* (2000) and *Ghosts of Memory: Essays on Remembrance and Relatedness* (2007). She has conducted fieldwork in Malaysia and Scotland, most recently on ideas about blood, based in hospital clinical pathology labs and blood banks in Penang.

**Gérard Delille** was a member of the Ecole française de Rome and submitted his doctoral thesis in 1982 at the Université de Paris I. He was directeur des études pour l'histoire moderne et contemporaine at the Ecole française de Rome before becoming directeur de recherches at the Centre national de la recherche scientifique in Paris, as well as directeur d'études at the Ecole des hautes études en sciences sociales. Between 1994 and 2002, he was professor at the European University Institute in Florence. His research interests are family, kinship, and alliance, as well as the history of southern Italy in the Middle Ages and in the early modern period. His recent publications include *Le maire et le prieur. Pouvoir central et pouvoir local en Méditerranée occidentale (Xe–XVIIIe siècle)* (Paris, 2003).

**Cornelia Essner** is Privatdozent for modern history at the Technische Universität Berlin. She has published many articles and some books about German colonialism and about the Third Reich. Her habilitation concerned Nazi anti-Semitism: *Die Nürnberger Gesetze oder die Verwaltung des Rassenwahns 1933–1945* (Paderborn, 2002).

**Sarah Franklin** holds the Chair in Sociology at the University of Cambridge, where she is currently involved in research on the history of mammalian developmental biology in the UK in the postwar period. She is the author of both *Embodied Progress: A Cultural Account of Assisted Conception* (1997) and *Dolly Mixtures: The Remaking of Genealogy* (2007). Her forthcoming book from Duke University Press is entitled *Biological Relatives: IVF, Stem Cells and the Future of Kinship.*

**Anita Guerreau-Jalabert** is directeur de recherche at the Institut de recherche et d'histoire des textes (Centre national de la recherche scientifique) in Paris, and former director of the Ecole nationale des chartes (Paris). She is currently director of the *Novum glossarium mediae latinitatis,* published by the Union académique internationale (Brussels). Her publications include *Histoire culturelle de la France: Tome 1, Le Moyen Age* (Paris, 1997) and many articles about kinship.

**Ann-Cathrin Harders** is assistant professor of ancient history at the University of Bielefeld; she also has been a research assistant at Freiburg and Heidelberg Universities. Her main research interests are family and kinship in Greece and Rome, also the wider social history of the Roman Republic and early imperial era as well as of monarchy in the Hellenistic period. She has published a monograph on Roman kinship, *Suavissima Soror. Untersuchungen zu den Bruder-Schwester-Beziehungen in der römischen Republik* (Munich, 2008).

**Christopher H. Johnson** is professor emeritus of history at Wayne State University in Detroit, Michigan. He is nearing completion of a book tentatively entitled "Becoming Bourgeois: Love, Kinship, and Power in Provincial France, 1670-1880." A parallel interest is the history of siblings, discourses of incest, and sensibility from 1750 to 1850. Johnson is also at work on a study of family conflict, ordinary women's search for rights, and the shifting perspectives of the law in Paris during the last decades of the Old Regime. His previous work, in working-class and economic history, includes *Utopian Communism in France: Cabet and the Icarians, 1839–1851* (Ithaca and New York, 1974) and *The Life and Death of Industrial Languedoc, 1700–1920: The Politics of De-Industrialization* (Oxford, 1995).

**Bernhard Jussen** has been professor of medieval history at Goethe University Frankfurt since 2008. He was professor at Bielefeld University and research fellow at the Max Planck Institute for History in Göttingen. In 2007 he was awarded the Leibniz Prize of the German Research Foundation. Jussen was guest professor at the University of Michigan Ann Arbor and at the École normale supérieure in Paris, visiting scholar at Harvard University, and fellow of the Wissenschaftskolleg zu Berlin. Among his publications: *Der Name der Witwe* (2000); *Spiritual Kinship as Social Practice* (2000); *Die Macht des Königs* (2005); *Atlas des historischen Bildwissens* (2009).

**Philippe Moreau** is professor of Latin language and literature at the Université de Paris Est Créteil, and former maître de conférences at the Sorbonne and at the École pratique des hautes études (IVᵉ section). He has published *Sur les murs de Pompéi. Choix d'inscriptions latines* (Paris, 1993) and *Incestus et prohibitae nuptiae. Conception romaine de l'inceste et histoire des prohibitions matrimoniales pour cause de parenté dans la Rome ancienne* (Paris, 2002), and edited *Corps romains* (Grenoble, 2002). He is also director of the *Revue de philologie* (Paris, Klincksieck). His research interests are kinship anthropology and lawmaking in ancient Rome.

**Teofilo F. Ruiz** is Distinguished Professor of History and of Spanish and Portuguese at University of California, Los Angeles. A recipient of Guggenheim, NEH, ACLS, and other fellowships, he was also a director of studies at the École des hautes études en sciences sociales in Paris. Among his most recent publications are *From Heaven to Earth* (Princeton, NJ, 2004); *Spain's Centuries of Crisis: 1300–1474* (Malden, MA, and Oxford, 2007); *The Terror of History* (Princeton, NJ, 2011); *A King Travels: Festive Traditions in Late Medieval and Early Modern Spain* (Princeton, NJ, 2012).

**David Warren Sabean** is Henry J. Bruman professor of German history at the University of California, Los Angeles. A graduate of the University of Wisconsin where he studied under George Mosse, Sabean has taught at the University of East Anglia, University of Pittsburgh, and Cornell, and he has been a fellow at the Max Planck Institute for History in Göttingen, the Maison des sciences de l'homme, and the Wissenschaftskolleg zu Berlin, the American Academy in Berlin, and the National Humanities Center in North Carolina. He is a fellow of the American Academy of Arts and Sciences. His publications include *Power in the Blood: Popular Culture and Village Discourse in Early Modern Germany* (Cambridge, 1984); *Property, Production, and Family in Neckarhausen, 1700–1870* (Cambridge, 1990); *Kinship in Neckarhausen, 1700–1870* (Cambridge, 1998). He is the co-editor with Simon Teuscher and Jon Mathieu of *Kinship in Europe: Approaches to Long-Term Development (1300–1900)* (Oxford and New York, 2007).

**Simon Teuscher** is professor of medieval history at the University of Zurich. He has been an assistant professor at the University of Basel and the University of California, Los Angeles; a visiting professor at the École des hautes études en sciences sociales in Paris and the Université de Neuchâtel; and a member of the Institute for Advanced Study, School of Historical Studies, at Princeton. His publications include *Lords' Rights and Peasant Stories: Writing and the Formation of Tradition in the Late Middle Ages* (Philadelphia, PA, 2012) and, together with David Sabean and Jon Mathieu, *Kinship in Europe: Approaches to Long-Term Development (1300–1900)* (Oxford and New York, 2007).

**Kath Weston** is professor of anthropology and women, gender, and sexuality at the University of Virginia. She has held visiting professorships at Cambridge University, Tokyo University, Harvard University, Brandeis University, and Wellesley College. Her publications include *Families We Choose: Lesbians, Gays, Kinship* (1991); *Traveling Light: On the Road with America's Poor* (2008); and *Gender in Real Time* (2002). She is currently working on two book projects: *The Intimacy of Resources: Technology, Affect, and Embodiment in the Synthesis of Nature* and *The Magic of Capital: A Cultural Critique of Circulation and Generation in Finance*.

# Index